Behavioural and Experimental Economics

GW00690731

The New Palgrave Economics Collection
Editors: Steven N. Durlauf, University of Wisconsin-Madison, USA & Lawrence E. Blume,
Cornell University, USA

Also in the series:
Economic Growth
Game Theory
Macroeconometrics and Time Series Analysis
Microeconometrics
Monetary Economics

Series Standing Order ISBN 978-0-230-24014-8 hardcover
Series Standing Order ISBN 978-0-230-24013-1 paperback

To receive future titles in this series as they are published quote one of the ISBNs listed above to set
up a standing order: contact your bookseller; write to Customer Services Department, Macmillan
Distribution Ltd, Houndmills, Basingstoke, Hampshire, RG21 6XS; or email orders@palgrave.com.

Kevin
Brady

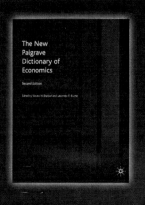

The New Palgrave Dictionary of Economics
Second Edition

Edited by Steven N. Durlauf and Lawrence E. Blume

The definitive resource for a new generation of economists

5.8 million words	1,872 articles	8 print volumes

1,506 contributors	7,680 page	1 dynamic online resource

Including articles by over 1,500 eminent contributors and providing a current overview of economics, this second edition of *The New Palgrave* is now available both in print and online.

The online *Dictionary* is a dynamic resource for economists which:

- Is regularly updated with new articles and updates to existing articles, along with new features and functionality

- Allows 24x7 access to members of subscribing institutions, outside library opening hours, on the move, at home or at their desk

- Offers excellent search and browse facilities, both full text and advanced, which make it possible to explore the Dictionary with great speed and ease

- Contains hyperlinked cross-references within articles, making it an indispensable tool for researchers and students

- Features carefully selected and maintained links to related sites, sources of further information and bibliographical citations

- Enables users to save searches, make personal annotations and bookmark articles they need to refer to regularly by using 'My Dictionary'

www.dictionaryofeconomics.com

Behavioural and Experimental Economics

Edited by
Steven N. Durlauf
University of Wisconsin-Madison, USA

Lawrence E. Blume
Cornell University, USA

First published 2010 by
PALGRAVE MACMILLAN

Palgrave Macmillan in the UK is an imprint of Macmillan Publishers Limited,
registered in England, company number 785998, of Houndmills, Basingstoke,
Hampshire RG21 6XS.

Palgrave Macmillan in the US is a division of St Martin's Press LLC,
175 Fifth Avenue, New York, NY 10010.

Palgrave Macmillan is the global academic imprint of the above companies
and has companies and representatives throughout the world.

Palgrave® and Macmillan® are registered trademarks in the United States,
the United Kingdom, Europe and other countries.

ISBN 978-0-230-23867-1   hardback
ISBN 978-0-230-23868-8   paperback

This book is printed on paper suitable for recycling and made from fully
managed and sustained forest sources. Logging, pulping and manufacturing
processes are expected to conform to the environmental regulations of the
country of origin.

A catalogue record for this book is available from the British Library.

A catalog record for this book is available from the Library of Congress.

10   9   8   7   6   5   4   3   2   1
19   18   17   16   15   14   13   12   11   10

Printed and bound in Great Britain by
CPI Antony Rowe, Chippenham and Eastbourne

Contents

List of Contributors

LISA ANDERSON
College of William and Mary, USA

JAMES ANDREONI
University of California San Diego, USA

SHERYL BALL
Virginia Polytechnic Institute and State University, USA

B. DOUGLAS BERNHEIM
Stanford University, USA

ROBERT BLOOMFIELD
Cornell University, USA

IRIS BOHNET
Harvard University, USA

ROB BOYD
University of California Los Angeles, USA

COLIN F. CAMERER
California Institute of Technology, USA

JEFFREY CARPENTER
Middlebury College, USA

CHRISTOPHER F. CHABRIS
Harvard University, USA

YAN CHEN
University of Michigan, USA

RACHEL T. A. CROSON
University of Texas at Dallas, USA

DOUGLAS D. DAVIS
Virginia Commonwealth University, USA

JOHN DUFFY
University of Pittsburgh, USA

ARMIN FALK
University of Bonn, Germany

DANIEL FRIEDMAN
University of California Santa Cruz, USA

SIMON GÄCHTER
University of Nottingham, UK

JACOB K. GOEREE,
California Institute of Technology, USA

FRANCESCO GUALA
The University of Exeter, UK

FARUK GUL
Princeton University, USA

WILLIAM T. HARBAUGH
University of Oregon, USA

GLENN W. HARRISON
University of Central Florida, USA

TECK H. HO
University of Pennsylvania, USA

CHARLES A. HOLT
University of Virginia, USA

DANIEL E. HOUSER
George Mason University, USA

GEORGE LOEWENSTEIN
Carnegie Mellon University, USA

JOHN H. KAGEL
Ohio State University, USA

DAVID I. LAIBSON
Harvard University, USA

JOHN O. LEDYARD
California Institute of Technology, USA

DAN LEVIN
Ohio State University, USA

JOHN A. LIST
University of Chicago, USA

GRAHAM LOOMES
University of East Anglia, UK

JACK OCHS
Indiana University, USA

THOMAS R. PALFREY
California Institute of Technology, USA

ANTONIO RANGEL
California Institute of Technology, USA

DAVID REILEY
University of Arizona, USA

SCOTT RICK
The University of Pennsylvania, USA

RAJIV SETHI
Columbia University, USA

JASON F. SHOGREN
University of Wyoming, USA

JONATHON P. SCHULDT
University of Michigan, USA

VERNON L. SMITH
George Mason University, USA

CHRIS STARMER
University of Nottingham, UK

LISE VESTERLUND
University of Pittsburgh, USA

RICK K. WILSON
Rice University, USA

General Preface

All economists of a certain age remember the "little green books". Many own a few. These are the offspring of *The New Palgrave: A Dictionary of Economics*; collections of reprints from *The New Palgrave* that were meant to deliver at least a sense of the *Dictionary* into the hands of those for whom access to the entire four volume, four million word set was inconvenient or difficult. *The New Palgrave Dictionary of Economics, Second Edition* largely resolves the accessibility problem through its online presence. But while the online search facility provides convenient access to specific topics in the now eight volume, six million word *Dictionary of Economics*, no interface has yet been devised that makes browsing from a large online source a pleasurable activity for a rainy afternoon. To our delight, *The New Palgrave*'s publisher shares our view of the joys of dictionary-surfing, and we are thus pleased to present a new series, the "little blue books", to make some part of the *Dictionary* accessible in the hand or lap for teachers, students, and those who want to browse. While the volumes in this series contain only articles that appeared in the 2008 print edition, readers can, of course, refer to the online *Dictionary* and its expanding list of entries.

The selections in these volumes were chosen with several desiderata in mind: to touch on important problems, to emphasize material that may be of more general interest to economics beginners and yet still touch on the analytical core of modern economics, and to balance important theoretical concerns with key empirical debates. The 1987 Eatwell, Milgate and Newman *The New Palgrave: A Dictionary of Economics* was chiefly concerned with economic theory, both the history of its evolution and its contemporary state. The second edition has taken a different approach. While much progress has been made across the board in the 21 years between the first and second editions, it is particularly the flowering of empirical economics which distinguishes the present interval from the 61 year interval between Henry Higgs' *Palgrave's Dictionary of Political Economy* and *The New Palgrave*. It is fair to say that, in the long run, doctrine evolves more slowly than the database of facts, and so some of the selections in these volumes will age more quickly than others. This problem will be solved in the online *Dictionary* through an ongoing process of revisions and updates. While no such solution is available for these volumes, we have tried to choose topics which will give these books utility for some time to come.

Steven N. Durlauf
Lawrence E. Blume

Introduction

Modern economics has flirted with psychology since its inception at the hands of Jevons, Edgeworth, Pareto and others. Much of Edgeworth's *Mathematical Psychics* was devoted to a careful examination of the Weber-Fechner law and its generalization, while Wicksell thought it would ultimately lead to a principal of interpersonal utility comparisons. The connection between psychophysics and economics continues to the present day, and can be seen in the influence of work in measurement theory by Luce, Tversky and others on decision theory and social choice. The connection between experimental psychology and economics, however, has been fitful. The first true choice theory experiments were done not by an economist, but by the psychologist L.L. Thurstone (1931). Thurstone, to whom we owe the random utility model which has been so fruitful in empirical microeconomics and which ultimately produced a Nobel Prize for Daniel McFadden, was urged on in this enterprise by Henry Schultz, who was greatly interested in the estimation of consumer demand. Thurstone presented this paper at a 1932 meeting of the Econometric Society, but it seems to have had little subsequent impact. The work of von Neumann and Morgenstern and subsequently Savage led to some interesting attempts to elicit preferences and beliefs such as those of Mosteller and Nogee (1951), and to some early and important criticisms of the emerging theory (Allais (1953), Ellsberg (1961)) but again this led to no sustained interest in experimental methods. Perhaps even at the time of *The New Palgrave: A Dictionary of Economics* (1987) one could write, as one contributor did, '. . . it may be said that scientific experiments (experimenta lucifera) are a very slight resource in economics.'[1] Today, however, modern social psychology brings much more to the table than psychophysics alone ever could. The relationship between economics and psychology has finally been consummated, and behavioural economics is its fruit. The limits of simple versions of rationality and the exploration of alternative behaviourally-based decision models is a thriving field of research. The increasing sophistication of brain studies in psychology has opened up the new frontier of neuroeconomics. In *The New Palgrave Dictionary of Economics, Second Edition*, John Dickhaut and Aldo Rustichini state that, 'Neuroeconomics aims at improving the science of major economic phenomena such as the formation of prices and the design and performance of institutions.' (See 'neuroeconomics', not reprinted here.) We expect a subsequent edition of the *Dictionary* will report on progress towards this goal. The subject of economics is more the group than the individual, and the relationship between experimental research and theories of interactive decision making has been more steady, and until recently more fruitful than that between psychology and choice theory, perhaps because some of the same people were involved on both sides of the relationship. One of the most influential pieces of research in modern social science is a game experiment conducted at the Rand Corporation by Melvin Dresher and Merrill Flood. This experiment introduced the prisoner's dilemma, so named by Albert Tucker, which is perhaps the only game with name recognition outside the community of social scientists. Market experiments have also been consistently present in economics, beginning with Harvard's Edward Chamberlin (1947) and Berkeley's Austin Hoggatt (1959). Vernon Smith reports in his entry, 'experimental methods in economics', reprinted here, that he began the work leading to Smith (1962) in 1956. Since then, the experiments have been very influential in the development of game theory (see 'individual learning in games'), mechanism design (see 'mechanism design experiments') and the design of markets (see 'matching and market design', not reprinted here). As the design of institutions has become an ever more central part of economics, experiments have become increasingly important as a means of probing their behaviour. With new modalities of instrumentation becoming available through PDA's and cellular phones, the boundaries between laboratory and field experiments will begin to blur, and perhaps to change entirely the face of empirical microeconomics.

1. C.F. Bastable (1987), 'Experimental methods in economics (i)'.

Steven N. Durlauf
Lawrence E. Blume

addiction

Economists were latecomers to the study of addiction, a concept which researchers in other disciplines usually define as including a loss of self-control, continuation of behaviour despite adverse consequences, and preoccupation or obsession with the substance or activity one is addicted to. Economists came late to the subject perhaps because the first two of these characteristics seem inconsistent with economists' rational choice paradigm.

This may be exactly what spurred Gary Becker, along with coauthor Kevin Murphy, to propose, in 1988, a 'rational account of addiction', which stimulated much subsequent research and theorizing by economists. Although not the first economic account of addiction, Becker and Murphy's model (referred to henceforth as B&M) was certainly the most influential, and has spawned a very lively line of research, theorizing and debate about addiction by economists.

Contributions of disciplines other than economics

Prior to B&M, scientists in a range of disciplines had already developed a rich tradition of research on addiction. For example, early studies by psychopharmacologists identified the actions of addictive drugs in the brain, and subsequent research by neuroscientists has uncovered the neural pathways through which addictive activities derive their motivational power (see, for example, Gardner and James, 1999; Lyvers, 2000). Sociologists have also been major contributors, conducting ethnographic and life-course studies of drug users that have identified many of the social influences on drug use. Psychologists have studied the widest range of different facets of drug abuse, including biological underpinnings and social, cognitive and emotional dimensions, and have also been in the forefront when it comes to treatment. Psychologists, as well as other health professionals, have tested a great diversity of treatments for addiction, including residential treatment, counselling, psychotherapy, drug therapies such as methadone, nicotine patches and antidepressants, aversive conditioning, and hypnosis. Taken together, these diverse lines of research have yielded a number of important, and often counter-intuitive, findings.

- Historic use of different types of drugs exhibits 'fads', rising then falling in popularity, sometimes repeatedly for a specific drug.
- Most drug users do not just use a single drug, but many different drugs.
- Many if not most drug abusers also suffer from other psychiatric conditions, such as anxiety or mood disorders, schizophrenia or antisocial personality disorder.
- Much if not most quitting occurs outside of treatment.
- It is not short-term withdrawal from drugs (for example, for a few days) that most addicts find difficult, but long-term abstinence, which tends to be punctuated by episodes of 'craving' which create an almost overwhelming motivation for drug use.

- Episodes of craving are often triggered by 'cues' – people or other stimuli that the addict associates with drug use.
- While approximately 20 per cent of a sample of veterans reported being addicted to heroin in Vietnam, and 45 per cent reported narcotic use, only one per cent remained addicted, and two per cent reported using narcotics after returning home (Robins, 1973); this finding radically changed prevailing views of the incidence of recovery from heroin addiction.
- Humans and other mammals voluntarily self-administer most of the same chemical compounds. (Hallucinogens, which some humans seek out but most animals avoid, are a major exception.)
- Although a small number of intense users account for a large fraction of drug use, most drug users consume at moderate or low rates, and do not become addicted in the sense of losing control, suffering adverse consequences or becoming obsessed with drug-taking.
- Many of the adverse health effects of illicit drugs, such as opiates, do not stem from physical effects of the drugs themselves, but from the difficulty of financing an illegal, and hence typically expensive, habit.
- Most addictions begin when people are in their teens or early twenties, and addicts often 'mature out' – quitting when they reach middle age. People rarely become addicted for the first time in middle or old age.

In addition to generating a wide range of interesting and important findings, researchers in disciplines other than economics have proposed a variety of theoretical perspectives on addiction. Some perspectives place great importance on the pleasure of drug-taking, the pain of withdrawal, or the motivational force of 'cue-conditioned' craving, while others view drug use as a form of self-medication for psychiatric conditions such as depression.

For better or for worse, economists' focus on addiction has been much narrower, at both the theoretical and the empirical levels. Most empirical work has involved estimating price elasticities of demand for drugs (often using aggregate consumption data), and most theoretical work has involved some type of generalization of Becker and Murphy's perspective.

Becker and Murphy's model

In Becker and Murphy's rational model of addiction, utility from an addictive good, $c(t)$, is assumed to depend on consumption of that good and on the degree of addiction $S(t)$. $S(t)$ changes according to the function $\dot{S}(t) = c(t) - \delta S(t)$, where the first term represents the impact of engaging in the addictive good on one's level of addiction, and the second represents the natural decline in addictedness when one desists. The individual is assumed to trade off consumption of the addictive good against consumption of other (non-addictive) goods, discounting for time delay in the conventional (exponential) fashion. The central insight of B&M is that people treat addictive goods no differently from the way they treat any good whose utility depends on consumption over time, trading them off against other goods based on current and future (anticipated) prices.

This model can accommodate a number of features of classical addiction, such as that being addicted lowers instantaneous utility $u_s < 0$, that it increases the instantaneous marginal utility of taking the drug $u_{cs} > 0$. Solving the model yields a number of implications, most importantly that it can be rational for an individual to maintain a positive rate of consumption of an addictive good.

Empirical tests of B&M have focused on the strong prediction that anticipated changes in future prices affect the current behaviour of addicts, which is counter-intuitive given that addicts are commonly seen as behaving myopically. The model is therefore typically tested by estimating what could be called the 'forward price elasticity' of various addictive substances. Consistent with Becker and Murphy's model, negative forward price elasticities have been found for alcohol, cigarettes, marijuana, opium, heroin and cocaine (for a review, see Pacula and Chaloupka, 2001), although the effect appears to be more consistent for adults than for youth.

Moving beyond Becker and Murphy

In proposing their rational account of addiction, Becker and Murphy initiated the study of addiction among economists, and made the key point that it is useful to think of addicts as solving a forward-looking optimization problem. However, the B&M model fails to incorporate a number of important features of addiction, and is either inconsistent with or fails to predict many salient features of addiction, including some of the stylized facts listed above. Responding to these limitations, economists have built upon the B&M model by relaxing some of its most extreme assumptions or incorporating more realistic assumptions that are often inspired by research in other disciplines.

One important generalization has been to examine the implications of relaxing the assumption of exponential time discounting. Gruber and Koszegi (2001; 2004), for example, propose a model in which time-inconsistent addicts have self-control problems: they would like to quit using but cannot force themselves to do so (see also O'Donoghue and Rabin, 1997). As in B&M, Gruber and Koszegi's model predicts that a rise in current or anticipated excise taxes will reduce use of addictive substances. However, although the models make similar behavioural predictions, they interpret the hedonic consequences of altered usage behaviour differently. B&M predicts that taxes on addictive substances – 'sin taxes' – make addicts worse off since the price of a good that they enjoy has risen. Gruber and Koszegi's model, on the other hand, predicts that the tax makes time-inconsistent addicts better off since it provides a valuable self-control device.

Since behavioural data cannot distinguish between the models, Gruber and Mullainathan (2005) bypassed the standard practice of measuring the impact of policy interventions by estimating price elasticities in favour of directly examining the impact of these interventions on subjective well-being. They did so by matching cigarette excise taxation data to surveys from the United States and Canada that contain data on self-reported happiness. Consistent with Gruber and Koszegi's model, Gruber and Mullainathan (2005) found that excise taxes on cigarettes make smokers happier.

Another implication of time inconsistency involves purchasing patterns. The B&M model predicts that addicts will behave in a time-consistent fashion and hence will buy in bulk to save time and money in satisfying their anticipated long-term habit. Wertenbroch (1998; 2003), however, found that consumers – even those who are not liquidity-constrained – often purchase 'vice' items, such as cigarettes, in small quantities in an attempt to control their intake of the harmful substance.

Other research has questioned the assumption that addicts begin drug taking with full knowledge of the consequences. For example, Slovic (2000a; 2000b) has argued that people take up cigarette smoking in part because they underestimate the health risks, although Viscusi (2000) counters that any error is actually in the opposite direction – that smokers *overestimate* the health risks of smoking. Pointing to a somewhat different type of underestimation, Loewenstein (1999) has argued, based on a wide range of evidence, that potential drug users underestimate their own proneness to addiction because they underestimate the motivational force of drug craving.

Finally, a recent line of theoretical models, while also building on the insights of Becker and Murphy, has incorporated evidence from the psychological literature on cue-conditioned craving and from neuroscience. For example, Laibson (2001) proposes a model of addiction that incorporates the role of cue-conditioned craving. In his model, environmental cues that become associated with drug use, when encountered by an ex-addict, produce surges of craving (like sudden changes in $S(t)$ in B&M). Bernheim and Rangel (2004) develop a model of addiction that is particularly closely grounded in neuroscience research and that is perhaps the most radical departure from B&M. Their model is based on the idea that repeated experience with drugs sensitizes individuals to environmental cues that trigger mistaken usage.

So far, economists are still playing catch-up with researchers in other disciplines when it comes to their understanding of addiction or their influence on policy. Thus, a large fraction of empirical research on drug use by economists has focused on price elasticities. While price is one determinant of drug use, it is arguably not the most important, or even the most amenable to manipulation through the instruments of policy. Nevertheless, economic models of addiction have made great strides, building on Becker and Murphy's seminal contribution with new models that incorporate many of the insights and findings generated by research in other disciplines.

GEORGE LOEWENSTEIN AND SCOTT RICK

See also **intertemporal choice.**

We thank Caroline Acker, Ted O'Donoghue and Antonio Rangel for helpful suggestions.

Bibliography

Becker, G. and Murphy, K. 1988. A theory of rational addiction. *Journal of Political Economy* 96, 675–700.

Bernheim, B. and Rangel, A. 2004. Addiction and cue-triggered decision processes. *American Economic Review* 94, 1558–90.

Gardner, E. and James, D. 1999. The neurobiology of chemical addiction. In *Getting Hooked: Rationality and Addiction*, ed. J. Elster and O.-J. Skog. Cambridge: Cambridge University Press.

Gruber, J. and Koszegi, B. 2001. Is addiction 'rational?' Theory and evidence. *Quarterly Journal of Economics* 116, 1261–305.

Gruber, J. and Koszegi, B. 2004. A theory of government regulation of addictive bads: tax levels and tax incidence for cigarette excise taxation. *Journal of Public Economics* 88, 1959–87.

Gruber, J. and Mullainathan, S. 2005. Do cigarette taxes make smokers happier? *Advances in Economic Analysis & Policy* 5, 1–43.

Laibson, D. 2001. A cue-theory of consumption. *Quarterly Journal of Economics* 116, 81–119.

Loewenstein, G. 1999. A visceral account of addiction. In *Getting Hooked: Rationality and Addiction*, ed. J. Elster and O.-J. Skog. Cambridge: Cambridge University Press.

Lyvers, M. 2000. 'Loss of control' in alcoholism and drug addiction: a neuroscientific interpretation. *Experimental and Clinical Psychopharmacology* 8, 225–45.

O'Donoghue, T. and Rabin, M. 1997. Addiction and self control. In *Addiction: Entries and Exits*, ed. J. Elster. New York: Russell Sage Foundation.

Pacula, R. and Chaloupka, F. 2001. The effects of macro-level interventions on addictive behavior. *Substance Use and Misuse* 36, 1901–22.

Robins, L. 1973. *The Vietnam Drug User Returns*. Washington, DC: U.S. Government Printing Office.

Slovic, P. 2000a. What does it mean to know a cumulative risk? Adolescents' perceptions of short-term and long-term consequences of smoking. *Journal of Behavioral Decision Making* 13, 259–66.

Slovic, P. 2000b. Rejoinder: the perils of Viscusi's analyses of smoking risk perceptions. *Journal of Behavioral Decision Making* 13, 273–76.

Viscusi, W. 2000. Comment: the perils of qualitative smoking risk measures. *Journal of Behavioral Decision Making* 13, 267–71.

Wertenbroch, K. 1998. Consumption self-control via purchase quantity rationing of virtue and vice. *Marketing Science* 17, 317–37.

Wertenbroch, K. 2003. Self-rationing: self-control in consumer choice. In *Time and Decision: Economic and Psychological Perspectives on Intertemporal Choice*, ed. G. Loewenstein, D. Read and R. Baumeister. New York: Russell Sage Foundation.

altruism in experiments

Unlike experiments on markets or mechanisms, experiments on altruism are about an individual motive or intention. This raises serious obstacles for research. How do we define an altruistic act, and how do we know altruism when we see it?

The philosopher Thomas Nagel provides this definition of altruism: 'By altruism I mean not abject self-sacrifice, but merely a willingness to act in the consideration of the interests of other persons, without the need of ulterior motives' (1970, p. 79). Notice that there are two parts to this definition. First, the act must be in the consideration of others. It may or may not imply sacrifice on one's own part, but it does require that the consequences for someone else affect one's own choice. The second aspect is that one does not need 'ulterior motives' rooted in selfishness to explain altruistic behaviours. Of course, ulterior motives may exist alongside altruism, but they cannot be the only motives.

If this is our definition of altruism, then how do we know altruism when we see it? The answer, unfortunately, is necessarily a negative one – we only know when we do not see it. Altruism is part of the behaviour that you cannot capture with a specifically defined ulterior motive. Experimental investigation of altruism is thus focused around eliminating any possible ulterior motives rooted in selfishness. One of the central motives that potentially confounds altruism is the warm-glow of giving, that is, the utility one gets simply from the act of giving *without* any concern for the interests of others (Andreoni, 1989; 1990). While it is possible that warm-glow exists apart from altruism, it seems most likely that the two are complements – the stronger your desire to act unselfishly, the greater the personal satisfaction from doing so. Indeed, the two may be inextricably linked. Having a personal identity as an altruist may necessarily precede altruistic acts, and maintaining that identity can only come from actually being generous.

In what follows we will highlight the main experimental evidence regarding choices made in the interests of others, and the systematic attempts in the literature to rule out ulterior motives for these choices. Since these serious and repeated attempts to rule out ulterior motives have not been totally successful, the experimental evidence, like Thomas Nagel, favours the possibility of altruism.

Laboratory experiments with evidence of altruism

In describing the games below, we adopt the convention of using Nash equilibrium to refer to the prediction that holds if all subjects are rational money-maximizers.

Prisoner's Dilemma

There have been thousands of studies using Prisoner's Dilemma (PD) games in the psychology and political science literatures, all exploring the stubborn nature of cooperation (Kelley and Stanelski, 1970). Roth and Murnigham (1978) explored PD games under paid incentives and with a number of different payoff conditions. Their study confirmed to economists that cooperation is robust.

Sceptics noted, however, that cooperation need not be caused by altruism. First, inexperience and initial confusion may cause subjects to cooperate. Second, subjects in a finitely repeated version of the game may cooperate if they each believe there is a chance someone actually is altruistic. Behaviourally this 'sequential equilibrium reputation hypothesis' (Kreps et al., 1982) does not actually require subjects to be altruistic, but only that they believe that they are sufficiently likely to encounter such a person.

Andreoni and Miller (1993) explore these two factors by asking subjects to play 20 separate ten-period repeated PD games. A control treatment had subjects constantly changing partners, thus unable to build reputations. They find significant evidence for reputations, but that these alone cannot explain the level of cooperation, especially at the end of the experiment. Rather, they estimate that about 20 per cent of subjects actually need to be altruistic to support the equilibrium findings. This finding is corroborated in other repeated games, such as Camerer and Weigelt's (1988) moral hazard game, McKelvey and Palfrey's (1992) centipede game, and in a two-period PD of Andreoni and Samuelson (2006).

Public goods
Linear public goods games have incentives that make them resemble a many-person PD game. Individuals have an endowment m which they each must allocate between themselves and a public account. Each of the n members of the group earns α for each dollar allocated to the public account. By design, $0 < \alpha < 1$, so giving nothing is a dominant strategy, but $\alpha n > 1$, so giving m is Pareto efficient.

The results of these games are that average giving is significantly above zero, even as we change n, m and α (Isaac and Walker, 1988; Isaac, Walker and Williams; 1994) and whether the play is with the same group of 'partners' or with randomly changing groups of 'strangers' (Andreoni, 1988). Hence, reputations play little role in public goods games (Andreoni and Croson, 2008; Palfrey and Prisbrey, 1996).

In his review of this literature, Ledyard (1995) notes that, with a dominant strategy of giving zero, any error or variance in the data could mistakenly be viewed as altruism. Thus, to determine what drives giving one needs to confirm that subjects understand the dominant strategy but choose to give anyway.

Andreoni (1995) develops a design to separate 'kindness' from 'confusion' in linear public goods games. Rather than paying subjects for their absolute performance, in one treatment he paid subjects by their relative performance. Converting subjects' ranks into their payoffs converts a positive-sum game to a zero-sum game. It follows that even altruists have no incentive to cooperate when paid by rank (that is, under the usual definition of altruism where people love themselves at least as much as they love others). Cooperation by subjects in the treatment group, therefore, provides a measure of confusion. Andreoni finds that both kindness and confusion are significant, and about half all cooperation in public goods games is from people who understand free riding but choose to give anyway.

To establish that giving is deliberate, however, does not necessarily mean it is based in altruism; it could, instead, be from warm-glow. Two papers, using similar experimental designs but different data analysis methods, explore this question by separating the marginal net return that a gift to the public good has for the giver and for the recipient. The 'internal return' experienced by the giver should affect warm-glow and altruism, but the 'external return' received by the others affects only altruism. Palfrey and Prisbrey (1997) find that warm-glow dominates altruism, while Goeree, Holt and Laury (2002) find mostly altruism. Combining this evidence, it appears that both motives are likely to be significant.

Another way to test for the presence of altruism and warm-glow is to choose a manipulation that would have different predictions in the two regimes. Andreoni (1993) looks at the complete crowding out hypothesis, which states that a lump-sum tax, used to increase government spending on a public good, will reduce an altruist's voluntary contributions by the amount of the tax. He employs a public goods game with an interior Nash equilibrium. Suppose subjects care only about the payoffs of other subjects (altruism). Then if we force subjects to make a minimum contribution below the Nash equilibrium, this should simply crowd out their chosen gift, leaving the total gift unchanged. If they get utility from the act of giving (warm-glow), by contrast, crowding out should be incomplete. Andreoni finds crowding at 85 per cent, which is significantly different from both zero and 100 percent. This confirms the findings from the last paragraph; both warm-glow and altruism are evident in experiments on public goods. Similar findings are presented in Bolton and Katok (1998) and Eckel, Grossman and Johnston (2005).

Dictator games
This line of research began with the ultimatum game, where a proposer makes an offer on the split of a sum of money. If the responder accepts, the offer is implemented, while if she rejects both sides get nothing. Guth, Schmittberger and Schwarze (1982) find that proposers strike fair deals and leave money on the table. Is this altruism, or just fear of rejection? To answer this question Forsythe et al. (1994) also examine behaviour in a dictator game that cuts out the second stage, leaving selfish proposers free to keep the whole pie for themselves, and leaving altruists unconstrained to give a little or a lot. While keeping the entire endowment is the modal choice in the dictator game, a significant fraction of people give money away. On average, people share about 25 per cent of their endowment. This seems to indicate significant altruism.

Again, researchers have explored numerous non-altruistic explanations. One is that, while the dictator's identity is unknown to the recipient, it is not unknown to the researcher. This lack of 'social distance' could cause the selfish but self-conscious subjects to give when they would prefer not to. Hoffman et al. (1994) take elaborate steps to increase the anonymity and confidentiality of the subjects so that even the researcher cannot know their choices for sure. They find that this decreases giving to about 10 per cent of endowments. However, this 'double anonymous' methodology creates problems of its own. Bolton, Katok and Zwick (1998) argue that greater anonymity makes the participants sceptical about whether the transfers will be carried out. Bohnet and Frey (1999) find that reducing the social distance increases equal splits greatly, but in their anonymous treatments giving again averages 25 per cent (see also Rege and Telle, 2004).

Andreoni and Miller (2002) take a different approach. They note that, if altruism is a deliberate choice, then it should follow the neoclassical principles of revealed preference. They gave subjects a menu of several dictator 'budgets', each with different 'incomes' and different 'prices' of transferring this income to another anonymous subject. By checking choices against the generalized axiom of revealed preference, they show that indeed most subjects are rational altruists, that is, they have consistent and well-behaved preferences for altruistic giving in a dictator game. They also show substantial heterogeneity across subjects, with preferences ranging from utilitarian (maximizing total payments to both subjects) to Rawlsian (equalizing payments to both subjects). Interestingly, men and women are on average equally altruistic in this study, but vary significantly in response to price. Andreoni and Vesterlund (2001) show that men are more likely to be utilitarian, and women are more likely to be Rawlsian. This implies that men are significantly more generous when giving is cheap (that is, it costs the giver less than one to give one), but women are significantly more altruistic when giving is expensive (costs greater than or equal one to give one). Which is the fairer sex, therefore, depends on the price of giving (see also Eckel and Grossman, 1998, on dictator games when the price is one).

Trust games and gift exchange
When someone buys a loaf of bread from a baker, there is a moment when one party has both the bread and the money and the incentive to take both. Why don't they? Similarly, why are some car mechanics truthful, and why do some workers put in an honest effort even when they are not monitored? These questions have been studied under names of trust games and gift exchange.

In the trust game, two players are endowed with M each. A sender chooses to pass x to a receiver. A receiver receives kx, where $k > 1$. The receiver then chooses a y to pass back to the sender. Senders earn $M - x + y$, while receivers earn $M + kx - y$. Since $y = 0$ is a dominant strategy for receivers, $x = 0$ is the subgame perfect equilibrium strategy for senders. That is, since the baker keeps both the bread and the money, no exchange is attempted. Despite this dire prediction, x and y are often positive, and y is typically increasing in x. While there is tremendous variance, the average y is often slightly below the average x (Berg, Dickhaut and McCabe, 1995).

The gift exchange game is a nonlinear version of the trust game above. Fehr, Kirchsteiger and Riedl (1993) adapted the Akerlof (1982) labour market model of efficiency wages. Some subjects play the roles of firms and offer labour contracts to workers. The contracts stipulate a wage and an expected effort level of workers. Since effort is costly and unobservable, it should be minimal. The subjects playing the role of firms should expect low effort, and offer low wages. However, in the experiment wages are high and effort rises with the wage offer, just as Akerlof predicted.

Trust and gift exchange games are often used to argue for the importance of reciprocity. Reciprocity is, however, an ulterior motive – giving in order to either generate or relieve an obligation is not altruism by the definition in our introduction. How much of the exchange can be attributed to altruism alone? Cox (2004) separates these motives by comparing senders in a trust game with those in a dictator game. As dictators have no ulterior motive of generating an obligation, their behaviour can be used to estimate the altruism of senders. For receivers he uses a control group whose x is determined at random by the experimenter. These receivers have no obligation to the sender, thus their transfers serve as a measure of the receivers' altruism. Cox finds that 60 per cent of an average sender's x and 42 per cent of the average receiver's y is motivated by altruism. Thus, while reciprocity is clearly present, altruism is not replaced in this exchange (see also Charness and Haruvy, 2002; Gneezy, Guth and Verboven, 2000).

While some have criticized whether gift exchange in the laboratory is robust to small changes in parameters and presentation (Charness, Frechette and Kagel, 2006), others have challenged gift exchange in the field. List (2006) looks for gift exchange on the trading floor of a sports card market. He conducts a series of experiments that move incrementally from a standard laboratory game with a neutral presentation to actual exchanges on the floor. While he finds that gift exchange (higher-quality product in return for higher price) is not totally extinguished in the actual market, he also finds that reputation is far more important in determining the quality provided by sellers. Gneezy and List (2006) follow up with a labour market experiment. They recruited students to do a one-day job working in a library. The treatment group was told, unexpectedly, that their wage would be 167 per cent of the agreed wage. These subjects were significantly more productive in the first 90 minutes of work than the control subjects. However, after a one-hour lunch break, there was no difference between the productivity of treatment and control. They conclude that gift exchange in actual labour markets may have no long-term effects.

Conclusion

There is ample consistent evidence of altruism in experiments. This follows both from studies that have taken great effort to remove any ulterior motives, as well as studies that provide manipulations that should influence altruism. While the existence and importance of altruism seem well established in the laboratory, many questions that could help us understand and amplify altruism remain unanswered.

First, where do altruistic preferences come from? One notion is that they come from culture. Evidence of this is suggested by differences in behaviour in experiments in different countries (Roth et al., 1991; Henrich et al., 2001). Another notion is that they are acquired as part of psychological development and socialization, as seen in economic experiments using children as subjects (Harbaugh and Krause, 2000). A third possibility for altruism is that we are innately wired to care. Harbaugh, Mayr and Burghart (2007) use fMRI to show that neural activation in the ventral striatum is very similar when money goes to the subject and when it goes to a charity, and that the relative activations actually predict who will give. Tankersley, Stowe and Huettel (2007) show that posterior superior temporal sulcus activation is higher for people who report more helping behaviour outside the lab.

Second, is altruism significant outside the laboratory? The laboratory is, after all, a unique environment. Field experiments on fundraising, such as List and Lucking-Reiley (2002), show the potential of this method for finding good evidence of altruism outside the laboratory, but without giving up all experimental control.

Finally, how does altruism combine with other ulterior motives? Are warm-glow and altruism inextricably linked, and can we use mechanisms that act on warm-glow to amplify altruism and overcome free riding? Does voting to force everyone to provide a public good provide a warm-glow benefit to the voters? Economic experiments may be a productive method for answering these questions, and for using the knowledge of altruism that results to improve the institutions within which altruist economic agents interact.

JAMES ANDREONI WILLIAM T. HARBAUGH AND LISE VESTERLUND

See also **experimental economics, history of; public goods experiments.**

Bibliography
Akerlof, G.A. 1982. Labor contracts as partial gift exchange. *Quarterly Journal of Economics* 97, 543–69.
Andreoni, J. 1988. Why free ride? Strategies and learning in public goods experiments. *Journal of Public Economics* 37, 291–304.
Andreoni, J. 1989. Giving with impure altruism: applications to charity and Ricardian equivalence. *Journal of Political Economy* 97, 1447–58.
Andreoni, J. 1990. Impure altruism and donations to public goods: a theory of warm-glow giving. *Economic Journal* 100, 464–77.
Andreoni, J. 1993. An experimental test of the public-goods crowding-out hypothesis. *American Economic Review* 83, 1317–27.
Andreoni, J. 1995. Cooperation in public-goods experiments: kindness or confusion? *American Economic Review* 85, 891–904.
Andreoni, J. and Croson, R. 2008. Partners versus strangers: the effect of random rematching in public goods experiments. In *Handbook of Experimental Economics Results*, ed. V. Smith and C. Plott. New York: North-Holland, forthcoming.
Andreoni, J. and Miller, J.H. 1993. Rational cooperation in the finitely repeated prisoner's dilemma: experimental evidence. *Economic Journal* 103, 570–85.
Andreoni, J. and Miller, J.H. 2002. Giving according to GARP: an experimental test of the consistency of preferences for altruism. *Econometrica* 70, 737–53.
Andreoni, J. and Samuelson, L. 2006. Building rational cooperation. *Journal of Economic Theory* 127, 117–54.
Andreoni, J. and Vesterlund, L. 2001. Which is the fair sex? Gender differences in altruism. *Quarterly Journal of Economics* 116, 293–312.
Berg, J., Dickhaut, J. and McCabe, K. 1995. Trust, reciprocity, and social history. *Games and Economic Behavior* 10, 122–42.
Bohnet, I. and Frey, B.S. 1999. Social distance and other-regarding behavior in dictator games: comment. *American Economic Review* 89, 335–9.

Bolton, G.E. and Katok, E. 1998. An experimental test of the crowding out hypothesis: the nature of beneficent behavior. *Journal of Economic Behavior and Organization* 37, 315–31.

Bolton, G.E., Katok, E. and Zwick, R. 1998. Dictator game giving: rules of fairness versus acts of kindness. *International Journal of Game Theory* 27, 269–99.

Camerer, C. and Weigelt, K. 1988. Experimental tests of a sequential equilibrium reputation model. *Econometrica* 56, 1–36.

Charness, G., Frechette, G.R. and Kagel, J.H. 2004. How robust is laboratory gift exchange? *Experimental Economics* 7, 189–205.

Charness, G. and Haruvy, E. 2002. Altruism, equity, and reciprocity in a gift-exchange experiment: an encompassing approach. *Games and Economic Behavior* 40, 203–31.

Cox, J.C. 2004. How to identify trust and reciprocity. *Games and Economic Behavior* 46, 260–81.

Eckel, C.C. and Grossman, P.J. 1998. Are women less selfish than men? Evidence from dictator experiments. *Economic Journal* 108, 726–35.

Eckel, C.C., Grossman, P.J. and Johnston, R.M. 2005. An experimental test of the crowding out hypothesis. *Journal of Public Economics* 89, 1543–60.

Fehr, E., Kirchsteiger, G. and Riedl, A. 1993. Does fairness prevent market clearing? An experimental investigation. *Quarterly Journal of Economics* 108, 437–59.

Forsythe, R., Horowitz, J.L., Savin, N.E. and Sefton, M. 1994. Fairness in simple bargaining experiments. *Games and Economic Behavior* 6, 347–69.

Gneezy, U. Guth, W. and Verboven, F. 2000. Presents or investments? An experimental analysis. *Journal of Economic Psychology* 21, 481–93.

Gneezy, U. and List, J.A. 2006. Putting behavioral economics to work: testing for gift exchange in labor markets using field experiments. *Econometrica* 74, 1365–84.

Goeree, J.K., Holt, C.A. and Laury, S.K. 2002. Private costs and public benefits: unraveling the effects of altruism and noisy behavior. *Journal of Public Economics* 83, 255–76.

Guth, W. Schmittberger, R. and Schwarze, B. 1982. An experimental analysis of ultimatum bargaining. *Journal of Economic Behavior and Organization* 3, 367–88.

Harbaugh, W.T., Mayr, U. and Burghart, D. 2007. Neural responses to taxation and voluntary giving reveal motives for charitable donations. *Science*, forthcoming.

Harbaugh, W.T. and Krause, K. 2000. Children's altruism in public good and dictator experiments. *Economic Inquiry* 38, 95–109.

Henrich, J., Boyd, R., Bowles, S., Camerer, C., Fehr, E., Gintis, H. and McElreath, R. 2001. In search of homo economicus: behavioral experiments in 15 small-scale societies. *American Economic Review* 91, 73–8.

Hoffman, E., McCabe, K., Shachat, K. and Smith, V.L. 1994. Preferences, property rights and anonymity in bargaining games. *Games and Economic Behavior* 7, 346–80.

Isaac, M.R. and Walker, J.M. 1988. Group size effects in public goods provision: the voluntary contributions mechanism. *Quarterly Journal of Economics* 103, 179–99.

Isaac, M.R., Walker, J.M. and Williams, A.W. 1994. Group size and the voluntary provision of public goods: experimental evidence utilizing large groups. *Journal of Public Economics* 54, 1–36.

Kelley, H.H. and Stanelski, A.J. 1970. Social interaction basis of cooperators' and competitors' beliefs about others. *Journal of Personality and Social Psychology* 16, 66–91.

Kreps, D., Milgorm, P., Roberts, J. and Wilson, R. 1982. Rational cooperation in the finitely repeated prisoners' dilemma. *Journal of Economic Theory* 27, 245–52.

Ledyard, J.O. 1995. Public goods: a survey of experimental research. In *The Handbook of Experimental Economics*, ed. J.H. Kagel and A.E. Roth. Princeton: Princeton University Press.

List, J.A. 2006. The behavioralist meets the market: measuring social preferences and reputation effects in actual transactions. *Journal of Political-Economy* 114, 1–37.

List, J.A. and Lucking-Reiley, D. 2002. The effects of seed money and refunds on charitable giving: experimental evidence from a university capital campaign. *Journal of Political Economy* 110, 215–33.

McKelvey, R.D. and Palfrey, T.R. 1992. An experimental study of the centipede game. *Econometrica* 60, 803–36.

Nagel, T. 1970. *The Possibility of Altruism*. Oxford: Clarendon Press.

Palfrey, T.R. and Prisbrey, J.E. 1996. Altruism, reputation and noise in linear public goods experiments. *Journal of Public Economics* 61, 409–27.

Palfrey, T.R. and Prisbrey, J.E. 1997. Anomalous behavior in public goods experiments: how much and why? *American Economic Review* 87, 829–46.

Rege, M. and Telle, K. 2004. The impact of social approval and framing on cooperation in public good situations. *Journal of Public Economics* 88, 1625–44.

Roth, A.E. and Murnigham, J.K. 1978. Equilibrium behavior and repeated play of the prisoner's dilemma. *Journal of Mathematical Psychology* 17, 189–98.

Roth, A.E. Prasnikar, V. Okuno-Fujiwara, M. and Zamir, S. 1991. Bargaining and market behavior in Jerusalem, Ljubljana, Pittsburgh, and Tokyo: an experimental study. *American Economic Review* 81, 1068–95.

Tankersley, D. Stowe, C.J. and Huettel, S.A. 2007. Altruism is associated with an increased neural response to agency. *Nature Neuroscience* 10, 150–1.

auctions (experiments)

Experimental work in auctions interacts with theory, providing a basis for testing and modifying theoretical developments. It has advantages and disadvantages relative to empirical work with field data, so that we view the two as complimentary. Experimental work is used increasingly as a test bed for new auction formats such as the Federal Communication Commission's (FCC) sale of spectrum (air-wave) rights.

Until recently most of theoretical and experimental work was devoted to single-unit demand auctions. With the success of the FCC's spectrum auctions, much of the interest has shifted to auctions in which individual bidders demand multiple units. Experimental work in this area is still in its infancy. In keeping with the historical development of the field, we first report on single-unit demand auctions and then move to multi-unit demand auctions and Internet auctions.

Single-unit, private-value auctions

Initial experimental research on auctions focused on the independent private values (IPV) model investigating the revenue equivalence theorem. In the IPV model each bidder knows his valuation of the item with certainty, bidders' valuations are drawn identically and independently from each other, and bidders know the distribution from which their rivals' values are drawn (but not their values) and the number of bidders. Under the revenue equivalence theorem the four main auction formats – first- and second-price sealed-bid auctions, English and Dutch auctions – yield the same average revenue for risk neutral bidders. Further, first-price sealed-bid and Dutch auctions are theoretically isomorphic – they yield the same revenue for each auction trial regardless of risk preferences – as are second-price sealed-bid and English clock auctions. These isomorphisms are particularly attractive as it is hard to control bidders' risk preferences. These theoretical results are also quite surprising and counter-intuitive as the Dutch auction starts with a high price which is lowered until a bidder accepts at that price. And in the English auctions the price starts low and increases until only one bidder is left standing and pays the price where the next-to-last bidder dropped out; while in a first- (second-) price sealed-bid auction the high bidder wins the item and pays the highest (second-highest) bid.

An experimental session typically consists of 20–40 auction periods under a given auction institution. Subjects' valuations are determined randomly prior to each auction period (by the experimenter) and are private information. Valuations are typically independent and identical draws (i.i.d) from a *uniform* distribution. In each period the high bidder earns a profit equal to his value less the auction price; other bidders earn zero profit. Bids are commonly restricted to be non-negative and rounded to the nearest penny. Theory does not specify what information feedback bidders ought to get after each auction. Although such information is unimportant in a one-shot auction, it may be important, even critical, to learning given that experimental sessions typically consist of a number of auction periods. Information feedback usually differs between different experimenters, with almost all experimenters reporting back the auction price to all bidders and own earnings to the winning bidder.

Strategic equivalence usually fails between the relevant auction formats: Coppinger, Smith and Titus (1980) and Cox, Roberson and Smith (1982) found higher prices in first-price than in Dutch auctions (about five per cent higher) with these differences holding across auctions with different numbers of bidders. Further, bidding was significantly above the risk-neutral Nash equilibrium (RNNE) in the first-price auctions for all numbers of bidders $n > 3$, which is consistent with risk-averse bidders.

Kagel, Harstad and Levin (1987) reported failures of strategic equivalence in second-price and English clock auctions, with winning bids in the second-price auctions averaging 11 per cent *above* the predicted equilibrium price. In contrast, market prices converge rapidly to the predicted equilibrium in the clock auctions. Bidding above value in second-price auctions is widespread, with 62 per cent of all bids above values, 30 per cent of all bids essentially equal to value (within five cents of it), and eight per cent of all bids below it (Kagel and Levin, 1993). (In clock auctions price rises by fixed increments with bidders counted as active until they drop out – and are not permitted to re-enter the auction. This format insures clear information flows as a consequence of announcing irrevocable drop-out prices.)

Bidding above value in second-price auctions is attributable to a number of factors: (*a*) it is sustainable since average profits are positive, (*b*) figuring out the dominant strategy is not that obvious, and (*c*) the feedback from losses that would promote the dominant bidding strategy is weak (Kagel, Harstad and Levin, 1987). Subsequent research generalizes the superiority of the (dynamic) clock auction format compared to the (static) sealed-bid format to Vickrey-style auctions in which bidders demand multiple units. The closer conformity to equilibrium outcomes in the clock auctions results from the clock format in conjunction with bidders knowing that the auction ends when the next-to-last bidder drops out. This induces bidders to remain active as long as the clock price is less than their value (as they have nothing to lose by remaining active and might win the item) and to drop out once the price is greater than their value (as they will lose money for sure should they win the item) (Kagel and Levin, 2006).

Efficiency in private value auctions can be measured by the percentage of auctions won by the high-value holder. In Cox, Roberson and Smith (1982) 88 per cent of the first-price auctions were Pareto efficient compared with 80 per cent of the Dutch auctions. In contrast, efficiency in first- and second-price auctions may be quite comparable; for example, 82 per cent of the first-price auctions and 79 per cent of the second-price auctions reported in Kagel and Levin (1993) were Pareto efficient. More work needs to be devoted to comparing efficiency across auction institutions.

A number of papers have explored bidding above the RNNE in first-price sealed-bid auctions, questioning the risk-aversion interpretation. This has generated some heated debate (see the December 1992 issue of the *American Economic Review*). Isaac and James (2000) compare estimates of risk preferences from first-price auctions with estimates using the Becker–DeGroot–Marshak (BDM) procedure for comparably risky choices. The Spearman rank–correlation coefficient between individual subject risk parameters is significantly *negatively* correlated under the two procedures. Subjects whose bids in the first-price auction are relatively risk neutral remain risk neutral under BDM, but those who are relatively risk averse in the first-price auction become relatively risk loving under BDM. The net result is that *aggregate* measures of risk preferences show that bidders are risk averse in the first-price auction but risk neutral, or moderately risk loving, under the BDM procedure. Although it is well known from the psychology literature that different elicitation procedures will yield somewhat different quantitative predictions, a negative correlation between measures seems rather astonishing. (See Dorsey and Razzolini, 2003, for a similar investigation.)

Neugebauer and Selten (2006) compare treatments with different information feedback: (i) a bidder only learns if s/he won the auction or not, (ii) the winning bid (market price) is revealed to bidders whether they win or not; and (iii) the winning bid is revealed to bidders and the winner learns the second highest bid as well. They find that average bids are highest under treatment (ii) and exceed the RNNE for every given market size. In contrast, bidding above the RNNE does not occur consistently, or is not as strong, in the other two treatments. They use 'learning direction theory' to argue that the information feedback in (ii) promotes bidding above the RNNE. However, the result for treatment (iii) contrasts with results from Kagel, Harstad and Levin (1987) and Dyer, Kagel and Levin (1989a), who find consistent bidding above the RNNE when providing bidders with all bids and valuations following each auction. Perhaps the best conclusion at this point is that subjects typically act 'as if' they are risk averse in first-price auctions, while the underlying basis of their behaviour remains open to interpretation.

In spite of the reported deviations from equilibrium outcomes reported above, the comparative static implications of the IPV model tend to hold (albeit with varying levels of noise). Bidding in first-price auctions increases regularly in response to increased numbers of bidders. For example, in a series of first-price sealed-bid auctions, 86 per cent of subjects increased their bids when the number of bidders increased from five to ten, with the majority of these increases (60 per cent) being statistically significant, with no subjects decreasing their bids by a statistically significant amount (Battalio, Kogut and Meyer, 1990). More aggressive bidding in response to increased numbers of rivals would seem to be a natural reaction, and can be rationalized by plausible ad hoc rules of thumb.

Kagel and Levin (1993) provide a more stringent test of the comparative static implications of the IPV model using a third-price auction in which the high bidder wins the item and pays the third-highest bid. In this case the model predicts that bids will be *above* values and will be *reduced* in response to increases in n. They find that 85–90 per cent of all bids are above value compared with 58–67 per cent in second-price auctions and less than 0.5 per cent in first-price auctions. Further, comparing auctions with $n = 5$ and $n = 10$ (i) in first-price auctions *all* bidders increased their bids on average (average increase of $0.65 per auction; $p < .01$), (ii) in second-price auctions the majority of bidders did not change their bids on average (average decrease of $0.04; $p>.10$), and (iii) in third-price auctions 46 per cent of all subjects *decreased* their bids on average (average decrease of $0.40 per auction; $p<.05$). Even stronger qualitative support for the theory is reported when the calculations are restricted to valuations lying in the top half of the domain of valuations (where bidders have a realistic chance of winning and might be expected to take bidding more seriously). Thus, although a number of bidders in third-price auctions clearly err in response to increased numbers of rivals by increasing, or not changing, their bids, the change in pricing rules has relatively large and statistically significant effects on bidders' responses in the *direction* that Nash equilibrium bidding theory predicts. This experiment also illustrates one of the great strengths of the experimental method as there are no third-price auctions outside the lab, where it was developed for the explicit purpose of providing unusual, counter-intuitive predictions to use in testing the theory. The results are increased confidence in the fundamental 'gravitational' forces underlying the theory, in spite of violations of its point predictions. The latter could be the result of some uncontrolled factor impacting on behaviour and/or simple miscalibration on subjects' part.

Single-unit common value auctions

In common value auctions (CVA) the value of the item is the same to all bidders. What makes common value auctions interesting is that bidders receive signals (estimates) that are correlated (affiliated) with the value of the item but they do not know its true value. Mineral rights auctions (for example, outer continental shelf – OCS – oil lease auctions) are usually modelled as a common value auction. There is a common value element to most auctions. Bidders for a painting may purchase it for their own pleasure, a private value element, but also for investment and eventual resale, the common value element.

Experimental research on CVAs has focused on the 'winner's curse'. Although all bidders obtain unbiased estimates of the item's value, they typically win in cases where they have (one of) the highest signal value. Unless this adverse selection problem is accounted for, it will result in winning bids that are systematically too high, earning below normal or negative profits – a disequilibrium phenomenon. Oil companies claim they fell prey to the winner's curse in early OCS lease sales, with similar claims made in a variety of other settings (for example, free agency markets for professional athletes and corporate takeovers). Economists are naturally sceptical of such claims as they involve out-of-equilibrium play. Experiments clearly show the presence of a winner's curse for inexperienced bidders under a variety of circumstances and with different experimental subjects: average undergraduate or MBA students (Bazeramn and Samuelson, 1983; Kagel and Levin, 1986), extremely bright (Cal Tech) undergraduates (Lind and Plott, 1991), experienced professionals in a laboratory setting (Dyer, Kagel and Levin, 1989b), and auctions in which it is common knowledge that one bidder knows, with certainty, the value of the item (Kagel and

Levin, 1999). Further, these deviations from equilibrium predictions cannot be explained by simple miscalibration on bidders' part as the theory's comparative static implications are systematically violated when bidders suffer from a winner's curse; for example, bidder responses to additional information or increased numbers of rivals.

Kagel et al. (1989) find that inexperienced bidders suffer a pervasive winner's curse in first-price, sealed-bid auctions. For the first nine auctions, profits averaged minus $2.57 compared with the RNNE prediction of $1.90, with only 17 per cent of all auctions having positive profits. This is not a simple matter of bad luck as 59 per cent of all bids, and 82 per cent of the high bids, were above the expected value of the item conditional on winning the auction. Although public information in first-price auctions is predicted to raise sellers' revenue, it reduces it for inexperienced bidders as subjects use the public information to help overcome the winner's curse (Kagel and Levin, 1986). Similarly, 'public information' reduces revenue in English clock auctions when bidders suffer from a winner's curse (Levin, Kagel and Richard, 1996). Further, experienced bidders appear to adjust to the winner's curse through a 'hot stove' learning process: with the losses, bids are lowered and losses are mitigated, or eliminated, but there is no real understanding of the adverse selection problem. For example, an increase in n generates higher individual bids, although theory predicts a slight reduction (Kagel and Levin, 1986). Efforts to explain the winner's curse in terms of limited liability for losses and/or the 'joy of winning' fail as well (Kagel and Levin, 1991; Holt and Sherman, 1994). In short, inexperienced subjects do not perform well in pure common value auctions.

Experienced subjects learn to overcome the worst effects of the winner's curse, earning positive average profits. But these rarely exceed 65 per cent of the RNNE profit, and virtually all subjects are *not* best responding to their rivals' overly aggressive bids (Kagel and Richard, 2001). However, once bidders overcome the worst effects of the winner's curse, public information raises sellers' revenue, English auctions raise more revenue than sealed-bid auctions, and a number of other comparative static implications of the theory are satisfied as well (Kagel and Levin, 2002). Experienced bidders learn to overcome the winner's curse through a combination of individual learning and market selection process whereby bankrupt bidders self-select out of further experimental sessions. Ability as measured by composite SAT/ACT scores (standardized college entrance exam scores) matters in terms of avoiding the winner's curse, with the biggest and most consistent impact resulting from those with *below median* scores being more susceptible to the winner's curse. Economics and business majors consistently bid more aggressively than others (thus, lose more), and women, at least initially, are much more susceptible to a winner's curse than men. However, there is still a winner's curse even for the best-calibrated demographic and ability groups (Casari, Ham and Kagel, 2007).

Experiments combining common-value and private-value elements

Goeree and Offerman (2002) provide the only experimental study to date in which the object's expected value depends on both private and common value elements. (The difficulty here is in combining private and common value information into a single statistic that maps into a bid.) Actual bids lie in between the RNNE benchmark of fully rational bidding and the naive benchmark in which subjects completely fail to account for the winner's curse. The winner's curse effect is more pronounced the less important a bidder's private value is relative to the common value. Realized efficiency is roughly at the level predicted under the RNNE, with the winner's curse only raising seller revenue and cutting into bidder profits. This occurs because (*a*) almost all bidders suffer from a winner's curse and (*b*) the degree of suffering is roughly the same across bidders, so that the size of the private value element serves to dictate who wins the item.

In an almost common value auction one bidder, the advantaged bidder, has an added private value for the item, unlike all the other (regular) bidders who care only about the common value. With only two bidders, even a tiny private value advantage is predicted to have an explosive effect in second-price sealed-bid auctions: the advantaged bidder always wins and revenue decreases dramatically as the regular bidder lowers her bid to protect against a winner's curse. This effect extends to a variety of English auctions that start with more than two bidders, raising serious concerns about the English auction format (Klemperer, 1998). Three experiments have looked at almost common value auctions using both second-price sealed-bid and clock auctions (Avery and Kagel, 1997; Rose and Levin, 2005; and Rose and Kagel, 2005). In all cases the response to the private value advantage has been proportional rather than explosive. This is true even with experienced bidders who earn a respectable share of RNNE profits in pure common value first-price and clock auctions (Rose and Kagel, 2005). The apparent reason for these failures is that bidders do not fully appreciate the adverse selection effect conditional on winning, which is exacerbated for regular bidders with an advantaged rival. As such, the behavioural mechanism underlying the explosive effect is not present, and there are no forces at work to replace it.

Internet auctions

Internet auctions provide new opportunities to conduct experiments to study old and new puzzles. Lucking-Reiley (1999) has used the Internet to sell collectable trading cards under the four standard auction formats, testing the revenue equivalence theorem. He finds that Dutch auctions produce 30 per cent higher revenue than first-price auctions, a reversal of previous laboratory results, and that English and second-price auctions produce roughly equivalent revenue. These results are interesting but lack the controls present in more standard laboratory experiments; that is, there may well be a common value element to the trading cards, and Dutch auctions provide an opportunity to use the game cards immediately, which cannot be done until the fixed closing date in the first-price auctions. Garratt, Walker and Wooders (2004) conduct a second-price auction, recruiting subjects with substantial experience bidding on eBay. Using induced valuations, they find that average bids are close to valuations, but those with prior experience as *sellers* tend to underbid and those with prior experience as *buyers* tend to overbid.

In eBay auctions which have a fixed closing time many bidders *snipe* (submit bids seconds before the closing time), while other bidders increase their bids over time in response to higher bids. This seems puzzling since eBay has a number of characteristics similar to a second-price auction. In addition, there is substantially more last-minute bidding for comparable (private-value) items in eBay than in Amazon auctions, which automatically extend the deadline in response to last-minute bids. Roth and Ockenfels (2002) argue that sniping results from the fixed deadline in eBay, suggesting at least two rational reasons for sniping. Because there are differences between eBay and Amazon other than their ending rules, they conduct a laboratory experiment in which the only difference between auction institutions is the ending rule – a dynamic eBay auction with a .8 (1.0) probability that a late bid will be accepted (eBay.8 and eBay1, respectively) and an Amazon-style auction with a .8 probability that a late bid will be accepted, in which case the auction is automatically extended (Ariely, Ockenfels and Roth, 2005). The results show quite clearly that there is more late bidding in both eBay auctions than in the Amazon auction. Further, there is significantly more late bidding in eBay1 than in eBay.8, which at least rules out one possible rational explanation for sniping – implicit collusion on the part of snipers in an effort to get the item at rock-bottom prices since not all last-minute bids will be recorded (due to congestion) at the website.

Salmon and Wilson (2008) investigate the Internet practice of second-chance offers to non-winning bidders when selling multiple (identical) items. They compare a two-stage game with a second-price auction followed by an ultimatum game between the seller and the second-highest bidder with a sequential English auction. As predicted, the auction-ultimatum game mechanism generates more revenue than the sequential English auction.

Multi-unit demand auctions

Most of the work on multi-unit demand auctions has been devoted to mechanism design issues, in particular dealing with problems created by complementarities, or synergies, between items. Absent package bidding, the latter can create an 'exposure' problem whereby efficient outcomes require submitting bids above the stand-alone values for individual units since the value of the package is more than the sum of the individual values. Correcting for this problem by permitting package bids increases the complexity of the auction significantly, and creates a 'threshold' problem whereby 'small' bidders (for example, those with only local markets) could, in combination, potentially outbid a large competitor who can internalize the complementarities. But the small bidders have no means to coordinate their bids. Leading examples of this line of research are Porter et al. (2003), Kwasnica et al. (2005), and Goeree, Holt and Ledyard (2006). Much more work remains to be done in this area.

JOHN H. KAGEL AND DAN LEVIN

Bibliography

Ariely, D., Ockenfels, A. and Roth, A.E. 2005. An experimental analysis of ending rules in internet auctions. *RAND Journal of Economics* 36, 890–907.

Avery, C. and Kagel, J.H. 1997. Second-price auctions with asymmetric payoffs: an experimental investigation. *Journal of Economics and Management Strategy* 6, 573–604.

Battalio, R.C., Kogut, C.A. and Meyer, D.J. 1990. Individual and market bidding in a Vickrey first-price auction: varying market size and information. In *Advances in Behavioral Economics*, vol. 2, ed. L. Green and J.H. Kagel. Norwood, NJ: Ablex Publishing.

Bazeramn, M.H. and Samuelson, W.F. 1983. I won the auction but don't want the prize. *Journal of Conflict Resolution* 27, 618–34.

Casari, M., Ham, J.C. and Kagel, J.H. 2007. Selection bias, demographic effects and ability effects in common value auction experiments. *American Economic Review* 97, 1278–304.

Coppinger, V.M., Smith, V.L. and Titus, J.A. 1980. Incentives and behavior in English, Dutch and sealed-bid auctions. *Economic Inquiry* 43, 1–22.

Cox, J., Roberson, B. and Smith, V.L. 1982. Theory and behavior of single object auctions. In *Research in Experimental Economics*, ed. V.L. Smith. Greenwich: JAI Press.

Dorsey, R. and Razzolini, L. 2003. Explaining overbidding in first price auctions using controlled lotteries. *Experimental Economics* 6, 123–40.

Dyer, D., Kagel, J.H. and Levin, D. 1989a. Resolving uncertainty about the number of bidders in independent private-value auctions: an experimental analysis. *RAND Journal of Economics* 20, 268–79.

Dyer, D., Kagel, J.H. and Levin, D. 1989b. A comparison of naive and experienced bidders in common value offer auctions: a laboratory analysis. *Economic Journal* 99, 108–15.

Garratt, R., Walker, M. and Wooders, J. 2004. Behavior in second-price auctions by highly experienced eBay buyers and sellers. Working Paper No. 1181, Department of Economics, UC Santa Barbara.

Goeree, J.K., Holt, C.A. and Ledyard, J.O. 2006. *An Experimental Comparison of the FCC's Combinatorial and Non-Combinatorial Simultaneous Multiple Round Auctions.* Prepared for the Wireless Telecommunications Bureau of the Federal Communications Commission. Online. Available at HTTP://WIRELESS.FCC.GOV/AUCTIONS/DATA/PAPERSANDSTUDIES/FCC_FINAL_REPORT_071206.PDF, accessed 1 February 2007.

Goeree, J.K. and Offerman, T. 2002. Efficiency in auctions with private and common values: an experimental study. *American Economic Review* 92, 625–43.

Holt, C.A., Jr. and Sherman, R. 1994. The loser's curse and bidder's bias. *American Economic Review* 84, 642–52.

Isaac, M. and James, D. 2000. Just who are you calling risk averse? *Journal of Risk and Uncertainty* 20, 177–87.

Kagel, J.H., Harstad, R.M. and Levin, D. 1987. Information impact and allocation rules in auctions with affiliated private values: a laboratory study. *Econometrica* 55, 1275–304.

Kagel, J.H. and Levin, D. 1986. The winner's curse and public information in common value auctions. *American Economic Review* 76, 894–920.

Kagel, J.H. and Levin, D. 1991. The winner's curse and public information in common value auctions: reply. *American Economic Review* 81, 362–9.

Kagel, J.H. and Levin, D. 1993. Independent private value auctions: bidder behavior in first-, second- and third-price auctions with varying numbers of bidders. *Economic Journal* 103, 868–79.

Kagel, J.H. and Levin, D. 1999. Common value auctions with insider information. *Econometrica* 67, 1219–38.

Kagel, J.H. and Levin, D. 2001. Behavior in multi-unit demand auctions: experiments with uniform price and dynamic Vickrey auctions. *Econometrica* 69, 413–54.

Kagel, J.H. and Levin, D. 2002. Bidding in common value auctions: a survey of experimental research. In *Common Value Auctions and the Winner's Curse.* Princeton: Princeton University Press.

Kagel, J.H. and Levin, D. 2006. Implementing efficient multi-object auction institutions: an experimental study of the performance of boundedly rational agents. Mimeo, Ohio State University.

Kagel, J.H., Levin, D., Battalio, R. and Meyer, D.J. 1989. First-price common value auctions: bidder behavior and the winner's curse. *Economic Inquiry* 27, 241–58.

Kagel, J.H. and Richard, J.F. 2001. Super-experienced bidders in first-price common value auctions: rules of thumb, Nash equilibrium bidding and the winner's curse. *Review of Economics and Statistics* 83, 408–19.

Klemperer, P. 1998. Auctions with almost common values: the 'wallet game' and its applications. *European Economic Review* 42, 757–69.

Kwasnica, A.M., Ledyard, J.O., Porter, D. and DeMartini, C. 2005. A new and improved design for multiobject iterative auctions. *Management Science* 51, 419–34.

Levin, D., Kagel, J.H. and Richard, J.F. 1996. Revenue effects and information processing in English common value auctions. *American Economic Review* 86, 442–60.

Lind, B. and Plott, C.R. 1991. The winner's curse: experiments with buyers and with sellers. *American Economic Review* 81, 335–46.

Lucking-Reiley, D. 1999. Using field experiments to test equivalence between auction formats: magic on the internet. *American Economic Review* 89, 1062–80.

Neugebauer, T. and Selten, R. 2006. Individual behavior of first-price auctions: the importance of information feedback in computerized experimental markets. *Games and Economic Behavior* 54, 183–204.

Porter, D., Rassenti, S., Roopnarine, A. and Smith, V. 2003. Combinatorial auction design. *Proceedings of the National Academy of Sciences* 100, 11153–7.

Rose, S.L. and Kagel, J.H. 2005. Bidding in almost common value auctions: an experiment, mimeographed. Mimeo, Ohio State University.

Rose, S.L. and Levin, D. 2005. An experimental investigation of the explosive effect in common value auctions. Mimeo, Ohio State University.

Roth, A.E. and Ockenfels, A. 2002. Last-minute bidding and the rules for ending second-price auctions: evidence from eBay and Amazon auctions on the internet. *American Economic Review* 92, 1093–103.

Salmon, T.C. and Wilson, B.J. 2008. Second chance offers versus sequential auctions: theory and behavior. *Economic Theory* 34, 47–67.

behavioural economics and game theory

In traditional economic analysis, as well as in much of behavioural economics, the individual's motivations are summarized by a utility function (or a preference relation) over possible payoff-relevant outcomes while his cognitive limitations are described as incomplete information. Thus, the standard economic theory of the individual is couched in the language of constrained maximization and statistical inference.

The approach gains its power from the concise specification of payoff-relevant outcomes and payoffs as well as a host of auxiliary assumptions. For example, it is typically assumed that the individual's preferences are well behaved: that is, they can be represented by a function that satisfies conditions appropriate for the particular context such as continuity, monotonicity, quasi-concavity, and so on. When studying behaviour under uncertainty, it is often assumed that the individual's preference obeys the expected utility hypothesis. More importantly, it is assumed that the individual's subjective assessments of the underlying uncertainty are reasonably close to the observed distributions of the corresponding variables. Even after all these bold assumptions, the standard model would say little if the only relevant observation regarding the utility function is one particular choice outcome. Thus, economists will often assume that the same utility function is relevant for the individual's choices over some stretch of time during which a number of related choices are made. One hopes that these observations will generate enough variation to identify the decision-maker's (DM's) utility function. If not, the analyst may choose to utilize choice observations from different contexts to identify the individual's preferences or make parametric assumptions. The analyst may even pool information derived from observed choices of different individuals to arrive at a representative utility function.

1. Experimental challenges to the main axioms of choice theory

The simplest type of criticism of the standard theory accepts the usual economic abstractions and the standard framework but questions specific assumptions within this framework.

1.1 The independence axiom

Allais (1953) offers one of the earliest critiques of standard decision-theoretic assumptions. In his experiment, he provides two pairs of binary choices and shows that many subjects violate the expected utility hypothesis, in particular, the independence axiom. Allais's approach differs from the earlier criticisms: Allais questions an explicit axiom of choice theory rather than a perceived implicit assumption such as 'rationality'. Furthermore, he does so by providing a simple and clear experimental test of the particular assumption.

Subsequent research documents related violations of the independence axiom and classifies them. Researchers have responded to Allais's critique by developing a class of models that either abandons the independence axiom or replaces it with weaker alternatives. The agents in these models still maximize their preference and still reduce uncertainty to probabilistic assessments (that is, they are probabilistically sophisticated), but have preferences over lotteries that fail the independence axiom.

Non-expected utility preferences pose a difficulty for game theory: because many non-expected utility theories do not lead to quasi-concave utility functions, standard fixed point theorems cannot be used to establish the existence of Nash equilibrium. Crawford (1990) shows that if one interprets mixed strategies not as random behaviour but as the opponents' uncertainty regarding this behaviour, then the required convex-valuedness of the best response correspondence can be restored and existence of Nash equilibrium can be ensured.

In dynamic games, abandoning the independence axiom poses even more difficult problems. Without the independence axiom, conditional preferences at a given node of an extensive form game (or a decision-tree) depend on the unrealized payoffs earlier in the game. The literature has dealt with this problem in two ways: first, by assuming that the DM maximizes his conditional preference at each node (for a statement and defence of this approach, see Machina, 1989). This approach leads to dynamically consistent behaviour, since the DM ends up choosing the optimal strategy for the reduced (normal form) game. However, it is difficult to compute optimal strategies once conditional preference depends on the entire history of unrealized outcomes. The second approach rejects dynamic consistency and assumes that at each node the DM maximizes his unconditional preference given his prediction of future behaviour. Thus, in the second approach, each node is treated as a distinct player and a subgame perfect equilibrium of the extensive form game is computed. Game-theoretic models that abandon the independence axiom have favoured the second approach. Such models have been used to study auctions.

1.2 Redefining payoffs: altruism and fairness

The next set of behavioural criticisms question common assumptions regarding deterministic outcomes. Consider the *ultimatum game*: Player 1 chooses some amount $x \leq 100$ to offer to Player 2. If Player 2 accepts the offer, 2 receives x and 1 receives $100-x$; If 2 rejects, both players receive 0. Suppose the rewards are measured in dollars and Player 1 has to make his offer in multiples of a dollar. It is easy to verify that if the players care only about their own financial outcome, there is no subgame perfect Nash equilibrium of this game in which Player 1 chooses $x>1$. Moreover, in every equilibrium, any offer $x>0$ must be accepted with probability 1. Contrary to these predictions, experimental evidence indicates that small offers are often rejected. Hence, subjects in the Player 2 role resent either the unfairness of the (99,1) outcome, or Player 1's lack of generosity. Moreover, many experimental subjects anticipate this response and make more generous offers to ensure acceptance. Even in the version of this game in which Player 2 does not have the opportunity to reject (that is,

Player 1 is a *dictator*), Player 1 often acts altruistically and gives a significant share to Player 2.

More generally, there is empirical evidence that suggests that economic agents care not only about their physical outcomes but also about the outcomes of their opponents and how the two compare. Within game theory, this particular behavioural critique has been influential and has led to a significant theoretical literature on social preferences (see, for example, Fehr and Schmidt, 1999).

1.3 Redefining the objects of choice: ambiguity, timing of resolution of uncertainty, and preference for commitment

The next set of behavioural criticisms points out how the standard definition of outcome or consequence is inadequate. The literature on ambiguity questions probabilistic sophistication; that is, the idea that all uncertainty can be reduced to probability distributions. Ellsberg (1961) provides the original statement of this criticism. Consider the following choice problem: there are two urns; the first contains 50 red balls and 50 blue balls; the second contains 100 balls, each of which is either red or blue. The DM must select an urn and announce a colour. Then a ball will be drawn from the urn he selects. If the colour of the ball is the same as the colour the DM announces, he wins 100 dollars. Otherwise the DM gets zero. Experimental results indicate that many DMs are indifferent between (urn 1, red) and (urn 1, blue) but they strictly prefer either of these choices to (urn 2, red) and (urn 2, blue). If the DM were probabilistically sophisticated and assigned probability p to choosing a red ball from urn 1 and q to choosing a red ball from urn 2, the preferences above would indicate that $p = 1-p$, $p > q$, and $p > 1-q$, a contradiction. Hence, many DMs are not probabilistically sophisticated.

Ellsberg's experiment has lead to choice-theoretic models where agents are not probabilistically sophisticated and have an aversion to ambiguity; that is, the type of uncertainty associated with urn 2. Recent contributions have investigated auctions with ambiguity-averse bidders and mechanism design with ambiguity aversion.

Other developments in behavioural choice theory that fall into this category have had limited impact on game-theoretic research. For example, Kreps and Porteus (1978) introduce the notion of a temporal lottery to analyse economic agents' preference over the timing of resolution of uncertainty. The Kreps–Porteus model has been extremely influential in dynamic choice theory and asset pricing but has had less impact in strategic analysis.

Kreps (1979) takes as his primitive individuals' preferences over sets of objects. Hence, an object similar to the indirect utility function of demand theory defines the individual. Kreps uses this framework to analyse preference for flexibility. So far, there has been limited analysis of preference for flexibility in strategic problems.

Gul and Pesendorfer (2001) use preferences over sets to analyse agents who have a preference for commitment (an alternative approach to preference for commitment is discussed in Section (3.2)). The GP model has been used to analyse some mechanism design problems.

2. Limitations of the decision-maker

The work discussed in Section 1 explores alternative formulations of economic consequences to identify preference-relevant considerations that are ignored in standard economic analysis. The work discussed in this section provides a more fundamental challenge to standard economics. This research seeks alternatives to common assumptions regarding economic agents' understanding of their environments and their cognative/computational abilities.

2.1 Biases and heuristics

Many economic models are stated in subjectivist language. Hence probabilities, whether they represent the likelihood of future events or the individual's own ignorance of past events, are the DMs' personal beliefs rather than objective frequencies. Similarly, the DM's utility function is a description of his behaviour in a variety of contingencies rather than an assessment of the intrinsic value of the possible outcomes. Nevertheless, when economists use these models to analyse particular problems, the subjective probabilities (and sometimes other parameters) are often calibrated or estimated by measuring objective frequencies (or other objective variables).

Psychology and economics research has questioned the validity of this approach. Tversky and Kahneman (1974) identify systematic biases in how individuals make choices under uncertainty. This research has led to an extensive literature on heuristics and biases. Consider the following:

(a) Which number is larger $P(A|B)$ or $P(A \cap C|B)$? Clearly, $P(A|B)$ is the larger quantity; conditional on B or unconditionally, $A \cap C$ can never be more likely than A. Yet, when belonging to set C is considered 'typical' for a member of B, many subjects state that $A \cap C$ conditional on B is more likely than A conditional on B.

(b) Randomly selected subjects are tested for a particular condition. In the population, 95 per cent are healthy. The test is 90 per cent accurate; that is, a healthy subject tests negative and a subject having the condition tests positive with probability 0.9. If a randomly chosen person tests positive, what is the probability that he is ill? In such problems, subjects tend to ignore the low prior probability of having the condition and come up with larger estimates than the correct answer (less than one-third in this example).

Eyster and Rabin's (2005) analysis of auctions offers an example of a strategic model of biased decision-making. This work focuses on DMs' tendency to overemphasize their own (private) information at the expense of the information that is revealed through the strategic interaction.

2.2 Evolution and learning

As in decision theory, it is possible to state nearly all the assumptions of game theory in subjectivist language (see, for example, Aumann and Brandenburger, 1995). Hence, one can define Nash equilibrium as a property of players' beliefs. Of course, Nash equilibrium beliefs (together with utility maximization) will impose restrictions on observable behaviour, but these restrictions will fall short of demanding that the observed frequency of actions profiles constitute a Nash equilibrium. The theory of evolutionary games searches for dynamic mechanisms that lead to equilibrium behaviour, where equilibrium is identified with observable decisions (as opposed to beliefs) of individuals. The objective is to describe how equilibrium may emerge and which equilibria are more likely to emerge through repeated interaction in a setting where the typical epistemic assumptions of equilibrium analysis fail initially. Thus, such models are used both to justify Nash (or weaker) equilibrium notions and to justify refinements of these notions.

2.3 Cognitive limitations and game theory
Some game theoretic solution concepts require iterative procedures. For example, computing rationalizable outcomes in normal form games or finding backward induction solutions in extensive form games involves an iterative procedure that yields a smaller game after each step. The process ends when the final game, which consists exclusively of actions that constitute the desired solution, is reached. In principle, the number of steps needed to reach the solution can be arbitrarily large. Ho, Camerer and Weigelt (1998) observe that experimental subjects appear to carry out at most the first two steps of these procedures.

   This line of work focuses both on organizing observed violations of standard game theoretic solutions concepts and interpreting the empirical regularities as the foundation of a behavioural notion of equilibrium.

3. Alternative models of the individual
The work discussed in this section poses the most fundamental challenge to the standard economic model of the individual. This work questions the usefulness of constrained maximization as a framework of economic analysis, or at least argues for a fundamentally different set of constraints.

3.1 Prospect theory and framing effects
Consider the following pair of choices (Tversky and Kahneman, 1981): an unusual disease is expected to kill 600 people. Two alternative programmes to combat the disease have been proposed.

   Programme A will save 200; with Programme B, there is a one-third probability that 600 people will be saved, and a two-thirds probability that no one will be saved.

   Next, consider the following restatement of what would appear to be the same options:

   If Programme C is adopted 400 people will die; with Programme D, there is a one-third probability that nobody will die, and a two-thirds probability that 600 people will die.

Among subjects given a choice between A and B, most choose the safe option A, while the majority of the subjects facing the second pair of choices choose the risky option D.

Kahneman and Tversky's (1979) prospect theory combines issues discussed in Sections (1.1) and (2.2), with a more general critique of standard economic models, or at least of how such models are used in practice. Thus, while a standard model might favour a level of abstraction that ignores the framing issue above, Kahneman and Tversky (1979) argue that identifying the particular frame that the individual is likely to confront should be central to decision theory. In particular, these authors focus on the differential treatment of gains and losses. Prospect theory defines preferences not over lotteries of terminal wealth but over gains and losses, measured as differences from a status quo. In applications, the status quo is identified in a variety of ways.

For example, Köszegi and Rabin (2005–6) provide a theory of the status quo and utilize the resulting model to study a monopoly problem. In their theory, the DM's optimal choice becomes the status quo. Thus, the simplest form of the Köszegi–Rabin model defines optimal choices from a set A as $C(A) = \{x \in A | U(x, x) \geq U(y, x) \forall y \in A\}$. Hence, $x \in A$ is deemed to be a possible choice from A if the DM who views x as his reference point does not strictly prefer some other alternative y.

The three lines of work discussed below all represent a fundamental departure from the standard modelling of economic decisions: they describe behaviour as the outcome of a game even in a single person problem.

3.2 Preference reversals

Strotz (1955–6) introduces the idea of dynamic inconsistency: the possibility that a DM may prefer to consume x in period 2 to consuming y in period 1, if he makes the choice in period 0, but may have the opposite preference if he makes the choice in period 1. Strotz suggests that the appropriate way to model dynamically inconsistent behaviour is to assume that the period 0 individual treats his period 1 preference (and the implied behaviour) as a constraint on what he can achieve. Thus, suppose the period 0 DM has a choice between committing to z for period 2 consumption, or rejecting z and giving his period 1 self the choice between x in period 2 and y in period 1. Suppose also that the period 0 self prefers x to z and z to y while the period 1 self prefers y to x. Then, the Strotz model would imply that the DM ends up consuming z in period 2: the period 0 self realizes that if he does not commit to z, his period 1 self will choose y over x, which, for the period 0 self, is the least desirable outcome. Therefore, the period 0 self will commit to z. Hence, dynamic inconsistency leads to a preference for commitment.

Peleg and Yaari (1973) propose to reconcile the conflict among the different selves of a dynamically inconsistent DM with a strategic equilibrium concept. Their reformulation of Strotz's notion of consistent planning has facilitated the application of Strotz's ideas to more general settings, including dynamic games.

3.3 Imperfect recall

An explicit statement of the perfect recall assumption and analysis of its consequences (Kuhn, 1953) is one of the earliest contributions of extensive form game theory. In contrast, the analysis of forgetfulness, that is, extensive form games where the individual forgets his own past actions or information, is relatively recent (Piccione and Rubinstein, 1997).

Piccione and Rubinstein observe that defining optimal behaviour for players with imperfect recall is problematic and propose a few alternative definitions (1997). Subsequent work has focused on what they call the multi-selves approach. In the multi-selves approach to imperfect recall, as in dynamic inconsistency, each information set is treated as a separate player. Optimal behaviour is a profile of behavioural strategies and beliefs at information sets such that the beliefs are consistent with the strategy profile and each behavioural strategy maximizes the corresponding agent's payoff given his beliefs and the behaviour of the remaining agents. Hence, the multi-selves approach leads to a prediction of behaviour that is analogous to perfect Bayesian equilibrium.

3.4 Psychological games

Harsanyi (1967–8) introduces the notion of a type to facilitate analysis of the interaction of players' information in strategic problems. He argues that the notion of a type is flexible enough to accommodate all uncertainty and asymmetric information that is relevant in games. Geanakoplos, Pearce and Stacchetti (1989) observe that if payoffs are 'intrinsically' dependent on beliefs and beliefs are determined in equilibrium, then types cannot be defined independently of the particular equilibrium outcome. Their notion of a psychological game and type (for psychological games) allows for this interdependence between equilibrium expectations and payoffs.

Gul and Pesendorfer (2006) offer an alternative framework for dealing with interdependent preferences. In their analysis, players care not only about the physical consequences of their actions on their opponents, but also about their opponents' attitudes towards such consequences, and their opponents' attitudes towards others' attitudes towards such consequences, and so on. Gul and Pesendorfer provide a model of interdependent preference types similar to Harsanyi's interdependent belief types to analyse situations in which preference interdependence may arise not from the interaction of (subjective) information but from the interaction of the individuals' attitudes towards the well-being of others.

3.5 Neuroeconomics

The most comprehensive challenge to the standard economic modelling of the individual comes from research in neuroeconomics. Neuroeconomists argue that no matter how much the standard conventions are expanded to accommodate behavioural phenomena, it will not be enough: understanding economic behaviour requires studying the physiological, and in particular, neurological mechanisms behind choice. Recent experiments relate choice-theoretic variables to levels of brain activity, the type of choices to the parts of the brain that are engaged when making these choices, and hormone levels to behaviour (Camerer, 2006) provide a concise summary of recent research in neuroeconomics).

Neuroeconomists contend that 'neuroscience findings raise questions about the usefulness of some of the most common constructs that economists commonly use, such as risk aversion, time preference, and altruism' (Camerer, Loewenstein and Prelec, 2005). They argue that neuroscience evidence can be used directly to falsify or validate specific hypotheses about behaviour. Moreover, they claim that organizing choice theory and game theory around the abstractions of neuroscience will lead to better theories. Thus, neureconomics proposes to change both the language of game theory and what constitutes its evidence.

4. Conclusion

The interaction of behavioural economics and game theory has had two significant effects: first, it has broadened the subject matter and set of acceptable approaches to strategic analysis. New modelling techniques such as equilibrium notions that explicitly address biases have become acceptable and new questions such as the effect of ambiguity aversion in auctions have gained interest. More importantly, behavioural approaches have altered the set of empirical benchmarks – the stylized facts – that game theorists must address as they interpret their own conclusions.

FARUK GUL

See also **altruism in experiments; prospect theory; preference reversals.**

Bibliography

Allais, M. 1953. Le comportement de l'homme rationnel devant le risque: critique des postulats et axiomes de l'ecole Americaine. *Econometrica* 21, 503–46.
Aumann, R.J. and Brandenburger, A. 1995. Epistemic conditions for Nash equilibrium. *Econometrica* 63, 1161–80.
Camerer, C.F., Loewenstein, G. and Prelec, D. 2005. Neuroeconomics: how neuroscience can inform economics. *Journal of Economic Literature* 43, 9–64.
Camerer, C.F. 2007. Neuroeconomics: using neuroscience to make economic predictions. *Economic Journal.*
Crawford, V.P. 1990. Equilibrium without independence. *Journal of Economic Theory* 50, 127–54.
Ellsberg, D. 1961. Risk, ambiguity, and the savage axioms. *Quarterly Journal of Economics* 75, 643–69.
Eyster, E. and Rabin, M. 2005. Cursed equilibrium. *Econometrica* 73, 1623–72.
Fehr, E. and Schimdt, K. 1999. A theory of fairness, competition and cooperation. *Quarterly Journal of Economics* 114, 817–68.
Geanakoplos, J., Pearce, D. and Stacchetti, E. 1989. Psychological games and sequential rationality. *Games and Economic Behavior* 1, 60–80.
Gul, F. and Pesendorfer, W. 2001. Temptation and self-control. *Econometrica* 2001, 1403–35.
Gul, F. and Pesendorfer, W. 2006. The canonical type space for interdependent preferences. Working paper. Princeton University.
Harsanyi, J. 1967–8. Games with incomplete information played by Bayesian players. *Management Science* 14, 159–82, 320–34, 486–502.

Ho, T., Camerer, C. and Weingelt, K. 1998. Iterated dominance and iterated best responses in p-beauty contests. *American Economic Review* 88, 947–69.

Kahneman, D. and Tversky, A. 1979. Prospect theory: an analysis of decision under risk. *Econometrica* 47, 263–92.

Köszegi, B. and Rabin, M. 2006. A model of reference-dependent preferences, *Quarterly Journal of Economics* 121, 1133–66.

Kreps, D.M. 1979. A preference for flexibility. *Econometrica* 47, 565–76.

Kreps, D.M. and Porteus, E.L. 1978. Temporal resolution of uncertainty and dynamic choice theory. *Econometrica* 46, 185–200.

Kuhn, H.W. 1953. Extensive games and the problem of information. In *Contributions to the Theory of Games*, vol. 2. Princeton, NJ: Princeton University Press.

Machina, M. 1989. Dynamic consistency and non-expected utility models of choice under uncertainty. *Journal of Economic Literature* 1622–68.

O'Donoghue, T. and Rabin, M. 1999. Doing it now or later. *American Economic Review* 103–24.

Peleg, B. and Yaari, M.E. 1973. On the existence of a consistent course of action when tastes are changing. *Review of Economic Studies* 40, 391–401.

Piccione, M. and Rubinstein, A. 1997. On the interpretation of decision problems with imperfect recall. *Games and Economic Behavior* 20, 3–24.

Strotz, R.H. 1955–6. Myopia and inconsistency in dynamic utility maximization. *Review of Economic Studies* 23, 165–80.

Tversky, A. and Kahnemann, D. 1974. Judgment under uncertainty: Heuristic and biases. *Science* 85, 1124–31.

Tversky, A. and Kahneman, D. 1981. The framing of decisions and the psychology of choice. *Science* 211, 453–8.

behavioural finance

Mounting evidence suggests that a variety of trading strategies generate returns that are larger than permitted by the reigning theory of efficient financial markets. Defenders of efficient markets theory argue that the anomalies represent methodological errors, and in many cases they appear to have been correct. In cases where the anomalies appear robust, the debates turn to two other questions. First, why would investors make systematic trading errors that could result in mispricing? Second, why wouldn't smarter traders exploit those errors, thereby driving prices to appropriate levels? Many answers to the first question have relied heavily on the branch of psychology called 'behavioural decision theory', which has led to the entire body of research being dubbed 'behavioural finance' even though there is rarely much behavioural content in the literatures identifying pricing anomalies and explaining why price errors are not eliminated by smarter traders.

The next section of this article discusses the empirical evidence that market prices deviate from levels that would reflect perfectly rational traders acting in competitive markets (the 'anomalies' literature). I then discuss literatures that document how behavioural forces can explain these anomalies, and that examine why irrational traders might influence prices in competitive markets. I conclude by suggesting some promising future directions in behavioural finance.

Anomalies

In 1968, two accounting professors reported that markets react sharply to earnings announcements over the course of a few days, and then continue drifting in the same direction for the better part of a year (Ball and Brown, 1968). This post-earnings-announcement drift (PEAD) appeared to provide an easy opportunity for making money: one could create a hedged portfolio that is long in firms that have just announced good news and short in firms that have just announced bad news, so that it earns positive returns from no net investment.

The fact that prices react at all to earnings was surprising enough, given that earnings was then viewed as an accounting fiction describing past events, with no bearing on the future cash flows of the firm that should entirely determine firm value. (Accounting 'fictions' like earnings and book value are now known to provide important information about future cash flows, spawning a large field of financial accounting research.) But the subsequent drift was even more surprising, as it flew in the face of the recently developed efficient markets hypothesis (EMH), subsequently codified by Gene Fama (1970). The EMH relies on competition among investors to assert that strategies based on public information cannot earn returns after adjusting for risk. If all investors know that holding the PEAD portfolio would allow for excess returns, they would compete to hold the portfolio, and drive prices to the level needed to eliminate those returns.

PEAD has turned out to be one of the first – and most robust – of a large number of market anomalies. Initial explanations for PEAD were that the predictable returns simply reflect the expected returns that investors demand to compensate for the risk the PEAD portfolio would impose on them. Such arguments were made much more difficult by Bernard and Thomas (1990), who showed that about half the returns to the PEAD portfolio were experienced in the three-day windows surrounding the two subsequent earnings announcements. Thus, any risk-based explanation would require firms with extremely good or bad earnings news to experience dramatic changes in systematic risk for only a few days a year, several months in the future. The alternative explanation, proffered by Bernard and Thomas, was that investors simply did not understand the implications of current earnings for future earnings – an assertion that has been repeatedly supported by studies of analysts' earnings estimates and laboratory experiments. Researchers were successful enough in ruling out the risk explanation, and in tying future returns to the information content of current earnings, so that Fama (1998, p. 304) concluded that PEAD 'has survived robustness checks', and was possibly 'above suspicion'.

Three other robust anomalies seem more likely to reflect compensation for risk than mispricing: the book-to-market effect, the size effect and the momentum effect. The book-to-market ratio is the ratio of a firm's net assets (as reported on the firm's balance sheet) to the total market value of the firm's outstanding stock. Firms with low book-to-market ratios earn substantially higher returns than those with high book-to-market ratios (the book-to-market effect), as if the market value reverts over time to the value indicated by the accounting statements. Firms with small market capitalization earn higher returns than firms with large market capitalization (the size effect), as if small firms are consistently underpriced. Stocks that move strongly upwards or downwards over a three- to six-month period are very likely to continue moving in that direction over a subsequent three to six months (the momentum effect), as if the market responds slowly to changes in value.

Distinguishing risk and mispricing is difficult for book-to-market and size and momentum effects because researchers have no hypothesis that the mispricing will be corrected at some particular moment. (In contrast, the theory explaining PEAD suggests that mispricing will be revealed and corrected upon subsequent earnings announcements). Proponents of efficient markets have provided evidence that book-to-market and size capture systematic risk, and have expanded the traditional asset pricing model to include book-to-market, size and (less frequently) momentum as risk factors. However, analysts appear to view book-to-market as an indicator of mispricing rather than risk, as indicated by examinations of analyst reports and controlled experiments.

Researchers in finance and accounting have identified a host of other pricing anomalies. Here is a selective sampling of some of the most well known, all of which remain controversial:

- *Long-term price reversal.* Stocks that move strongly over a three- to five-year period are very likely to reverse a portion of those movements over a following three- to five-year period (DeBondt and Thaler, 1985). Evidence for long-term reversal tends to be more controversial than evidence for short-term momentum, because longer horizons make it harder to guarantee appropriate computation of risk-adjusted returns.

- *The equity premium puzzle.* A diversified portfolio of equity securities should earn higher returns than a portfolio of bonds, because of the additional risk equities impose on investors. However, the equity premium appears far too large relative to the associated risk (Mehra and Prescott, 1985).

- *The home bias puzzle.* Both institutional and individual investors tend to hold a disproportionate amount of their portfolios in firms based in their own countries and regions. This may reflect a bias to purchase familiar stocks (Huberman, 2001), or the inside information held by local investors (Coval and Moskowitz, 2001).

- *Excessive volatility and excessive volume.* Shiller (1981) has argued that market prices are excessively volatile, relative to the volatility of fundamentals. Many others, including Kandel and Pearson (1995), have argued that trade volume is far too high to be explained by traditional theory, in light of the Milgrom and Stokey (1982) 'no-trade theorem', which proves that, in the absence of non-informational motivations for trade, such as a need for liquidity or sharing of risk, markets should not include any trade.

- *The accruals anomaly.* Firms' earnings can be decomposed into cash flows and accruals (defined as earnings minus cash flows). Sloan (1996) showed that firms with large positive accruals earn lower future returns than firms with large negative accruals, as if investors are unaware that accruals – which do not represent cash flows and are easily manipulated by managers – reverse rapidly.

Individual behaviour

The variety of market anomalies has led some to doubt the validity of the EMH, but few researchers are likely to let go of the efficient markets perspective without a coherent and parsimonious theory of when to predict which types of anomalies. One branch of psychology, called 'behavioural decision theory' (BDT), appears particularly well-suited to imposing regular structure on otherwise ad hoc results. BDT researchers have shown that a variety of apparently irrational behaviours can be explained by a relatively parsimonious set of theories. For their part, behavioural finance researchers have sought to use empirical and experimental studies to show that behavioural theories can describe the actions of individual investors (as well as managers), and to use theoretical methods to show that a small set of behavioural theories can account for the wide variety of market anomalies. Four streams of results feature most prominently in behavioural finance: prospect theory, miscalibration, pattern recognition and limited attention.

Prospect theory

Throughout the 1970s, Amos Tversky and Daniel Kahneman published a series of papers characterizing how people value outcomes. This research ultimately resulted in a mathematical representation of subjective (hedonic) value called 'prospect theory' (Kahneman and Tversky, 1979), for which Kahneman won the 2002 Nobel Prize in economics (Amos Tversky died in 1996). Prospect theory emphasizes three features of the value function: that the hedonic value of an outcome is determined by whether the outcome is a gain or loss relative to the agent's reference point; that the negative hedonic value of a loss more than offsets the positive hedonic value of a gain of the same size; and that the marginal effect of increasing a gain (or loss) is decreasing in the size of the gain (or loss).

Prospect theory yields a variety of predictions that describe individual behaviour well, and that can also account for several market anomalies. Prospect theory helps to explain a common behaviour termed the 'disposition effect' (Shefrin and Statman, 1985) – traders will close out profitable investments quickly, to lock in gains, while holding on to their losing investments or perhaps even invest more in them, in hopes that the investment will turn around. Let us assume that a trader has bought a stock at 50 dollars, and that it is now priced at 80 dollars. Using the 50-dollar purchase price as a reference point, the trader has a 30-dollar gain, and (because the marginal effect of increasing a gain is decreasing in the size of the gain) the agent is risk-averse, and will want to close the position quickly to avoid risk. If the price fell to 20 dollars, however, the trader has a 30-dollar loss, and (because the marginal effect of increasing a loss is decreasing in the size of the loss) the agent is risk seeking, and will want to keep the position open to take on more risk.

Terry Odean (1998a) has shown clear evidence of the disposition effect among thousands of individual investors at a brokerage firm. Unfortunately for the investors, selling winners and holding on to losers is nearly the opposite of the profitable momentum strategy, which involves buying recent winners and selling recent losers. As a result, the stocks the investors held subsequently underperformed the stocks they sold. The disposition effect does not seem restricted to amateurs. Coval and Shumway (2005) show that professional commodity traders who have net losses near the end of the day tend to trade quite aggressively until trading closes, and take on significant risk. Finally, Frazzini (2006) ties the disposition effect back to price anomalies by providing evidence that disposition effects drive short-term momentum, because the relatively rapid selling of winners slows reactions to good news, while the tendency to hold losers slows reactions to bad news.

The disposition effect is driven by the different curvatures of the value function in the loss and gain realms. Curvature is important when investors evaluate the risk of relatively small changes in wealth. Investors who evaluate the risk of large wealth changes are influenced instead by the different average slopes of the value function in the loss and gain realms. Because the average slope is flatter in the realm of gains, investors with large gains in hand are likely to appear less risk-averse than those with losses or small gains. Evidence from experiments (Thaler and Johnson, 1990) and game show contestants (Gertner, 1993) are consistent with this 'house money' effect, named after the exaggerated risk tolerance of the behaviour of gamblers who have won money from the house, and therefore are risking only the house's money. Barberis, Huang and Santos (2001) show that the house money effect can account for both short-term momentum and long-term reversal. Short-term momentum arises because traders demand more compensation for risk after price declines, further depressing prices, while demanding less compensation for risk after price increases, further inflating prices. Similar reasoning shows that the house money effect can account for the book-to-market effect and an exaggerated equity premium.

While prospect theory is a relatively parsimonious and powerful theory, its predictions are highly sensitive to assumptions about how people identify benchmarks against which to measure gains and losses, and under what circumstances they might evaluate gains and losses of portfolios, rather than of individual securities. The field of 'mental accounting' (Barberis, Huang and Thaler, 2006) addresses such questions.

Miscalibrated confidence

Financial models of trade traditionally assume that agents have confidence calibrated to reflect the precision of their information. Experiments show that people rarely satisfy this requirement. People tend to be overconfident in their ability to predict events when they have very poor information, while people who are asked easy questions tend to be underconfident. Psychologists call this tendency the 'hard–easy' effect (Griffin and Tversky, 1992); Bloomfield, Libby and Nelson (2000) call it 'moderated confidence' because confidence is moderated from the optimal level towards a prior belief of moderate data reliability, as if people are rational Bayesians with imperfect information about the reliability of their data.

Because financial outcomes are so hard to predict, people are likely to be overconfident, rather than under-confident. Indeed, evidence of overconfidence is widespread. Odean (1999) finds that individual investors trade far too frequently, apparently overconfident in their ability to identify mispriced securities. Malmendier and Tate (2005) find that many executives are overconfident in their firms' futures (as evidenced by their failure to exercise stock options before expiration), and further show that more overconfident executives are more likely to engage in value-reducing mergers.

Theoretical and experimental research has shown that calibration errors can account for a variety of known anomalies. Gervais and Odean (2001) and Odean (1998b) examine how overconfidence can lead to excessive trading. Daniel, Hirshleifer and Subrahmanyam (1998) show that overconfidence can account for both overreactions and underreactions to information. In a similar vein, Bloomfield, Libby and Nelson (2003) show that overconfident inferences from old earnings numbers, which have little information content once newer numbers are available, lead to both post-earnings-announcement drift and overreactions to earnings trends.

Pattern recognition

The human mind has a gift for finding order in chaos, even when objective analysis shows no order to be found. In such cases, people show remarkable consistency in the order they perceive. People fall prey to the gambler's fallacy when they expect that a coin that has come up 'heads' many times in a row is then more likely to come up 'tails' because such streaks are typically short-lived. People fall prey to the 'hot-hand' fallacy when they mistakenly believe that basketball players who have made ten free throws in a row are especially likely to make the next, even though this is not the case (a professional basketball player's free throw performance is not distinguishable from a random series with a constant mean). The tendency to see patterns in random sequences is likely to be particularly important in financial markets, where competitive pressures force market prices to follow a random walk (after risk premia are accounted for). Despite the randomness in stock movements, many investors subscribe to 'technical analysis' trading strategies (and expensive newsletters) based on elaborate patterns like 'head and shoulders' and 'cup with handle', even though systematic research has found little evidence that such patterns can predict future stock movements.

Barberis, Shleifer and Vishny (1998) claim that people who observe a random walk are likely to fluctuate between beliefs in the gambler's fallacy (in which any trends are quickly reversed) and beliefs in the hot hand (in which trends continue), depending on how many reversals in price they have seen in recent periods. They then prove that such beliefs can account for both short-term price momentum and long-term price reversal. Bloomfield and Hales (2002) find experimental support for that assumption.

Limited attention

A fundamental tenet of cognitive science is that people have limited cognitive resources, implying that their attention to financial information and investment opportunities may be determined by economically irrelevant factors such as how information is presented or how often it is talked about by others. Experiments have found that even experienced analysts draw conclusions that are coloured by seemingly irrelevant aspects of how financial information is presented (Hirst and Hopkins, 1998). Employees' decisions on how to invest their defined contribution pension funds are dramatically influenced by how the options are presented (Benartzi and Thaler, 2001), while their decision to enrol in such plans at all are dramatically increased by a policy that makes investment the default option, so that enrolment requires no attention at all (Benartzi and Thaler, 2004).

Limited attention may determine how stocks come in and out of favour, and provides a natural explanation for the home bias puzzle – people naturally notice local firms more readily than distant firms. Limited attention may also explain the tendency of firms to attract attention (and trading volume) when their earnings are growing rapidly, but be ignored when they perform poorly for long periods. Lee and Swaminathan (2000) argue that such tendencies might explain short-term momentum, and support their argument by showing that firms with low volume and strong returns show strong momentum in returns (as if they are underpriced while still neglected), while those with high volume and strong returns show long-term reversal (as if they are overpriced at the peak of attention).

Accounting researchers have been particularly interested in the effects of limited attention, because they may explain why people care so much about accounting regulations that alter only how information is presented, and not the information content of the complete accounting disclosure. A highly publicized example is the controversy over whether employee stock option costs should be deducted from reported earnings per share; in both cases, investors could gather all relevant information from the footnotes to the financial statements. Bloomfield (2002) argues that fewer investors attend to footnotes than to earnings, and that standard models of information aggregation predict that market prices less completely reveal information that is held by fewer investors – a result repeatedly confirmed in laboratory markets. This 'incomplete revelation hypothesis' runs counter to the EMH, which is typically applied to all public information regardless of how it is presented. However, accounting researchers have made considerable progress in understanding how different presentation options, such as the formating, isolation and ordering of text can alter investors' attention to and weighting of the information in that text (see, for example, Maines and McDaniel, 2000).

Limits to arbitrage

Studies of individual behaviour show that investors and managers make systematic errors of judgement, but do not explain how other investors fail to exploit, and thereby eliminate, any aggregate mispricing.

A number of studies have noted that arbitrage may be limited by risks that cannot be captured as risk factors in traditional asset pricing models. Even if a pricing error must eventually converge (as when two securities representing claims on the same underlying assets have different prices), such convergence may not be rapid, and may even be preceded by additional divergence. While asset pricing models like the capital asset pricing model (CAPM) conclude that such idiosyncratic risk does not affect price levels, Pontiff (2006) has argued forcefully that idiosyncratic risk still hinders the correction of price errors by effectively imposing a 'holding cost' on arbitrageurs. Idiosyncratic risk restricts arbitrage most severely when a trader uses borrowed capital to engage in arbitrage, because a short-term loss may result in a margin call, or may lead the investors to infer that the arbitrageur has a poor strategy, and therefore withdraw their funds (Shleifer and Vishny, 1997). DeLong et al. (1990) take these arguments one step further: they assume that the noise in returns is driven by irrational traders, and then show that these traders still earn sufficient returns for them to survive indefinitely.

Another line of literature notes that rational arbitrageurs might earn greater profits by exacerbating price errors rather than disciplining them. Abreu and Brunnermeier (2002) construct a model in which irrational traders drive prices too high, a fact that eventually becomes known to every arbitrageur. Because arbitrageurs do not know whether other arbitrageurs have yet learned of the overpricing, each one continues to 'ride the bubble' after they learn of the overpricing, rather than pop it, because they expect others to do so as well. As a result, the arbitrageurs continue magnifying the bubble even after each individual arbitrageur knows that prices are too high.

The preceding explanations of limited arbitrage are largely devoid of behavioural content – the price errors that fail to be corrected could arise from any cause, including completely random trading. However, researchers do occasionally examine how specific biases can limit arbitrage opportunities. Overconfidence, in particular, has been shown to be difficult to arbitrage. For example, Kyle and Wang (1997) show that overconfident traders can effectively gain 'elbow room' in a market, just as a trader in a Cournot oligopoly game can benefit by committing to aggressive production, and forcing others to produce less. As a result, overconfident traders earn enough trading gains to persist.

Conclusion and future directions

This history of behavioural finance fits well within Kuhn's (1962) narrative of scientific revolution. Early researchers uncovered results that were anomalous within the paradigm of efficient markets; as they became convinced that the anomalies were not simply the result of methodological error, researchers sought a new paradigm that could encompass the anomalies, as well as the predictions of the traditional theory. This new paradigm assumes that markets include some participants who optimize their expected utility, along with others whose susceptibility to psychological forces leads them to behave suboptimally.

No behavioural alternative will ever rival the coherence, parsimony and power of traditional efficient markets theory, because psychological forces are too complex. Thus, behavioural researchers in finance must devote themselves to the 'normal science' suggested by their new paradigm: documenting and refining our understanding of how psychological forces influence individual behaviour in financial settings, and how those behaviours affect market phenomena. This will require much more attention to behavioural psychology than is evident in the existing body of research. (As of 2007, few papers in behavioural finance rely on psychological research published after the 1970s.) Perhaps more importantly, advances in behavioural finance will require more attention to the details of market microstructure, which influence individual behaviour, and how those behaviours affect market-level phenomena. Finally, researchers in behavioural finance can expand their scope beyond describing the behaviour of investors and prices in highly competitive asset markets. Behavioural theories are likely to have greater ability to explain phenomena in settings that provide fewer opportunities for others to exploit (and thereby eliminate) suboptimal outcomes. For example, decisions on how to hire and compensate executives, and on when and how to raise and invest capital, seem particularly susceptible to behavioural analysis (as in Shefrin, 2005).

ROBERT BLOOMFIELD

See also **behavioural economics and game theory; prospect theory.**

Bibliography

Abreu, D. and Brunnermeier, M.K. 2002. Synchronization risk and delayed arbitrage. *Journal of Financial Economics* 66, 341–60.

Ball, R. and Brown, P. 1968. An empirical evaluation of accounting income numbers. *Journal of Accounting Research* 6, 159–78.

Barberis, N., Huang, M. and Thaler, R.H. 2006. Individual preferences, monetary gambles and stock market participation: a case for narrow framing. *American Economic Review* 96, 1069–90.

Barberis, N., Shleifer, A. and Vishny, R. 1998. A model of investor sentiment. *Journal of Financial Economics* 49, 307–43.

Barberis, N., Huang, M. and Santos, T. 2001. Prospect theory and asset prices. *Quarterly Journal of Economics* 116, 1–53.

Benartzi, S. and Thaler, R.H. 2001. Naïve diversification strategies in defined contribution savings plans. *American Economic Review* 91, 79–98.

Benartzi, S. and Thaler, R.H. 2004. Save more tomorrow TM: using behavioral economics to increase employee saving. *Journal of Political Economy* 112, S164–S187.

Bernard, V.I. and Thomas, J. 1990. Evidence that stock prices do not fully reflect the implications of current earnings for future earnings. *Journal of Accounting and Economics* 13, 305–41.

Bloomfield, R. and Hales, J. 2002. Predicting the next step of a random walk: experimental evidence of regime-shifting beliefs. *Journal of Financial Economics* 65, 397–415.

Bloomfield, R. 2002. The incomplete revelation hypothesis: implications for financial reporting. *Accounting Horizons* 16, 233–44.

Bloomfield, R., Libby, R. and Nelson, M.W. 2003. Over-reliance on previous years' earnings. *Contemporary Accounting Research* 20, 1–31.

Bloomfield, R., Libby, R. and Nelson, M.W. 2000. Underreactions, overreactions and moderated confidence. *Journal of Financial Markets* 3, 113–37.

Coval, J. and Moskowitz, T. 2001. The geography of investment: informed trading and asset prices. *Journal of Political Economy* 109, 811–41.

Coval, J.D. and Shumway, T. 2005. Do behavioral biases affect prices? *Journal of Finance* 60, 1–34.

Daniel, K., Hirshleifer, D. and Subrahmanyam, A. 1998. Investor psychology and security market under- and overreaction. *Journal of Finance* 53, 1839–86.

DeBondt, W.F.M. and Thaler, R.H. 1985. Does the stock market overreact? *Journal of Finance* 40, 793–807.

DeLong, J.B., Shleifer, A., Summers, L.H. and Waldmann, R.J. 1990. Noise trader risk in financial markets. *Journal of Political Economy* 98, 703–38.

Fama, E.F. 1970. Efficient capital markets: a review of theory and empirical work. *Journal of Finance* 25, 383–417.

Fama, E.F. 1998. Market efficiency, long-term returns, and behavioral finance. *Journal of Financial Economics* 49, 283–306.

Frazzini, A. 2006. The disposition effect and underreaction to news. *Journal of Finance* 61, 2017–46.

Gertner, R. 1993. Game shows and economic behavior: risk taking on 'card sharks'. *Quarterly Journal of Economics* 151, 507–21.

Gervais, S. and Odean, T. 2001. Learning to be overconfident. *Review of Financial Studies* 14, 1–27.

Griffin, D. and Tversky, A. 1992. The weighing of evidence and the determinants of confidence. *Cognitive Psychology* 24, 411–35.

Hirst, D.E. and Hopkins, P.E. 1998. Comprehensive income reporting and analysts' valuation judgments. *Journal of Accounting Research* 36(Supplement), 47–75.

Huberman, G. 2001. Familiarity breeds investment. *Review of Financial Studies* 14, 659–80.

Kahneman, D. and Tversky, A. 1979. Prospect theory: an analysis of decision under risk. *Econometrica* 47, 263–92.

Kandel, E. and Pearson, N.D. 1995. Differential interpretation of public signals and trade in speculative markets. *Journal of Political Economy* 103, 831–72.

Kuhn, T.S. 1962. *The Structure of Scientific Revolutions.* Chicago: University of Chicago Press.

Kyle, A. and Wang, F.A. 1997. Speculation duopoly with agreement to disagree: can overconfidence survive the market test? *Journal of Finance* 52, 2073–90.

Lee, C.M.C. and Swaminathan, B. 2000. Price momentum and trading volume. *Journal of Finance* 55, 2017–33.

Maines, L.A. and McDaniel, L.S. 2000. Effects of comprehensive-income characteristics on nonprofessional investors' judgments: the role of financial-statement presentation format. *Accounting Review* 75, 179–207.

Malmendier, U. and Tate, G. 2005. CEO overconfidence and corporate investment. *Journal of Finance* 60, 2661.

Mehra, R. and Prescott, E.C. 1985. The equity premium: a puzzle. *Journal of Monetary Economics* 15, 145–61.

Milgrom, P. and Stokey, N. 1982. Information, trade and common knowledge. *Journal of Economic Theory* 26, 17–27.

Odean, T. 1998a. Are investors reluctant to realize their losses? *Journal of Finance* 53, 1775–98.

Odean, T. 1998b. Volume, volatility, price, and profit when all traders are above average. *Journal of Finance* 53, 1887–934.

Odean, T. 1999. Do investors trade too much? *American Economic Review* 89, 1279–98.

Pontiff, J. 2006. Costly arbitrage and the myth of idiosyncratic risk. *Journal of Accounting and Economics* 42, 35–52.

Shefrin, H. 2005. *Behavioral Corporate Finance.* New York: McGraw-Hill/Irwin.

Shefrin, H. and Statman, M. 1985. The disposition to sell winners too early and ride losers too long: Theory and evidence. *Journal of Finance* 40, 777–90.

Shiller, R.J. 1981. Do stock prices move too much to be justified by subsequent changes in dividends? *American Economic Review* 71, 421–36.

Shleifer, A. and Vishny, R.W. 1997. The limits of arbitrage. *Journal of Finance* 52, 35–55.

Sloan, R. 1996. Do stock prices fully reflect information in accruals and cash flows about future earnings? *Accounting Review* 71, 289–315.

Thaler, R.H. and Johnson, E.J. 1990. Gambling with the house money and trying to break even: the effects of prior outcomes on risky choice. *Management Science* 36, 643–60.

behavioural game theory

Analytical game theory assumes that players choose strategies which maximize the utility of game outcomes, based on their beliefs about what others players will do, given the economic structure of the game and history; in equilibrium, these beliefs are correct. Analytical game theory is enormously powerful, but it has two shortcomings as a complete model of behaviour by people (and other possible players, including non-human animals and organizations).

First, in complex naturally occurring games, equilibration of beliefs is unlikely to occur instantaneously. Models of choice under bounded rationality, predicting initial choices and equilibration with experience, are therefore useful.

Second, in empirical work, only received (or anticipated) payoffs are easily measured (for example, prices and valuations in auctions, or currency paid in an experiment). Since games are played over *utilities* for received payoffs, it is therefore necessary to have a theory of social preferences – that is, how measured payoffs determine players' utility evaluations – in order to make predictions.

The importance of understanding bounded rationality, equilibration and social preferences is provided by hundreds of experiments showing conditions under which predictions of analytical game theory are sometimes approximately satisfied, and sometimes badly rejected (Camerer, 2003). This article describes an emerging approach called 'behavioural game theory', which generalizes analytical game theory to explain experimentally observed violations. Behavioural game theory incorporates bounds on rationality, equilibrating forces, and theories of social preference, while retaining the mathematical formalism and generality across different games that has made analytical game theory so useful. While behavioural game theory is influenced by laboratory regularities, it is ultimately aimed at a broad range of applied questions such as worker reactions to employment terms, evolution of market institutions, design of auctions and contracts, animal behaviour, and differences in game-playing skill.

Social preferences

Let us start with a discussion of how preferences over outcomes of game can depart from pure material self-interest. In an ultimatum game a Proposer is endowed with a known sum, say ten dollars, and offers a share to another player, the Responder. If the Responder rejects the offer they both get nothing. The ultimatum game is a building block of more complex natural bargaining and a simple tool to measure numerically the price that Responders will pay to punish self-servingly unfair treatment.

Empirically, a large fraction of subjects rejects low offers of 20 per cent or so. Proposers fear these rejections reasonably accurately, and make offers around 40 per cent rather than very small offers predicted by perceived self-interest. (The earliest approximations of whether Proposers offer expected profit-maximizing offers, by Roth et al. 1991, suggested they did. However, those estimates were limited by the method of presenting Responders only with specific offers; since low offers are rare, it is hard to estimate the rejection rate of low offers accurately and hence hard to know conclusively whether offers are profit-maximizing. Different methods, and cross-population data used in Henrich et al., 2005, established that offers are too generous, even controlling for risk-aversion of the Proposers.) This basic pattern scales up to much higher stakes (the equivalent of months of wages) and does not change much when the experiment is repeated, so it is implausible to argue that subjects who reject offers (often highly intelligent college students) are confused.

It is crucial to note that rejecting two dollars out of ten dollars is a rejection of the *joint* hypothesis of utility-maximization and the auxiliary hypothesis that player i's utility depends on only her own payoff x_i. An obvious place to repair the theory is to create a parsimonious theory of social preferences over (x_i, x_j) (and possibly of other features of the game) which predicts violations of self-interest across games with different structures. I will next mention some other empirical regularities, then turn to a discussion of such models of these regularities.

In ultimatum games, it appears that norms and judgements of fairness can depend on context and culture. For example, when Proposers earn the right to make the offer (rather than respond to an offer) by winning at a pre-play trivia game, they feel entitled to offer less – and Responders seem to accept less (Hoffman et al., 1994). Two comparative studies of small-scale societies show interesting variation across cultures. Subjects in a small Peruvian agricultural group, the Machiguenga, offer much less than those in other cultures (typically 15–25 per cent) and accept low offers. Across 15 societies, equality of average offers is positively related to the degree of cooperation in economic activity (for example, do men hunt collectively?) and to the degree of impersonal market trading (Henrich et al., 2005).

Ultimatum games tap negative reciprocity or vengeance. Other games suggest different psychological motives which correspond to different aspects of social preferences. In dictator games, a Proposer simply dictates an allocation of money and the Responder must accept it. In these games, Proposers offer less than in ultimatum games (about 15 per cent of the stakes on average), but offers vary widely with contextual labels and other variables (Camerer, 2003, ch. 2). In trust games, an Investor risks some of her endowment of money, which is increased by the experimenter (representing a return on social investment) and given to an anonymous Trustee. The Trustee pays back as much of the increased sum as she likes to the Investor (perhaps nothing) and keeps the rest. Trust games are models of opportunities to gain from investment with no legal protection against moral hazard by a business partner. Self-interested Trustees will never pay back money; self-interested Investors with equilibrium beliefs will anticipate this and invest nothing. In fact, Investors typically risk about half their money, and Trustees pay back slightly less than was risked (Camerer, 2003, ch. 2). Investments reflect expectations of repayment, along with altruism toward Investors (Ashraf, Bohnet and Piankov, 2006) and an aversion to 'betrayal' (Bohnet and Zeckhauser, 2004). Trustee payback is consistent with positive reciprocity, or a moral obligation to repay a player who risked money to benefit the group.

Importantly, competition has a strong effect in these games. If two or more Proposers make offers in an ultimatum game, and a single Responder accepts the highest offer, then the only equilibrium is for the Proposers to offer almost all the money to the Responder (the *opposite* of the prediction with one Proposer). In the laboratory this Proposer competition occurs rapidly, resulting in a very unfair allocation – almost no earnings for Proposers (for example, Camerer and Fehr, 2006). Similarly, when there is competition among Responders, at least one Responder accepts low offers and Proposers seem to anticipate this effect and offer much less. These regularities help explain an apparent paradox, why the competitive model based on self-interest works so well in explaining market prices in experiments with three or more traders on each side of the market. In these markets, traders with social preferences cannot make choices which reveal a trade-off of self-interest and concern for fairness. The parsimonious theory in which agents have social preferences can therefore explain both fairness-type effects in bilateral exchange and the absence of those effects in multilateral market exchange.

A good social preference theory should explain all these facts: rejections of substantial offers in ultimatum games, lower Proposer offers in dictator games than in ultimatum games, trust and repayment in trust games, and the effects of competition (which bring offers closer to the equilibrium self-interest prediction).

In 'inequality-aversion' theories of social preference, players prefer more money and also prefer that allocations be more equal (judged by differences in payoffs – Fehr and Schmidt, 1999 – or by deviations from payoff shares and equal shares – Bolton and Ockenfels, 2000). In a related 'Rawlsitarian' approach, players care about a combination of their own payoffs, the minimum payoff (à la Rawls) and the total payoff (utilitarian) (Charness and Rabin, 2002). These simple theories account relatively well for the regularities mentioned above across games, with suitable parameter values.

Missing from the inequality aversion and Rawlsitarian theories is a reaction to the intentions of players. Intentions seem to be important because players are much less likely to reject unequal offers that are created by a random device or third party than equivalently unequal offers proposed by a player who benefits from inequality (for example, Blount, 1995; Falk, Fehr and Fischbacher, 2007). In reciprocity theories which incorporate intentions, player A forms a judgement about whether another player B has sacrificed to benefit (or harm) her (for example, Rabin, 1993). A likes to reciprocate, repaying kindness with kindness, and meanness with vengeance. This idea can also explain the results mentioned above, and the effects of intentions shown in other studies.

A newer class of theories focused on 'social image' – that is, player A cares about whether another player B believes A adheres to a norm of fairness. For example, Dufwenberg and Gneezy (2000) show that Trustee repayments in a trust game are correlated with the Trustee's perception of what he or she thought the Investor expected to be repaid. These models hinge on delicate details of iterated beliefs (A's belief about B's belief about A's fairness), so they are more technically complicated but can also explain a wider range of results (see Bénabou and Tirole, 2006; Dillenberger and Sadowski, 2006). Models of this sort are also better equipped to explain deliberate avoidance of information. For example, in dictator games where the dictator can either keep nine dollars or can play a ten-dollar dictator game (knowing the Recipient will *not know* which path was chosen), players often choose the easy nine dollar payment (Dana, Cain and Dawes, 2006). Since they could just play the ten-dollar game and keep all ten dollars, the ten-dollars sacrifice is presumably the price paid to avoid knowing that another person knows you have been selfish (see also Dana, Weber and Kuang, 2007).

Social preference utility theories and social image concerns like these could be applied to explain charitable contribution, legal conflict and settlement, wage-setting and wage dispersion within firms, strikes, divorces, wars, tax policy, and bequests by parents to siblings. Explaining these phenomena with a single parsimonious theory would be very useful and important for policy and welfare economics.

Limited strategic thinking and quantal response equilibrium

In complex games, equilibrium analysis may predict poorly what players do in unique games, or in the first period of a repeated game. Disequilibrium behaviour is important to understand if equilibration takes a long time, and if initial behaviour is important in determining which of several multiple equilibria will emerge. Two types of theories are prominent: cognitive hierarchy theories of different limits on strategic thinking; and theories which retain the assumption of equilibrium beliefs but assume players make mistakes, choosing strategies with higher expected payoff deviations less often.

Cognitive hierarchy theories describe a 'hierarchy' of strategic thinking and constrain how the hierarchy works to make precise predictions. Iterated reasoning surely is limited in the human mind because of evolutionary inertia in promoting high-level thinking, because of constraints on working memory, and because of adaptive motives for overconfidence in judging relative skill (stopping after some steps of reasoning, believing others have reasoned less). Empirical evidence from many experiments with highly skilled subjects suggests that 0–2 steps of iterated reasoning are most likely in the first period of play. A simple illustration is the 'p-beauty contest' game (Nagel, 1995; Ho, Camerer and Weigelt, 1998). In this game, several players choose a number in the interval [0,100]. The average of the numbers is computed, and multiplied by a value p (say 2/3). The player whose number is closest to p times the average wins a fixed prize.

In equilibrium players are never surprised what other players do. In the p-beauty contest game, this equilibrium condition implies that all players must be picking p times what others are choosing. This equilibrium condition only holds if everyone chooses 0 (the Nash equilibrium, consistent with iterated dominance). Figure 1 shows data from a game with $p = 7$ and compares the Nash prediction (choosing 0) and the fit of a cognitive hierarchy model (Camerer, Ho and Chong, 2004). In this game, some players choose numbers scattered from 0 to 100, many others choose p times 50 (the average if others are expected to choose randomly) and others choose p^2 times 50. When the game is played repeatedly with the same players (who learn the average after each trial), numbers converge toward zero, a reminder that equilibrium concepts do reliably predict where an adaptive process leads, even if they do not predict the starting point of that process.

In cognitive hierarchy theories, players who do k steps of thinking anticipate that others do fewer steps. Fully specifying these theories requires specifying what 0-step players do, what higher-step players think, and the statistical distribution of players' thinking levels. One type of theory assumes players who do k steps of thinking believe others do k-steps (Nagel, 1995; Stahl and Wilson, 1995; Costa-Gomes, Crawford and Broseta, 2001). This specification is analytically tractable (especially in games with $n >$ two players) but implies that as players do more thinking their beliefs are further from reality. Another specification assumes increasingly rational expectations – k-level players truncate the actual distribution $f(k)$ of k-step thinkers and guess accurately the relative proportions of thinkers doing 0 to $k-1$ steps of thinking. Camerer, Ho and Chong (2004) and earlier studies show how these cognitive hierarchy theories can fit experimental data from a wide variety of games, with similar thinking-step parameters across games.

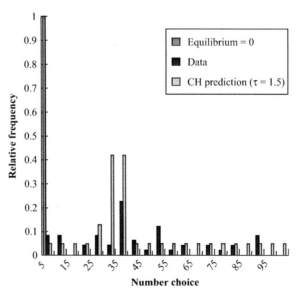

Figure 1   Number choices and theoretical predictions in beauty contest games. *Note*: Players choose numbers from 0 to 100 and the closest number to 0.7 times the average wins a fixed prize. *Source*: Camerer and Fehr (2006).

These cognitive hierarchy theories ignore the benefits and costs of thinking hard. Costs and benefits can be included by relaxing Nash equilibrium, so that players respond stochastically to expected payoffs and choose better responses more often then worse ones, but do not maximize. Denote player i's beliefs about the chance that other players j will choose strategy k by $P_i(s_j^k)$. The expected payoff of player i's strategy s_i^h is $E(s_i^h) = \sum_k P_i(s_j^k)\pi_i(s_i^h, s_j^k)$ (where $\pi_i(x,y)$ is i's payoff if i plays x and j plays y). If player i responds with a logit choice function, then $P_i(s_i^h) = \exp(\lambda E(s_i^h))/\sum_k \exp(\lambda E(s_i^k))$. In this kind of 'quantal response' equilibrium (QRE), each player's beliefs about choice probabilities of others are consistent with actual choice probabilities, but *players do not always choose the highest expected payoff strategy (and λ parameterizes the degree of responsiveness; larger λ implies better response)*. QRE fits a wide variety of data better than Nash predictions (McKelvey and Palfrey, 1995; 1998; Goeree and Holt, 2001). It also circumvents some technical limits of Nash equilibrium because players always tremble but the degree of trembling in strategies is linked to expected payoff differences.

Learning

In complex games, it is unlikely that equilibrium beliefs arise from introspection or communication. Therefore, theorists have explored the mathematical properties of various rules under which equilibration might occur when rationality is bounded.

Much research is focused on population evolutionary rules, such as replicator dynamics, in which strategies which have a payoff advantage spread through the population (for example, Weibull, 1995). Schlag and Pollock (1999) show a link between imitation of successful players and replicator dynamics.

Several individual learning rules have been fit to many experimental data-sets (see INDIVIDUAL LEARNING IN GAMES). Most of these rules can be expressed as difference equations of underlying numerical propensities or attractions of stage-game strategies which are updated in response to experience. The simplest rule is choice reinforcement, which updates chosen strategies according to received payoffs (perhaps scaled by an aspiration level or reference point). These rules fit surprisingly well in some classes of games (for example, with mixed strategy equilibrium, so that all strategies are played and reinforced relatively often) and in environments with little information, where agents must learn payoffs from experience, but can fit quite poorly in other games. A more complex rule is weighted fictitious play (WFP), in which players form beliefs about what others will do in the future by taking a weighted average of past play, and then choose strategies with high expected payoffs given those beliefs (Cheung and Friedman, 1997). Camerer and Ho (1999) showed that WFP with geometrically declining weights is mathematically equivalent to generalized reinforcement in which unchosen strategies are reinforced as strongly as chosen ones. Building on this insight, they create a hybrid called experience weighted attraction (EWA). The original version of EWA has many parameters because it includes all the parameters used in the various special cases it hybridizes. The EWA form fits modestly better in some games (it adjusts carefully for overfitting by estimating parameters on part of the data and then forecasting out-of-sample), especially those with rapid learning across many strategies (such as pricing). In response to criticism about the number of free parameters, Ho, Camerer, and Chong (2007) created a version with zero *learning parameters (just a response sensitivity λ as in QRE)* by replacing parameters by 'self-tuning' functions of experience.

Some interesting learning rules do not fit neatly into the class of strategy-updating difference equations. Often it is plausible to think that players are reinforcing learning *rules* rather than strategies (for example, updating the reinforcement rule or the WFP rule; see Stahl, 2000). In many game it is also plausible that people update history-dependent strategies (like tit for tat; see Erev and Roth, 2001; McKelvey and Palfrey, 2001). Selten and Buchta (1999) discuss a concept of 'direction learning' in which players adjust based on experience in a 'direction' when strategies are numerically ordered.

All the rules described above are naive (called 'adaptive') in the sense that they do not incorporate the fact that other players are learning. Models which allow players to be 'sophisticated' and anticipate learning by other players (Stahl, 1999; Chong, Camerer and Ho, 2006) often fit better, especially with experienced subjects. Sophistication is particularly important if players are matched together repeatedly – as workers in firms, firms in strategic alliances, neighbours, spouses, and so forth. Then players have an incentive to take actions that 'strategically teach' an adaptive player what to do. Models of this sort have more moving parts but can explain some basic stylized facts (for example, differences in repeated-game play with fixed 'partner' and random 'stranger' matching of players) and fit a little better than equilibrium reputational models in trust and entry deterrence games (Chong, Camerer and Ho, 2006).

Conclusion

Behavioural game theory uses intuitions and experimental evidence to propose psychologically realistic models of strategic behaviour under rationality bounds and learning, and incorporates social motivations in valuation of outcomes. There are now many mathematical tools available in both of these domains that have been suggested by or fit closely to many different experimental games: cognitive hierarchy, quantal-response equilibrium, many types of learning models (for example, reinforcement, belief learning, EWA and self-tuning EWA), and many different theories of social preference based on inequality aversion, reciprocity, and social image. The primary challenge in the years ahead is to continue to compare and refine these models – in most areas, there is still lively debate about which simplifications are worth making, and why – and then apply them to the sorts of problems in contracting, auctions, and signalling that equilibrium analysis has been so powerfully applied to.

A relatively new challenge is to understand communication. Hardly any games in the world are played without some kind of pre-play messages (even in animal behaviour). However, communication is so rich that understanding how communication works by pure deduction is unlikely to succeed without help from careful empirical observation. A good illustration is Brandts and Cooper (2007), who show the nuanced ways in which communication and incentives, together, can influence coordination in a simple organizational team game.

COLIN F. CAMERER

See also **experimental economics; individual learning in games.**

Bibliography

Ashraf, N., Bohnet, I. and Piankov, N. 2006. Decomposing trust and trustworthiness. *Experimental Economics* 9, 193–208.

Bénabou, R. and Tirole, J. 2006. Incentives and prosocial behavior. *American Economic Review* 96, 1652–78.

Blount, S. 1995. When social outcomes aren't fair – the effect of causal attributions on preferences. *Organizational Behavior and Human Decision Processes* 63, 131–44.

Bohnet, I. and Zeckhauser, R. 2004. Trust, risk and betrayal. *Journal of Economic Behavior & Organization* 55, 467–84.

Bolton, G.E. and Ockenfels, A. 2000. ERC: a theory of equity, reciprocity, and competition. *American Economic Review* 90, 166–93.

Brandts, J. and Cooper, A. 2007. It's what you say, not what you pay: an experimental study of manager-employee relationships in overcoming coordination failure. *Journal of the European Economic Association* (forthcoming).

Camerer, C.F. 2003. *Behavioral Game Theory: Experiments on Strategic Interaction*. Princeton: Princeton University Press.

Camerer, C.F. and Fehr, E. 2006. When does 'economic man' dominate social behavior? *Science* 311, 47–52.

Camerer, C.F. and Ho, T.H. 1999. Experience-weighted attraction learning in normal form games. *Econometrica* 67, 827–74.

Camerer, C.F., Ho, T.-H. and Chong, J.-K. 2004. A cognitive hierarchy model of games. *Quarterly Journal of Economics* 119, 861–98.

Charness, G. and Rabin, M. 2002. Understanding social preferences with simple tests. *Quarterly Journal of Economics* 117, 817–69.

Cheung, Y.-W. and Friedman, D. 1997. Individual learning in normal form games: some laboratory results. *Games and Economic Behavior* 19, 46–76.

Chong, J.-K., Camerer, C.F. and Ho, T.H. 2006. A learning-based model of repeated games with incomplete information. *Games and Economic Behavior* 55, 340–71.

Costa-Gomes, M., Crawford, V.P. and Broseta, B. 2001. Cognition and behavior in normal-form games: an experimental study. *Econometrica* 69, 1193–235.

Dana, J., Cain, D.M. and Dawes, R.M. 2006. What you don't know won't hurt me: costly (but quiet) exit in dictator games. *Organizational Behavior and Human Decision Processes* 100, 193–201.

Dana, J.D., Weber, R.A. and Kuang, J.X. 2007. Exploiting moral wiggle room: behavior inconsistent with a preference for fair outcomes. *Economic Theory*. (forthcoming).

Dillenberger, D. and Sadowski, P. 2006. *Ashamed to Be Selfish*. Princeton: Princeton University Press.

Dufwenberg, M. and Gneezy, U. 2000. Measuring beliefs in an experimental lost wallet game. *Games and Economic Behavior* 30, 163–82.

Erev, I. and Roth, A.E. 2001. On simple reinforcement learning models and reciprocation in the prisoner dilemma game. In *The Adaptive Toolbox*, ed. G. Gigerenzer and R. Selten. Cambridge: MIT Press.

Falk, A., Fehr, E. and Fischbacher, U. 2007. Testing theories of intentions – fairness matters. *Games and Economic Behavior* (forthcoming).

Fehr, E. and Schmidt, K.M. 1999. A theory of fairness, competition, and cooperation. *Quarterly Journal of Economics* 114, 817–68.

Goeree, J.K. and Holt, C.A. 2001. Ten little treasures of game theory and ten intuitive contradictions. *American Economic Review* 91, 1402–22.

Henrich, J. et al. 2005. 'Economic man' in cross-cultural perspective: behavioral experiments in 15 small-scale societies. *Behavioral and Brain Sciences* 28, 795–815.

Ho, T.H., Camerer, C.F and Chong, J.-K. 2007. Self-tuning experience weighted attraction learning in games. *Journal of Economic Theory* 133, 177–98.

Ho, T.H., Camerer, C.F. and Weigelt, K. 1998. Iterated dominance and iterated best response in experimental 'p-beauty contests'. *American Economic Review* 88, 947–69.

Hoffman, E., McCabe, K., Shachat, K. and Smith, V. 1994. Preferences, property-rights, and anonymity in bargaining games. *Games and Economic Behavior* 7, 346–80.

McKelvey, R.D. and Palfrey, T.R. 1995. Quantal response equilibria for normal form games. *Games and Economic Behavior* 10, 6–38.

McKelvey, R.D. and Palfrey, T.R. 1998. Quantal response equilibria for extensive form games. *Experimental Economics* 1, 9–41.

McKelvey, R.D. and Palfrey, T.R. 2001. *Playing in the Dark: Information, Learning, and Coordination in Repeated Games*. Princeton: Princeton University Press.

Nagel, R. 1995. Unraveling in guessing games: an experimental study. *American Economic Review* 85, 1313–26.

Rabin, M. 1993. Incorporating fairness into game-theory and economics. *American Economic Review* 83, 1281–302.

Roth, A.E., Prasnikar, V., Okuno-Fujiwara, M. and Zamir, S. 1991. Bargaining and market behavior in Jerusalem, Ljubljana, Pittsburgh, and Tokyo: an experimental study. *American Economic Review* 81, 1068–95.

Schlag, K.H. and Pollock, G.B. 1999. Social roles as an effective learning mechanism. *Rationality and Society* 11, 371–97.

Selten, R. and Buchta, J. 1999. Experimental sealed bid first price auctions with directly observed bid functions. In *Games and Human Behavior: Essays in Honor of Amnon Rapoport*, ed. D.V. Budescu, I. Erev and R. Zwick. Mahwah, NJ: Lawrence Erlbaum.

Stahl, D. 1999. Sophisticated learning and learning sophistication. Working paper, University of Texas.

Stahl, D.O. 2000. Rule learning in symmetric normal-form games: theory and evidence. *Games and Economic Behavior* 32, 105–38.

Stahl, D.O. and Wilson, P. 1995. On players' models of other players: theory and experimental evidence. *Games and Economic Behavior* 10, 218–54.

Weibull, J. 1995. *Evolutionary Game Theory*. Cambridge, MA: MIT Press.

behavioural public economics

Interest in the field of psychology and economics has grown in recent years, stimulated largely by accumulating evidence that the neoclassical model of consumer decision-making provides an inadequate description of human behaviour in many economic situations. Scholars have begun to propose alternative models that incorporate insights from psychology and neuroscience. Some of the pertinent literature focuses on behaviours commonly considered 'dysfunctional', such as addiction, obesity, risky sexual behaviour, and crime. However, there is also considerable interest in alternative approaches to more standard economic problems such as saving, investing, labour supply, risk-taking, and charitable contributions.

Behavioural public economics (BPE) is the label used to describe a rapidly growing literature that uses this new class of models to study the impact of public policies on behaviour and well-being (see Bernheim and Rangel, 2006a, for a more comprehensive review).

Background: the neoclassical approach to public economics

Public economic analysis requires us to formulate models of human decision-making with two components – one describing choices, and the other describing well-being. Using the first component, we can forecast the effects of policy reforms on individuals' actions, as well as on prices and allocations. Using the second component, we can determine whether these changes benefit consumers or harm them.

The neoclassical approach assumes that individuals' choices can be described *as if* generated by the maximization of a well-defined and stable utility function subject to feasibility and informational constraints. Neoclassical welfare analysis proceeds from the premise that, when evaluating policies, the government should act as each individual's proxy, extrapolating his preferred choices from observed decisions in related situations. This premise justifies the use of the *as-if* utility function as a gauge of well-being. In effect, this approach uses the same model for positive and normative analysis.

Within the neoclassical paradigm, government policy can affect behaviour and welfare only if it changes the decision maker's information or budget constraint. For example, vaccination campaigns may influence behaviour by providing information concerning the risks of a disease and the advantages of taking preventive action, while cigarette taxes may alter choices by raising the cost of smoking.

From the neoclassical perspective, government intervention in private markets is justified to enforce property rights, correct market failures, and address inequity by redistributing resources. Standard examples of interventions motivated by market failures include the use of taxes and subsidies to correct externalities, the provision of public goods, and the introduction of social insurance when private risk sharing is inefficient.

The accomplishments of neoclassical public economics, such as the theories of optimal income taxation and corrective environmental policy, are considerable. However, there is growing concern that this paradigm does not adequately address a number of important public policy challenges – for example, what to do about 'self-destructive' behaviours such as substance abuse, or about the apparently myopic choices of those who save 'too little' for retirement. Since the neoclassical welfare criterion respects all voluntary consumer choices (conditional on the information in the consumer's possession), it rules out the possibility of enhancing well-being by correcting 'poor' choices (except through the provision of information).

The behavioural approach to public economics

A key feature of BPE is the potential divergence of positive and normative models. Even when it is assumed that individuals are endowed with well-behaved lifetime preferences, decision processes may translate these preferences to choices imperfectly. To conduct positive analysis, one employs a model of the potentially imperfect decision process. To conduct normative analysis, one uses a well-defined welfare relation. In stark contrast to the neoclassical approach, the welfare relation may prescribe an alternative other than the one that the individual would choose for himself, at least under some conditions.

The analysis of addiction presented in Bernheim and Rangel (2004) illustrates this approach. Our model assumes that people attempt to optimize given their preferences, but randomly encounter conditions that trigger systematic mistakes, the likelihood of which evolves with previous substance use. The model is based on the following three premises. First, use among addicts is sometimes a mistake and sometimes rational. Second, experience with an addictive substance sensitizes an individual to environmental cues that trigger mistaken usage. Third, addicts understand their susceptibility to cue-triggered mistakes and attempt to manage the process with some degree of sophistication. The first two premises are justified by a body of research in psychology and neuroscience, which shows that, after repeated exposure to an addictive substance, the brain tends to overestimate the hedonic consequences of drug consumption upon encountering environmental cues that are associated with past use. The third premise is justified by behavioural evidence indicating that users are often surprisingly sophisticated and forward looking.

The (β,δ)-model of intertemporal choice (Strotz, 1956; Phelps and Pollack, 1968; Laibson, 1997; O'Donoghue and Rabin, 1999; 2001) also illustrates the BPE approach. Psychologists have found that people often act as if they attach disproportionate importance to immediate rewards relative to future rewards, especially in situations where cognitive systems are overloaded. (For a recent review of this literature, see Frederick, Loewenstein and O'Donoghue, 2002; Loewenstein, Read and Baumister, 2003.) To capture this tendency, the (β,δ)-model assumes that, in each period t, individuals behave as if they maximize a utility function of the form

$$u(c_t) + \beta \left[\sum_{k=t+1}^{T} \delta^{k-t} u(c_k) \right],$$

where $0 < \beta < 1$. In this framework, the parameter β represents the degree of *present bias* or *myopia*. The neoclassical model corresponds to the special case where $\beta = 1$. With $\beta < 1$, behaviour is dynamically inconsistent. This complicates positive analysis, since behaviour no longer corresponds to the solution of single utility maximization problem.

Many analysts interpret present bias as a mistake. They argue that the individual's underlying well-being actually corresponds to the preferences revealed through choices that do not involve immediate rewards:

$$U(c_1, \dots, c_T) = \sum_{t=0}^{T} \delta^t u(c_t).$$

Under this interpretation, $\beta < 1$ creates a tendency to consume excessively in the present.

These examples illustrate some important conceptual and methodological aspects of BPE. First, with behaviour and welfare modelled separately, BPE allows for the possibility of mistakes. In contrast to a neoclassical analyst, a BPE analyst can pose questions that presuppose possible divergences between behaviour and preferences, such as whether Americans save too little for retirement, or whether addicts engage in self-destructive behaviour. Within the BPE framework, one can test the hypothesis that individuals maximize their well-being, and measure the magnitude of their errors. Second, to justify either a positive representation of choice or a particular welfare criterion, a BPE analyst relies on evidence from psychology and neuroscience. This evidence can help economists pin down underlying preferences by identifying the mechanisms responsible for the decision-making errors. Good structural models of decision-making processes may also improve the quality of out-of-sample behavioural predictions, which are often required for policy evaluation.

Behavioural policy analysis

BPE models are extensions of neoclassical models. Thus, they imply that public policy can modify behaviour by changing budget constraints and/or information. For example, cigarette prices affect cigarette consumption in the Bernheim–Rangel addiction model, and savings are responsive to interest rates in most specifications of the (β, δ)-model.

In addition, the BPE framework introduces new channels through which public policy can affect behaviour and welfare. In particular, it allows for the possibility that some public policies can influence behaviour *directly* by activating particular cognitive processes, even when they leave budget constraints and information unchanged.

For example, Brazil and Canada require every pack of cigarettes to display a prominent, viscerally charged image depicting some deleterious consequences of smoking, such as lung disease and neonatal morbidity. Since the consequences of smoking are well known, this policy has no effect in information or budget constraints. And yet the Bernheim–Rangel theory of addiction allows for the possibility that a sufficiently strong counter-cue could reduce the probability of a mistake by triggering thought processes that induce users to resist cravings. When successful, this policy affects behaviour by activating particular cognitive processes.

Another striking example involves the effects of default options in employee-directed pension plans. A 'default option' is the outcome resulting from inaction. For a neoclassical consumer, choices depend only on preferences, information, and constraints. Consequently, in the absence of significant transaction costs, default options should be inconsequential. However, in the context of decisions concerning saving and investment, defaults seem to matter a great deal. For example, with respect to 401(k) plans (employer-sponsored retirement savings accounts in the United States that receive preferential tax treatment), there is considerable evidence that default options affect participation rates, contribution rates, and portfolios (Madrian and Shea, 2001; Choi, Laibson and Madrian, 2004). Yet, arguably, a default neither affects opportunities (since transaction costs are low) nor provides new information.

While BPE models admit traditional justifications for government intervention in private markets (the enforcement of property rights, the correction market failures, and the redistribution of resources), they also introduce novel justifications. For example, public policy may improve welfare by reducing the size, likelihood, or consequences of mistakes. As shown in the next two sections, this can lead to conclusions that are strikingly at odds with those generated by the neoclassical model.

Example: addiction policy

In the neoclassical theory of rational addiction (Becker and Murphy, 1988), government intervention may be justified *only* when it corrects market failures involving addictive substances, such as second-hand smoking, or when it combats ignorance or misinformation. In contrast, in our model of addiction (Bernheim and Rangel, 2004), government intervention may also be justified when it reduces the frequency, magnitude, and consequences of mistakes. These considerations give rise to a number of non-standard policy implications.

Limitations of informational policy. In practice, public education campaigns (such as anti-smoking and anti-drug initiatives) have achieved mixed results. Our view of addiction highlights a fundamental limitation of informational policy: contrary to standard theory, one cannot assume that even a highly knowledgeable addict always makes informed choices. Information about the consequences of substance abuse may affect initial experimentation with drugs, but cannot alter the neurological mechanisms through which addictive substances subvert deliberative decision-making.

Beneficial harm reduction. If addiction results from randomly occurring mistakes, various interventions can serve social insurance objectives by ameliorating some of its worst consequences. For instance, subsidization of rehabilitation centres and treatment programmes (particularly for the indigent) can moderate the financial impact of addiction and promote recovery. Likewise, the free distribution of clean needles can moderate the incidence of diseases among heroin addicts. In some cases, it may even be beneficial to make substances available to severe addicts at low cost, a policy used in some European countries.

Counterproductive disincentives. Policies such as 'sin taxes' strive to discourage use by making substances costly. This is potentially justifiable on the grounds that use generates negative externalities. Even higher taxes (whether implicit or explicit) might be justified if they also reduce 'unwanted' use. Unfortunately, the compulsive use of addictive substances is probably much less sensitive to costs and consequences than is deliberative use. Consequently, imposing costs on users in excess of the standard Pigouvian levy will likely distort deliberate choices detrimentally, without significantly reducing problematic compulsive usage. In addition, policies that impose high costs on use may thwart social insurance objectives by exacerbating the consequences of uninsurable risks associated with the use of addictive substances, such as poverty and prostitution. Accordingly, for some substances the optimal rate of taxation for addictive substances may be significant *lower* than that the standard Pigouvian levy (see Bernheim and Rangel, 2005, for simulation results).

Policies affecting cues. Since environmental cues appear to trigger addictive behaviours, public policy can also influence use by changing the cues that people normally encounter. One approach involves the elimination of problematic cues. For example, advertising and marketing restrictions of the type imposed on sellers of tobacco and alcohol suppress one possible artificial trigger for compulsive use. Since one person's decision to smoke may trigger another, confining use to designated areas may reduce unintended use. Another approach involves the creation of counter-cues, which we discussed above. Policies that eliminate problematic cues or promote counter-cues are potentially beneficial because they combat compulsive use while imposing minimal inconvenience and restrictions on rational users.

Facilitation of self-control. Most behavioural theories of addiction potentially justify policies that provide better opportunities for self-regulation without making particular choices compulsory. In principle, this helps those who are vulnerable to compulsive use without encroaching on the freedoms of those who would deliberately choose to use. Laws that limit the sale of a substance to particular times, places, and circumstances may facilitate self-regulation. Well-designed policies could in principle accomplish this objective more effectively. For example, a number of states have enacted laws allowing problem gamblers to voluntarily ban themselves from casinos. Alternatively, if a substance is available only by prescription, and if prescription orders are filled on a 'next day' basis, then deliberate forward-looking planning becomes a prerequisite for availability. In the absence of a pervasive black market, recovering heroin addicts could self-regulate problematic compulsive use by carefully choosing when, and when not, to file requests for refills.

Example: savings policy

The (β,δ)-model of savings also exemplifies the novel policy insights generated by the BPE approach. For example, this model implies that many individuals will save too little for retirement, and that there may be Pareto improving policy interventions even in the absence of capital market distortions – a conclusion that is at odds with the neoclassical framework. Other notable implications include the following:

Mandatory savings policies. Within the (β,δ) framework, compulsory saving may be welfare-enhancing if it fully crowds out private saving (in the form of liquid assets) at some point during the life cycle (Imrohoroglu, Imrohoroglu and Joines, 2003; Diamond and Koszegi, 2003). This provides a rationale for mandatory savings programmes, which are pervasive across the world, and which are more difficult to justify within the neoclassical framework.

Saving subsidies. On the assumption that (*a*) the population includes some individuals with self-control problems and (*b*) the social welfare function is continuous and concave, a small subsidy for saving financed with lump-sum taxes is welfare improving (O'Donoghue and Rabin, 2006; Krusell, Kuruscu and Smith, 2000; 2002). Intuitively, the subsidy produces a first-order improvement in the well-being of individuals with self-control problems (since they save too little), and only a second-order reduction in the well-being of those without self-control problems. This provides a possible rationale for tax-favoured savings programmes, such as, in the United States, 401(k) plans and Individual Retirement Accounts (IRAs).

Credit restrictions. Introducing restrictions on the availability of credit, for example, by regulating the distribution of revolving credit lines and mandating credit ceilings, can potentially enhance the well-being of those with self-control problems. For example, Laibson, Repetto and Tobacman (2004) estimate that the representative (β,δ) consumer would be willing to pay $2000 at the age of 20 to exclude himself from the credit card market.

Behavioural public economics circa 2006

As of 2006, the rapidly growing field of BPE has demonstrated its value by enhancing our understanding of public policy in several areas, including savings and addiction. Nevertheless, the literature is still in its infancy. As time passes, we anticipate that the methods and tools of BPE will contribute new insights in these areas, as well as to other difficult public policy issues involving poverty, crime, corruption, violence, obesity, and charitable giving, among others.

In addition to providing new insights concerning the effects of familiar policies, research in BPE can also guide the design of new policies. One obvious goal is to reduce the frequency of mistakes among those who behave suboptimally without interfering with the choices of those who behave optimally. Some recent fieldwork by

Thaler and Bernartzi (2004), who advocate a savings programme called Save More Tomorrow, illustrates the potential value of this approach. In this programme, a worker can allocate a portion of her future salary increases towards retirement savings. Subsequently, she is allowed to change this allocation at a negligible transaction cost. In practice, 78 per cent of those who were eligible for the plan chose to participate, 80 per cent of participants remained in the plan through the fourth pay raise, and the average contribution rate for programme participants increased from 3.5 per cent to 13.6 per cent over the course of 40 months.

To date, progress in BPE has been somewhat hampered by the absence of a general framework for behavioural welfare analysis. Analysts tend to devise and justify welfare criteria on a case-by-case basis, rather than through the application of general principles. Ongoing research aims to fill this gap (see Bernheim and Rangel, 2006b).

B. DOUGLAS BERNHEIM AND ANTONIO RANGEL

See also **addiction; behavioural game theory; public goods experiments.**

Bibliography

Becker, G. and Murphy, K. 1988. A theory of rational addiction. *Journal of Political Economy* 96, 675–700.

Bernheim, B.D. and Rangel, A. 2004. Addiction and cue-triggered decision processes. *American Economic Review* 94, 1558–90.

Bernheim, B.D. and Rangel, A. 2005. From neuroscience to public policy: a new economic view of addiction. *Swedish Economic Policy Review* 12, 11–46.

Bernheim, B.D. and Rangel, A. 2006a. Behavioral public economics: welfare and policy analysis with fallible decision-makers. In *Economic Institutions and Behavioral Economics*, ed. P. Diamond and H. Vartiainen. Princeton: Princeton University Press, (forthcoming).

Bernheim, B.D. and Rangel, A. 2006b. Toward choice-theoretic foundations for behavioral welfare economics. *American Economic Review Papers and Proceedings*, (forthcoming).

Choi, J., Laibson, D. and Madrian, B. 2004. Plan design and 401(k) savings outcomes. *National Tax Journal* 57, 275–98.

Diamond, P. and Koszegi, B. 2003. Quasi-hyperbolic discounting and retirement. *Journal of Public Economics* 87, 1839–72.

Frederick, S., Loewenstein, G. and O'Donoghue, T. 2002. Time discounting and time preference: a critical review. *Journal of Economic Literature* 40, 351–401.

Imrohoroglu, S., Imrohoroglu, A. and Joines, D. 2003. Time inconsistent preferences and social security. *Quarterly Journal of Economics* 118, 745–84.

Krusell, P., Kuruscu, B. and Smith, A. 2000. Tax policy with quasi-geometric discounting. *International Economic Journal* 14(3), 1–40.

Krusell, P., Kuruscu, B. and Smith, A. 2002. Equilibrium welfare and government policy with quasi-geometric discounting. *Journal of Economic Theory* 105, 42–72.

Laibson, D. 1997. Golden eggs and hyperbolic discounting. *Quarterly Journal of Economics* 112, 443–77.

Laibson, D., Repetto, A. and Tobacman, J. 2004. Estimating discount functions from lifecycle consumption choices. Working paper, Harvard University.

Loewenstein, G., Read, D. and Baumister, R., eds. 2003. *Time and Decision: Economic and Psychological Perspectives on Intertemporal Choice*. New York: Russell Sage Foundation.

Madrian, B. and Shea, D. 2001. The power of suggestion: inertia in 401(k) participation and savings behavior. *Quarterly Journal of Economics* 116, 1149–87.

O'Donoghue, T. and Rabin, M. 1999b. Doing it now or later. *American Economic Review* 89, 103–24.

O'Donoghue, T. and Rabin, M. 2001. Choice and procrastination. *Quarterly Journal of Economics*, 121–60.

O'Donoghue, T. and Rabin, M. 2006. Optimal sin taxes. *Journal of Public Economics* 90, 1825–49.

Phelps, E. and Pollack, R. 1968. On second-best national savings and game equilibrium growth. *Review of Economic Studies* 35, 185–99.

Strotz, R.H. 1956. Myopia and inconsistency in dynamic utility maximization. *Review of Economic Studies* 23, 165–80.

Thaler, R.H. and Bernartzi, S. 2004. Save more for tomorrow: using behavioral economics to increase employee savings. *Journal of Political Economy* 112, S164–S187.

collective choice experiments

Duncan Black (1948) and Kenneth Arrow (1963) raised the key question of collective choice: if people have different preferences for policy outcomes are there general mechanisms that can (always) aggregate those preferences in consistent and coherent ways? The answer is 'no'. Starting from simple premises involving individual transitivity, aggregate Pareto optimality and non-dictatorship there is no collective choice mechanism that yields a socially transitive outcome. Such a finding is startling given the confidence placed in democratic institutions that rely on voting mechanisms to choose a single outcome from many possible outcomes.

Experimentalists have thoroughly explored different institutions that can be used to aggregate preferences. Political economists who straddle both economics and political science have carried out much of this work. Their concern is with situations where actors who have opposed interests have to settle on a single outcome and with the properties of the institution used to produce an outcome. This article first turns to the institutional mechanisms by which individuals settle on a collective outcome. The second topic turns to electoral mechanisms used in representative democracies.

Spatial committee experiments

In the late 1960s theoretical papers by Davis and Hinich (1966) and Plott (1967) described a social choice environment for spatial committees. Those committees consist of a well-defined multidimensional policy space, with actors holding fixed preferences over the dimensions, and policies represented as points in the space. Using rules that mimic many parliamentary systems, these theoretical papers demonstrate that a Condorcet winner (a policy that can defeat all others under pairwise voting) exists only under rare distributions of voters' preferences. Plott (1967) establishes the conditions under which a Condorcet winner will exist and he makes the connection between this and a Nash equilibrium of a spatial committee game. Like others, he concludes that an equilibrium is rare in multidimensional spatial committee games.

Early spatial committee experiments by Berl et al. (1976) and Fiorina and Plott (1978) provide evidence that when a Condorcet winner exists, subjects choose it or outcomes that are close to it. In games where there is no such equilibrium (which is the most common case), subjects select outcomes that scatter in the policy space. These initial empirical findings, coupled with experiments by Laing and Olmsted (1978) and McKelvey, Ordeshook and Winer (1978), defined the standard for conducting spatial committee experiments. Subsequent experiments have adopted almost identical procedures.

The standard experimental design introduces a two-dimensional policy space. The orthogonal dimensions are arbitrary (X and Y in most settings) and typically range from zero to 200 or more units. Every point in the space characterizes a policy. Preferences over outcomes are induced by assigning each subject a payoff function mapping earnings in dollars to each point in the space. While many payoff functions have been tested, most experimenters have settled on a quadratic loss function, with monetary payoffs decreasing as a function of distance from a subject's ideal point. Usually five subjects are assigned different ideal points in the space, and it is the arrangement of these ideal points that allows the experimenter to manipulate, whether a Condorcet winner exists or not. Subjects are given an initial status quo and then allowed to introduce amendments. Voting takes place following an amendment, with the winner becoming (or remaining) the new status quo. Amending takes place in between votes. A motion to adjourn, passed under a voting rule, constitutes the stopping rule for the committee decision. This serves as the standard institution for subsequent spatial committee experiments. Changing these basic institutional rules became the way to test theories of collective choice.

Experimental results in the absence of equilibrium are both frustrating and profitable. Frustration arises over the fact that committee choices tend to be clustered in similar regions of the policy space. While there appears to be some pattern to the outcomes, the process by which these outcomes arise has not been fully characterized (but see the attempt by Bianco et al., 2006). Profitably, these empirical results led theorists and experimenters to add agenda control to the structure of the game. This led to a distinction between preference-induced and structure-induced equilibrium. For example, Plott and Levine (1978) showed the effectiveness of agenda control both in the laboratory and in a natural setting. Awarding agenda power created a structure-induced equilibrium and laboratory subjects converged to it. Recent experimental work by Frechette, Kagel and Lehrer (2003) illustrates that the equilibrium favours agenda setters.

Theoretical work by Buchanan and Tullock (1962) led experimentalists to examine whether changing the proportion of actors needed to pass a policy had any effect. Experiments by Laing and Slotznick (1983) showed that moving from simple majority rule (50 per cent plus 1) to supermajority majority rule (67 per cent) resulted in many equilibria and that subjects chose them. Schofield (1985), among others, provided the theoretical basis for when an equilibrium exists as a function of the dimensionality of the policy space, the voting rule and the distribution of voters' preferences. These theoretical findings spurred experimentalists to examine other changes to the standard committee experiment. For example Wilson and Herzberg (1987) theoretically predicted and experimentally demonstrated that when a single player holds veto power, that player's ideal point is the equilibrium. Haney, Herzberg and Wilson (1992) empirically show committee choices converging to equilibrium when a weighted voting rule is used. Such a rule requires that a single player always be included in a coalition. These results are representative of the kind of work that has dominated the experimental spatial committee agenda.

Experiments on spatial committees have added to a clearer understanding of institutional mechanisms. Experimental results demonstrate that changing who has the power to set the agenda, how the agenda is built, how many votes are needed and whether players enjoy veto powers, matters.

Electoral mechanisms

A second area of interest for collective choice experimentalists is with electoral mechanisms. Three broad directions have been taken that treat different aspects of representative democracies. The first is concerned with candidate behaviour. At the heart of this research is the question of whether candidate positions will converge to equilibrium when it exists. The second direction is concerned with voter behaviour, particularly how voters behave when they have little information about candidate positions. The final direction deals with the way in which electoral rules determine the likelihood that 'types' of candidates are elected, where types usually refer to racial and ethnic minority candidates.

The initial experimental work on candidate behaviour focused on candidates who cared only about winning and varied the information conditions that the candidates have about the preferences of voters. Most experiments use a unidimensional policy space that guarantees an equilibrium. This equilibrium is defined by the policy preference of the median voter. In the experiments elections are sequential, with two candidates announcing positions in the policy space and voters choosing between the candidates. Voters are assigned ideal points in the policy space, the winning candidate is required to implement the announced policy and voters are paid an amount that decreases with the distance of the winning position from their ideal point. Candidates are paid only if they win. Once the election is over another election is held with candidates free to change their previously announced policy. Not surprisingly, all candidates quickly adopt the position of the median voter when they are fully informed about voter preferences. Under incomplete information about voters, candidates also converge to the median voter's position, by responding to feedback about the vote share accruing to different policy positions, as in McKelvey and Ordeshook (1985). If candidates have policy preferences whereby their earnings depend not only on winning but also on implementing a policy close to their own preferred position, then the median voter result no longer holds (see the experimental results by Morton, 1993).

When voters are uninformed about candidate positions, are they able to cast accurate ballots? With minimal information, such as biased endorsements or polls, subjects do very well at inferring candidate positions. Lupia and McCubbins (1998) and Morton and Williams (2001) consider various aspects of voter information and show that voters are able to quickly determine the positions of candidates and cast their vote accordingly.

Finally, several experiments have focused on differing electoral mechanisms and what they mean for the type of candidates that gain election. For example Gerber, Morton and Rietz (1998) compare two voting mechanisms in an experiment to test whether one or the other disadvantages a racial or ethnic minority candidate. A form of cumulative voting (in which voters can cast more than a single vote) leads to more minority candidates being elected. This should be no surprise to collective choice theorists who have long noted that different electoral mechanisms lead to predictable variation in outcomes. Cox (1997) offers an extended discussion of such mechanisms.

What we know

Collective choice experiments provide several insights. First, when a Nash equilibrium of the underlying game exists it is a strong predictor of the outcome of the experiment. The second finding is that when there is no Nash equilibrium for the underlying game, subjects choose outcomes that cluster in predictable areas of the policy space, but the process by which that occurs is not settled. At the same time, experimentalists have implemented institutional mechanisms altering such games, thereby producing an equilibrium that subjects choose. Often those institutional changes benefit one actor (for example, by assigning agenda control to a particular player). A third finding is that incomplete information does not prevent convergence to equilibrium for either candidate platform choice or voter behaviour. The fourth finding returns to Arrow's original insight: voting mechanisms can be manipulated to achieve predictable, but very different, outcomes. It all depends on the mechanism that is implemented.

RICK K. WILSON

See also **experimental economics.**

Bibliography
Arrow, K.J. 1963. *Social Choice and Individual Values*. New Haven: Yale University Press.
Berl, J.E., McKelvey, R.D., Ordeshook, P.C. and Winer, M.D. 1976. An experimental test of the core in a simple n-person cooperative nonsidepayment game. *Journal of Conflict Resolution* 20, 453–76.
Bianco, W.T., Lynch, M.S., Miller, G.J. and Sened, I. 2006. 'A theory waiting to be discovered and used': a reanalysis of canonical experiments on majority rule decision making. *Journal of Politics* 68, 837–50.
Black, D. 1948. On the rationale of group decision making. *Journal of Political Economy* 56, 22–34.
Buchanan, J. and Tullock, G. 1962. *Calculus of Consent*. Ann Arbor: University of Michigan Press.
Cox, G.W. 1997. *Making Votes Count: Strategic Coordination in the World's Electoral Systems*. New York: Cambridge University Press.
Davis, O.A. and Hinich, M.J. 1966. A mathematical model of policy formation in a democratic society. In *Mathematical Applications in Political Science*, ed. J.L. Bernd. Dallas, TX: Southern Methodist University.
Fiorina, M.P. and Plott, C.R. 1978. Committee decisions under majority rule: an experimental study. *American Political Science Review* 72, 575–98.
Frechette, G., Kagel, J.H. and Lehrer, J.H. 2003. Bargaining in legislatures: an experimental investigation of open versus closed amendment rules. *American Political Science Review* 97, 221–32.
Gerber, E.R., Morton, R.B. and Rietz, T.A. 1998. Minority representation in multimember districts. *American Political Science Review* 92, 127–44.

Haney, P., Herzberg, R. and Wilson, R.K. 1992. Advice and consent: unitary actors, advisory models and experimental tests. *Journal of Conflict Resolution* 36, 603–33.

Laing, J.D. and Olmsted, S. 1978. An experimental and game theoretic study of committees. In *Game Theory and Political Science*, ed. P.C. Ordeshook. New York: New York University Press.

Laing, J.D. and Slotznick, B. 1983. Winners, blockers, and the status quo: simple collective decision games and the core. *Public Choice* 40, 263–79.

Lupia, A. and McCubbins, M.D. 1998. *The Democratic Dilemma: Can Citizens Learn What They Need To Know?* Cambridge: Cambridge University Press.

McKelvey, R.D. and Ordeshook, P.C. 1985. Sequential elections with limited information. *American Journal of Political Science* 29, 480–512.

McKelvey, R.D., Ordeshook, P.C. and Winer, M.D. 1978. The competitive solution for n-person games without transferable utility with an application to competitive games. *American Political Science Review* 72, 599–615.

Morton, R.B. 1993. Incomplete information and ideological explanations of platform divergence. *American Political Science Review* 87, 382–92.

Morton, R.B. and Williams, K.C. 2001. *Learning by Voting: Sequential Choices in Presidential Primaries and Other Elections*. Ann Arbor, MI: University of Michigan Press.

Plott, C.R. 1967. A notion of equilibrium and its possibility under majority rule. *American Economic Review* 57, 787–806.

Plott, C.R. and Levine, M.E. 1978. A model of agenda influence on committee decisions. *American Economic Review* 68, 146–60.

Schofield, N. 1985. *Social Choice and Democracy*. Heidelberg: Springer.

Wilson, R.K. and Herzberg, R.Q. 1987. Negative decision powers and institutional equilibrium: experiments on blocking coalitions. *Western Political Quarterly* 40, 593–609.

coordination problems and communication

Lewis (1969) defined a *coordination equilibrium* as a Nash equilibrium in which no agent would be better off if any other agent had chosen a different action. When there are multiple coordination equilibria, agents face an obvious coordination problem. The resolution of coordination problems rests upon individuals coming to understand the intentions of one another. The most explicit way of developing this understanding is for the individuals to communicate with one another. Common knowledge of a language must precede communication. Even with common knowledge of a language, individuals may not be bound to do what they say they will do. In such circumstances, talk is 'cheap'.

When will the receiver, having received a message from a sender, behave differently from how the receiver would have behaved if no message had been sent? According to Farrell and Rabin (1996) *highly credible* messages will not be ignored. A message that signals an intention to take action X is highly credible if it satisfies two conditions: it is (*a*) *self-signalling* and (*b*) *self-committing*. A message that the sender is taking action X is self-signalling if, and only if, it is both true and it is in the sender's interest to have it believed to be true. A message is self-committing if a belief by the receiver that the message is true creates an incentive for the sender to do what the sender said he or she would do. A message that is self-committing, if believed, will lead to an outcome that is a Nash equilibrium. A message can be self-committing without being self-signalling. For example, in the classic game of Chicken, if one player announces that he will be Passive, that message is self-committing since, if it is believed by the receiver then the receiver's best response is to be Aggressive, and the best response of the sender to the receiver's aggression is to be Passive. However, the sender would prefer to have the receiver believe that the sender will play Aggression. So the message, 'I intend to play Passive', is not self-signalling because it is not in the interest of the sender to have the receiver believe it is true.

A message is *cheap talk* if the sender is not bound to do what the message says. Crawford (1998) provides a survey of a number of cheap talk experiments. In experiments with structured communication, either only one player may send a message (one-sided communication) or more than one player can send a message. When the payoff functions of the players are symmetrical, one-sided communication breaks the symmetry of the game without communication. This is sufficient to allow a very high level of coordination. Indeed, in such games one-sided communication is much more effective in promoting coordination that is simultaneous, two-sided communication. This suggests that, when payoff functions are symmetric but players have different preference orderings over equilibria, as in the Battle of the Sexes, the principal impact of one-sided communication is to create an extensive form game in which the symmetry is broken by designating one player as the first mover. In games with Pareto-ordered equilibria communication is not needed to break symmetry, but may be effective in reducing uncertainty about the intentions or, in Crawford's terms, to give 'reassurance'. Empirically this 'reassurance' appears to be most effective in achieving coordination on the Pareto-dominant equilibrium when communication is two-sided, but even one-sided communication has a positive effect on the likelihood of achieving the Pareto-optimal outcome. Furthermore, this effect has been found to be greater when a message was self-signalling than when such a message was only self-committing.

When there are multiple players each player must be interested in, and possibly condition his actions on, the entire message profile. Therefore, the concepts of self-signalling and self-committing messages may not have much meaning in this context. Nevertheless, there is some evidence that costless pre-play communication can help groups whose members repeatedly interact to achieve more efficient outcomes than is attainable without such communication (Blume and Ortmann, 2007).

A signal that is commonly observed may be used to coordinate actions even if the signal does not emanate from any of the players. Traffic signals play this role. We do as these signals say we should do because we believe that others will also do what the signals say they should do. This belief is reinforced by experience, so doing as the signals suggest has simply become a convention that is adopted by drivers. While this convention is backed by law, there is good reason to believe that it is so ingrained in people's expectations that they would continue to act as the signals suggest even in the absence of any law. Can signals be effective in coordinating actions when the signals are not sent by any of the players and do not themselves have any payoff consequences? Van Huyck, Gillette and Battalio (1992) found that, when a game has multiple coordination equilibria, all of which yield the same payoff, a signal from an outside 'moderator' that specifically says 'play a particular equilibrium' produces a very high degree of coordination on the suggested equilibrium, even though absent any signal there is a high frequency of coordination failure. However, in games where the equilibria are Pareto ordered the introduction of a recommendation to play any equilibrium other than the payoff-dominant equilibrium significantly reduces the degree of coordination that is achieved. The authors also found that when there was an equilibrium that provided equal payoff a recommendation to play an equilibrium with unequal payoffs had little influence on how the game was played. Evidently some features, such as symmetry, may be sufficiently strong focal points that the introduction of extrinsic signals may have little influence. Similarly, some features of a game may make some coordination equilibria, once achieved by repeated interaction, exceedingly difficult to displace through the introduction of communication, even if everyone would gain by moving to another coordination equilibrium (Cooper, 2006).

A 'sunspot' is a commonly observable event that may have been correlated in the past with different outcomes. For example, published forecasts may have this property. When agents coordinate their actions on a 'sunspot' the resulting equilibrium is called a 'sunspot equilibrium'. Marimon, Spear and Sunder (1993) devised an experiment to see whether they could generate a sunspot equilibrium where prices fluctuate with an extrinsic signal even though the fundamental parameter values remained fixed. During a 'training interval', the colour of a blinking light on a screen was perfectly correlated with a change in a parameter that induced changes in equilibrium prices. After this 'training period' the parameter value was fixed, but the signal continued to vary according to the same process. Prices continued to be volatile but there was little evidence that the variation in the sunspot variable had any effect on the observed price volatility. Duffy and Fisher (2005), using a quite different design, were able to induce sunspot equilibria under restricted conditions. They found that the semantics of the sunspot variable mattered. There were two fundamental equilibria in their design. One equilibrium had a high price, the other a low price. When the sunspot message was either 'high' or 'low' the outcomes of the actions were sometimes correlated with the message. But when the message was either 'sunshine' or 'rain' this correlation was never observed. Evidently, correlation of expectations with the signal depends upon how confident people are that everyone is interpreting the signal in the same way. They also found that information that is generated by observable actions subsequent to the observation of the signal itself tends to diminish the focal power of the signal.

Sometimes actions might 'speak' louder than words. In a Prisoners' Dilemma game the cooperative outcome is not a Nash equilibrium, but it does Pareto-dominate the Nash equilibrium. Since non-cooperation is a dominant strategy a message that one intends to play 'Cooperate' is neither self-committing nor self-signalling. Nevertheless, Duffy and Feltovich (2002) found that when this message was sent it tended to be truthful and also tended to induce a cooperative response. Similarly, when their past actions with other players were observable, subjects were more likely to cooperate than if neither communication nor observability was possible. Furthermore, observation increased the frequency of cooperative choices by more than cheap talk. This suggests that observability of past actions may sometimes be more effective than mere words in helping people achieve a good outcome.

JACK OCHS

See also **experimental economics.**

Bibliography

Blume, A. and Ortmann, A. 2007. The effects of costless pre-play communication: experimental evidence from games with Pareto-ranked equilibria. *Journal of Economic Theory* 132, 274–90.

Cooper, D. 2006. Are experienced managers experts at overcoming coordination failure? *Advances in Economic Analysis & Policy* 6(2), Article 6.

Crawford, V. 1998. A survey of experiments on communication via cheap talk. *Journal of Economic Theory* 78, 286–98.

Duffy, J. and Feltovich, N. 2002. Do actions speak louder than words? An experimental comparison of observation and cheap talk. *Games and Economic Behavior* 39, 1–27.

Duffy, J. and Fisher, E. 2005. Sunspots in the laboratory. *American Economic Review* 95, 510–29.

Farrell, J. and Rabin, M. 1996. Cheap talk. *Journal of Economic Perspectives* 10(3), 103–18.

Lewis, D. 1969. *Convention: A Philosophical Study.* Cambridge, MA: Harvard University Press.

Marimon, R., Spear, S. and Sunder, S. 1993. Expectationally driven market volatility: an experimental study. *Journal of Economic Theory* 61, 74–103.

Van Huyck, J., Gillette, A. and Battalio, R. 1992. Credible assignments in coordination games. *Games and Economic Behavior* 4, 606–26.

cross-cultural experiments

A large number of well-replicated results using a wide variety of experimental games are inconsistent with the assumption that people are money maximizers. Instead, people's behaviour is consistent with choices based on social preferences in which people place a positive value on fairness, reciprocity, or equity (see Camerer, 2003, for a review). For example, subjects typically make significant positive contributions in the public goods games, reject positive offers in the ultimatum game, and impose costly punishment in the third-party punishment game (see, Camerer, ch. 2, for descriptions of these games.) In some games these results are insensitive to framing and whether behaviour is anonymous to the experimenter ('double blind').

These experiments are open to two qualitatively different interpretations: It could be that pro-social behaviours like cooperation in the public goods game and punishment in the third-party punishment game reflect human nature. Cooperation in the public goods game could result from universal cognitive systems that cause people everywhere to behave as if all acts have reputational consequences, even when facts suggest no one will know what they have done. Punishment in the third-party punishment game could result from a pan-human motivational system that causes people to prefer outcomes that are fair or mutually beneficial, and to derive satisfaction from punishing unfair behaviour. However, with few exceptions experimental subjects have been university students in urbanized, industrial societies. Thus, it also could be that observed pro-social behaviour results from culturally evolved beliefs and values that are specific to such social environments. It is obviously of great importance to determine which of these two interpretations is correct.

To answer this question, a team of anthropologists and economists performed two rounds of experimental games in a wide range of cultural environments. The first round (Henrich et al., 2004; 2005) comprised a diverse group of 15 societies including peoples like the Aché and Hadza who live in nomadic foraging bands, the Achuar and Au who live in small villages and mix hunting and horticulture, Mongol and Sangu pastoralists, and sedentary Shona farmers in Zimbabwe. The ultimatum game was performed in all 15 societies, and the public goods game and the dictator game were performed in different subsets. The second round (Henrich et al., 2006) included a similar and overlapping range of 15 societies. Based on experience in the first round, experimental protocols were improved and standardized, and a greater effort was made to collect standardized data on individual characteristics. During the second round the ultimatum, dictator, and third-party punishment games were performed in all 15 societies. In addition complete strategies for second players in the ultimatum game and punishers in the third-party punishment game were elicited using the strategy method.

These experiments reveal a number of interesting results.

1. *Behaviour in non-Western populations can be quite different from that of Western university subjects.* Figure 1 shows the distribution of ultimatum game offers in the first round of experiments. The Pittsburgh data taken from Roth et al. (1991) are typical for university populations – the modal offer is 50 per cent but many subjects make somewhat lower offers. Behaviour in other populations can be very different. For example, modal offers are much lower among two lowland tropical forest groups; the Achuar and the Machiguenga are quite low. Interestingly, these very low offers were usually accepted, behaviour much closer to the predictions of money maximization than the behaviour of Western university subjects. Non-western populations also exhibited novel behaviours not seen in university populations. Figure 2 shows the rejection probabilities for different ultimatum game offers. Notice that in several populations increasing offer level above 50 per cent *increased* the rate of rejections, a phenomenon not observed among student subjects.

2. *Behavioural differences are correlated with group characteristics but not individual characteristics.* The ethnographers who performed most of these experiments have

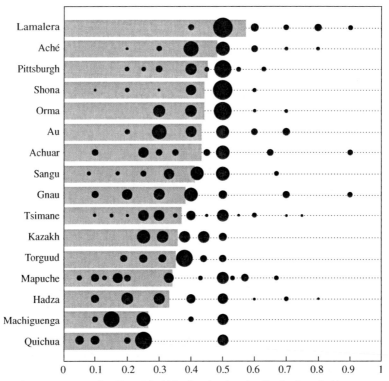

Figure 1   Ultimatum game offer. *Note*: A bubble plot showing the distribution of ultimatum game offers for each group. The diameter of the circle at each location along each row represents the proportion of the sample that made a particular offer. The right edge of the lightly shaded horizontal grey bar is the mean offer for that group. In the Machiguenga row, for example, the mode is 0.15, the secondary mode is 0.25, and the mean is 0.26. *Source*: Henrich et al. (2005).

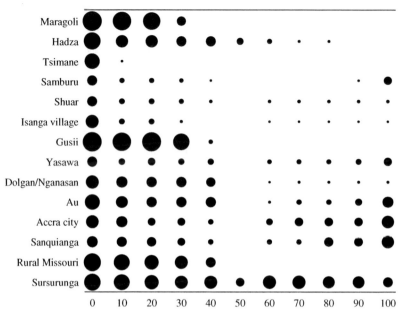

Figure 2   Ultimatum game rejection rates. *Note:* The diameter of the black circles is proportional to the fraction of offers that would have been rejected in the ultimatum game during the second round of experiments plotted as a function of the offer as a percentage of the maximum offer. For scale, note that the Gusii and Maragoli rejected all offers of zero. Notice that in all societies offering 50% of the stake minimizes the probability of rejection, but that in a number of societies increasing offers above 50% increases the rate of rejection. *Source:* Henrich et al. (2006).

studied these groups for many years and have detailed data on subjects about income, wealth, education, market contact, and a variety of other factors. None of these factors was significantly correlated with ultimatum game offers within social groups in first round, or offers or rejections in the second round. Because measures of wealth, income, and so on are not comparable across groups, these measures could not be aggregated to derive group characteristics. However, during the first round, ethnographers who were blind to the results ranked each of the groups along five dimensions: extent of cooperation in subsistence, degree of market contact, amount of privacy, amount of anonymity, and social complexity. We also had comparable data on settlement size. It turned out that market contact, settlement size, and social complexity were all highly correlated, so these were collapsed into a single variable labelled 'aggregate market contact'. Multiple linear regression showed that increasing aggregate market contact and cooperation in subsistence significantly predicted increased ultimatum game offers, and together the two variables accounted for more than half of the variance among groups in average offers.

3. *Variation in punishment predicts variation in altruism across societies.* In the third-party punishment game, an individual, the 'punisher' observes a dictator game and can punish the dictator at a cost to him or herself. The average minimum offer acceptable to the punisher in this game provides a measure of the level of punishment

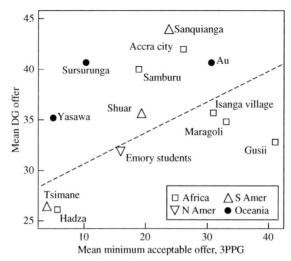

Figure 3   Mean minimum acceptable offer, third-party punishment game. *Note*: The mean offer in the dictator game for a society plotted against the mean value of the minimum acceptable offer in the third-party punishment game. The different symbols indicate continents. The size of each symbol is proportional to the number of DG pairs at each site. The dotted line gives the weighted regression line, with continental controls of mean dictator game offers against mean minimum acceptable offer in the third-party punishment game. *Source*: Henrich et al. (2006).

in that society. As is shown in Figure 3, this measure of punishment also predicts the level of altruism measured by dictator offers in the ordinary dictator game.

Taken together these results indicate that pro-social behaviour in economic experiments does not result from an invariant property of our species, and instead suggest that there are significant cultural differences between societies. The fact that ultimatum game behaviour is predicted by the average level of cooperation and average level of market contact further indicates that these cultural differences are not arbitrary, but may reflect economic, ecological and social differences between societies. However, the lack of correlation between individual characteristics and individual behaviour indicates that the differences between societies are not likely to be explained as the simple aggregation of individual experiences. Instead, it is more plausible that cultures evolve over time in response to the average conditions which they face, and that individual behaviour is, in turn, shaped by these cultural differences.

ROB BOYD

See also **experimental economics.**

Bibliography

Camerer, C. 2003. *Behavioral Game Theory: Experiments on Strategic Interaction*. Princeton: Princeton University Press.
Henrich, J.R.B., Bowles, S., Camerer, C., Fehr, E. and Gintis, H. 2004. *The Foundations of Human Sociality: Economic Experiments and Ethnographic Evidence from Fifteen Small-Scale Societies*. New York: Oxford University Press.

Henrich, J., Boyd, R., Bowles, S., Camerer, C., Fehr, E., Gintis, H., McElreath, R., Alvard, M., Barr, A., Ensminger, J., Hill, K., Gil-White, F., Gurven, M., Marlowe, F., Patton, J.Q., Smith, N. and Tracer, D. 2005. 'Economic man' in cross-cultural perspective: behavioral experiments in 15 small-scale societies. *Behavioral and Brain Sciences* 28, 795–855.

Henrich, J., McElreath, R., Barr, A., Ensminger, J., Barrett, C., Bolyanatz, A., Cardenas, J.C., Gurven, M., Gwako, E., Henrich, N., Lesorogol, C., Marlowe, F., Tracer, D. and Ziker, J. 2006. Costly punishment across human societies. *Science* 312, 1767–70.

Roth, A.E., Prasnikar, V., Okuno-Fujiwara, M. and Zamir, S. 1991. Bargaining and market behavior in Jerusalem, Ljubljana, Pittsburgh, and Tokyo: an experimental study. *American Economic Review* 81, 1068–95.

entitlements in laboratory experiments

Entitlements are rights granted by contract, law or practice. Under the assumption of pure self-interest, modelling games with entitlements is fairly straightforward; however, work in behavioural economics has consistently demonstrated the existence of other-regarding preferences, with strong effects of perceptions of what is fair. In the laboratory, behaviour is affected not only by the entitlement per se but also by the procedure by which entitlements come about. One form of laboratory entitlement is a more advantageous position in an economic game, where the advantage arises from a larger endowment, favourable exchange rules or greater decision-making authority. A second type of entitlement is a guaranteed payoff or a payoff floor. Experimental results show that the means by which entitlements are acquired is one cue that influences the nature of other-regarding behaviour. This is important both for understanding behaviour and the design of experiments.

In early experimental work on entitlements, Hoffman and Spitzer (1985) demonstrate that both the existence of an entitlement and its source determine economic outcomes. They study bilateral bargaining problems where one of the two subjects, called the 'controller', has unilateral authority to decide the outcome of a negotiation game in the event of disagreement. Authority is assigned based on either the outcome of a coin flip or the result of a simple test of a skill that is irrelevant to the experimental task. They find that controllers are most willing to exploit their power when they are assigned their role based on the skill test and are told that they 'earned' the right to be the controller – that is, that they have moral authority. These results are consistent with Burrows and Loomes (1994).

The subjects' behaviour illustrates Rawls's (1971) notion of 'desert', which requires that people deserve the conditions underlying their actions as well as the fruits of their actions. Thus subjects divided an endowment equally when the controller was chosen according to the flip of a coin and had low moral authority. On the other hand, both earning the right to be controller and higher moral authority triggered changes in observed allocations, so that outcomes favoured the controller. Entitlements that were earned or that involved 'morally unequal' agents were sufficient to trigger unequal outcomes. Equity theory developed by social psychologists is similar in spirit to this theory of justice.

Ideas of procedural fairness also affect perceptions of government entitlements. Fong (2001) looks at poll data on perceptions of poverty and opportunity, and finds that beliefs about others' effort, luck and opportunity play the largest role in determining support for government entitlement programmes. In particular these beliefs outweigh concerns about tax costs in supporting these programmes. These results are consistent with the experimental results discussed above, where low payoffs are acceptable if one displays low effort. If one's situation is determined by poor luck, however, one will give up some of one's earnings to increase the earnings of others.

A number of experimental studies on income redistribution examine Rawls's claim that individuals prefer an income redistribution rule that maximizes the position of the poorest member of society (Frohlich and Oppenheimer, 1990). Studies where subjects must choose a principle of distributive justice and a tax system in addition to participating in a production task find that people choose rules that maximize the productivity of society while maintaining a minimum floor for the worst off members. Subjects generate greater output in experiments where they are able to determine the entitlements for the worst off individual in their group, again demonstrating that the source of entitlements matters.

These results show that researchers need to pay attention to how entitlements are determined. This is a complication for theories of behavioural economics or psychological games. People do not have a pure taste for fair allocations; they are more self-interested, altruistic or fair according to circumstances that depend on how advantage arises. This behaviour is closely related to reciprocity, but that is often modelled as 'if you are nice to me I'll be nice to you' (Bowles and Gintis, 2001). In contrast, this collection of results can be interpreted as, 'I will respect your entitlement if you deserve it'.

A preference for procedural factors also complicates experimental design, since subjects behave in a more self-interested manner when entitlements are earned than when they are randomly assigned. Researchers must be careful to consider how subjects will interpret the rules by which advantages are assigned or they may risk introducing nuisance variables. Future work might deliberately award entitlements in a manner that subjects view as unjust to see whether that produces yet another pattern of behaviour.

SHERYL BALL

See also **behavioural game theory; experimental economics.**

Bibliography

Burrows, P. and Loomes, G. 1994. The impact of fairness on bargaining behavior. *Empirical Economics* 19, 201–21.
Bowles, S. and Gintis, H. 2001. The inheritance of economic status: education, class and genetics. In *Genetics, Behavior and Society*, ed. M. Feldman. In *International Encyclopedia of the Social and Behavioral Sciences*, ed. N. Smelser and P. Baltes. Oxford: Elsevier.
Fong, C. 2001. Social preferences, self-interest, and the demand for redistribution. *Journal of Public Economics* 82, 225–46.
Frohlich, N. and Oppenheimer, J.A. 1990. Choosing justice in experimental democracies with production. *American Political Science Review* 84, 461–77.
Hoffman, E. and Spitzer, M.L. 1985. Entitlements, rights and fairness: an experimental examination of subjects' concepts of distributive justice. *Journal of Legal Studies* 14, 259–97.
Lissowski, G., Tyszka, T. and Okrasa, W. 1991. Principles of distributive justice: experiments in Poland and America. *Journal of Conflict Resolution* 35, 98–119.
Rawls, J. 1971. *A Theory of Justice*. Cambridge, MA: Belknap, Harvard University Press.

experimental economics

> But I believe that there is no philosophical highroad in science, with epistemological signposts…we are in a jungle and find our way out by trial and error, building our road *behind* us as we proceed. We do not *find* signposts at crossroads, but our scouts *erect them*, to help the rest.
> —Max Born, *Experiment and Theory in Physics* (1943)

> … they were criticized [those studying observational learning in a social context] for being unscientific and performing *uncontrolled* experiments. In science, there's nothing 'worse' than an experiment that's uncontrolled.
> —Temple Grandin, *Animals in Translation* (2005, bracketed comments added).

The subject matter of this article is rationality in science particularly as it applies to experimental methods. In this context 'rationality' is commonly used to refer to a particular conception that Hayek (1967, p 85) has called:

> *Constructivist Rationality*, which, applied to individuals, associations or organizations, involves the conscious deliberate use of reason to analyze and prescribe actions judged to be better than alternative feasible actions that might be chosen; applied to institutions it involves the deliberate design of rule systems to achieve desirable performance. The latter include 'optimal design' where the intention is to provide incentives for agents to choose better actions than would result from alternative arrangements.

Rationality in socioeconomic systems, including scientific communities, cannot be adequately understood by restricting one's perspective to this traditional Cartesian framework. In the discussion that follows I want to draw upon a second conception of rationality:

> *Ecological rationality* refers to emergent order in the form of practices, norms and rules governing action by individuals, groups and institutions that are part of our cultural and biological heritage, created by human interactions, but not by conscious human design.

I have argued (Smith, 2003) that rationality in the economy depends on individuals whose behaviour is conditioned by cultural norms and emergent institutions that evolve from human experience, neither of which is ultimately derived from constructivist reason; although, clearly, constructivist ideas are important sources of variation for the gristmill of ecological selection. Parallel considerations apply to rationality in scientific method, the extension to be treated here.

Stated briefly, here is the argument that I will present: scientific methodology reveals a predominantly constructivist theme largely guided by the following:

- falsification criteria for hypotheses derived from theories;
- experimental designs for testing hypotheses;
- statistical tests; and
- liturgies of reporting style that have become standard in scientific papers.

But all tests of theory are necessarily joint tests of hypotheses derived from theory and the set of auxiliary hypotheses necessary to implement, construct and execute the tests: this is the well-known Duhem–Quine (D–Q) problem. Thus, whatever might be the testing rhetoric of scientists, they do not reject hypotheses, and their antecedent theories, on the basis of falsifying outcomes. But this is not cause for despair, let alone retreat into a narrow postmodern sea of denial in which science borders on unintended fraud. D–Q is a property of inquiry, a truth, and as such a source for deepening our understanding of what *is*, not a clever *touché* for exposing the rhetorical pretensions of science. But the failure of all philosophy of science programs to articulate a rational constructivist methodology of science that serves to guide scientists, or explain what they do, as well as what they say about what they do, does not mean that science is devoid of rationality or that scientific communities fail to generate rational programmes of scientific inquiry. Thus, scientists engage in commentary, reply, rebuttal and vigorous discussions over whether the design is appropriate, the test adequate, whether the procedures and measurements might be flawed, and the conclusions and interpretations correct. One must look to this conversation in the scientific community in asking whether and how science sorts out competing primary and auxiliary hypotheses after each new set of tests results are made available. If this conversation does not read like a theorem and its proof, and fails to reduce methodology to a consciously rigorous science of inquiry, this is because we can never reduce the testing enterprise to a simple up or down test of an isolated non-trivial hypothesis; so be it.

If emergent method is rational in science it must be a form of ecological rationality; this means that it rightly and inevitably grows out of the norms, practices and conversation that characterize meaningful interactions in the scientific community. Listen not only to what scientists say about what they do, ignoring the arrogant tone in their little knowledge, but also examine what they do. The power behind the throne of accomplishment in the human career is our *sociality*, and the unintended mansions that are built by that sociality. The long view of that career is in sharp focus: our accumulation of knowledge and its expression in technology enabled us to survive the Pleistocene, people the Earth, penetrate the heavens, and explore the ultimate particles and forces of matter, energy and life. That achievement hardly deserves to be described as either irrational or non-rational.

What does it mean to test a theory or a hypothesis derived from a theory? Scientists everywhere say and believe that the unique feature of science is that theories, if they are to be acceptable, require rigorous support from facts based on replicable observations. But the deeper one examines this belief the more elusive becomes the task of giving it precise meaning and content in the context of conventional rational programs of inquiry.

Can we derive theory directly from observations?

Prominent scientists through history have believed that the answer to this question is 'yes', and that this was their modus operandi. Thus, quoting from two of the most influential scientists in history:

> I frame no hypotheses; for whatever is not deduced from the phenomena ... have no place in experimental philosophy ... (in which) ... particular propositions are inferred from the phenomena ... (Isaac Newton, *Principia*, 1687; quoted in Segrè, 1984, p. 66)

> Nobody who has really gone into the matter will deny that in practice the world of phenomena uniquely determines the theoretical system, in spite of the fact that there is no theoretical bridge between phenomena and their theoretical principles. (Einstein, 1934, pp. 22–3)

But these statements are without validity. 'One can today easily demonstrate that there can be no valid derivation of a law of nature from any finite number of facts' (Lakatos, 1978, vol. 1, p. 2). Yet in economics critics of standard theory call for more empirical work on which to base development of *the* theory, and generally the idea persists that the essence of science is its rigorous observational foundation.

But how are the facts and theories of science to be connected so that each constructively informs and enriches the other?

Newton passionately believed not just that he was proffering lowly hypotheses, but that his laws were derived directly, by logic, from Kepler's discovery that the planets moved in ellipses. But Newton only showed that the path was an ellipse if there are $n = 2$ planets. Kepler was wrong in thinking that the planets followed elliptical paths, and to this day there is no solution for the $n(>2)$-body problem, and in fact the paths can be chaotic. Thus, when he published the *Principia*, Newton's model could not account for the motion of our nearest and most accurately observable neighbour, the moon, whose orbit is strongly influenced by both the sun and the earth.

Newton's sense of his scientific procedure is commonplace: one studies an empirical regularity (for example, the 'trade-off' between the rate of inflation and the unemployment rate), and proceeds to articulate a model from which a functional form can be derived that yields the regularity. In the above confusing quotation, Einstein seems to agree with Newton. At other times he appears to articulate the more qualified view that theories make predictions, which are then to be tested by observations (see his insightful comment below on Kaufmann's test of special relativity theory), while on other occasions his view is that reported facts are irrelevant compared to theories based on logically complete meta theoretical principles, coherent across a broad spectrum of fundamentals (see Northrup, 1969, pp. 387–408). Thus, upon receiving the telegraphed news that Eddington's 1919 eclipse experiments had 'confirmed' the general theory, Einstein showed it to a doctoral student who was jubilant, but he commented unmoved: 'I knew all the time that the theory was correct.' But what if it had been refuted? 'In that case I'd have to feel sorry for God, because the theory is correct' (quoted in Fölsing, 1997, p. 439).

The main theme I want to develop in this and subsequent sections is captured by the following quotation from a lowbrow source, the mythical character Phaedrus in *Zen and the Art of Motorcycle Maintenance*, '… the number of rational hypotheses that can explain any given phenomena is infinite' (Pirsig, 1981, p. 100).

Proposition 1 Particular hypotheses derived from any testable theory imply certain observational outcomes; the converse is false (Lakatos, 1978, vol. 1, pp. 2, 16, *passim*).

Theories produce mathematical theorems. Each theorem is a mapping from postulated statements (assumptions) into derived or concluding statements (the theoretical results). Conventionally, the concluding statements are what the experimentalist uses to formulate specific hypotheses (models) that motivate the experimental design that is implemented. The conditions that underpin the hypotheses are the objects of control in an economics experiment, insofar as they can be controlled. Since not every assumption can always be reproduced in the experimental design the problem of the 'controlled experiment' is one of trying to minimize the risk that the results will fail to be interpretable as a test of the theory because one or more assumptions were violated. An uncontrolled assumption that is postulated to hold in interpreting test results is one of many possible contingent auxiliary hypotheses to be discussed below.

The wellspring of testable hypotheses in economics and game theory is to be found in the marginal conditions defining equilibrium points or strategy decision functions that constitute a theoretical equilibrium. In games against nature the subject-agent is assumed to choose among alternatives in the feasible set that which maximizes his or her outcome (reward, utility or payoff), subject to the technological and other constraints on choice. Strategic games are solved by the device of reducing them to games against nature, as in a non-cooperative (Cournot–Nash) equilibrium (pure or mixed) where each agent is assumed to maximize his or her own outcome, given (subject to the constraints of) the maximizing behaviour of all other agents. The equilibrium strategy when used by all but agent i reduces i's problem to an own maximizing choice of that strategy. Hence, in economics, all testable hypotheses come from the marginal conditions (or their discrete opportunity cost equivalent) for maximization that define equilibrium for an individual or across individuals interacting through an institution. These conditions are implied by the theory from which they are derived, but given experimental observations consistent with (that is, supporting) these conditions there is no way to reverse the steps used to derive the conditions, and deduce the theory from a set of observations on subject choice. Behavioural point observations conforming to an equilibrium theory cannot be used to deduce or infer either the equations defining the equilibrium or the logic and assumptions of the theory used to derive the equilibrium conditions.

Suppose, however, that the theory is used to derive non-cooperative best reply functions for each agent that maps one or more characteristics of each individual into that person's equilibrium decision. Suppose next that we perform many repetitions of an experiment varying some controllable characteristic of the individuals, such as their assigned values for an auctioned item, and obtain an observed response for each value of the characteristic. This repetition of course must be assumed always to support equilibrium outcomes. Finally, suppose we use this data to estimate response functions obtained from the original maximization theory. First order conditions defining an optimum can always be treated formally as differential equations in the original criterion function. Can we solve these equations and 'deduce' the original theory?

An example is discussed in Smith, McCabe and Rassenti (1991) from first-price auction theory. Briefly the idea is this. Each of N individuals in a repeated auction game is assigned value $v_i(t)$ $(i = 1, \ldots, N; \quad t = 1, 2, \ldots, T)$ from a distribution, and on each trial, t, i bids $b_i(t)$. On each trial each i is assumed to choose a bid that maximizes expected utility.

$$\max_{0 \leq b_i \leq v_i} (v_i - b_i)^{r_i} G_i(b_i) \tag{1}$$

where r_i $(0 < r_i \leq 1)$ is i's measure of constant relative risk aversion, and $G_i(b_i)$ is i's probability belief that a bid of b_i will win. This leads to the first order condition,

$$(v_i - b_i)G_i'(b_i) - r_i G_i(b_i) = 0. \tag{2}$$

If all i have identical common rational probability expectations

$$G_i(b_i) = G(b_i). \tag{3}$$

This leads to a closed form equilibrium bid function (see Cox, Smith and Walker, 1988).

$$b_i = (N - 1)v_i/(N - 1 + r_i), \quad b_i \leq b = 1 - G(\bar{b})/G'(b), \quad \text{for all } i. \tag{4}$$

The data from experimental auctions strongly support linear subject bid rules of the form

$$b_i = \alpha_i v_i, \tag{5}$$

obtained by linear regression of b_i on v_i using the T observations on (b_i, v_i), for given N, with $\alpha_i = (N - 1)v_i/(N - 1 + r_i)$. Can we reverse the above steps, then integrate (2) to get (1)? The answer is 'no'. Equation (2) can be derived from maximizing either (1) or the criterion

$$(v_i - b_i)G(b_i)^{1/r_i}, \tag{1'}$$

in which subjective probabilities, rather than profit, are 'discounted' in computing the expectation. That is, without all the assumptions used to get (4), we cannot uniquely conclude (1). In (1') we have $G_i(b_i) = G(b_i)^{1/r_i}$ instead of (3), and this is not ruled out by the data.

In fact, instead of (1) or (1') we could have maximized

$$(v_i - b_i)^{\beta_i} G(b_i)^{\beta_i/r_i}, \quad \text{with} \quad r_i \leq \beta_i \leq 1 \tag{1'}$$

giving an infinite mixture of subjective utility and subjective probability models of bidding.

There is a special case of the above model that is reversible: all bidders are risk neutral with, $r_i = 1$. While that model is often defended in the abstract, and is the workhorse assumption for deriving theorems under uncertainty, it fails all the lab and field empirical tests known to me. Risk neutrality trivializes decisions by requiring all humans to have identical preferences. It fails because people are inherently heterogeneous in making decisions under uncertainty, and this empirical diversity is captured by an appearance (or a mirage) in the data of non-neutral 'risk'. Equation (1') above provides a hint of the manner in which individual diversity can appear in data interpretations that confound measures of risk with other sources of heterogeneity.

Thus, in general, we cannot backward infer from empirical equilibrium conditions, even when we have a large number of experimental observations, to arrive at the original parameterized model within the general theory. *The purpose of theory is precisely one of imposing much more structure on the problem than can be inferred from the data.* This is because the assumptions used to deduce the theoretical model contain more information, such as (3), than the data – the theory is underdetermined.

Economics: is it an experimental science?

All editions of Paul Samuelson's *Principles of Economics* refer to the inability of economists to perform experiments. This continued for a short time after William Nordhaus joined Samuelson as a coauthor. Thus, 'Economists ... cannot perform the controlled experiments of chemists and biologists because they cannot easily control other important factors' (Samuelson and Nordhaus, 1985, p. 8).

My favourite quotation, however, is supplied by one of the 20th century's foremost Marxian economists, Joan Robinson. To wit, 'Economists cannot make use of controlled experiments to settle their differences' (Robinson, 1979, p. 1319). Like Samuelson, she was not accurate – economists do indeed perform controlled experiments – but how often have they, or their counterparts in any science, used them to 'settle their differences?' Here she was expressing the popular image of science, which is indeed one in which 'objective' facts are the arbiters of truth that in turn 'settle' differences. The caricatured image is that of two scientists, who, disagreeing on a fundamental principle, go to the lab, do a 'crucial experiment', and learn which view is assuredly right. The hypothesis they are testing is not underdetermined by the test data. They do not argue about the result; their question is answered and they move on to a new topic that is not yet 'settled.'

Although these quotations provide telling commentaries on the state of the profession's knowledge of the development of experimental methods in economics since the 1950s, there is a deeper question of whether there are more than a very small number of non-experimentalists in economics that understand key features of our methodology. These are twofold: (*a*) employ a reward scheme to motivate individual behaviour in the laboratory within an economic environment defining gains from trade that are controlled by the experimenter – for example, the supply of and demand for an abstract item in an isolated market or an auction; and (*b*) use the observations to test predictive hypotheses derived from one or more models (formal or informal) of behaviour in these environments using the rules of a particular trading institution – for example, the equilibrium clearing price and corresponding exchange volume when subjects trade under some version of an oral or electronic double auction, posted pricing, sealed bidding, and so on. This differs from the way that economics is commonly researched, taught and practised, which implies that it is largely an a priori science in which economic problems come to be understood by thinking about them. This generates logically correct, internally consistent theories and models. The data of econometrics are then used for 'testing' between alternative model specifications within basic equilibrium theories that are not subject to challenge, or to estimate the supply and/or demand parameters assumed to generate data representing equilibrium outcomes by an unspecified process. (Leamer, 1978, and others have challenged the interpretation of this standard econometric methodology as a scientific 'testing' programme as distinct from a programme for specification searches of data.) Theories are not so much subject to doubt as used to impose restrictions on the data that allow parameters to be estimated. *Its constructivism all the way down.*

I want to report two examples indicating how counter-intuitive it has been for prominent economists to see the function of laboratory experiments in economics. The first example is contained in a quotation from Hayek whose Nobel citation was for his theoretical conception of the price system as an information system for coordinating agents with dispersed information in a world where no single mind or control centre possesses, or can ever have knowledge of, this information. His critique and rejection of mainstream quantitative methods, 'scientism', in economics are well known (see, for example, Hayek, 1942; 1945). But in his brilliant paper interpreting competition as a discovery process, rather than a model of equilibrium price determination, he argues:

> ... wherever the use of competition can be rationally justified, it is on the ground that we do not know in advance the facts that determine the actions of competitors ... competition is valuable only because, and so far as, its results are unpredictable and on the whole different from those which anyone has, or could have, deliberately aimed at.... The necessary consequence of the reason why we use competition is that, in those cases in which it is interesting, the validity of the theory can never be tested empirically. We can test it on conceptual models, and *we might conceivably test it in artificially created real situations, where the facts that competition is intended to discover are already known to the observer. But in such cases it is of no practical value, so that to carry out the experiment would hardly be worth the expense.* (F.A. Hayek, 1978, p. 255; emphasis added)

Hayek describes with clarity an important use (unknown to him) that has been made of experiments – testing competitive theory 'in artificially created real situations, where the facts which competition is intended to discover are already known to the observer' – then proceeds to completely fail to see how such an experiment could be used to test his own proposition that competition is a discovery procedure, under the condition that neither agents as a whole nor any one mind needs to know what each agent knows. Rather, his concern for dramatizing what is arguably the most important socio-economic idea of the 20th century seems to have caused him to interpret his suggested hypothetical experiment as 'of no practical value' since it would (if successful) merely reveal what the observer already knew!

I find it astounding that one of the most profound thinkers in the 20th century did not see the demonstration potential and testing power of the experiment he suggests for testing the proposition: with competition *no one in the market* need know in advance the actions of competitors, and that competition is valuable only because, and so far as, its results are unpredictable *by anyone in the market* and on the whole different from those which anyone *in the market* has, or could have, deliberately aimed at. Yet, unknown to me at the time, this is precisely what my first experiment conducted in January 1956, published later as 'Test 1', was all about (Smith, 1962).

I assembled a considerable number of experiments for a paper 'Markets as Economizers of Information: Experimental Examination of the "Hayek Hypothesis"', presented at the 50th Jubilee Congress of the Australian and New Zealand Association for the Advancement of Science, in Adelaide, Australia, 12–16 May 1980. A version of this paper was reprinted in Smith (1991, pp. 221–35). Here is what I called the Hayek Hypothesis. Strict privacy together with the trading rules of a market institution (the oral double auction in this case) is sufficient to produce efficient competitive market outcomes. The alternative was called the Complete Knowledge Hypothesis: competitive outcomes require perfectly foreseen conditions of supply and demand, a statement attributable to many economists, including Paul Samuelson who refers to 'foreseen changes in supply and demand' (Samuelson, 1966, p. 947 and *passim*), that can be traced back to W.S. Jevons in 1871. (Stigler, 1957, provides a historical treatment of the concept of perfect competition.) In this empirical comparison the Hayek Hypothesis was strongly supported. This theme had been visited earlier (before I had become aware or at least fully appreciative of Hayek's 1945 contribution that equilibrium theory was a tautology) in Smith (1976), wherein eight experiments comparing private information with complete information showed that complete information was neither necessary nor sufficient for convergence to a competitive equilibrium: complete information interfered with, and slowed, convergence compared with private information. Shubik (1959, pp. 169–71) had noted earlier, and correctly, the confusion inherent in ad hoc claims that perfect knowledge is a requirement of pure (or sometimes perfect) competition. The experimental proposition that private information increases support for non-cooperative, including competitive, outcomes applies not only to markets but also to the two-person extensive-form repeated games reported by McCabe, Rassenti and Smith (1998). Hence it is clear that without knowledge of the other's payoff it is not possible for players to identify and consciously coordinate on a cooperative outcome. Thus, as we have learned, payoff information is essential to conscious coordination in two-person interactions, but irrelevant, if not pernicious, in impersonal market exchange. We note in passing that the large number of experiments demonstrating the Hayek Hypothesis in no sense implies that there may not be exceptions (Holt, 1989). It's the other way around: this large set of experiments demonstrates clearly that there are exceptions almost everywhere to the Complete Knowledge Hypothesis, and these exceptions were not part of a prior design created to provide a counter example.

Holt and his coauthors have asked, 'Are there any conditions under which double-auction markets do not generate competitive outcomes? The only exception seems to be an experiment with a "market power" design reported by Holt, Langan and Villamil (1986) and replicated by Davis and Williams (1991)' (Davis and Holt, 1993, p. 154; also see Holt, 1989). The example reported in this exception was a market in which there was a constant excess supply of only one unit – a market with inherently weak equilibrating properties. Actually, there were two earlier reported exceptions, neither of which required market power: (a) one in which information about private circumstances is known by all traders (the alternative to the Hayek Hypothesis as stated above), and (b) an example in which the excess supply in the market was only two units. Exception (a) was reported in Smith (1980; 1991, pp. 104–5) and (b) in Smith (1991, p. 67). The above cited exceptions, attributed to market power, would need to be supplemented with comparisons in which there was just one unit of excess demand, but no market power, in order to show whether or not each exception was driven by market power, and not the fact that there is only one unit of excess supply which may be enabling of above equilibrium prices even is there is no market power. Sometimes missing in the standard toolkit of experimentalists are routines for challenging our own interpretation of data where there are confounding elements in the explanations of the results. But in this respect our methodology keeps getting better.

My second example involves the same principle as the first. It derives from a personal conversation in the early 1980s with one of my favorite Nobel Laureates in economics, a prominent theorist. In response to a question, I described the experimental public goods research I had been doing in the late 1970s and early 1980s comparing the efficacy of various public good mechanisms: Lindahl, Groves–Ledyard, the so-called auction election or mechanism. (See the public goods papers reprinted in Smith, 1991.) He wondered how I had achieved control over the efficient allocation as the benchmark used in these comparisons. So I explained what I had naively thought was commonly understood by then: I give each subject a payoff function (table) in monetary payoffs defined jointly over variable units of a public (common outcome) good, and variable units of a private good. This allows the experimenter to solve for the social optimum and then use the experimental data to judge the comparative performance of alternative public good incentive mechanisms. Incredibly, he objected that if, as the experimenter, I have sufficient information to know what constitutes the socially optimal allocation then I did not need a mechanism! I can just impose the optimal allocation! Baldly stated, economics is about deducing best actions from theory, not finding ways to test its propositions. So there I was, essentially an anthropologist on Mars, unable to convey to one of the best and brightest in the traditional ways of thinking that the whole idea of laboratory experiments was to evaluate mechanisms in an environment where *the Pareto optimal outcome was known by the experimental designer but not by the agents* so that performance comparisons could be made; that in the field such knowledge was never possible, and we had no criteria, other than internal theoretical properties such as incentive compatibility to judge the efficacy of the mechanism. He didn't get it; psychologically this testing procedure is not comprehensible if somehow your thinking has accustomed you to believe that allocation mechanisms require agents to have complete information, but not mechanism designers who presumably slipped through by assuming their agents were fully informed. In fact, with that worldview what is there to test in mechanism theory?

The issue of whether economics is an experimental science is moot among experimental economists who are, and should be, too busy having fun doing their work to reflect on the methodological implications of what they do. But when we do speak of methodology, as in comprehensive introductions to the field, what do we say? Quotations from impeccable sources will serve to introduce the concepts to be developed next. The first emphasizes that an important category of experimental work '... includes experiments designed to test the predictions of well articulated formal theories and to observe unpredicted regularities, in a controlled environment that allows these observations to be unambiguously interpreted in relation to the theory' (Kagel and Roth, 1995, p. 22). Experimental economists strongly believe, I think, that this is our most powerful scientific defence of experimental methods: we ground our experimental inquiry in the firm bedrock of economic or game theory. A second crucial advantage, recognizing that field tests involve hazardous joint tests of multiple hypotheses, is the sentiment that 'Laboratory methods allow a dramatic reduction in the number of auxiliary hypotheses involved in examining a primary hypothesis' (Davis and Holt, 1993, p. 16).

Hence the strongly held belief that, in the laboratory, we can test well-articulated theories, interpret the results unambiguously in terms of the theory, and do so with minimal, trivial or at least greatly reduced dependence on auxiliary hypothesis. This view and the idea that theories can be derived directly from observations are not unique to any science, but they are *illusions*. Fortunately, such illusions do not constitute a barrier to great scientific achievement because they appear to affect the rhetoric of science far more than its substance. Perhaps this is because the beliefs of scientists are important in reinforcing their commitment to discovery whether or not they are defensible. I cannot imagine that Newton would have been more accomplished if he had been methodologically more sophisticated.

What is the scientist's (qua experimentalist) image of what he does?

The standard experimental paper within and without economics uses the following format in outline form: (1) state the theory; (2) implement it in a particular context (with 'suitable' motivation in economics); (3) summarize the implications in one or more testable hypotheses; (4) describe the experimental design; (5) present the data and results of the hypothesis tests; (6) conclude that the experiments either reject or fail to reject the theoretical hypotheses. This format is shown in Figure 1. In the case in which we have two or more competing theories and corresponding hypotheses, the researcher offers a conclusion as to which one is supported by the data using some measure of statistical distance between the data and each of the predictive hypotheses, reporting which distance is statistically the shortest.

Suppes (1969; also see Mayo, 1996, ch. 5) has observed that there exists a hierarchy of models behind the process in Figure 1. The primary model or theory is contained in steps (1) and (2), which generate particular topical hypotheses that address primary questions. Experimental models are contained in (3) and (4). These serve to link the primary theory with data. Finally, we have data models, steps (5) and (6), that link operations on raw data (not the raw data itself) to the testing of experimental hypotheses.

This process describes much of the rhetoric of science, and reflects the self-image of scientists, but it does not adequately articulate what scientists actually do. Furthermore, the rhetoric does not constitute a viable, defensible and coherent methodology. But what we actually do, I believe, is highly defensible and on the whole positively affects what we think we know from experiment. Implicitly, as experimentalists, we understand that every step, (1)–(6), in the above process is

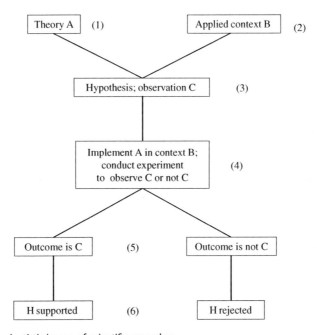

Figure 1   The scientist's image of scientific procedure

subject to judgments, learning from past experiments, our knowledge of protocols and technique, and to error. This is reflected in what we do as a professional community, if not in what we say about what we do in the standard scientific paper, or when we try to describe the science that we do.

As I have noted, the problem with the above image is known as the 'D–Q problem': experimental results always present a joint test of the theory (however well articulated, formally) that motivated the test, *and all the things you had to do to implement the test*. (For good discussions of the D–Q thesis and its relevance for experimental economics, see Soberg, 2005, and Guala, 2005, pp. 54–61 and *passim*. Soberg provides interesting theoretical results showing how the process of replication can be used, in the limit, to inductively eliminate clusters of alternative hypotheses and lend increasing weight to the conclusion that the theory itself is in doubt.) Thus, if theoretical hypothesis H is implemented with context specific auxiliary hypotheses required to make the test operational, $A_1, A_2, ..., A_n$; then it is $(H|A_1, A_2, ..., A_n)$ that implies observation C. If you observe not-C, this can be because any of the antecedents $(H; A_1, ..., A_n)$ can represent what is falsified. Thus, the interpretation of observations in relation to a theoretical hypothesis is *inherently and inescapably ambiguous*, contrary to our accustomed rhetoric.

The reality of what we do, and indeed must do, is implied by the truth that 'No theory is or can be killed by an observation. Theories can always be rescued by auxiliary hypotheses' (Lakatos, 1978, vol. 1, p. 34).

A D–Q example from physics

Here is a historical example from physics: in 1905 Kaufmann (cited in Fölsing, 1997, p. 205), a very accomplished experimentalist (in 1902 he showed that the mass of an electron is increased by its velocity!), published a paper 'falsifying' Einstein's special theory of relativity the same year in which the latter was published (Einstein, 1905). Subsequently, Einstein (1907) in a review paper reproduced Kaufmann's Figure 2, commenting that

> The little crosses above the [Kaufmann's] curve indicate the curve calculated according to the theory of relativity. In view of the difficulties involved in the experiment one would be inclined to consider the agreement as satisfactory. However, the deviations are systematic and considerably beyond the limits of error of Kaufmann's experiment. That the calculations of Mr. Kaufmann are error-free is shown by the fact that, using another method of calculation, Mr. Planck arrived at results that are in full agreement with those of Mr. Kaufmann. Only after a more diverse body of observations becomes available will it be possible to decide with confidence whether the systematic deviations are due to a not yet recognized source of errors or to the circumstance that the foundations of the theory of relativity do not correspond to the facts. (Einstein, 1907, p. 283)

Kaufmann was testing the hypothesis that (H|A) implies C, where H was an implication of special relativity theory, A was the auxiliary hypothesis that his context-specific test and enabling experimental apparatus was without 'a not yet recognized source of errors', C was the curve indicated by the 'little crosses', and not-C was Kaufmann's empirical curve (Einstein, 1907, Figure 2, p. 283).

Einstein's comment in effect says that either of the antecedents (H|A) represents what is falsified by Kaufmann's results. Others, such as Planck and Kaufmann himself, however, acknowledged that the observation might conceivably be in error (Fölsing, 1997, p. 205). Such acknowledgements are not unusual in the scientific community, which means that scientists informally recognize the D–Q problem as it arises in particular contexts, that it is part of the scientific conversation and that they seek solutions even if this modus operandi is not part of their rhetoric. Thus, in less than a year, Bucherer (see Fölsing, 1997, p. 207) showed that there indeed had been a 'problem' with Kaufmann's experiments and proceeded to obtain new results supporting Einstein's theory.

There is an important lesson in this example if we develop it a little more fully. Suppose Bucherer's experiments *had not changed Kaufmann's results enough to change the conclusion.* (There is never a shortage of claims that a given experimental result may be in doubt: see Mayo, 1996, for the imaginative arguments proffered by the Newtonians in response to Eddington's eclipse observations.) Then Einstein could still have argued that there may be 'a not yet recognized source of errors'. If so, the implication is that H is not falsifiable, for the same argument can be made after each new test in which the new results are outside the range of error for the apparatus! Recall that the deviations were alleged to be 'considerably beyond the limits of error of Kaufmann's experiment'. But here 'error' is used in the sense of internal variations arising from the apparatus and procedure, not in the sense that there is a problem with the apparatus or procedure itself. We can go still further in explicating the problem of testing H conditional on any A. The key is to note in this example the strong dependence of any test outcome on the *state of experimental knowledge*: Bucherer found a way to 'improve' Kaufmann's experimental technique so as to rescue Einstein's 'prediction'. But the predictive content of H (and therefore of the special theory) was inextricably bound up with A. Einstein's theory did not embrace any of the elements of Kaufmann's (or Bucherer's) *apparatus:* A is based on experimental knowledge of testing procedures and operations in the physics laboratory, and has nothing to do with the theory of relativity, a separate and distinct body of theoretically coherent knowledge.

A proposition and an economics example

Here is the most common casual empiricist objection to economics experiments: the payoffs are too small. This objection is one of several principal issues in a target article by Hertwig and Ortmann (2001), with comments by 34 experimental psychologists and economists. This objection sometimes is packaged with an elaboration to the effect that economic or game theory is about situations that involve large stakes, and you 'can't' study these in the laboratory. (Actually, of course, you can, but funding is not readily available.)

Suppose, therefore that we have the following:

- H (from theory): subjects will choose the equilibrium outcome (for example, Nash or subgame perfect).
- A (auxiliary hypothesis): payoffs are adequate to motivate subjects.

Proposition 2 Suppose a specific rigorous test rejects (H|A), and someone (say, T), protests that what must be rejected is A not H. Let E replicate the original experiment with an n-fold increase in payoffs. There are only two outcomes and corresponding interpretations , neither of which is comforting to the rhetorical image of science as conducting falsification tests of predictive hypotheses:

1. The test outcome is negative. Then T can imagine a still larger payoff multiple $N > n$, and still argue for rejecting A not H. But this implies that H *cannot be falsified*.
2. After repeated increases in payoffs, the test outcome is positive for some $N \geq n^*$. Then H has *no predictive content*. E, with no guidelines from the theory, has searched for and discovered an empirical payoff multiple, n^*, that 'confirms' the theory, but n^* is an *extra theoretical property of considerations outside H and the theory* that was being tested. Finding this multiple is not something for T or E to crow about, but rather an event that should send T or E back to his desk. The theory is inadequately specified to embrace the observations from all the experiments.

Proposition 2 holds independent of any of the following considerations:

- how well articulated, rigorous or formal the theory is; game theory in no sense constitutes an exception;
- how effective the experimental design is in reducing the number of auxiliary hypotheses – it only takes one to create the problem; and
- the character or nature of the auxiliary hypothesis – A can be anything not contained in the theory.

In experimental economics, reward adequacy is just one of a standard litany of objections to experiments in general and to many experiments in particular. Here are three additional categories in this litany:

1. *Subject sophistication.* The standard claim is that undergraduates are not sophisticated enough. They are not out there participating in the 'real world'. In the 'real world' where the stakes are large, such as in the FCC spectrum rights auctions, bidders use game theorists as consultants (Banks et al., 2003). (For an investigation of the hypothesis that undergraduates are insufficiently sophisticated, see McCabe and Smith, 2000, who report a comparison of undergraduate and graduate students, and these with economics faculty, in a two-person trust game. The first two groups were indistinguishable, and both earned more than the faculty because with greater frequency they risked defection in offering to cooperate, as against opting for the subgame perfect outcome.)

2. *Subjects need an opportunity to learn.* This is a common response from both experimentalists and theorists when you report the results of single play games in which 'too many' people cooperate. The usual proposed 'fix' is to do repeat single protocols in which distinct pairs play on each trial, and apply a model of learning to play non-cooperatively. (See McCabe, Rassenti and Smith, 1998, for a trust game with the option of punishing defection in which support for the cooperative outcome does not decrease in repeat single relative to single play across trials, and therefore subjects *do not* 'learn' to play non-cooperatively.) But there are many unanswered questions implicit in this auxiliary hypothesis: since repeat single protocols require large groups of subjects (20 subjects to produce a 10-trial sequence), have any of these games been run long enough to measure adequately the extent of learning? In single play two-person anonymous trust games data have been reported showing that group size matters; that is, it makes a difference whether you are running 12 subjects (6 pairs) or 24 subjects (12 pairs) simultaneously in a session (Burnham, McCabe and Smith, 2000). Also, in the larger groups pairs were found to be less trusting than in the small groups – perhaps not too surprising. But in repeat single games, in which a game is repeated with distinct pairs of subjects on each repetition, larger groups are needed for longer trial sequences. Hence, learning and group size as auxiliary hypotheses loses independence, and we have knotty new problems of complex joint hypothesis testing. The techniques, procedures and protocol tests we fashion for solving such problems are the sources of our experimental knowledge. All testing depends on, and is limited by, the state of that experimental knowledge at any given time. Over time it expands incrementally in the design problem-solving context of particular new testing challenges. This is a community development enterprise that is largely outside individual conscious awareness, but an integral part of the sociality of scientific change.

3. *Instructions are adequate* (or decisions are robust with respect to instructions, and so on). What does it mean for instruction to be adequate? Clear? If so, clear about what? What does it mean to say that subjects understand the instructions? Usually this is interpreted to mean that they can perform the task, which is judged by how they answer questions about what they are to do. In two-person interactions, instructions often matter so much that they must be considered a (powerful) treatment. (Thus, Hertwig and Ortmann, 2001, section 2, argue that scripts – instructions – are important for replication, and that 'ad-libbing' should be avoided.) Instructions can be important because they define context, and context matters. Ultimatum and dictator game experiments yield statistically and economically significant differences in results due to differing instructions and protocols (Hoffman et al., 1994; Hoffman, McCabe and Smith, 1996).

Positive economics: judge theories by their predictions not their assumptions

There is a methodological perspective associated with Milton Friedman (1953), which fails to provide an adequate foundation for experimental (field or laboratory) science, but which influenced economists for decades and still has some currency. Friedman's proposition is that the truth value of a theory should be judged by its testable and tested predictions not by its assumptions. This proposition is deficient for at least three reasons:

1. If a theory fails a test, we should ask why, not always just move on to seek funding for a different new project; obviously, one or more of its assumptions may be wrong, and it behoves us to design experiments that will probe conjectures about which assumptions failed. Thus, if first price auction theory fails a test is it a consequence of the failure of one of the axioms of expected utility theory, for example, the compound lottery axiom? If a subgame perfect equilibrium prediction fails, does the theory fail because the subjects do not satisfy the assumption that the agents choose dominant strategies? Or did the subjects fail to use backward induction? Or was it none of the above because the theory was irrelevant to how some motivated agents solve such problems in a world of bilateral (or multilateral) reciprocity in social exchange? When a theory fails there is no more important question to ask than what it is about the theory that has failed.
2. Theories may have the if-and-only if property that one (or more) of their 'assumptions' can be derived as implication(s) from one (or more) of their 'results'. These cases if trivial lead to the reversible property of testing illustrated above for risk-neutral agents bidding in first price auctions with linear density functions on value.
3. If a theory passes one or more tests, this need not be because its assumptions are correct. A subject may choose the subgame perfect equilibrium because she believes she is paired with a person that is not trustworthy, and not because she always chooses dominant strategies, or assumes that others always so choose or that this is common knowledge. This is why you are not done when a theory is corroborated by a test. You have examined only one point in the parameter space of payoffs, subjects, tree structure, and so on. Your results may be a freak accident of nature due to a complex of suitabilities or in any case may have other explanations.

In view of Proposition 2, what are experimentalists and theorists to do?

Consider first the example in which we have a possible failure of A: rewards are adequate to motivate subjects. Experimentalists should do what comes naturally, namely, do new experiments that increase rewards and/or lower decision costs by simplifying experiment procedures. The literature is full of examples (for surveys and interpretations see Smith and Walker, 1993; Camerer and Hogarth, 1999; Holt and Laury, 2001; Harrison, McInnes and Rutstroem, 2005).

Theorists should ask whether the theory is extendable to include A, so that the effect of payoffs is explicitly modelled. It is something of a minor scandal when economists – whose models predict the optimal outcome independently of payoff levels, and however gently rounded the payoff in the neighbourhood of the optimum is – object to an experiment because the payoffs are inadequate. What is adequate?

Why are payoff inadequacies a complaint rather than a spur to better and more relevant modelling of payoffs? A step toward modelling both H and A (as payoffs) is provided in Smith and Szidarovszky (2004). Economic intuition tells us that payoffs should matter. But if they do, it must mean that some cost, which is impeding equilibrium, is being overcome at the margin by higher payoffs. The natural psychological assumption is that there are cognitive costs of getting the best outcome, and more reward enables higher cognitive cost to be incurred to increase net return.

Generally, both groups must be aware that for any H, any A and any experiment, one can say that if the outcome of the experiment rejects (H|A), then both should assume that either H or A may be false, which is an obvious corollary to Proposition 2. This was Einstein's position concerning the Kaufmann results, and was the correct position, whatever later tests might show. After every test, either the theory (leading to H) is in error or the circumstances of the test, A, is in error.

The experimentalist has much to do, but primarily more experiments, which is precisely what experimentalists do in response to the many conjectures about what is wrong with the experiment – re-examine the instructions, payoffs, subjects, anything and everything the experimentalist did to formulate the test.

The theorist should also ask, especially if further tests continue to reject (H|A), whether the auxiliary hypothesis can be incorporated into the theory.

If the outcome fails to reject (H|A), the experimentalist should escalate the severity of the test. At some point does H fail? This identifies the limits of the theory's validity, and gives the theorist clues for modifying the theory.

Experimental knowledge drives our methods

Philosophers have written eloquently and argued intently over the implications of D–Q and related issues for the interpretation of science. Popper tried to demarcate science from pseudoscience with the basic rule requiring the scientist to specify in advance the conditions under which he will give up his theory. This is a variation on the idea of a so-called 'crucial experiment', a concept which cannot withstand examination (Lakatos, 1978, vol. 1, pp. 3–4, 146–8), as is evident from our Proposition 2.

The failure of all programmes attempting to articulate a defensible rational science of scientific method has bred postmodern negative reactions to science and scientists. These exercises and controversies make fascinating reading, and provide a window on the social context of science, but I believe they miss the essence of what is most important in the working lives of all practitioners. Popper was wrong in thinking he could demarcate science from pseudoscience by an exercise in logic, but that does not imply that the Popperian falsification rule failed as a milestone contribution to the scientific conversation; nor does it mean that 'anything goes' (Feyeraband, 1975). Rather, what one can say is much less open ended: anything goes only in so far as what can be concluded about *constructive rationality in science*. But the scientific enterprise is also about *ecological rationality in science*, which is about discovery, about probes into Max Born's 'jungle', about thinking outside the box and, as I shall argue below, about the technology of observation in science that renders obsolete long-standing D–Q problems while introducing new ones for a time.

You do not have to know anything about D–Q and statements like Proposition 2 to appreciate that the results of an experiment nearly always suggest new questions precisely because the interpretation of results in terms of the theory are commonly *ambiguous*. This ambiguity is reflected in the discussion whenever new results are presented at seminars and conferences. Without ambiguity there would be nothing to discuss. What is the response to this ambiguity? Invariably, if it is a matter of consequence, experimentalists design new experiments with the intention of confronting the issues in the controversy, and in the conflicting views that have arisen in interpreting the previous results. This leads to new experimental knowledge of how results are influenced, or not, by changes in procedures, context, instructions and control protocols. The new knowledge may include new techniques that have application to areas other than the initiating circumstance. This ecological process is driven by the D–Q problem, but practitioners need have no knowledge of the philosophy of science literature to take the right next steps, subject to error, in the laboratory.

This is because the theory or primary model that motivates the questions tells you nothing definitive or even very useful about precisely how to construct tests. Tests are based on extra theoretical intuition, conjectures, and experiential knowledge of procedures. The context, subjects, instructions, parameterization, and so on are determined outside the theory, and their evolution constitutes the experimental knowledge that defines our methodology. The forms taken by the totality of individual research testing programmes cannot be accurately described in terms of the rhetoric of falsification, no matter how much we speak of the need for theories to be falsifiable, stating in advance the conditions under which the theory will be rejected, the tests discriminating or 'crucial' and the results robust.

Whenever negative experimental results threaten perceived important new theoretical tests, the resulting controversies galvanize experimentalists into a search for different or better tests – tests that examine the robustness of the original results. Hence, Kaufmann's experimental apparatus was greatly improved by Bucherer, although there was no question about Kaufmann's skill and competence in laboratory technique. The point is that with escalated personal incentives, and a fresh perspective, scientists found improved techniques. This scenario is common as new challenges bring forth renewed effort. This process generates the constantly changing body of experimental and observational knowledge whose insights in solving one problem often carry over to applications in many others.

Just as often experimental knowledge is generated from curiosity about the properties of phenomena that we observe long before a body of theory exists that deals specifically with the phenomenon at issue. An example in experimental economics is the continuous double auction trading mechanism (Smith, 1962; 2003).

An example from physics is Brownian motion, discovered by the botanist Robert Brown in 1827, who first observed the unpredictable motion of small particles suspended in a fluid. This motion is what keeps them from sinking under gravity. This was 78 years before Einstein's famous paper (one of three) in 1905 developed the molecular kinetic theory that was able to account for it, although he did not know that the applicable observations of Brownian motion were already long familiar (see Mayo, 1996, ch. 7, for references and details). The long 'inquiry into the cause of Brownian motion has been a story of hundreds of experiments ... [testing hypotheses attributing the motion]...either to the nature of the particle studied or to the various factors external to the liquid medium ... '(Mayo, 1996, pp. 217–18). The essential point is 'that these early experiments on the possible cause of Brownian motion were not testing any full-fledged theories. Indeed it was not yet known whether Brownian motion would turn out to be a problem in chemistry, biology, physics, or something else. Nevertheless, a lot of information was turned up and put to good use by those later researchers who studied their Brownian motion experimental kits' (Mayo, 1996, p. 240). The problem was finally solved by drawing on the extensive bag of experimental tricks, tools and past mistakes that constitute 'a log of the extant experimental knowledge of the phenomena in question' (1996, p. 240).

Again, 'the infinitely many alternatives really fall into a few categories. Experimental methods (for answering new questions) coupled with experimental knowledge (for using techniques and information already learned) enable local questions to be split off and answered' (Mayo, 1996, p. 242).

The bottom line is that good-enough solutions emerge to the baffling infinity of possibilities, as new measuring systems emerge, experimental toolkits are updated, and understanding is sharpened. This bottom line also goes far towards writing the history of experimental economics and its many detailed encounters with data, and the inevitable ambiguity of subsequent inpt. And in most cases the jury remains in session on whether we are dealing with a problem in psychology (perception), economics (opportunity cost and strategy), social psychology (equality, equity or reciprocity), neuroscience (functional imaging and brain modeling) or all of the above. So be it.

The machine builders

Mayo's (1996) discussion and examples of experimental knowledge leave unexamined the question of how technology affects the experimentalist's toolkit. The heroes of science are neither the theorists nor the experimentalists but the unsung tinkers, mechanics, inventors and engineers who create the new generation of machines that make obsolete yesterday's observations and heated arguments over whether it is T or A that has been falsified. Scientists, of course, are sometimes a part of this creative destruction, but what is remembered in academic recognition is the new scientific knowledge they created, not the instruments they invented that made possible the new knowledge. Michael Faraday, 'one of the greatest physicists of all time' (Segrè, 1984, p. 134), had no formal scientific education. He was a bookbinder, who had the habit of reading the books that he bound. He was pre-eminently a tinker for whom 'some pieces of wood, some wire and some pieces of iron seemed to suffice him for making the greatest discoveries' (quoted from a letter by Helmholz in Segrè, 1984, p. 140). Yet he revolutionized how physicists thought about electromagnetic phenomena, invented the concept of lines of force (fields), and inspired Maxwell's theoretical contributions. 'He writes many times that he must experience new phenomena by repeating the experiments, and that reading is totally insufficient for him' (Segrè, 1984, p. 141). This is what I mean, herein, when I use the term 'experimental knowledge'. It is 'can do' knowledge acquired by trial, error and discovery. And it is what Mayo (1996) is talking about. It is also why doing experiments changed the way I thought about economics.

Technology and science

With the first moon landing, theories of the origin and composition of our lunar satellite, contingent on the state of existing indirect evidence, were upstaged by direct observation; the first Saturn probe sent theorists back to their desks and computers to re-evaluate her mysterious rings, whose layered richness had not been anticipated. Similar experiences have followed the results of ice core sampling in Greenland, and instrumentation for mapping the genome of any species. Galileo's primitive telescope opened a startling window on the solar system, as do Roger Angel's multiple mirror light-gathering machines (created under the Arizona football stadium) that open the mind to a view of the structure of the universe. (For a brief summary of the impact of past, current, and likely future effects of rapid change in optical and infrared (terrestrial and space) telescopes on astronomy see Angel, 2001.) The technique of tree ring dating, invented by an Arizona astronomer, has revolutionized the interpretation of archeological data from the last 5,000 years.

Yesterday's reductionisms, shunned by mainstream 'practical' scientists, create the demand for new deeper observations, and hence for the machines that can deliver answers to entirely new questions. Each new machine – microscope, telescope, Teletype, computer, the Internet, fMRI imaging – changes the way teams of users think about their science. The host of auxiliary hypotheses needed to give meaning to theory in the context of remote and indirect observations (inferring the structure of Saturn's ring from earth-based telescopes) are suddenly made irrelevant by deep and more direct observations of the underlying phenomena (fly by computer-enhanced photos). It's the machines that drive the new theory, hypotheses, and testing programmes that take you from atoms, to protons, to quarks. Yet with each new advance comes a blizzard of auxiliary hypotheses, all handcuffed to new theory, giving expression to new controversies seeking to rescue T and reject A, or to accept A and reject T.

Experimental economics and computer/communication technology

In 1976 when Arlington Williams (1980) created the first electronic double-auction software program for market experiments, all of us thought we were simply making it easier to run experiments, collect more accurate data, observe longer time series, facilitate data analysis, and so on. What were computerized were the procedures, recording and accounting that heretofore had been done manually. No one was anticipating how this tool might impact on and change the way we thought about the nature of doing experiments. But with each new electronic experiment we were 'learning' (affected by, but without conscious awareness of) the fact that traders could be matched at essentially zero cost, that the set of feasible rules that could be considered was no longer restricted by costly forms of implementation and monitoring, that vastly larger message spaces could be accommodated, and that optimization algorithms could now be applied to the messages to define new electronic market forms for trading energy, air emission permits, water and other network industries. In short, the transaction cost of running experimental markets became minuscule in comparison with the pre-electronic days, and this opened up new directions that previously had been unthinkable.

This quickly led to the concept of smart computer-assisted markets, which appeared in the early 1980s (Rassenti, 1981; Rassenti, Smith and Bulfin, 1982), extended conceptually to electric power and gas pipelines in the late 1980s (Rassenti and Smith, 1986; McCabe, Rassenti and Smith, 1989), with practical applications to electric power networks and the trading of emission permits across time and regions in the 1990s (Rassenti, Smith and Wilson, 2002). These developments continue as major new efforts in which the laboratory is used as a test bed for measuring, modifying, and further testing the performance characteristics of new institutional forms.

What is called e-commerce has spawned a rush to reproduce on the Internet the auction, retailing and other trading systems people know about from past experience. But the new experience of being able to match traders at practically zero cost is sure to change how people think about trade and commerce, and ultimately this will change the very nature of trading institutions. In the short run, of course, efforts to protect existing institutions will spawn efforts to shield them from entry by deliberately introducing cost barriers, but in the long run these efforts will be increasingly uneconomical.

Neuroscience carries the vision of changing the experimental study of individual, two-person interactive and market decision making. The neural correlates of decision making, how it is affected by rewards, cognitive constraints, working memory, institutions, repeat experience and a host of factors that in the past we could neither control or observe can in the future be expected to become an integral part of the way we think about and model decision making. Models of decision, now driven by game and utility theory, and based on trivial, patently false, models of mind, must take account of new models of cognitive, calculation and memory properties of mental function that are accessible to more direct observational inpt. Game-theoretic models assume consciously calculating, rational mental processes, but models of mind include non-self-aware processes just as accessible to neural brain imaging as the conscious. For the first time we may be able to give some observational content to the vague and slippery idea of 'bounded rationality' (see Camerer, Loewenstein and Prelec, 2005).

Conclusion

In principle the D–Q problem is a barrier to any defensible notion of a rational science that selects theories by a logical process of confrontation with scientific evidence. This is cause for joy not despair. Think how dull a life of science would be if, once we were trained, all we had to do was to turn on the threshing machine of science, feed it the facts, send its output to the printer, and run it through the formulas for writing a scientific paper.

As I see it, there is no rationally constructed science of scientific method. The attempt to do it has led to important insights and understanding, and has been a valuable exercise. But all construction must ultimately pass ecological or 'fitness' tests based on the totality of our experience. Control is of course important; it is why we do laboratory and field experiments. But control is always limited in scope, and above all the rhetoric of control should not restrict the examination and re-examination of our own assumptions, both in the theory and in its testing, or limit our capacity to think outside the professional box. We do this in the reality underneath our rhetoric because we cannot help it, so much is it part of our deep human sociality and the workings of our social brains.

VERNON L. SMITH

See also **experimental economics history of.**

Bibliography

Angel, R. 2001. Future optical and infrared telescopes. *Nature Insights* 409, 427–30.
Banks, J., Olson, M., Porter, D., Rassenti, S. and Smith, V. 2003. Theory, experiment and the Federal Communications Commission spectrum auctions. *Journal of Economic Behavior & Organization* 51, 303–50.
Born, M. 1943. *Experiment and Theory in Physics*. Cambridge: Cambridge University Press.
Burnham, T., McCabe, K. and Smith, V. 2000. Friend-or-foe intentionality priming in an extensive form trust game. *Journal of Economic Behavior & Organization* 43, 57–73.
Camerer, C.F. and Hogarth, R.M. 1999. The effects of financial incentives in experiments: a review and capital-labor-production framework. *Journal of Risk and Uncertainty* 19, 7–42.
Camerer, C., Loewenstein, G. and Prelec, D. 2005. Neuroeconomics: how neuroeconomics can inform economics. *Journal of Economic Literature* 43, 9–64.
Cox, J., Smith, V. and Walker, J. 1988. Theory and individual behavior of first price auctions. *Journal of Risk and Uncertainty* 1, 61–99. Reprinted in Smith (1991).
Davis, D. and Holt, C. 1993. *Experimental Economics*. Princeton: Princeton University Press.
Davis, D. and Williams, A. 1991. The Hayek hypothesis in experimental auctions: institutional effects and market power. *Economic Inquiry* 29, 261–74.
Einstein, A. 1905. On the electrodynamics of moving bodies. In *The Collected Papers of Albert Einstein*, vol. 2, trans. A. Beck, Princeton: Princeton University Press, 1989.
Einstein, A. 1907. On the relativity principle and the conclusions drawn from it. In *The Collected Papers of Albert Einstein*, vol. 2, trans. A. Beck, Princeton: Princeton University Press, 1989.
Einstein, A. 1934. *The World as I see it*. New York: Covici Friede Publishers.
Feyeraband, P. 1975. *Against Method*. London: Versa.
Fölsing, A. 1997. *Albert Einstein*. New York: Viking.
Friedman, M. 1953. *Essays in Positive Economics*. Chicago: University of Chicago Press.

Grandin, T. and Johnson, C. 2005. *Animals in Translation*. New York: Scriber.

Guala, F. 2005. *The Methodology of Experimental Economics*. Cambridge: Cambridge University Press.

Harrison, G., McInnes, J. and Rutstroem, L. 2005. Risk aversion and incentive effects: comment. *American Economic Review* 95, 897–901.

Hayek, F.A. 1942. Scientism and the study of society. *Economica*; reprinted in *The Counter-Revolution in Science*. Indianapolis: Liberty Press, 1979.

Hayek, F.A. 1945. The use of knowledge in society. *American Economic Review* 35, 519–30.

Hayek, F.A. 1967. *Studies in Philosophy, Politics and Economics*. London: Routledge & Kegan Paul.

Hayek, F.A. 1978. Competition as a discovery procedure. In *New Studies in Philosophy, Politics, Economics, and the History*. Chicago: Chicago University Press. Reprinted in *The Essence of Hayek*. Stanford: Hoover Institution Press, 1984.

Hertwig, R. and Ortmann, A. 2001. Experimental practices in economics. *Behavioral and Brain Sciences* 24, 383–451.

Hoffman, E., McCabe, K. and Smith, V. 1996. On expectations and the monetary stakes in ultimatum games. *International Journal of Game Theory* 25, 289–301.

Hoffman, E., McCabe, K., Shachat, K. and Smith, V. 1994. Preferences, property rights and anonymity in bargaining games. *Games and Economic Behavior* 7, 346–80.

Holt, C. 1989. The exercise of market power in experiments. *Journal of Law and Economics* 32S, 107–30.

Holt, C., Langan, L. and Villamil, A. 1986. Market power in oral double auction experiments. *Economic Inquiry* 24, 107–23.

Holt, C. and Laury, S. 2001. Varying the scale of financial incentives under real and hypothetical conditions. *Behavioral and Brain Sciences* 24, 417–18.

Kagel, J. and Roth, A. 1995. *Handbook of Experimental Economics*. Princeton: Princeton University Press.

Kahneman, D., Knetsch, J. and Thaler, R. 1986. Fairness as a constraint on profit seeking: entitlements in the market. *American Economic Review* 76, 728–41.

Lakatos, I. 1978. *The Methodology of Scientific Research Programmers*, 2 vols. Cambridge: Cambridge University Press.

Leamer, E. 1978. *Specification Searches*. New York: Wiley.

Mayo, D. 1996. *Error and the Growth of Experimental Knowledge*. Chicago: University of Chicago Press.

McCabe, K., Rassenti, S. and Smith, V.L. 1989. Designing smart computer assisted markets for gas networks. *European Journal of Political Economy* 5, 259–83.

McCabe, K., Rassenti, S. and Smith, V.L. 1998. Reciprocity, trust and payoff privacy in extensive form bargaining. *Games and Economic Behavior* 24, 10–24. Reprinted in Smith (2000).

McCabe, K. and Smith, V. 2000. A comparison of naïve and sophisticated subject behavior with game theoretic prediction. *Proceedings National Academy of Sciences* 97, 3777–81.

Northrup, F.S.C. 1969. Einstein's conception of science. In *Albert Einstein: Philosopher–Scientist*, ed. P.A. Schilpp. LaSalle, IL: Open Court.

Pirsig, R.M. 1981. *Zen and the Art of Motorcycle Maintenance*. New York: Banton Books.

Rassenti, S. 1981. O-1 decision problems with multiple resource constrains: algorithms and applications. Ph.D. thesis, University of Arizona.

Rassenti, S. and Smith, V. 1986. Electric utility deregulation. In *Pricing Electric Gas and Telecommunication Services*. Washington, DC: Institute for the Study of Regulation.

Rassenti, S., Smith, V. and Bulfin, R. 1982. A combinatorial auction mechanism for airport time slot allocation. *Bell Journal of Economics* 13, 402–17.

Rassenti, S., Smith, V. and Wilson, B. 2002. Using experiments to inform the privatization/deregulation movement in electricity. *Cato Journal* 21, 515–44.

Robinson, J. 1979. What are the questions? *Journal of Economic Literature* 15, 1318–39.

Samuelson, P. 1966. Intertemporal price equilibrium: a prologue to the theory of speculation. In *The Collected Papers of Paul A. Samuelson*, vol. 2, ed. J. Stiglitz. Cambridge, MA: MIT Press.

Samuelson, P. and Nordhaus, W. 1985. *Economics*. New York: McGraw-Hill.

Segrè, E. 1984. *From Falling Bodies to Radio Waves*. New York: Freeman.

Shubik, M. 1959. *Strategy and Market Structure*. New York: Wiley.

Smith, V.L. 1962. An experimental study of competitive market behavior. *Journal of Political Economy* 70, 111–37.

Smith, V.L. 1965. Experimental auction markets and the Walrasian hypothesis. *Journal of Political Economy* 73, 387–93.

Smith, V.L. 1976. Experimental economics: induced value theory. *American Economic Review Proceedings* 66, 274–79. Reprinted in Smith (1980; 1991).

Smith, V.L. 1980. *Evaluation of Econometric Models*. New York: Academic Press.

Smith, V.L. 1991. *Papers in Experimental Economics*. New York: Cambridge University Press.

Smith, V.L. 2000. *Bargaining and Market Behavior. Essays in Experimental Economics*. New York: Cambridge University Press.

Smith, V. 2003. Constructivist and ecological rationality in economics. *American Economic Review* 93, 465–508.

Smith, V., McCabe, K. and Rassenti, S. 1991. Lakatos and experimental economics. In *Appraising Economic Theories*, ed. N. De Marchi and M. Blaug. London: Edward Elgar.

Smith, V.L. and Szidarovszky, F. 2004. Monetary rewards and decision cost in strategic interactions. In *Models of a Man: Essays in Memory of Herbert A. Simon*, ed. M. Augier and J. March. Cambridge MA: MIT Press.

Smith, V. and Walker, J. 1993. Monetary rewards and decision cost in experimental economics. *Economic Inquiry* 31, 245–61. Best Article Award, Western Economic Association, 1993.

Soberg, M. 2005. The Duhem–Quine thesis and experimental economics: a reinpt. *Journal of Economic Methodology* 12, 581–97.

Stigler, G. 1957. Perfect competition, historically contemplated. *Journal of Political Economy* 65, 1–17.

Suppes, P. 1969. Models of data. In *Studies in the Methodology and Foundations of Science*. Dordrecht: Reidel.

Williams, A. 1980. Computerized double-auction markets: some initial experimental results. *Journal of Business* 53, 235–57.

experimental economics, history of

Experimental economics has experienced one of the most stunning methodological revolutions in the history of science. In just a few decades, economics has been transformed from a discipline where the experimental method was considered impractical, ineffective and largely irrelevant to one where some of the most exciting advancements are driven by laboratory data.

Like many other new developments in the social sciences during the second half of the 20th century, experimental economics is largely a by-product of the combination of massive investments in science, a fertile intellectual culture and socio-political conditions in the 1940s and 1950s in the United States. Although it is possible in principle to identify earlier experimental or proto-experimental work being done in economics and psychology (see Roth, 1995), there is hardly any direct intellectual, personal or institutional continuity between these isolated episodes and today's fully institutionalized experimental programme.

A proper history of experimental economics is yet to be written, and one challenge faced by historians of the discipline is its strikingly interdisciplinary character. The rise of experimental economics takes the form of several, partly independent and partly intertwined threads that can be brought under a single coherent narrative only with difficulty. It is partly for this reason that most of the existing historical literature consists of personal recollections or reconstructions of individual trajectories rather than of a collective enterprise. It is possible, however, to identify some key moments and achievements that have helped to establish experimentation as a legitimate method of investigation in economics.

Historical background and early years

The traditional view of economics as a primarily non-experimental science was outlined in the methodological writings of 19th-century economists. John Stuart Mill (1836, p. 124), for example, identifies several practical obstacles to the use of the experimental method, in particular the impossibility of controlling key economic variables and of keeping background conditions fixed so that the effect of manipulating each cause in isolation can be checked. This was Mill's main justification for adopting the so-called 'a priori deductive' method, a mix of introspection and theoretical reasoning, to determine what an idealized *homo oeconomicus* would do in given circumstances. Despite various changes in economists' methodological rhetoric and practice, it took a century and a half for philosophical scepticism towards experimentation to fade away.

Like many methodological revolutions in science, the experimental turn in economics was primarily made possible not by a change in philosophical perspective but by a number of innovations at the level of scientific practice and theoretical commitment. At a very general level, in the middle of the 20th century economics was in the process of becoming a 'tool-based' science (Morgan, 2003): from the old, discursive 'moral science' of political economy, it was changing into a discipline where models, statistics and mathematics played the role both of instruments and, crucially, of *objects* of investigation. During this conceptual revolution economists came to accept that the path towards the understanding of a real-world economy might have to go through the detailed analysis of several tools that had apparently only a vague resemblance to the final target of investigation. Theoretical models and computer simulations entered the economists' toolkit first, with laboratory experiments following shortly after.

The birth of experimental economics owes much to the publication of von Neumann and Morgenstern's *Theory of Games and Economic Behavior* (1944) and to the subsequent developments of game and decision theory. Although game theory is often seen primarily as a contribution to the theoretical corpus of economics, this was not how it was perceived at the time. Von Neumann and Morgenstern's work initially found fertile ground in a community of scientists devoted to the simultaneous development of a great variety of approaches and research methods and interested in their application to solve scientific, policy, and management problems across the disciplinary boundaries – from conflict resolution in international relations to group psychology, cybernetics, and the organization of the firm, to name just a few.

'Gaming' – playing game-theoretic problems for real – was common practice in the mathematical community at Princeton in the 1940s and 1950s, and quickly spread elsewhere as game theory increased in popularity. This practice did not involve sophisticated experimental design, but was conceived mainly as a useful way of illustrating game theoretic puzzles, as well as a check on abstract speculation and a guide to the theoretician's intuitions. Traces of this attitude can be found in the writings of some pioneers in game theory in the 1950s, who explicitly advocated a combination of formal theorizing and empirical evidence of various kinds, and engaged in (mostly casual) forms of experimenting to back up their theoretical claims (see, for example, Schelling, 1960; Shubik, 1960).

The first event devoted specifically to 'The Design of Experiments in Decision Processes' was a 1952 two-month seminar sponsored by the Ford Foundation, organized in Santa Monica by a group of researchers at the University of Michigan. The seminar's location was intended to facilitate the participation of members of the RAND Corporation, a think tank sponsored by the US Air Force, where among others Merrill Flood was conducting game-theoretic experiments (including famously the first Prisoner's Dilemma experiments). It is difficult to assess at all precisely the role of the Santa Monica seminar in the birth of experimental economics because, apart from an important minority, most of the published papers (in Thrall, Coombs and Davis, 1954) are theoretical rather than experimental in character. Several later protagonists, however, first became familiar with the idea of experiments in economics through the Santa Monica seminar, which therefore functioned as a catalyst in various indirect ways (see Smith, 1992).

The most extensive experimental projects of the 1950s were pursued at Penn State, Michigan, and Stanford. In collaboration with Lawrence Fouraker, the psychologist Sidney Siegel conducted a systematic investigation of bargaining behaviour at Pennsylvania State University, trying to combine what he took to be the most advanced aspects of economics (the theory) and psychology (the experimental method). The project came to an abrupt end with Siegel's death in 1961, but the resulting book (Siegel and Fouraker, 1960) won the American Academy of Arts and Sciences best monograph prize. Siegel and Fouraker's experiments focused on several aspects of bargaining behaviour, but are particularly significant for the systematic study of variations in the monetary payoffs and in the information made available to the subjects. Interestingly, this research project was rather disconnected from current developments in axiomatic bargaining theory, focusing instead on testing various hypotheses from the psychological literature. 'Level of aspiration theory' emerged eventually as the best predictor of bargaining behaviour.

From the point of view of experimental design, Siegel is often credited with being the first experimenter to highlight the importance of using real incentives to motivate subjects but, with hindsight, his experiments with Fouraker are also remarkable for the implementation of strict between-subjects anonymity. The latter practice would become very common in later experimental economics, usually as an attempt to implement economic theory's standard atomistic assumptions (especially the ban on other-regarding preferences). Contrary to the standard economic theory, Fouraker and Siegel recognized that interpersonal reactions do matter, but left a systematic investigation of their effects for later research.

More or less simultaneously, Ward Edwards at Michigan pioneered the experimental study of expected utility theory, as axiomatized in the second edition of von Neumann and Morgenstern's *Theory of Games* (1947). Amos Tversky, a student of Edwards and Coombs, would play a major role in the institutionalization of behavioural economics two decades later, as we shall see. In the mid-1950s an interdisciplinary group was also at work on the new theory of individual decision making, under the heading of the Stanford Value Project. Donald Davidson and Pat Suppes (both to become famous later for their contributions to philosophy) published with Siegel one of the first monographs of experimental decision theory (Davidson, Suppes and Siegel, 1957). At the centre of their research were measurement issues, in particular the implementation of learning theory and Frank Ramsey's method for measuring utilities and subjective probabilities.

Another major centre of interdisciplinary research in those years was the Carnegie group working on the psychology of organizations. Herbert Simon – working at Carnegie and the RAND Corporation, himself a participant in the Santa Monica seminar – is usually credited with being a pivotal player in this connection, although his influence on experimental economics is mostly indirect. The Carnegie group made use of a variety of methodologies, among which experimental 'role playing', 'business games', and simulations were central. In their larger projects, like the Carnegie Tech Management Game, human decision makers took managerial decisions in an environment simulated by a computer. Although primarily devised for pedagogic and illustrative purposes, such games were also used to shed light on the 'boundedly rational' processes of decision making that guide behaviour in big organizations. There is little continuity, however, between this body of work and contemporary experimental economics, with Simon playing a role more as a source of moral support and intellectual inspiration than as a direct contributor to experimental research.

The most famous experimental discovery of this period is due to a scholar who was to have little to do with later developments in experimental economics. Maurice Allais had been developing in France his own version of utility theory as a cardinal measurable quantity well before the publication of the *Theory of Games*. At a conference he organized in Paris in 1952, during a lunch break Allais presented Leonard Savage with a 'questionnaire' that was to become famous as the 'Allais paradox' experiment. When Savage gave answers that were inconsistent with the expected utility model he himself supported, Allais was encouraged to extend his questionnaire and to circulate it more widely.

The results were partially published in French in *Econometrica* (Allais, 1953) but received little attention in the short term. The main immediate result of the Allais experiment was Savage's switch to a purely normative defence of expected utility (Jallais and Pradier, 2005). Milton Friedman at the time was developing his methodology of positive economics which accorded no importance to the accuracy of the models of individual decision used to predict aggregate phenomena; and Allais's chauvinistic polemic against the 'American School' probably did little to attract sympathy. For about two decades Allais did not pursue research in this area any further.

The only large-scale experimental research project in Europe during this period was led by Reinhard Selten in Frankfurt, under the auspices of Heinz Sauermann. Like other early game theorists, Selten was convinced that the theory could contribute to the solution of important social science problems only if used in conjunction with empirical evidence. Indeed, even his most celebrated theoretical achievement (the concept of subgame perfection) was conceived in the context of a larger experimental project (see Selten, 1995).

The last piece of the puzzle of experimental economics in the 1950s is at the same time the most important and the most idiosyncratic. Vernon Smith had been experimenting at Purdue since 1956, focusing on the properties of different market institutions and their effects on the convergence towards equilibrium (see Smith, 1981). Smith had an engineering background and, unlike most experimenters at the time, did not approach experiments from a game-theoretic perspective. In the 1940s and 1950s Edward Chamberlin at Harvard had been performing little classroom experiments for illustrative purposes, to show his graduate students the falsity of the competitive theory of markets. Although the results of such experiments had been published in the *Journal of Political Economy* (1948), nobody at the time, including Chamberlin, attributed particular scientific value to them. Smith was the exception: a few years after leaving graduate school he came to question the design used by

Chamberlin and to test the robustness of the 'no convergence' results to variations in the exchange institution and repetition of the task.

Overcoming several obstacles, Smith managed to publish his counter-experiments to Chamberlin (Smith, 1962). For many years Smith led the only experimental project carried on fully within the boundaries of the economics discipline. In the early 1960s his work received funding from the National Science Foundation, but, apart from a brief attempt to collaborate with the Carnegie group (see Lee, 2004), his work in this phase was mostly carried out in isolation. One important exception is Smith's brief but important encounter with Sidney Siegel at Stanford in 1961. Smith perceived Siegel as much more advanced in methodological matters, and took from him several insights in experimental design that were to become the hallmark of economic experimentation (Smith, 1981; 1992).

From the underground to the big bang

Like other innovations of the previous two decades, experimental economics went through a period of slow, quiet growth in the 1960s. Some early contributors, like Allais, disappeared from the scene; others, like Smith, quit experimenting for some time (1967–74) and generally struggled to find an audience. Some areas, like social dilemmas and bargaining experiments, were booming in psychology but had little impact on the economics literature (see Leonard, 1994). In the 1970s, however, the landscape of experimental economics changed considerably, partly thanks to the formation of a few key partnerships. During 1968–9 Amos Tversky began collaborating with Daniel Kahneman at the Hebrew University, initially on judgement and then on decision making. In Europe, by 1972, Selten had moved to Bielefeld and started a collaboration with Werner Güth, later author of the first experiments on the ultimatum game. Allais in the meantime returned to expected utility in 1974, and was persuaded to publish a full report in English of his 1952 results (in Allais and Hagen, 1979). Allais's legacy would also begin to bear some fruits on the theoretical front. The late 1970s and early 1980s were characterized by a proliferation of alternative models to expected utility, mostly inspired by the experimental evidence that had been accumulated up until then.

After the happy anarchy of the earlier period, the 1970s were marked by the beginning of some controversies and the partial separation of the experimental community into sub-disciplines. In 1974 an article by Tversky and Kahneman in *Science* was widely read as a challenge to the view that human beings were rational agents, and, although it made experiments on judgement and decision making enter the intellectual debate at large, it also fed some deep cross-disciplinary misconceptions. A few years later Lichtenstein and Slovic's seminal experiments on preference reversals were introduced into the economics literature by Grether and Plott (1979), kicking off a series of theoretical and experimental papers that would fill the pages of the *American Economic Review* for years.

Charles Plott had been in close contact with Vernon Smith since the early 1960s, and started to run experiments a decade later, after his move to Caltech. Their collaboration led not only to important experimental projects but also to the creation of the Caltech laboratory and the training of the second and third generations of experimental economists. An important outcome of this period was also the attempt to systematize the methodology of experimental economics around a set of rules or 'precepts' of experimental design (Smith, 1976; 1982). Smith in these papers highlighted the importance of monetary incentives to control subjects' preferences, a practice that he had borrowed from Siegel – a psychologist – but that ironically was to become the main distinguishing feature of the 'economic' way of experimenting, as opposed to the more liberal 'psychological' way. With hindsight these methodological papers are also striking for their effective use of the language and conceptual framework of mechanism design theory. In this sense they reflected Smith's (and Plott's) attitude towards the use of experiments to tackle real-world problems of institutional design and policymaking (see Guala, 2005).

With the slow exhaustion of general equilibrium theory, the turmoil in macroeconomics, and an increasing disillusionment about econometrics, the 1970s created the conditions for the seeds of the 1940s and 1950s to finally blossom. Experimental economists were in a position to take advantage of this situation. By the early 1980s most of the 'paradigmatic' experiments that would inform subsequent research had already been published (Smith and Plott's experiments on auctions and markets, Lichtenstein and Slovic (1971) on preference reversals, Plott and others on public goods (Isaac, McCue and Plott, 1985), Güth on the ultimatum game (Güth, Schmittberger and Schwartz, 1982), Alvin Roth and others on bargaining (Roth and Malouf, 1979)). Consolidation meant also differentiation. A persistent low-intensity conflict at the methodological and theoretical level led to the creation of so-called 'behavioural economics'. Whereas experimental economics refers primarily to a method of investigation, the work of behavioural economists is unified by a substantial project of revision of economic theory (especially the replacement of *homo oeconomicus* with a more realistic psychological model), with experimentation constituting a major but by no means exclusive source of evidence.

The history of experimental economics in the 1980s and 1990s is the story of a booming research programme, increasingly influential within the discipline and the social sciences at large, expanding in new directions – neuroscience, for example – and attracting some of the most talented graduate students. Together with game theorists, experimenters have also been increasingly involved in policymaking, notably by contributing to the design of new market institutions for the allocation of sensitive goods – from telecommunication licences to space stations, airport slots, and physicians and surgeons (see Roth, 2002). In 2002 the Nobel Memorial Prize in economics awarded to Vernon Smith and Daniel Kahneman provided official acknowledgement of this remarkable revolution.

FRANCESCO GUALA

See also **behavioural game theory; experimental economics; field experiments.**

Bibliography

Allais, M. 1953. La psychologie de l'homme rationnel devant le risque: critique des postulats et axiomes de l'école Américaine. *Econometrica* 21, 503–46.

Allais, M. and Hagen, O., eds. 1979. *Expected Utility Hypothesis and the Allais Paradox*. Dordrecht: Reidel.

Chamberlin, E.H. 1948. An experimental imperfect market. *Journal of Political Economy* 56, 95–108.

Davidson, D., Suppes, P. and Siegel, S. 1957. *Decision Making: An Experimental Approach*. Stanford: Stanford University Press.

Grether, D. and Plott, C. 1979. Economic theory of choice and the preference reversal phenomenon. *American Economic Review* 69, 623–38.

Guala, F. 2005. *The Methodology of Experimental Economics*. New York: Cambridge University Press.

Güth, W., Schmittberger, R. and Schwartz, B. 1982. An experimental analysis of ultimatum bargaining. *Journal of Economic Behavior and Organization* 3, 363–88.

Isaac, R., McCue, K. and Plott, C. 1985. Public goods provision in an experimental environment. *Journal of Public Economics* 26, 51–74.

Jallais, S. and Pradier, P. 2005. The Allais paradox and its immediate consequences for expected utility theory. In *The Experiment in the History of Economics*, ed. P. Fontaine and R. Leonard. London: Routledge.

Lee, K. 2004. Rationality, minds, and machines in the laboratory: a thematic history of Vernon Smith's experimental economics. Ph.D. thesis, University of Notre Dame.

Leonard, R. 1994. Laboratory strife: higgling as experimental science in economics and social psychology. In *Higgling*, ed. N. De Marchi and M. Morgan. Durham. NC: Duke University Press.

Lichtenstein, S. and Slovic, P. 1971. Reversals of preference between bids and choices in gambling decisions. *Journal of Experimental Psychology* 89, 46–55.

Mill, J.S. 1836. On the definition of political economy and the method of investigation proper to it. In *Collected Works of John Stuart Mill*, Vol. 4. Toronto: University of Toronto Press, 1967.

Morgan, M. 2003. Economics. In *The Cambridge History of Science, Volume 7: The Modern Social Sciences*, ed. T. Porter and D. Ross. Cambridge: Cambridge University Press.

Neumann, J. Von and Morgenstern, O. 1944. *The Theory of Games and Economic Behavior*, 2nd edn. Princeton: Princeton University Press, 1947.

Roth, A. 1995. Introduction to experimental economics. In *The Handbook of Experimental Economics*, ed. J. Kagel and A. Roth. Princeton: Princeton University Press.

Roth, A. 2002. The economist as engineer: game theory, experimentation, and computation as tools for design economics. *Econometrica* 70, 1341–78.

Roth, A. and Malouf, M. 1979. Game-theoretic models and the role of information in bargaining. *Psychological Review* 86, 574–94.

Schelling, T. 1960. *The Strategy of Conflict*. Cambridge, MA: Harvard University Press.

Selten, R. 1995. Autobiography. In *Les Prix Nobel/The Nobel Prizes 1994*. Stockholm: Nobel Foundation.

Shubik, M. 1960. Bibliography on simulation, gaming, artificial intelligence and allied topics. *Journal of the American Statistical Association* 55, 736–51.

Siegel, S. and Fouraker, L. 1960. *Bargaining and Group Decision Making*. New York: McGraw-Hill.

Smith, V. 1962. An experimental study of competitive market behavior. *Journal of Political Economy* 70, 111–37.

Smith, V. 1976. Experimental economics: induced value theory. *American Economic Review* 66, 274–7.

Smith, V. 1981. Experimental economics at Purdue. In *Papers in Experimental Economics*. Cambridge: Cambridge University Press.

Smith, V. 1982. Microeconomic systems as an experimental science. *American Economic Review* 72, 923–55.

Smith, V. 1992. Game theory and experimental economics: beginnings and early influences. In *Towards a History of Game Theory*, ed. E. Weintraub. Durham, NC: Duke University Press.

Thrall, R., Coombs, C. and Davis, R., eds. 1954. *Decision Processes*. New York: Wiley.

Tversky, A. and Kahneman, D. 1974. Judgment under uncertainty: heuristics and biases. *Science* 185, 1124–30.

experimental labour economics

Scientific progress relies on testing theories. In labour economics different data sources are available for performing such tests. An important distinction is between circumstantial data and experimental or questionnaire data. Circumstantial data is the by-product of uncontrolled, naturally occurring economic activity. In contrast, experimental data is created explicitly for scientific purposes under controlled conditions. In labour economics, the data most commonly and traditionally used is circumstantial data such as unemployment rates or data on wages, education, or income, complemented by survey data. Labour economists have only recently started to use laboratory experiments.

Laboratory experiments have several important advantages in comparison with data sets typically used in labour economics. A key advantage is the unparalleled opportunity to control crucial aspects of the economic environment. This includes control over information conditions, technology, market structure, and trends in economic fundamentals. Control over the decision environment makes it possible to identify the theoretical equilibrium in an experimental labour market, which is basically impossible with field data. Knowing the equilibrium allows the study of convergence properties, stability and efficiency. Experiments are particularly useful for investigating the economic consequences of important labour market institutions, such as minimum wages or employment protection legislations. The reason is that experiments allow the exogenous changes of institutions, holding everything else constant. In the field, by contrast, institutions are always adopted endogenously. Econometric strategies such as instrumenting for policy changes with political variables can help ameliorate this problem, but do not achieve the unequivocal exogenous variation provided by a laboratory experiment. Laboratory experiments also make it possible to observe behaviour at the level of individual economic agents. This is important given that theoretical predictions typically involve such micro behaviours. For example, it is possible to directly observe individual reservation wages or individual wage bargaining behaviour. Yet another advantage is that with laboratory experiments one can study, at relatively low cost, institutions that do not yet exist. Analogous to experimental tests of new medicines, where the medication is administered to a small subset of the population initially, laboratory experiments can be used as a first step, before experimenting with institutions in the field. Finally, experimental evidence is replicable, which is a prerequisite in establishing solid empirical knowledge.

Data-sets and the comparative advantage of laboratory experiments

Although we believe that laboratory experiments offer important advantages for studying institutions, and should thus be exploited more often, it is important to recognize that there are also drawbacks to this method, which calls for a complementary use of different methods. A potential disadvantage is limited generalizability. Note, however, that this critique holds with respect to any data-set, given that any empirical observation is time and space contingent. Another concern is that experiments may be overly simple, missing potentially relevant aspects of the labour market. This is in fact both a problem and an advantage of experiments. Just as economic models are simpler than reality, so experiments are designed to simplify as much as possible, without losing the essentials. Thus, simplicity need not be a defect of an experiment. The key challenge, just as in the case of building economic models, is to include those features that are essential to the question at hand.

Examples

In this section we discuss a selected set of examples of experiments that were designed to shed light on important issues in labour economics. The examples concern the nature of the employment relationship and its contractual regulation, wage rigidity, performance incentives and their potentially detrimental effects, and labour market institutions.

The employment relation

The employment relation is an incomplete contract, which typically leaves many important aspects unspecified. This holds in particular for the content of work effort, which is unregulated and thereby non-enforceable by third parties. Contractual incompleteness gives opportunistic agents an incentive to shirk and therefore leads to an inefficiently low surplus. Thus, voluntary cooperation is necessary to ensure efficiency. Akerlof (1982) argued that many employment relationships are therefore governed by a gift exchange: the firm pays a higher wage than necessary to keep the employee, and the employee returns the gift by providing above minimum effort. Akerlof supported his arguments by a case study and casual observations.

The gift-exchange game by Fehr, Kirchsteiger and Riedl (1993) provided the first experimental test of the existence of gift exchanges in the framework of a formal game-theoretic model designed to mimic an incomplete employment contract. In their experiment, participants assumed the roles of 'workers' and 'firms'. A firm made a wage offer that a worker could accept. If the worker accepted, he or she had then to choose a costly effort level. Parameters were such that a self-interested worker would always choose the lowest possible effort, since effort was costly. In turn, the firm had no incentive to pay an above-minimal wage, because a self-interested worker would shirk anyway. The results of numerous experiments in this framework showed, however, that wages and effort levels are positively correlated. Higher wages were reciprocated by higher effort levels, a finding which is consistent with the gift-exchange argument by Akerlof. This observation is also consistent with field evidence regarding the link between personnel policy and work morale (Bewley, 1999).

In these experiments the employment relationship was modelled as a one-shot game, because this allows an unambiguous prediction under the joint assumptions of rationality and self-interest. Yet in reality, employment relationships are long-term relationships. To test the impact of repeated interaction, Gächter and Falk (2002) conducted the gift-exchange experiment in the form of repeated games in which the same firm–worker pair interacted for ten periods. These repeated games were compared with one-shot games in which each firm was matched with ten different workers. The results showed a significantly higher effort in the repeated game than in the one-shot games. Gächter and Falk showed that the reason for this result is that in the repeated games the selfish types imitate the reciprocal types. This result provides support for theoretical arguments (for example, MacLeod and Malcomson, 1998) that incomplete employment relations allow for implicit incentives for non-opportunistic behaviour.

In the experiments by Gächter and Falk (2002) the experimenter determined the duration of the employment relationship exogenously. In reality, however, the duration of employment relationships arises endogenously. Contract theory suggests that the duration might be linked to contractual incompleteness. Specifically, when contracts are incomplete, a long-term relationship provides implicit incentives that constrain opportunistic behaviour – an argument supported by the cited experimental evidence. If contracts are complete then implicit incentives are not necessary to constrain opportunism. Thus, employment relationships will tend to be short term under contractual completeness. Brown, Falk and Fehr (2004) tested these arguments experimentally and found strong support for them.

Efficiency wages, wage rigidity, and involuntary unemployment
Efficiency wage theories explain why even in the absence of market interventions wages might be downwardly rigid, causing involuntary unemployment. Akerlof's (1982) gift-exchange theory is one efficiency wage theory that can explain involuntary unemployment. The main idea is simple. If gift exchanges exist, then firms have no incentive to lower wages because this would lead to low performance. Thus, paying high wages is profitable to the firm – wages are downwardly rigid and can cause involuntary unemployment. Fehr et al. (1998) demonstrated the behavioural validity of this argument experimentally.

Fehr and Falk (1999) provide the most stringent confirmation that gift exchanges can lead to downward wage rigidity. In their experiment an employment relationship was embedded in a 'double auction' market institution in which there were more workers than firms. This institution is known for its competitive properties; under complete contracts experimental double auction markets tend to clear very quickly. In the Fehr–Falk experiments both workers and firms could make wage offers. This enables us to observe whether workers underbid each other and firms therefore have the possibility of employing a worker at a low wage. There was indeed fierce competition among workers who underbid each other down to the theoretically predicted wage. Underbidding occurred in both treatments, the 'complete contract treatment' and the 'incomplete contract treatment'. In the latter, the striking finding was that firms did not take advantage of the possibility of paying low wages; instead they deliberately paid very high wages. The workers' reciprocal effort choice explains why firms had an incentive to pay high wages. In the control experiments with complete contracts gift exchanges were precluded by design and actual wages were very close to market clearing wages. Thus, incomplete contracts and gift exchange can explain wage rigidity and involuntary unemployment.

Performance incentives (and their detrimental effects)
Compensation and performance incentives have always been central topics in labour economics. Compensation may take different forms. The simplest form is a piece rate where a worker receives a certain wage for each unit she produces. Compensation may also depend on relative performance and be coupled with the possibility of moving up the career ladder. Tournament theory (Lazear and Rosen, 1981) is an important theoretical framework for understanding career incentives and relative performance incentives.

Bull, Schotter and Weigelt (1987) provide the first experimental analysis of piece rate and tournament incentives. They designed their experiments so that the incentive schemes were directly comparable, that is, the predicted effort level was the same both under piece rates and under tournament incentives. The results confirmed the theoretical predictions in both treatments. As it turned out, however, the support for tournament theory is weaker than for piece rate theory. In various treatment conditions these authors find that average effort choices converged close to the equilibrium prediction, but the variance was up to 30 times higher under tournament incentives than under the piece rate system.

The results by Bull, Schotter and Weigelt (1987) provide clear evidence that incentives influence behaviour very strongly. However, numerous experiments as well as field evidence (Bewley, 1999) suggest that employment relationships are also governed by 'good will' and voluntary cooperation. This raises the question how explicit performance incentives affect voluntary cooperation – a fertile area of current research in experimental labour economics. A nice illustration of the potentially dysfunctional effects of introducing explicit incentives is the field experiment by Gneezy and Rustichini (2000). These authors studied the parents' response to the introduction of a fixed fine for picking up their children too late from kindergarten. The experiment lasted for 20 weeks and there were two conditions. In the baseline condition no fine existed. In the treatment condition the experimenters implemented a fixed fine after week four for picking up a child too late. The fine was removed after week 16. From week seven onwards, there was a steep *increase* in the number of latecomers until their number was roughly twice as high as in the baseline condition. Moreover, when the fine was removed at the end of week 16 the number of tardy parents remained roughly twice as high as in the baseline condition. This result clearly contradicts standard incentive theory, which predicts that the introduction of the fine should lower the incidence of late coming. A likely explanation of this finding is that the implicit contract that governed the employment relationship was changed from a good-will-based one to a market-like transaction, in which 'a fine is a price' and parents bought the commodity of being late.

Labour market institutions

A particularly important advantage of laboratory experiments concerns the possibility to test the economic effects of (labour market) institutions in a controlled way. An example of such an institutional test is the paper on minimum wages by Falk, Fehr and Zehnder (2006). In their experiment firms make wage offers to workers in labour markets either with or without minimum wages. The key insight of their study is that minimum wages may affect the reservation wages of workers in a non-trivial way: first, when minimum wages are introduced, workers stipulate reservation wages above the level of the minimum wage level, because being paid at just the level of the minimum wage is considered unfair. Second, while the introduction of a minimum wage increases reservation wages, the removal of a minimum wage legislation changes reservation wages only marginally. These findings help explain several empirical minimum wage puzzles. First, there exists an anomalously low utilization of sub-minimum wages in situations where employers actually could pay workers less than the minimum; second there exist so-called spillover effects, that is, wages are often increased by an amount in excess of that necessary for compliance with the minimum wage; and third, minimum wages do not always cause a decrease in employment, in particular if the minimum wage increase is modest (see also Card and Krueger, 1995).

The finding that minimum wages affect workers' fairness perceptions of wages is also supported by Brandts and Charness (2004) who introduced a minimum wage in the context of an experimental labour market with worker moral hazard where workers' fairness concerns drive effort. They show that workers provide less effort for the same wage level in the presence of the minimum wage. This supports the view that the impact of minimum wages on workers' attributions of fairness intentions to firms partially shapes their effort responses.

Concluding remarks

Experimental economics is a method of empirical investigation, not a separate subfield of economics. Experimental methods can therefore in principle be utilized in all areas of economics. In this article we have illustrated some selected applications of experimental methods to important issues in labour economics. Further discussions of the issues raised here can be found in Fehr and Gächter (2000), Gächter and Fehr (2002), Fehr and Falk (2002), Falk and Fehr (2003) and Falk and Huffman (2007).

ARMIN FALK AND SIMON GÄCHTER

See also **behavioural economics and game theory; reciprocity and collective action.**

Bibliography

Akerlof, G. 1982. Labor contracts as partial gift exchange. *Quarterly Journal of Economics* 97, 543–69.

Bewley, T. 1999. *Why Wages Don't Fall in a Recession.* Cambridge, MA: Harvard University Press.

Brandts, J. and Charness, G. 2004. Do labour market conditions affect gift exchange? Some experimental evidence. *Economic Journal* 114, 684–708.

Brown, M., Falk, A. and Fehr, E. 2004. Relational contracts and the nature of market interactions. *Econometrica* 72, 747–80.

Bull, C., Schotter, A. and Weigelt, K. 1987. Tournaments and piece rates: an experimental study. *Journal of Political Economy* 95, 1–33.

Card, D. and Krueger, A. 1995. *Myth and Measurement: The New Economics of the Minimum Wage.* Princeton, NJ: Princeton University Press.

Falk, A. and Fehr, E. 2003. Why labor market experiments? *Labor Economics* 10, 399–406.

Falk, A., Fehr, E. and Zehnder, C. 2006. Fairness perceptions and reservation wages: the behavioral effects of minimum wage laws. *Quarterly Journal of Economics* 121, 1347–81.

Falk, A. and Huffman, D. 2007. Studying labor market institutions in the lab: minimum wages, employment protection and workfare. *Journal of Institutional and Theoretical Economics* 163, 30–45.

Fehr, E. and Falk, A. 1999. Wage rigidity in a competitive incomplete contract market. *Journal of Political Economy* 107, 106–34.

Fehr, E. and Falk, A. 2002. The psychological foundations of incentives. *European Economic Review* 46, 687–724.

Fehr, E. and Gächter, S. 2000. Fairness and retaliation: the economics of reciprocity. *Journal of Economic Perspectives* 14(3), 159–81.

Fehr, E., Kirchler, E., Weichbold, A. and Gächter, S. 1998. When social norms overpower competition – gift exchange in experimental labor markets. *Journal of Labor Economics* 16, 324–51.

Fehr, E., Kirchsteiger, G. and Riedl, A. 1993. Does fairness prevent market clearing? An experimental investigation. *Quarterly Journal of Economics* 108, 437–60.

Gächter, S. and Falk, A. 2002. Reputation and reciprocity: consequences for the labour relation. *Scandinavian Journal of Economics* 104, 1–27.

Gächter, S. and Fehr, E. 2002. Fairness in the labour market: a survey of experimental results. In *Surveys in Experimental Economics. Bargaining, Cooperation and Election Stock Markets,* ed. B. Friedel and M. Lehmann-Waffenschmidt. Heidelberg and New York: Physica.

Gneezy, U. and Rustichini, A. 2000. A fine is a price. *Journal of Legal Studies* 29, 1–17.

Lazear, P. and Rosen, S. 1981. Rank-order tournaments as optimum labor contracts. *Journal of Political Economy* 89, 841–64.

MacLeod, B. and Malcomson, J. 1998. Motivation and markets. *American Economic Review* 88, 388–411.

experimental macroeconomics

Experimental macroeconomics is a subfield of experimental economics that makes use of controlled laboratory methods to understand aggregate economic phenomena and to test the specific assumptions and predictions of macroeconomic models. Surveys of experimental macroeconomics are found in Ochs (1995), Duffy (1998) and Ricciuti (2004). Macroeconomic topics that have been studied in the laboratory include convergence to Walrasian competitive equilibrium (Lian and Plott, 1998), growth and development (Lei and Noussair, 2002; Capra et al., 2005), specialization and trade (Noussair, Plot and Riezman, 1995), Keynesian coordination failures (Cooper, 1999; Van Huyck, Battalio and Beil, 1990), the use of money as a medium of exchange (Brown, 1996; Duffy and Ochs, 1999; 2002) and as a store of value (McCabe, 1989; Lim, Prescott and Sunder, 1994; Marimon and Sunder, 1993; 1994), exchange rate determination (Arifovic, 1996; Noussair, Plot and Riezman, 1997), money illusion (Fehr and Tyran, 2001), asset price bubbles and crashes (Smith, Suchanek and Williams, 1988; Lei, Noussair and Plott, 2001; Hommes et al., 2005) sunspots (Marimon, Spear and Sunder, 1993; Duffy and Fisher, 2005), bank runs (Schotter and Yorulmazer, 2003; Garratt and Keister, 2005), contagions (Corbae and Duffy, 2006), speculative currency attacks (Heinemann, Nagel and Ockenfels, 2004), and the economic impact of various fiscal and monetary policies (Riedl and Van Winden, 2001; Arifovic and Sargent, 2003; Marimon and Sunder, 1994; Bernasconi and Kirchkamp, 2000).

The use of laboratory experiments, involving small groups of subjects interacting with one another for short periods of time, to analyse aggregate, economy-wide phenomena or to test macroeconomic model predictions or assumptions might be met with some scepticism. However, there are many insights to be gained from controlled laboratory experimentation that cannot be obtained using standard macroeconometric approaches, namely, econometric analyses of the macroeconomic data reported by government agencies. Often the data most relevant to testing a macroeconomic model are simply unavailable. There may also be identification, endogeneity and equilibrium selection issues that cannot be satisfactorily addressed using econometric methods. Indeed, Robert Lucas (1986) was the first macro-economist to make such observations, and he invited laboratory tests of rational expectations macroeconomic models; much of the subsequent experimental macroeconomics literature may be viewed as a response to Lucas's (1986) invitation. It is also worth noting that experimental methodologies have been improbably applied to the study of many other aggregate phenomena including astronomy, epidemiology, evolution, meteorology, political science and sociology.

Insights from macroeconomic experiments

To date, experimental macroeconomics research has yielded some important insights, including an understanding of when equilibration works, when it fails, and the means by which equilibrium selection or coordination problems are resolved. Equilibration, the process by which competitive equilibrium is achieved, is often ignored by modern macroeconomic modellers, who typically assume that market clearing is friction-free and instantaneous. Experimentalists, following the lead of Smith (1962), have explored mechanisms such as the double auction, the availability of information, futures markets and other means by which this equilibration might be achieved or enhanced (see, for example, Forsythe, Palfrey and Plott, 1982; Plott and Sunder, 1982; Sunder, 1995 for partial equilibrium approaches; and Lian and Plott, 1998 for a general equilibrium approach). A general finding is that, with enough trading experience and information feedback about transaction prices, bids, and asks, even small populations of five to ten subjects can learn to trade at prices and achieve efficiency consistent with competitive equilibrium in a large class of market environments. Indeed, the institutional rules, for instance of the double auction, may be all that is necessary to assure equilibration, as shown in the zero-intelligence trader approach of Gode and Sunder (1993).

Experimental insights regarding equilibration have enabled experimentalists to design market environments where equilibration may fail to obtain; in its place are observed price bubbles and crashes (Smith, Suchanek and Williams, 1988; Lei, Noussair and Plott, 2001; Hommes et al., 2005). Explaining these laboratory asset price bubbles has proved challenging. Lei, Noussair and Plott (2001) show that speculative motives alone cannot explain bubble formation and suggest that it may have more to do with subject boredom. Duffy and Ünver (2006) suggest that anchoring effects may factor in subjects' bidding up of prices until binding budget constraints force a crash. A further puzzle is that experienced subjects in laboratory asset markets learn to avoid price bubbles and crashes, and generally price assets in line with fundamental values. An explanation for why bubbles and crashes occur among inexperienced but not experienced subjects has yet to be provided. Experiments with mixtures of experienced and inexperienced subjects show no tendency for bubbles to arise (Dufwenberg, Lindqviist and Moore, 2005).

In environments with multiple equilibria, theory is typically silent as to which equilibrium agents will select or whether there will be transitions between equilibria. Understanding how agents coordinate on an equilibrium is of great interest to macroeconomists, as coordination problems are thought to play an important role in the persistence of business cycle fluctuations. Experimental evidence can and has been used to address the issue of which, among multiple equilibria, is most likely to be achieved, and why.

For instance, Van Huyck, Battalio and Beil (1990) have shown how minimum effort, team production payoff functions can lead to Keynes-type coordination failures – that is, coordination by groups of subjects on Pareto inferior equilibria. Such inefficiencies do not arise from conflicting objectives or from asymmetries of information; rather, they arise from individuals' *strategic uncertainty* with regard to the actions of other market participants. Similarly, Duffy and Ochs (1999; 2002) report that subjects have no difficulty coordinating on efficient monetary exchange equilibria in Kiyotaki–Wright-type money-search models when theory calls for the use of fundamental, cost-minimizing strategies, but subjects have much greater difficulty coordinating on efficient monetary equilibria that require them to employ more costly and forward-looking, speculative strategies, due perhaps to the unwillingness of other subjects to adopt those same speculative strategies.

Not all the experimental evidence points to inefficiencies in macro-coordination problems. Marimon and Sunder (1993) show that when subjects are presented with a Laffer-curve-type trade-off between two inflation rates, the efficient, low-inflation equilibria is more likely to be selected than is the inefficient, high-inflation equilibrium. They show that the low-inflation equilibrium is stable under the adaptive learning dynamics that subjects use whereas the high-inflation equilibrium is not. Similarly, Arifovic and Sargent (2003) study behaviour in a Kydland–Prescott model of expected inflation output trade-offs and find that a majority of subjects acting in the role of central bank are able to choose policies so as to induce subjects, in the role of the public, to coordinate their expectations on the efficient but time-inconsistent Ramsey equilibrium. Still, they report occasional instances of 'back-sliding' to the less efficient, time-consistent Nash equilibrium.

Finally, Duffy and Fisher (2005) explore subjects' use of non-fundamental 'sunspot' variables as coordination devices in an environment with multiple equilibria. They show that, when information is highly centralized, as in a call market, subjects use realizations of a sunspot variable as a device for coordinating on low- or high-price equilibria, but that this coordination mechanism may break down when information is more decentralized, as in a double auction, or when the mapping from realizations of the sunspot variable to the action space is unclear.

Methodological issues

Methodologically, macroeconomic experiments typically involve some kind of centralized market-clearing mechanism through which subjects interact with one another, for instance as buyers or sellers, or both. The double auction market mechanism (Friedman and Rust, 1991) is the most commonly used market-clearing mechanism, as it allows for continuous information on bids, asks, transaction prices and volume – information which is thought to be critical to rapid equilibration and high levels of allocative efficiency (Lian and Plott, 1998; Noussair, Plott and Riezman, 1995; 1997). The simultaneous, sealed-bid 'call' market version of this mechanism has also been used by some researchers (Cason and Friedman, 1997; Duffy and Fisher, 2005; Capra et al., 2005).

Some less centralized market mechanisms have also been used. For instance, Brown (1996), Duffy and Ochs (1999; 2002) study a money-search model in which subjects are randomly paired and may trade goods with one another at a fixed exchange rate. In addition, game-theoretic models are also commonly employed, especially in studies of coordination failure, contagion and speculative attacks (Van Huyck, Battalio and Beil, 1990; Corbae and Duffy, 2006; Heinemann, Nagel and Ockenfels, 2004).

A hallmark of modern macroeconomic modelling is the characterization of the economy using recursive dynamical systems where expectations of future endogenous variables determine current outcomes. Several experimental researchers testing such models have found it useful to separate subjects' forecast decisions from market-trading decisions. For instance, Marimon and Sunder (1993; 1994; 1995) and Hommes et al. (2005) elicit subjects' forecasts of the next period's price level. Using these individual forecasts, they determine subjects' individual demands for the consumption good in the current period and, as supply is fixed, they simultaneously determine the current period price. Similarly, Adam (2007) elicits forecasts of inflation one and two periods ahead, consistent with the monetary sticky price model that he investigates; these expectations are then used to determine output and inflation in the current period. Marimon and Sunder (1994) refer to this type of experimental design as a 'learning to forecast' framework, which they contrast with a 'learning to optimize' framework. Of course, in macroeconomic models, it is assumed that agents are able to both forecast and optimize at the same time.

Many macroeconomic models have representative agents and infinite horizons or an infinity of agents and goods which pose some challenges for laboratory implementation and testing of theoretical predictions. The representative agent assumption has been examined by Noussair and Matheny (2000) and Lei and Noussair (2002). They compare consumption and investment decisions made by individual subjects operating as 'representative agent-social planners' in the standard Cass–Koopmans optimal growth framework with the decisions made by groups of subjects who first trade shares of capital via a double-auction market clearing mechanism and then allocate their income between consumption and investment. They find that the double-auction market mechanism results in allocations that are far closer to the theoretical predictions than are the decisions made by subjects in the representative agent role attempting to solve the optimization problem on their own.

To implement infinite horizons, researchers have adopted two designs. One design, used for example by Marimon and Sunder (1993), is to recruit subjects for a fixed period of time but terminate the session early, without advance notice, following the end of some period of play. As Marimon and Sunder use a forward-looking dynamic model, they use the one-step-ahead forecasts made by a subset of subjects who are paid for their forecast accuracy to determine final period allocations. A second design is to introduce a constant small probability, $1-\delta$, that each period will be the last one played in a sequence, and allow enough time for several indefinite sequences to be played in an experimental session (Duffy and Ochs, 1999; 2002; Lei and Noussair, 2002; Capra et al., 2005). This design has the advantage of inducing both the stationarity associated with an infinite horizon and discounting of future payoffs at rate $(1-\delta)/\delta$ per period (equivalently a discount *factor* of δ). Related to the infinite horizon problem, overlapping generations models, as studied by Marimon and Sunder (1993; 1994; 1995) and Marimon, Spear and Sunder (1993) have an infinity of agents (and goods). Marimon and Sunder cope with this difficulty by recycling subjects – allowing each subject to live several two-period lives over the course of an indefinite sequence of periods. Marimon and Sunder (1993) argue that this repeated entry and exit of subjects does not induce any strategic opportunities that are not already present in the overlapping generations model without 'rebirth'. Indeed, the need for a large number of agents to study macroeconomic behaviour is a common issue confronted by researchers. However, results from many double auction experiments suggest that competitive equilibrium can be quickly achieved with as few as three to five subjects operating on each side of the market. Similarly, while search models of money assume a continuum of agents, Duffy and Ochs (2002) argue that the strategic incentives generated by having finite subject populations do not alter the equilibrium predictions of those models under the assumption of a continuum of agents.

Perhaps the most difficult methodological issue is the external validity of macroeconomic experimental findings. While external validity is generally a problem for all experimental economists, it might be regarded as a greater problem for macro-experimentalists seeking to explain economy-wide aggregate macroeconomic phenomena using necessarily small-scale laboratory evidence. Experimental macroeconomists have several responses to this issue. First, as noted earlier, modern macroeconomic models have explicit microfoundations as to how individual agents make decisions (for example, agents recognize the relevant trade-offs, form rational expectations) which can be directly tested in the laboratory. Indeed, in the laboratory one can be more certain about micro-level *causal relationships*, that is, that an experimenter induced change in a variable is the source of any observed change in subject behaviour as opposed to some other, unaccounted-for factors. Macroeconometric analyses of field data cannot claim the same degree of *internal validity*. A second response is to make use of highly experienced subjects – those who have participated in the same experiment many times – as a means of better proxying real-world behaviour. As noted earlier, asset price bubbles and crashes seem to disappear with experienced subjects. A third response has been to use parametric forms or calibrations of macroeconomic models that are of interest to macroeconomists, or to present subjects with real macroeconomic data as part of the experimental design (for example, Bernasconi, Kirchkamp and Parulo, 2004). Finally, many experimentalists would argue that all experimental work, including macroeconomic experiments, should be judged by the findings obtained and not by biases concerning the suitability of laboratory versus other empirical methods, all of which have their strengths and weaknesses.

JOHN DUFFY

See also **behavioural finance; coordination problems and communication; experimental economics.**

Bibliography

Adam, K. 2007. Experimental evidence on the persistence of output and inflation. *Economic Journal* 117, 603–36.

Arifovic, J. 1996. The behavior of the exchange rate in the genetic algorithm and experimental economies. *Journal of Political Economy* 104, 510–41.

Arifovic, J. and Sargent, T.J. 2003. Laboratory experiments with an expectational Phillips curve. In *Evolution and Procedures in Central Banking*, ed. D.E. Altig and B.D. Smith. Cambridge: Cambridge University Press.

Bernasconi, M. and Kirchkamp, O. 2000. Why do monetary policies matter? An experimental study of saving and inflation in an overlapping generations model. *Journal of Monetary Economics* 46, 315–43.

Bernasconi, M., Kirchkamp, O. and Paruolo, P. 2004. Do fiscal variables affect fiscal expectations? Experiments with real world and lab data. SPF 504 Discussion Paper No. 04–26: University of Mannheim.

Brown, P.M. 1996. Experimental evidence on money as a medium of exchange. *Journal of Economic Dynamics and Control* 20, 583–600.

Capra, C.M., Tanaka, T., Camerer, C.F., Munyan, L., Sovero, V., Wang, L. and Noussair, C. 2005. The impact of simple institutions in experimental economies with poverty traps. Working paper.

Cason, T.N. and Friedman, D. 1997. Price formation in single call markets. *Econometrica* 65, 311–45.

Cooper, R.W. 1999. *Coordination Games*. Cambridge: Cambridge University Press.

Corbae, D. and Duffy, J. 2006. Experiments with network formation. Working paper.

Duffy, J. 1998. Monetary theory in the laboratory. *Federal Reserve Bank of St. Louis Economic Review* 80, 9–26.

Duffy, J. and Fisher, E.O.N. 2005. Sunspots in the laboratory. *American Economic Review* 95, 510–29.

Duffy, J. and Ochs, J. 1999. Emergence of money as a medium of exchange: an experimental study. *American Economic Review* 89, 847–77.

Duffy, J. and Ochs, J. 2002. Intrinsically worthless objects as media of exchange: experimental evidence. *International Economic Review* 43, 637–73.

Duffy, J. and Ünver, U. 2006. Asset price bubbles and crashes with near-zero-intelligence traders. *Economic Theory* 27, 537–63.

Dufwenberg, M., Lindqviist, T. and Moore, E. 2005. Bubbles and experience: an experiment. *American Economic Review* 95, 1731–7.

Fehr, E. and Tyran, J.-F. 2001. Does money illusion matter? *American Economic Review* 91, 1239–62.

Forsythe, R., Palfrey, T.R. and Plott, C.R. 1982. Asset valuation in an experimental market. *Econometrica* 58, 537–68.

Friedman, D. and Rust, J. 1991. *The Double Auction Market: Institutions, Theories and Evidence*. Cambridge, MA: Perseus Publishing.

Garratt, R. and Keister, T. 2005. Bank runs: an experimental study. Working paper, University of California, Santa Barbara.

Gode, D.K. and Sunder, S. 1993. Allocative efficiency of markets with zero intelligence traders: market as a partial substitute for individual rationality. *Journal of Political Economy* 101, 119–37.

Heinemann, F., Nagel, R. and Ockenfels, P. 2004. The theory of global games on test: experimental analysis of coordination games with public and private information. *Econometrica* 72, 1583–99.

Hommes, C.H., Sonnemans, J., Tuinstra, J. and van de Velden, H. 2005. Coordination of expectations in asset pricing experiments. *Review of Financial Studies* 18, 955–80.

Lei, V. and Noussair, C.N. 2002. An experimental test of an optimal growth model. *American Economic Review* 92, 549–70.

Lei, V., Noussair, C.N. and Plott, C.R. 2001. Nonspeculative bubbles in experimental asset markets: lack of common knowledge of rationality vs. actual irrationality. *Econometrica* 69, 831–59.

Lian, P. and Plott, C.R. 1998. General equilibrium, markets, macroeconomics and money in a laboratory experimental environment. *Economic Theory* 12, 21–75.

Lim, S.S., Prescott, E.C. and Sunder, S. 1994. Stationary solution to the overlapping generations model of fiat money: experimental evidence. *Empirical Economics* 19, 255–77.

Lucas, R.E. 1986. Adaptive behavior and economic theory. *Journal of Business* 59, S401–S426.

Marimon, R., Spear, S.E. and Sunder, S. 1993. Expectationally driven market volatility: an experimental study. *Journal of Economic Theory* 61, 74–103.

Marimon, R. and Sunder, S. 1993. Indeterminacy of equilibria in a hyperinflationary world: experimental evidence. *Econometrica* 61, 1073–107.

Marimon, R. and Sunder, S. 1994. Expectations and learning under alternative monetary regimes: an experimental approach. *Economic Theory* 4, 131–62.

Marimon, R. and Sunder, S. 1995. Does a constant money growth rule help stabilize inflation? Experimental evidence. *Carnegie-Rochester Conference Series on Public Policy* 43, 111–56.

McCabe, K.A. 1989. Fiat money as a store of value in an experimental market. *Journal of Economic Behavior and Organization* 12, 215–31.

Noussair, C.N. and Matheny, K.J. 2000. An experimental study of decisions in dynamic optimization problems. *Economic Theory* 15, 389–419.

Noussair, C.N., Plott, C.R. and Riezman, R.G. 1995. An experimental investigation of the patterns of international trade. *American Economic Review* 85, 462–91.

Noussair, C.N., Plott, C.R. and Riezman, R.G. 1997. The principles of exchange rate determination in an international financial experiment. *Journal of Political Economy* 105, 822–61.

Ochs, J. 1995. Coordination problems. In *The Handbook of Experimental Economics*, ed. J.H. Kagel and A.E. Roth. Princeton: Princeton University Press.

Plott, C.R. and Sunder, S. 1982. Efficiency of experimental security markets with insider information: an application of rational-expectations models. *Journal of Political Economy* 90, 663–98.

Ricciuti, R. 2004. Bringing macroeconomics into the lab. Working paper No. 26, International Centre for Economic Research.

Riedl, A. and van Winden, F. 2001. Does the wage tax system cause budget deficits? A macro-economic experiment. *Public Choice* 109, 371–94.

Schotter, A. and Yorulmazer, T. 2003. On the severity of bank runs: an experimental study. Working paper, Center for Experimental Social Science, New York University.

Smith, V.L. 1962. An experimental study of competitive market behavior. *Journal of Political Economy* 70, 111–37.

Smith, V.L., Suchanek, G.L. and Williams, A.W. 1988. Bubbles, crashes, and endogenous expectations in experimental spot asset markets. *Econometrica* 56, 1119–51.

Sunder. 1995. Experimental asset markets: a survey. In *The Handbook of Experimental Economics*, ed. J.H. Kagel and A.E. Roth. Princeton: Princeton University Press.

Van Huyck, J.B., Battalio, R.C. and Beil, R.O. 1990. Tacit coordination games, strategic uncertainty, and coordination failure. *American Economic Review* 80, 234–48.

experimental methods in economics

Historically, the method and subject matter of economics have presupposed that it was a non-experimental (or 'field observational') science more like astronomy or meteorology than physics or chemistry. Based on general, introspectively 'plausible', assumptions about human preferences, and about the cost and technology based supply response of producers, economists have sought to understand the functioning of economies, using observations generated by economic outcomes realized over time. The data of the astronomer is of this same type, but it would be wrong to conclude that astronomy and economics are methodologically equivalent. There are two important differences between astronomy and economics which help to illuminate some of the methodological problems of economics. First, based upon parallelism (the maintained hypothesis that the same physical laws hold everywhere), astronomy draws on all the relevant theory from classical mechanics and particle physics – theory which has evolved under rigorous laboratory tests. Traditionally, economists have not had an analogous body of tested behavioural principles that have survived controlled experimental tests, and which can be assumed to apply with insignificant error to the microeconomic behaviour that underpins the observable operations of the economy. Analogously, one might have supposed that there would have arisen an important area of common interest between economics and, say, experimental psychology, similar to that between astronomy and physics, but this has only started to develop in recent years.

Second, the data of astronomy are painstakingly gathered by professional observational astronomers for scientific purposes, and these data are taken seriously (if not always non-controversially) by astrophysicists and cosmologists. Most of the data of economics has been collected by government or private agencies for non-scientific purposes. Hence astronomers are directly responsible for the scientific credibility of their data in a way that economists have not been. In economics, when things appear not to turn out as expected the quality of the data is more likely to be questioned than the relevance and quality of the abstract reasoning. Old theories fade away, not from the weight of falsifying evidence that catalyses theoretical creativity into developing better theory, but from lack of interest, as intellectual energy is attracted to the development of new techniques and to the solution of new puzzles that remain untested.

At approximately the mid-20th century, professional economics began to change with the introduction of the laboratory experiment into economic method. In this embryonic research programme economists (and a psychologist, Sidney Siegel) became directly involved in the design and conduct of experiments to examine propositions implied by economic theories of markets. For the first time this made it possible to introduce *demonstrable* knowledge into the economist's attempt to understand markets.

This laboratory approach to economics also brought to the economist direct responsibility for an important source of scientific data generated by controlled processes that can be replicated by other experimentalists. This development invited economic theorists to submit to a new discipline, but also brought an important new discipline and new standards of rigour to the data gathering process itself.

An untested theory is simply a hypothesis. As such it is part of our *self*-knowledge. Science seeks to expand our knowledge of *things* by a process of testing this type of self-knowledge. Much of economic theory can be called, appropriately, 'ecclesiastical theory'; it is accepted (or rejected) on the basis of authority, tradition, or opinion about assumptions, rather than on the basis of having survived a rigorous falsification process that can be replicated.

Interest in the replicability of scientific research stems from a desire to answer the question 'Do you see what I see?' Replication and control are the two primary means by which we attempt to reduce the error in our common knowledge of economic processes. However, the question 'Do you see what I see?' contains three component questions, recognition of which helps to identify three different senses in which a research study may fail to be replicable:

(1) *Do you observe what I observe?* Since economics has traditionally been confined to the analysis of non-experimental data, the answer to this question has been trivially, 'yes'. We observe the same thing because we use the same data. This non-replicability of our traditional data sources has helped to motivate some to turn increasingly to experimental methods. We can say that you have replicated my experiments if you are unable to reject the hypothesis that your experimental data came from the same population as mine. This means that the experimenter, his/ her subjects, and/or procedures are not significant treatment variables.

(2) *Do you interpret what we observe as I interpret it?* Given that we both observe the same, or replicable data, do we put the same interpretation on these data? The interpretation of observations requires theory (either formal or informal), or at least an empirical interpretation of the theory in the context that generated the data. Theory usually requires empirical interpretation either because (i) the theory is not developed directly in terms of what can be observed (e.g. the theory may assume risk aversion which is not directly observable), or (ii) the data were not collected for the purpose of testing, or estimating the parameters of a theory. Consequently, failure to replicate may be due to differences in interpretation which result from different meanings being ascribed to the theory. Thus two researchers may apply different transformations to raw field data (e.g. different adjustments for the effect of taxes), so that the results are not replicable because their theory interpretations differ.

(3) *Do you conclude what I conclude from our interpretation?* The conclusions reached in two different research studies may be different even though the data and their

interpretation are the same. In economics this is most often due to different model specifications. This problem is inherent in non-experimental methodologies in which, at best, one usually can estimate only the parameters of a prespecified model and cannot credibly test one model or theory against another. An example is the question of whether the Phillips' curve constitutes a behavioural trade-off between the rates of inflation and unemployment, or represents an equilibrium association without causal significance.

I. Markets and market experiments

Markets and how they function constitute the core of any economic system, whether it is highly decentralized – popularly, a 'capitalistic' system, or highly centralized – popularly, a 'planned' system. This is true for the decentralized economy because markets are the spontaneous institutions of exchange that use prices to guide resource allocation and human economic action. It is true for the centralized economy because in such economies markets always exist or arise in legal form (private agriculture in Russia) and clandestine or illegal form (barter, bribery, the trading of favours, and underground exchange in Russia, Poland and elsewhere). Markets arise spontaneously in all cultures in response to the human desire for betterment (to 'profit') through exchange. Where the commodity or service is illegal (prostitution, gambling, the sale of liquor under Prohibition or of marijuana, cocaine, etc.) the result is not to prevent exchange, but to raise the risk and therefore the costs of exchange. This is because enforcement is itself costly, and it is never economical for the authorities (whether Soviet or American) even to approximate perfect enforcement. The spontaneity with which markets arise is perhaps no better illustrated than when (1979–80) US airlines for promotional purposes issued travel vouchers to their passengers. One of these vouchers could be redeemed by the bearer as a cash substitute in the purchase of new airline tickets. Consequently vouchers were of value to future passengers. Furthermore, since (as Hayek would say) the 'circumstances of time and place' for the potential redemption of vouchers were different for different individuals, there existed the preconditions for the active voucher market that was soon observed in all busy airports. Current passengers with vouchers who were unlikely to be travelling again soon held an asset worth less to themselves than to others who were more certain of their future or impending travel plans. The resulting market established prices that were discounts from the redemption or 'face' value of vouchers. Sellers who were unlikely to be able to redeem their vouchers preferred to sell them at a discount for cash. Buyers who were reasonably sure of their travel plans could save money by purchasing vouchers at a discount. Thus the welfare of every active buyer and seller increased via this market. Without a market, many – perhaps most – vouchers would not have been exercised and would thus have been 'wasted'.

The previous paragraph illustrates a fundamental hypothesis (theorem) of economics: the ('competitive') market process yields welfare improving (and, under certain limiting ideal conditions, welfare maximizing) outcomes. But is the hypothesis 'true', or at least very probably true? (Lakatos (1978) would correctly ask 'Has it led to an empirically progressive research programme?') I think it is 'true', but how do I know this? Do you see what I see? A Marxist does not see what I see in the above interpretation of a market. The young student studying economics does not see what I see, although if they continue to study economics eventually they (predictably) come to see what I see (or, at least, they say they do). Is this because we have inadvertently brainwashed them? The gasoline consumer does not see what I see. They see themselves in a *zero* sum game with an oil company: any increase in price merely redistributes wealth from the consumer to the company, which is not 'fair' since the company is richer. What I see in a market is a *positive* sum game yielding gains from exchange, which constitutes the fundamental mechanism for creating, not merely redistributing wealth. The traditional method by which the economist gets others to see this 'true' function of markets is by logical arguments (suppose it were not true, then …), examples, and 'observations', such as are contained in my description of the voucher market, in which what is 'observed' is hortatively described and interpreted in terms of the hypothesis itself. But if this knowledge of the function of markets is 'true', can it be demonstrated? Experimentalists claim that laboratory experiments can provide a uniquely important technique of demonstration for supplementing the theoretical interpretation of field observations.

I conducted my first experiment in the spring of 1956. Since then hundreds of similar, as well as environmentally richer experiments have been conducted by myself and by others. In 1956, my introductory economics class consisted of 22 science and engineering students, and although this might not have been the 'large number' traditionally thought to have been necessary to yield a competitive market, I though it was large enough for a practice run to initiate a research programme capable of falsifying the standard theory. I conducted the experiment before lecturing on the theory and 'behaviour' of markets in class so as not to 'contaminate' the sample. The 22 subjects were each assigned one card from a well-shuffled deck of 11 white and 11 yellow cards. The white cards identified the sellers, and the yellow cards identified the buyers. Each white card carried a price, known only to that seller, which represented that seller's minimum selling price for one unit, and each yellow card identified a price, known only to that buyer, representing that buyer's maximum buying price for one unit. On the left of Figure 1 is listed these so-called 'limit' prices, identified by buyer, B1, B2 etc. (in descending order, D) and by seller, S1, S2 etc. (in ascending order, S). To keep things simple and well controlled each buyer (seller) was informed that he/she was a buyer (seller) of at most one unit of the item in each of several trading periods. Thus demand, D (supply, S) was 'renewed' in each trading period as a steady state flow, with no carry-over in unsatisfied demand (or unsold stock), from one period to the next. In the airline voucher example, imagine the vouchers being issued, followed by trading; the vouchers then expire, new vouchers are issued, traded and so on. In the experiment, suppose real motivation is provided by promising to pay (in cash) to each buyer the difference between that buyer's assigned limit buying price and the price actually paid in each period that a unit is purchased in the market. Thus

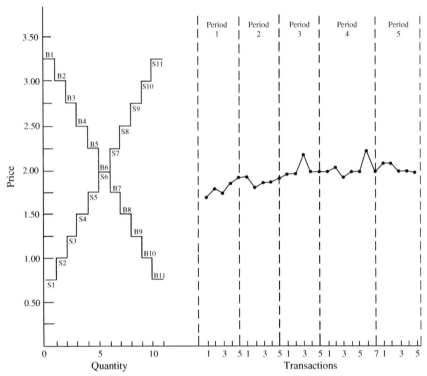

Figure 1

suppose seller 5 sells their unit to buyer 2 at the price 2.25. Then buyer 2 earns a 'profit' of $0.75 from this exchange. In this way we induce on each buyer a value (or hypothesized willingness-to-pay) equal to the assigned limit buy price. Similarly, suppose each seller is paid the difference between that seller's actual sales price and assigned limit price ('cost', or willingness-to-sell) in each trading period that a unit is sold. Thus in the previous exchange example, seller 5 earns $0.50 from the transaction.

This experimental procedure operationalizes the market preconditions that (1) 'the circumstances of time and place' for each economic agent are dispersed and known only to that agent (as in the above voucher market) and (2) agents have a secure property right in the objects of trade and the private gains ('profits') from trade (an airline travel voucher was transferable and redeemable by any bearer). The reader should note that 'profit' is identified as much with the act of buying as with that of selling. This is because 'profit' is the surplus earned by a buyer who buys for less than his willingness-to-pay, just as a seller's 'profit' is the surplus earned when an item is sold for more than the amount for which they are willing to sell. Willingness-to-sell need not have, and usually does not have anything to do with accounting 'cost', or production 'cost', from which one computes accounting profit. Willingness-to-sell, like willingness-to-buy, is determined by the immediate circumstances of each agent. Hence, a passenger might be prepared to pay the regular full fare premium on a first-class ticket for an emergency trip to visit a sick relative. The accountant's concept of profit cannot be applied to the passenger's decision any more than it can be applied to that of a passenger willing to sell a voucher at a deep discount. In what follows I will use the term 'buyer's surplus' or 'seller's surplus' instead of 'profit' to refer to the gains from exchange enjoyed by buyers or sellers because the term 'profit' is so strongly, exclusively and misleadingly associated with selling activities.

Now let us interpret the previously cited fundamental theorem of economics in the context of the experimental design contained in Figure 1. We note first that the ordered set of seller (buyer) limit prices defines a supply (demand) function (Figure 1). A supply (demand) function provides a list of the total quantities that sellers (buyers) would be willing to sell (buy) at corresponding hypothetical fixed prices. Neither of these functions is capable of being observed, scientifically, in the field. This is because the postulated limit prices are inherently private and not publicly observable. We could poll every potential seller (buyer) of vouchers in Chicago's O'Hare airport on 20 December 1979 to get each person's reported limit price, but we would have no way of validating the 'observations' thus obtained. Referring to Figure 1, we see that in my 1956 experiment, sellers (hypothetically) were just willing to sell three units at price 1.25, nine units at 2.75 and so on. Similarly buyers (hypothetically) were just willing to buy four units at 2.50, seven units at 1.75 and so on. If seller 3 is indifferent between selling and not selling at 1.25, and if every seller (buyer) is likewise indifferent at his/her limit price, then any particular unit may not be sold (purchased) at this limit price. One means of dealing with this problem in laboratory markets is to promise to pay a small 'commission', say 5 cents, to each buyer and seller for each unit bought or sold. Thus seller 3 has a small inducement to sell at 1.25 if he can do no better, and buyer 6 has a small inducement to buy at 2.00 if she can do no better.

Economic theory defines the competitive equilibrium as the price and corresponding quantity that clears the market; that is, it sets the quantity that sellers are willing to sell equal to the quantity that buyers are willing to buy. This assumes that the subjective cost of transacting is zero; otherwise any units with limit prices equal to the competitive equilibrium price will not exchange. In Figure 1 this competitive equilibrium price is 2.00. If the 5 cent 'commission' paid to each trading buyer and seller is sufficient to compensate for any subjective cost of transacting, then buyer 6 and seller 6 will each trade and the competitive equilibrium quantity exchanged will be 6 units. At the competitive equilibrium price, buyer 1 earns a surplus of $3.25 - 2.00 = 1.25$ (plus commission) per period and so on. Total surplus, which measures the maximum possible gains from exchange, or maximum wealth *created* by the existence of the market institution, is 7.50 per period, at the competitive equilibrium.

If by some miracle the competitive equilibrium price and exchange quantity were to prevail in this market, sellers 1–6 would sell, buyers 1–6 would buy, while sellers 7–11 would make no sales and buyers 7–11 would make no purchases. It might be thought that this is unfair – the market should permit some or all of the 'submarginal' buyers (sellers) 7–11 to trade – or that more wealth would be created if there were more than six exchanges. But these interpretations are wrong. By definition, buyer 10 is not willing to pay more than 1.00. Consequently, it is a peculiar notion of fairness to argue that buyer 10 should have as much priority as buyer 1 in obtaining a unit. In the airline voucher example, this would mean that a buyer who is unlikely to redeem a voucher should have the same priority as a buyer who is likely to redeem a voucher. One can imagine a market in which, say, buyer 1 is paired with seller 9 at price 3.00, buyer 2 with seller 8 at price 2.75, and so on with nine units traded. If this were to occur it would mean buyers 7–9, who are less likely to use vouchers, have purchased them, and sellers 7–9, who initially held vouchers, and were more likely to use them than buyers 7–9, have sold their vouchers. Furthermore, this allocation yields additional possible gains from exchange, and is thus *not sustainable*, even if it were thought to be desirable. That is, buyer 9, who bought from seller 1 at price 1.00, could resell the unit to seller 9 (who sold her unit to buyer 2), at price (say) 2.00. Why? Because, by definition a voucher is worth 2.75 to seller 9 and only 1.25 to buyer 9. Similar additional trades can be made by buyers (sellers) 7 and 8. The end result would be that buyers 1–6 and sellers 7–11 would be the terminal holders of vouchers, just as if the competitive equilibrium had been reached initially.

Hence, either the competitive equilibrium prevails, or if inefficient trades occur at dispersed prices, then further 'speculative' gains can be made by some buyers and sellers. If these gains are fully captured the end result is the same allocation as would occur at the competitive equilibrium price and quantity.

Having specified the environment (individual private values) of our experimental market, what remains is to specify an exchange institution. In my 1956 experiment I elected to use trading rules similar to those that characterize trading on the organized stock and commodity exchanges. These markets use the 'double oral auction' procedure. In this institution as soon as the market 'opens' any buyer is free to announce a bid to buy and any seller is free to announce an offer to sell. In the experimental version each bid (offer) is for a single unit. Thus a buyer might say 'buy, 1.00', while a seller might say 'sell, 5.00', and it is understood that the buyer bids 1.00 for a unit and the seller offers to sell one unit for 5.00. Bids and offers are freely announced and can be modified. A contract occurs if any seller accepts the bid of any buyer, or any buyer accepts the offer of any seller. In the simple experimental market, since each participant is a buyer or seller of at most one unit per trading period, the contracting buyer and seller drop out of the market for the remainder of the trading period, but return to the market when a new trading 'day' begins. The experimenter announces the close of each trading period and the opening of the subsequent period, with each trading period timed to extend, say, five minutes. Each contract price is plotted on the right of Figure 1 for the five trading periods of the experiment. This result was not as expected. The conventional view among economists was that a competitive equilibrium was like a frictionless ideal state which could not be conceived as actually occurring, even approximately. It could be conceived of occurring only in the presence of an abstract 'institution' such as a Walrasian *tâtonnement* or an Edgeworth recontracting procedure. It was for teaching, not believing.

From Figure 1 it is evident that in the strict sense the competitive equilibrium was not attained in any period, but the accuracy of the competitive equilibrium theory is easily comparable to that of countless physical processes. Certainly, the data clearly do not support the monopoly, or seller collusion model. The total return to sellers is maximized when four units are sold at price 2.50. Similarly, the monopsony, or buyer collusion model requires four units to exchange at price 1.50.

Since 1956, several hundred experiments using different supply and demand conditions, experienced as well as inexperienced subjects, buyers and sellers with multiple unit trading capacity, a great variation in the numbers of buyers and sellers, and different trading institutions, have established the replicability and robustness of these results. For many years at the University of Arizona and Indiana University we have been using various computerized (the PLATO system) versions of the double 'oral' auction, developed by Arlington Williams, in which participating subjects trade with each other through computer terminals. These experiments establish that the 1956 results are robust with respect to substantial reductions in the number of buyers and sellers. Most such experiments use only four buyers and four sellers, each capable of trading several units. Some have used only two sellers, yet the competitive equilibrium model performs very well under double auction rules. Figure 2 shows the supply and demand design and the market results for a typical experiment in which subjects trade through PLATO computer terminals under computer-monitored double auction rules.

In addition to its antiquarian value, Figure 1 illustrates the problem of monitoring the rules of a 'manual' experiment. Observe that in period 4 there were seven contracts which are recorded as occurring in the price range between $1.90 and $2.25. This is not possible since there are only six buyers with limit buy prices above $1.90. Either a buyer violated his budget constraint, or the experimenter erred in recording a price in his first experiment. In Figure 2 there is plotted each contract (an accepted bid if the contract line passes through a 'dot'; an accepted offer if the line passes through a 'circle') and the bids ('dots') and offers ('circles') that preceded each accepted bid or offer. One of the several advantages of computerized experimental markets is that the complete data of the market (all bids, offers, and contracts at their time of execution) are recorded accurately and non-invasively, and all experimental rules are enforced perfectly. In particular the violation of a budget constraint revealed in Figure 1, which is a perpetual problem with manually executed experiments, is not a problem when trading is perfectly computer monitored.

The rapid convergence shown in Figures 1 and 2 has not always extended to trading institutions other than the double auction. For example, the 'posted offer' pricing mechanism (associated with most retail markets), in which sellers post take it or leave it non-negotiable prices at the beginning of each period, yields higher prices and less efficient allocations than the double auction. This difference in performance becomes smaller with experienced subjects and with longer trading sequences in a given

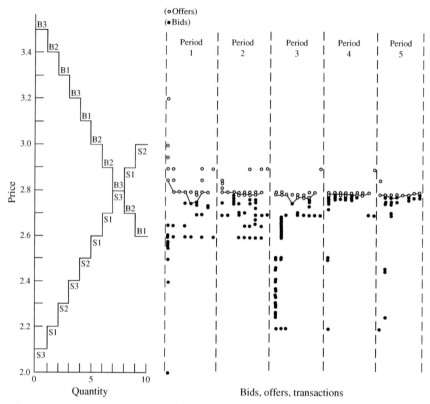

Figure 2

experiment (Ketcham et al., 1984). Similarly, a comparison of double auction with a sealed bid-offer auction finds the latter to be less efficient and to deviate more from the competitive equilibrium predictions (Smith et al., 1982). Thus, institutions have been demonstrated to make a difference in what we observe. The data and analysis strongly suggest that institutions make a difference because the rules (legal environment) make a difference, and the rules make a difference because they affect individual incentives.

II. Brief interpretive history of the development of experimental economics

The two most influential early experimental studies represent the two most primary poles of experimental economics: the study of individual preference (choice) under uncertainty (Mosteller and Nogee, 1951) and of market behaviour (Chamberlin, 1948). The investigation of uncertainty and preference has focused on the testing of von Neumann–Morgenstern–Savage subjective expected utility theory. Battalio, Kagel and others have pioneered in the testing of the Slutsky–Hicks commodity demand and labour supply preferences using humans (1973) and animals (1975). A series of large-scale field experiments in the 1970s extended the experimental study of individual preference to the measurement of the effect of the negative income tax and other factors on labour supply and to the measurement of the demand for electricity, housing and medical services.

Since the human species has been observed to participate in market exchange for thousands of years, the experimental study of market behaviour is central to economics. Preferences are not directly observable, but preference theory, as an abstract construct, has been *postulated* by economists to be fundamental to the explanation and understanding of market behaviour. In this sense the experimental study of group market behaviour depends upon the study of individual preference behaviour. But this intellectual history should not obscure the fact that the study of markets and the study of preferences need not be construed as inseparable. Adam Smith clearly viewed the human 'propensity to truck, barter and exchange' (and *not* the existence of human preferences) as axiomatic to the scientific study of economic behaviour. Obversely, the work of Battalio and Kagel showing that animals behave as if they had Slutsky–Hicks preferences makes it plain that substitution behaviour is an important cross species characteristic, but that such phenomena need not be associated with market exchange.

A significant feature of Chamberlin's (1948) original work is that it concerned the study of behaviourally complete markets; that is all trades, including purchases as well as sales, were executed by active subject agents. This feature has continued in the subsequent bilateral bargaining experiments of Siegel and Fouraker (1960) and in market experiments (Smith, 1962, 1982; Williams and Smith, 1984) such as those discussed in section I. This feature was not present in the early and subsequent experimental oligopoly literature (Hoggatt, 1959; Sauermann and Selten, 1959; Shubik, 1962; Friedman, 1963), in which the demand behaviour of buyers was simulated, that is, programmed from a specified demand function conditional on the prices selected in each 'trading' period by the sellers. This simulation of demand behaviour is justified as an intermediate step in testing models of seller price behaviour that assume passive, simple maximizing, demand-revelation behaviour by buyers. But the conclusions of such experimental studies should not be assumed to be applicable, even provisionally, to any observed complete market without first showing that the experimental results are robust with respect to the substitution of subject buyers for simulated buyers.

III. The functions of market experiments in microeconomic analysis

A conceptual framework for clarifying some uses and functions of experiments in microeconomics can be articulated by suitable modification and adaptation (Smith, 1982) of the concepts underlying the adjustment process, as in the welfare economics literature (see references to Hurwicz and Reiter in Smith, 1982). In this literature a microeconomic environment consists of a list of agents $\{1, \ldots, N\}$, a list of commodities and resources $\{1, \ldots, K\}$, and certain characteristics of each agent i, such as the agent's preferences (utility) u_i, technological (knowledge) endowment T^i, and commodity endowment w_i. Thus agent i is defined by the triplet of characteristics $E^i = (u^i, T^i, w^i)$ defined on the K-dimensional commodity space. A microeconomic *environment* is defined by the collection $E = (E^1, \ldots, E^N)$ of these characteristics. This collection represents a set of primitive circumstances that condition agents' interaction through institutions. The superscript i, besides identifying a particular agent, also means that these primitive circumstances are in their *nature* private: it is the individual who likes, works, knows and makes.

There can be no such thing as a credible institution-free economics. Institutions define the property right rules by which agents communicate and exchange or transform commodities within the limits and opportunities inherent in the environment, E. Since markets require communication to effect exchange, property rights in messages are as important as property rights in goods and ideas. An institution specifies a language, $M = (M^1, \ldots, M^N)$, consisting of message elements $m = (m^1, \ldots, m^N)$, where M^i is the set of messages that can be sent by agent i (for example, the range of bids that can be sent by a buyer). An institution also defines a set of allocation rules $h = (h^1(m), \ldots, h^N(m))$ and a set of cost imputation rules $c = (c^1(m), \ldots, c^N(m))$, where h^i(m) is the commodity allocation to agent i and $c^i(m)$ is the payment to be made by i, each as a function of the messages sent by all agents. Finally, the institution defines a set of adjustment process rules (assumed to be common to all agents), $g(t_0, t, T)$, consisting of a starting rule, $g(t_0, \cdot, \cdot)$, a transition rule, $g(\cdot, t, \cdot)$, governing the sequencing of messages, and a stopping rule, $g(\cdot, \cdot, T)$, which terminates the exchange of messages and triggers the allocation and cost imputation rules. Each agent's property rights in communication and exchange is thus defined by $I^i = (M^i, h^i(m), c^i(m), g(t_0, t, T))$. A microeconomic *institution* is defined by the collection of these individual property right characteristics, $I = (I^1, \ldots, I^N)$.

A microeconomic *system* is defined by the conjunction of an environment and an institution, $S = (E, I)$. To illustrate a microeconomic system, consider an auction for a single indivisible object such as a painting or an antique vase. Let each of N agents place an independent, certain, monetary value on the item $v_1, \ldots, v_N$, with agent i knowing his own value, v_i, but having only uncertain (probability distribution) information on the values of others. Thus $E^i = (v^i; P(v), N)$. If the exchange institution is the 'first price' sealed-bid auction, the rules are that all N bidders each submit a single bid any time between the announcement of the auction offering at t_0, and the closing of bids, at T. The item is then awarded to the maker of the highest bid at a price equal to the amount bid. Thus, if the agents are numbered in descending order of the bids, the first price auction institution $I_1 = I_1^1 = [h^1(m) = 1, c^1(m) = b_1]$ and $I_1^i = [h^i(m) = 0, c^i(m) = 0]$, $i > 1$, where $m = (b_1, \ldots, b_N)$ consists of all bids tendered. That is, the item is awarded to the high bidder, $i = 1$, who pays b_1, and all others receive and pay nothing. This contrasts with the 'second price' sealed-bid auction $I_2 = (I_2^1, \ldots, I_2^N)$ in which $I_2^1 = [h^1(m) = 1, c^1(m) = b_2]$ and $I_2^i = [h^i(m) = 0, c^i(m) = 0]$, $i > 1$; that is, the highest bidder receives the allocation but pays a price equal to the second highest bid submitted.

Another example is the English or progressive oral auction, whose rules are discussed under the entry AUCTIONS (EXPERIMENTS). It should be noted that the 'double oral' auction, used extensively in stock and commodity trading and in the two experimental markets discussed in section I, is a two-sided generalization of the English auction.

A microeconomic system is activated by the behavioural choices of agents in the set M. In the static, or final outcome, description of an economy, agent *behaviour* can be defined as a function (or correspondence) $m^i = \beta^i(E^i|I)$ carrying the characteristics E^i of agent i into a message m^i, conditional upon the property right specifications of the operant institution I. If all exchange-relevant agent characteristics are included in E^i, then $\beta \equiv \beta^i$ for all i. Given the message-sending behaviour of each agent, $\beta(E|I)$, the institution determines the outcomes

$$h^i(m) = h^i[\beta(E^1|I), \ldots, \beta(E^N|I)]$$

and

$$c^i(m) = c^i[\beta(E^1|I), \ldots, \beta(E^N|I)].$$

Within this framework we see that agents do not choose allocations directly; agents choose messages with institutions determining allocations under the rules that carry messages into allocations. (You cannot choose to 'buy' an auctioned item; you can only choose to raise the standing bid at an English auction or submit a particular bid in a sealed bid auction.) However, the allocation and cost imputation rules may have important incentive effects on behaviour, and therefore messages will in general depend on these rules. Hence, market outcomes will result from the conjunction of institutions' and agents' behaviour.

A proper theory of agents' behaviour allows one to deduce a particular β function based on assumptions about the agent's environment and the institution, and his motivation to act. Auction theory is perhaps the only part of economic theory that is fully institution specific. For example, in the second price sealed bid auction it is a dominant strategy for each agent simply to bid his or her value; that is

$$b^i = \beta(E^i|I_2) = \beta(v_i|I_2) = v_i, \quad i = 1, \ldots, N.$$

The resulting outcome is that $b_1 = v_1$ is the winning bid and agent 1 pays the price v_2. Similarly, in the English auction, agent 1 will eventually exclude agent 2 by raising the standing bid to v_2 (or somewhat above), and obtain the item at this price. In the first price auction Vickrey proved that if each agent maximizes expected surplus ($v_i - b_i$) in an environment with $P(v) = v$ (the v_i are drawn from a constant density on $[0, 1]$), then we can deduce the noncooperative equilibrium bid function, $b_i = \beta(E^i|I_1) = \beta[v_i; P(v), N|I_1] = (N - 1)v_i/N$ (see the entry on AUCTIONS (EXPERIMENTS) for a more complete discussion).

With the above framework it is possible to explicate the roles of theory and experiment, and their relationship, in a progressive research programme (Lakatos, 1978) of economic analysis. But to do this we must first ask two questions:

(1) 'Which of the elements of a microeconomic system are not observable?' The nonobservable elements are (i) preferences, (ii) knowledge endowments, and (iii) agent message behaviour, $\beta(E^i|I)$. Even if messages are available and recorded, we still cannot observe message behaviour functions because we cannot observe, or vary, preferences. The best we can do with field observations of outcomes is to interpret them in terms of models based on assumptions about preferences (Cobb-Douglas, constant elasticity of substitution, homothetic), knowledge (complete, incomplete, common), and behaviour (cooperative, noncooperative). Any 'tests' of such models must necessarily be joint tests of all of these unobservable elements. More often the econometric exercise is parameter estimation, which is conditional upon these same elements.

(2) 'What would we like to know?' We would like to know enough about how agents' behaviour is affected by alternative environments and institutions so that we can classify them according to the mapping they provide into outcomes. Do some institutions yield Pareto optimal outcomes, and/or stable prices, and, if so, are the results robust with respect to alternative environments?

These two questions together tell us that what we want to know is inaccessible in natural experiments (field data) because key elements of the equation are unobservable and/or cannot be controlled. If laboratory experiments are to help us learn what we want to know, certain precepts that constitute proposed sufficient conditions for a valid controlled microeconomic experiment must be satisfied:

(1) *Non-satiation* (or monotonicity of reward). Subject agents strictly prefer any increase in the reward medium, π; that is $U_i(\pi_i)$ is monotone increasing for all *i*.

(2) *Saliency*. Agents have the unqualified right to claim rewards that increase (decrease) in the good (bad) outcomes, x_i, in an experiment; the institution of an experiment renders these rewards salient by defining outcomes in terms of the message choices of agents. In both the field and the laboratory it is the institution that induces value on messages, given each agent's (subjective) value of commodity outcomes.

In the laboratory we use a monetary reward function to induce utility value on the abstract accounting outcomes ('commodities') of an experiment. Thus, agent *i* is given a concave schedule, $V_i(x_i)$, defining the 'redemption value' in dollars for x_i units purchased in an experimental market, and is assured of receiving a net payment equal to $V_i(x_i)$ less the purchase prices of the x_i units in the market. If the x_i units are all purchased at price *p* (which is the assumption used to derive a hypothetical demand schedule) the agent is paid $\pi_i = V_i(x_i) - px_i$, with utility $u^i(x_i) = U_i(\pi_i(x_i))$. In defining demand it is assumed that the agent directly chooses x_i (that is $x_i = m_i$). Therefore, if *i* maximizes $u^i(x_i) = U_i[V_i(x_i) - px_i]$, then at a maximum we have $U_i'[V_i'(x_i) - p] = 0$, giving the demand function $x_i = V_i'^{(-1)}(p)$ if $U_i' > 0$, where $V_i'^{(-1)}$ is the inverse of *i*'s marginal redemption value of x_i units. (The same procedure for a seller using a cost function $C_j(x_j)$ and paying $px_j - C_j(x_j)$ allows one to induce a marginal cost supply of *j*.) This illustration generalizes easily: if the joint redemption value is $V_i(x_i, y_i)$ for two abstract commodities (x_i, y_i), $u^i = U_i[V^i(x_i, y_i)]$ induces an indifference map given by the level curves of $V^i(x_i, y_i)$, on (x_i, y_i), with marginal rate of substitution $U'_i V^i_x / U'_i V^i_y = V^i_x / V^i_y$, if $U'_i > 0$. If $V^i(x_i, X)$ the reward function, with x_i a private and X a common (public) outcome good, we are able to control preferences in the study of public good allocation mechanisms, or if

$$X = \sum_{i=1}^{N} x_i$$

we are poised to study allocation with an 'atmospheric' externality (Coursey and Smith, 1985).

The first two precepts are sufficient to allow us to assert that we have created a microeconomic sysem $S = (E, I)$ in the laboratory. But to assure that we have created a controlled microeconomy, we need two additional precepts:

(3) *Dominance.* Own rewards dominate any subjective costs of transacting (or other motivation) in the experimental market.

   As with any person, subject agents may have variables other than money in their utility functions. In particular, if there is cognitive and kinesthetic (observe the traders on a Stock Exchange floor) disutility associated with the message-transaction process of the institution, then utility might be better written $U_i(\pi_i, m^i)$. To the extent that this is so we induce a smaller demand on i with the payoff $V_i(x_i)$ than was computed above, and we lose control over preferences. As a practical matter experimentalists think the problem can usually be finessed by using rewards that are large relative to the complexity of the task, and by adopting experimental procedures that reduce complexity (e.g. using the computer to record decisions, perform needed calculations, provide perfect recall, etc.). Another approach, as noted in Section I, is to pay a small commission for each trade to compensate for the subjective transaction costs.

(4) *Privacy.* The subjects in an experiment each receive information only on his/her own reward schedule.

   This precept is used to provide control over interpersonal utilities (payoff externalities). Real people may experience negative or positive utilities from the rewards of others, and to the extent that this occurs we lose control over induced demand, supply and preference functions. Remember that the reward functions have the same role in an experiment that preference functions have in the economy, and the latter preferences are private and non-observable.

If our interest is confined to testing hypotheses from theory, we are done. Precepts (1)–(4) are sufficient to provide rigorous tests of the theorist's ability to model individual and market behaviour. But one naturally asks if replicable results from the laboratory are transferable to field environments. This requires:

(5) *Parallelism.* Propositions about behaviour and/or the performance of institutions that have been tested in one microeconomy (laboratory or field) apply also to

other microeconomies (laboratory or field) where similar *ceteris paribus* conditions hold.

Astronomy, meteorology, biology and other sciences use the maintained hypothesis that the same physical laws hold everywhere. Economics postulates that when the environment and institution are the same, behaviour will be the same; that is, behaviour is determined by a relatively austere subset of life's parameters. Whether this is 'true' is an empirical question. Hence, when one experimentalist studies variations on the treatment variables of another it is customary to replicate the earlier work to check parallelism. Similarly, one must design field experiments, or devise econometric models using non-experimental field data, that provide tests of the transferability of experimental results to any particular market in the field. Only in this way can questions of parallelism be answered. They are not answered with speculations about alleged differences between the experimental subject's behaviour and (undefined) 'real world' behaviour. The experimental laboratory *is* a real world, with real people, real institutions, real payoffs and commodities just as real as stock certificates and airline travel vouchers, both of which have utility because of the claim rights they legally bestow on the bearer.

IV. Classifying the application of experimental methods

There are many types of experiments and many fields of economic study to which experimental methods have been applied.

The experimental study of auctions makes the most extensive use of models of individual behaviour based explicitly on the message requirements of the different institutions. This literature provides test comparisons of predicted behaviour, $\hat{m}^i = \beta^i(E_i|I)$, with observations on individual choice, $\hat{m}^i = \beta^i(\hat{E}^i|I)$ for given realizations, $\hat{E}^i$ (such as values, $\hat{v}_i$, where they are assigned at random). The large literature on experimental double auctions makes no such individual comparisons, because the theoretical literature had not yielded tractable models of individual bid-offer behaviour (but recent contributions by Friedman (1984), and Wilson (1984) are providing such models). Here as in most other areas of experimental research the comparisons are between the predicted price–quantity outcomes of static theory (such as competitive, monopoly, and Cournot models), and observed outcomes. But double auctions have been studied (see references in Smith, 1982) in a variety of environments; for example, the effect of price floors and ceilings have been examined (see references in Plott, 1982). In all cases these studies are making comparisons. In *nomotheoretical* experiments one compares theory and observation, whereas in *nomoempirical* experiments one compares the effect of different institutions and/or environments as a means of documenting replicable empirical 'laws' that may stimulate modelling energy in new directions. The idea that formal theory must precede meaningful observation does not account for most of the historical development of science. *Heuristic* or exploratory experiments that provide empirical probes of new topics and new experimental methods should not be discouraged.

In industrial organization, and antitrust economics, experimental methods have been applied to examine the effects of monopoly, conspiracy, and alleged anticompetitive practices, and to study the concept of natural monopoly and its relation to scale economics, entry cost and the contestable markets hypothesis (see references in Plott, 1982; Smith, 1982; Coursey et al., 1984).

An important development in the experimental study of allocation processes has been the extension of experimental market methods to majority rule (and other) committee processes, and to market-like group processes for the provision of goods which have public or common outcome characteristics (loosely, public goods). These studies have examined public good allocation under majority (and Roberts') rules for committee including the effect of the agenda (see the references to Fiorina and Plott, and Levine and Plott in Smith, 1982), and under compensated unanimity processes suggested by theorists (see the references in Coursey and Smith, 1985). Generally, this literature reports substantial experimental support for the theory of majority rule outcomes, the theory of agenda processes (the sequencing of issues for voting decisions), and for incentive compatible models of the provision of public goods.

VERNON L. SMITH

See also **preference reversals.**

Bibliography

Battalio, R., Kagel, J., Winkler, R., Fisher, E., Basmann, R. and Krasner, L. 1973. A test of consumer demand theory using observations of individual consumer purchases. *Western Economic Journal* 11, 411–28.

Chamberlin, E. 1948. An experimental imperfect market. *Journal of Political Economy* 56, 95–108.

Coursey, D., Isaac, M., Luke, M. and Smith, V. 1984. Market contestability in the presence of sunk (entry) costs. *RAND Journal of Economics* 15(1), 69–84.

Coursey, D. and Smith, V. 1985. Experimental tests of an allocation mechanism for private, public or externality goods. *Scandinavian Journal of Economics* 86, 468–84.

Friedman, D. 1984. On the efficiency of experimental double auction markets. *American Economic Review* 74, 60–72.

Friedman, J. 1963. Individual behavior in oligopolistic markets: an experimental study. *Yale Economic Essays* 3, 359–417.

Hoggatt, A. 1959. An experimental business game. *Behavioral Science* 4(3), 192–203.

Kagel, J., Battalio, R., Rachlin, H., Green, L., Basmann, R. and Klemm, W. 1975. Experimental studies of consumer behavior using laboratory animals. *Economic Inquiry* 13(1), 22–38.

Ketcham, J., Smith, V. and Williams, A. 1984. A comparison of posted-offer and double-auction pricing institutions. *Review of Economic Studies* 51, 595–614.

Lakatos, I. 1978. *The Methodology of Scientific Research Programmes, Philosophical Papers*, vol. 1, ed. J. Worrall and G. Currie. Cambridge: Cambridge University Press.

Mosteller, F. and Nogee, P. 1951. An experimental measurement of utility. *Journal of Political Economy* 59, 371–404.

Plott, C. 1982. Industrial organization theory and experimental economics. *Journal of Economic Literature* 20, 1485–527.

Sauermann, H. and Selten, R. 1959. Ein Oligopolexperiment. *Zeitschrift für die Gesamte Staatswissenschaft* 115, 427–71.

Shubik, M. 1962. Some experimental non zero sum games with lack of information about the rules. *Management Science* 81, 215–34.

Siegel, S. and Fouraker, L. 1960. *Bargaining and Group Decision Making.* New York: McGraw-Hill.

Smith, V. 1962. An experimental study of competitive market behavior. *Journal of Political Economy* 70, 111–37.

Smith, V. 1982. Microeconomic systems as experimental science. *American Economic Review* 72, 923–55.

Smith, V., Williams A., Bratton, K. and Vannoni, M. 1982. Competitive market institutions: double auctions versus sealed bid-offer auctions. *American Economic Review* 72, 58–77.

Williams, A. and Smith, V. 1984. Cyclical double-auction markets with and without speculators. *Journal of Business* 57(1) Pt 1, 1–33.

Wilson, R. 1984. Multilateral exchange. Working Paper No. 7, Stanford University, August.

experimental methods in environmental economics

Environmental policy is designed within the confluence of markets, missing markets, and no markets. Within this mixture, economists offer working rules to help make outcomes more efficient, usually based on ideas formed by rational choice theory. The rules ask decision-makers to compare benefits in relation to costs, to account for the risks and gains across time and space for winners and losers, to facilitate the movement of resources from low-value uses to high-value uses, and to equate incremental gains per cost across policy actions. The environmental economic challenge is to find effective decision rules that will help move an economy towards efficient resource allocation in the face of market failure, for example, externalities, non-rival consumption, non-excludable net benefits, nonconvexities and asymmetric information (see Hanley, Shogren and White, 2007).

Experimental methods have proven to be a useful tool in addressing this challenge. Environmental economists used experimental methods relatively early on, following the lead of Vernon Smith, Charles Plott and other pioneers. Experimental methods began to take hold in the 1980s, primarily in the area of non-market valuation (see Bohm, 1972; Bennett, 1983; Knetsch and Sinden, 1984; Coursey, Hovis and Schulze, 1987). Today, experimental economic research is commonplace in environmental economic discussions and research programmes, with data being generated both in the laboratory and field (see for example the research in Cherry, Kroll and Shogren, 2007). Experiments in this area can be grouped broadly into two categories, *institutional* and *valuation*. Institutional experiments test-bed new institutions such as marketable pollution permits and ambient non-point pollution taxes prior to implementation; valuation experiments use the laboratory or field to study how people value goods and services that are not otherwise bought and sold in markets.

Institutional experiments build on traditional designs to test the efficiency of alternative exchange mechanisms under different economic circumstances. Usually the institutions under examination are those theoretically argued to correct for some market failure. Benefits and costs in these institutional experiments are *induced* by the experimenter – buyers have pre-assigned resale values; sellers have designated induced costs; and the goal is to measure the efficiency of a set of alternative incentive schemes.

In contrast, valuation experiments flip the institutional experiment on its head, using experimental methods to elicit preferences for some particular private or public good given alternative market and non-market circumstances. Here eliciting *homegrown* preferences or values – those residing within the minds of people – is of ultimate interest. Research in value elicitation has been environmental economics' most unique contribution to experimental economics. The work has produced insight into how the framing of a question affects values, how different demand-revealing incentives elicit different values, and how unintentional cues affect a person's value for a good. Consider now a few examples of institutional and valuation experiments used in environmental economics.

Institutional experiments

Institutional experiments focus on evaluating market and non-market solutions to environmental problems. The key to these institutional experiments rests in the dialogue between the laboratory and potential or actual applications to environmental policy. For decades, environmental policy around the globe has been proposed and implemented in the real world with minimal input from insight gathered using experimental economics methods. Today, however, this is changing. Researchers are now using experiments to help understand and affect policy development, and this link between the laboratory and policy is probably more rigorously explored in environmental economics than any other area (Bohm, 2003).

Institutional environmental economic experiments can be categorized as three broad areas – institutions to provide incentives to control externality problems that arise from pollution or land use; institutions to increase the voluntary provision of public goods, such as climate change, or to manage effectively common property, such as fishing zones; and institutions designed to manage resources through negotiation and cooperation, that is, the Coase theorem. We now briefly consider each in turn, starting with early work, moving to current applications, and general principles.

First, experiments examining economic solutions to externality problems began in earnest with Plott's (1983) work on Pigovian taxation. Plott designed a competitive market of buyers and sellers who trade a valuable good. After first establishing that traders ignored negative social costs in a competitive market, he explored whether Pigovian taxes or tradable permits could equate private incentives with social costs. Both increased efficiency with repeated trading periods and quickly hit 100 per cent efficiency. Since then there has been an explosion of work examining incentive systems in a variety of settings, producing a growing and positive dialogue between policy proposals and insight from experimental studies.

Probably the most active area today remains the experimental work that tests the efficiency of tradable permit systems. Experimental methods have evaluated the efficacy of different trading rules in a variety of settings (for example, Bohm and Carlén, 1999). An important early example is the US Environmental Protection Agency's Acid Rain emission trading. This work revealed a basic flaw in the original design of the permit auction run by the Environmental Protection Agency (EPA) (see Cason, 1995; Cason and Plott, 1996). The laboratory results revealed how the EPA could increase the efficiency of the auction by changing how permits were allocated. Originally, buyers and sellers submitted bids and offers for emission permits, and the EPA set the market price discriminatively off the demand curve by first matching the seller with the lowest offer to the buyer with the highest bid. The matching then continued with the second lowest offer to the second highest bid, and so on, until the equilibrium quantity is reached. Rational sellers should see through this auction, and begin capturing rents by understating their true offer so they would be matched with a high bidder. Cason's laboratory results confirmed this intuition – sellers undercut each other to get into the high end of the market. The end result was an inefficient auction. Such lessons can be profitable, but insight like this should be made available before the regulatory tool is already in place, thus avoiding wasting resources due to inefficient design features. (For another important example comparing alternative trading institutions, see the tests of the RECLAIM market for the Los Angeles Basin by Ishikida et al., 2000).

Land conservation is a second area in which experimentally informed market designs have improved policy implementation. The Bush Tender auctions were designed to conserve land in Australia by creating a market where landowners bid to set aside specific units of land. Cason and Gangadharan (2004) examine how information about environmental benefits and a market clearing auction mechanism affect efficiency. Their results reveal an interesting pattern: people who did not know the environmental benefits provided by their private land were less likely to bid strategically in a conservation auction. Private ignorance reduces public expenditures. Based on this they suggest a provocative policy – a regulator might restrict the biological information publicly provided to landowners prior to running the auction. Another example of test-bedding is Parkhurst et al.'s (2002) agglomeration-bonus and smart-subsidy coordination game experiments, which illustrate an incentive scheme that can induce private landowners to create contiguous protected areas voluntarily. They compare a *smart subsidy* proposal, which creates an explicit link between neighbouring landowners with adjacent parcels, in relation to two standard policy options, compulsion and a standard fixed-fee subsidy. Their results show that a no-bonus mechanism always created fragmented habitat, whereas with the bonus, players found the first-best habitat reserve.

Second, environmental policy has long confronted the inherent efficiency issues associated with public goods and common property resources. These experimental games capture the elemental economic problem that drives many environmental goods: non-rival and non-exclusive consumption lead to free riding and inefficient production levels. Experimental evidence reveals neither complete free riding nor full cooperation (Ledyard, 1995). As noted by Ostrom (2000), three types of people commonly inhabit public-good and common-property experiments: the standard rational egoists, the conditional cooperators, and the willing punishers. Conditional cooperators cooperate when they expect others to reciprocate; otherwise they do not. Within the standard game (see PUBLIC GOODS EXPERIMENTS) rules can be manipulated to induce more or less cooperation depending on the mix of subject types, marginal payoffs, group size, communication, and voting with third-party enforcement.

For global environmental goods like climate change, a key policy issue is the impact on efficiency when a collective agreement has costly third-party enforcement. Punishment of free riders is a second-order public good; cooperation means bearing some private cost to sanction others. One relevant policy question is whether an institution based on a voting rule with a punishment mechanism can work to increase contributions to a public good. Kroll, Cherry and Shogren (2007) examined this in the laboratory and observed that voting alone does not increase cooperation; rather, if voters can pay to punish violators, contributions increase significantly. Overall efficiency for a voting-with-punishment rule exceeds the level observed for a voting-without-punishment rule. This result has implications for how policymakers think about institutions such as International Environmental Agreements (IEA), which are more likely to be successful if one nation is willing to act like the 'global police', and pay the costs of punishing violators (Barrett, 2003).

Another real-world policy issue is whether policymakers can use economic incentive devices in real-world applications to reveal public good demand (Bohm, 1972). Any proposed system has to 'work' – to provide the good when benefits exceed the provision costs – and has to be straightforward enough to be implemented in the field, characteristics that can be tested in the laboratory. One such mechanism is the *provision point* mechanism: if contributions meet or exceed a targeted provision cost, the public good is supplied to the group; otherwise, it is not. In a design that mimics field conditions, Rondeau, Schulze and Poe (1999) explored a mechanism in which contributions are returned if costs were not met. Their results suggest the provision point mechanism was 'demand revealing in aggregate' for a large group with heterogeneous preferences, suggesting that a relatively simple mechanism could be used in the field to elicit preferences, leading to the efficient provision of a public good.

Third, many observers and policymakers see place-based collaboration and bargaining as the future of environmental policy – arguing for more local control through negotiation and accountability (for example, Sabel, Fung and Karkkainen, 2000). Collaborative decision-making groups have begun to flourish in rural settings such as the western United States, and now number in the hundreds, ranging from informal grass-roots gatherings to government-mandated advisory councils. To an economist, this is the direct application of the Coase theorem – parties in dispute negotiating on a jointly acceptable agreement over resource use. Starting with Hoffman and Spitzer (1982), researchers have used experimental methods to test the robustness of collaborative decision-making underlying the Coase theorem. Hoffman and Spitzer's initial results supported the Coase theorem in that bargains were highly efficient. Harrison and McKee (1985) confirmed that Coasean bargaining under unilateral and joint property rights regimes can be efficient. Both experiments assumed the transaction costs of bargaining were zero. Recent experimental work has explored how bargaining efficiency is affected by positive transaction costs and addition friction due to large numbers of bargainers, property right insecurity, delay costs, imperfect contract enforcement, asymmetric information, and uncertain final authority. The lesson from over two decades of Coase bargaining research is that people have to address the nature of transaction costs and friction.

We illustrate using Rhoads and Shogren's (2003) policy-driven Coasean bargaining experiment. Experts see two elements of consensus-based environmental protection as crucial for effective regulatory outcomes: *final authority*, so that a collaborative agreement is binding; and *information symmetry*, in which bargainers create a common information pool about player payoffs. Their results are consistent with the findings of the experts: final authority and information symmetry were necessary conditions for efficient Coasean bargaining. Without final authority, efficiency falls by two-thirds, and falls further with asymmetric information. If the policy objective is to make a negotiated agreement efficient, the policy challenge is to understand the trade-offs associated with granting or denying final authority to the local bargainers.

In summary, the general principle in institutional environmental economics experiments that has emerged over the years is that the germ of a good idea can be codified into a bad one if the rules of implementation trigger unintended incentives that undercut the efficiency of the system. Experimental methods can be used to reveal which good ideas are actually beneficial to control externalities, provide public goods, and facilitate collaboration – and which ideas are ultimately counterproductive.

Valuation experiments

Economists also use experimental methods to understand better the behavioural underpinnings of environmental valuation. Experiments can be used to address incentive and contextual questions that arise in assessing values through direct statements of preferences. Three general areas have emerged: rational valuation, direct elicitation of values, and exploring the effectiveness of hypothetical non-market valuation surveys (see Shogren, 2006).

First, economists assume people can provide rational statements of their preferences and values towards the environment. Rather than assume that people make rational choices and reveal consistent values for environmental protection, environmental economists use experiments to examine whether people's choices and stated values meet these criteria. Enough evidence of behavioural anomalies now exists to undercut this presumption (Kahneman and Tversky, 2000). Without an exchange institution to arbitrage his or her irrational choices, the unsocialized person can engage in behaviours inconsistent with rational choice theory (see Akerlof, 1997).

The key behavioural regularity that potentially undercuts all valuation work is the WTP–WTA gap. Rational choice theory suggests that with small income effects and many available substitutes, the willingness to pay (WTP) for a commodity and the willingness to accept (WTA) compensation to sell the same commodity should be about equal. But evidence suggests that WTA exceeds WTP by up to tenfold. The experimental WTP–WTA work can be divided into two camps: research that suggests the gap is based on a psychological *endowment effect* and that which points to weak market institutions. A person who assigns greater value to a good he or she already owns exhibits the endowment effect, which leads to higher WTA to sell the good than WTP to buy the identical good (Kahneman, Knetsch and Thaler, 1990). The market experience explanation says that people have naive expectations about what they can sell the good for outside an active market place. This experimental work showed that market-like experience can remove the gap (see Shogren et al., 1994; 2001).

Second, valuation experiments are used to measure actual values for public and private goods (Lusk and Shogren, 2007). Direct valuation experiments are designed so that people buy and sell actual goods to elicit real values, in which researchers test how alternative exchange institutions affect these values. They entail real payments and binding budget constraints, and use auctions to sell goods for money, albeit within a stylized setting. Experimental designs are used to understand the balance between laboratory control and natural context, enabling researchers to learn things about behaviour that would have been impossible to discover from alternative tools. Subtle changes in experimental procedure affect behaviour, such as paying people before as opposed to after bidding, reporting the market-clearing price, and the novelty of the good.

Third, in the 1980s, Coursey and Schulze (1986) hoped the laboratory would be used more to test-bed field surveys. Today, in 2007, experiments are commonly employed to address problems in stated preference surveys such as hypothetical bias, calibration, surrogate bidding, and incentive compatibility. For instance, experiments have revealed time and again that *hypothetical bias* is real – people frequently promise more than they actually deliver. Experimental work has focused on trying to measure the degree of bias and what methods can be used to eliminate or reduce it in survey work. A good example is Cummings and Taylor (1999) who find that they can remove the hypothetical bias by telling a respondent about it.

In summary, choices and economic values emerge in the social context of an active exchange institution, and thus the measurement of value should not be separated from the interactive experience provided by an exchange institution. Institutions and the institutional context matter because experience can make rational choice more transparent to a person. Institutions also dictate the rules under which exchange occurs, and these rules can differ across settings. People can interpret differently the information conveyed by such settings. The reality is that most people make allocation decisions in several institutional settings each day – markets, missing markets, and unidentified markets. How does this institutional mix affect how people make their choices and form or state their preferences for environmental protection? This question is fundamental because it gives a reason for the purposeful actions underlying all valuation work.

Experimental work like the *rationality spillover* treatments in Cherry, Crocker and Shogren (2003) reveal that exposure to competition and discipline is needed to achieve rationality. In becoming rational, people refine their statements of value to better match their preferences. The contact with others who are making similar decisions in an exchange institution puts in context the economic maxim that choices have consequences and stated values have meaning for environmental valuation. Relying on rational theory to guide environmental valuation and policy makes more sense if people make, or act as if they make, consistent and systematic choices about certain and risky events. Valuation work in the laboratory needs to continue to address the economic conditions under which the presumption of rationality is supported and when it is not, which in turn has implications for the values we directly elicit.

Concluding remarks

Through the use of experimental methods, environmental economists now understand better how people learn about and react to incentives, institutions and information. They can compare how decisions are made with and without real economic commitments, within and without active exchange institutions, and with and without signals of value. They can then delve into what the results suggest for *ex ante* questionnaire design, *ex post* statistical evaluation, and, more importantly perhaps, economic theory itself. The environmental economics literature continues to follow the classic experimental strategy: start simply and add complexity slowly so as to understand which factors matter, and why.

In addition, all experiments in environmental economics reveal the perpetual tension between *control* and *context*. At the core, the experimental method is about *control*. One controls the experimental circumstances by trying to change only one variable at a time, which will reduce problems of confounding. Without control, it is unclear whether unpredicted behaviour is due to a poor theory or experimental design, or both. In contrast, others argue that *context* is desirable to avoid a setting that is too sterile and too removed from reality for something so real as environmental policy. Context affects participants' motivation.

Finally, as evidence continues to accumulate, a clearer and more definitive picture will emerge of how our institutions affect the efficiency and perceived value of environmental policies. The future of experimental work will be to design institutions that address the combination of market failure and behavioural anomalies. Otherwise we could find environmental economics falling into a new second-best problem: if we correct market failure without addressing behavioural biases, we might actually reduce overall social welfare.

JASON F. SHOGREN

See also **experimental economics; public goods experiments; value elicitation.**

Bibliography

Akerlof, G. 1997. Social distance and social decisions. *Econometrica* 65, 1005–27.
Barrett, S. 2003. *Environment and Statecraft: The Strategy of Environmental Treaty-Making.* New York: Oxford University Press.
Bennett, J. 1983. Validating revealed preferences. *Economic Analysis and Policy* 13, 2–17.
Bohm, P. 1972. Estimating demand for public goods: an experiment. *European Economic Review* 3, 111–30.
Bohm, P. 2003. Experimental evaluations of policy instruments. In *Handbook of Environmental Economics*, vol. 1, ed. K.G. Mäler and J. Vincent. Amsterdam: North-Holland, pp. 438–60.
Bohm, P. and Carlén, B. 1999. Emission quota trade among the few: laboratory evidence of joint implementation among committed countries. *Resource and Energy Economics* 21, 43–66.
Cason, T. 1995. An experimental investigation of the seller incentives in the EPA's emission trading auction. *American Economic Review* 85, 905–22.
Cason, T. and Plott, C. 1996. EPA's new emissions trading mechanism: a laboratory evaluation. *Journal of Environmental Economics and Management* 30, 133–60.

Cason, T. and Gangadharan, L. 2004. Auction design for voluntary conservation programs. *American Journal of Agricultural Economics* 86, 1211–7.

Cherry, T., Crocker, T. and Shogren, J. 2003. Rationality spillovers. *Journal of Environmental Economics and Management* 45, 63–84.

Cherry, T., Kroll, S. and Shogren, J. 2007. *Experimental Methods, Environmental Economics.* London: Routledge.

Coase, R. 1960. The problem of social cost. *Journal of Law and Economics* 3, 1–44.

Coursey, D. and Schulze, W. 1986. The application of laboratory experimental economics to the contingent valuation of public goods. *Public Choice* 49, 47–68.

Coursey, D., Hovis, J. and Schulze, W. 1987. The disparity between willingness to accept and willingness to pay measures of value. *Quarterly Journal of Economics* 102, 679–90.

Cummings, R. and Taylor, L. 1999. Unbiased value estimates for environmental goods: a cheap talk design for the contingent valuation method. *American Economic Review* 83, 649–65.

Hanley, N., Shogren, J. and White, B. 2007. *Environmental Economics in Theory and Practice*, 2nd edn. London and New York: Palgrave.

Harrison, G. and McKee, M. 1985. Experimental evaluation of the Coase theorem. *Journal of Law and Economics* 28, 653–70.

Hoffman, E. and Spitzer, M. 1982. The Coase theorem: some experimental tests. *Journal of Law and Economics* 25, 73–98.

Ishikida, T., Ledyard, J., Olson, M. and Porter, D. 2000. Experimental testbedding of a pollution trading system: southern California's RECLAIM emissions market. In *Research in Experimental Economics*, vol. 8, ed. R.M. Isaac. Greenwich, CN: JAI Press, Elsevier Science.

Kahneman, D., Knetsch, J. and Thaler, R. 1990. Experimental tests of the endowment effect and the Coase theorem. *Journal of Political Economy* 98, 1325–48.

Kahneman, D. and Tversky, A. 2000. *Choices, Values and Frames.* Cambridge: Cambridge University Press.

Knetsch, J. and Sinden, J.A. 1984. Willingness to pay and compensation demanded: experimental evidence of an unexpected disparity in measures of values. *Quarterly Journal of Economics* 99, 507–21.

Kroll, S., Cherry, T. and Shogren, J. 2007. Voting, punishment and public goods. *Economic Inquiry* 45, 557–70.

Ledyard, J. 1995. Public goods: a survey of experimental research. In *Handbook of Experimental Economics*, ed. J. Kagel and A. Roth. Princeton, NJ: Princeton University Press.

Lusk, J. and Shogren, J. 2007. *Experimental Auctions: Methods and Applications in Economic and Marketing Research.* New York: Cambridge University Press.

Ostrom, E. 2000. Collective action and the evolution of social norms. *Journal of Economic Perspectives* 14(3), 137–48.

Parkhurst, G., Shogren, J., Bastian, C., Kivi, P., Donner, J. and Smith, R. 2002. Agglomeration bonus: an incentive mechanism to reunite fragmented habitat for biodiversity conservation. *Ecological Economics* 41, 305–28.

Plott, C. 1983. Externalities and corrective policies in experimental markets. *Economic Journal* 93, 106–27.

Rhoads, T. and Shogren, J. 2003. Regulation through collaboration: final authority and information symmetry in environmental Coasean bargaining. *Journal of Regulatory Economics* 24, 63–89.

Rondeau, D., Schulze, W. and Poe, G. 1999. Voluntary revelation of the demand for public goods using a provision point mechanism. *Journal of Public Economics* 72, 455–70.

Sabel, C., Fung, A. and Karkkainen, B. 2000. *Beyond Backyard Environmentalism.* Boston, MA: Beacon Press.

Shogren, J. 2006. Experimental methods and valuation. In *Handbook of Environmental Economics*, vol. 2. ed. K.G. Mäler and J. Vincent. Amsterdam: North-Holland.

Shogren, J., Shin, S., Hayes, D. and Kliebenstein, J. 1994. Resolving differences in willingness to pay and willingness to accept. *American Economic Review* 84, 255–70.

Shogren, J., Cho, S., Koo, C., List, J. Park, C., Polo, P. and Wilhelmi, R. 2001. Auction mechanisms and the measurement of WTP and WTA. *Resource and Energy Economics* 23, 97–109.

experiments and econometrics

1. Introduction

'Experimetrics' refers to formal procedures used in designed investigations of economic hypotheses. A series of pathbreaking experimetric contributions by Ronald A. Fisher, written largely during the 1920s and early 1930s, elucidated fundamental concepts in the design and analysis of experiments (see, for example, Box, 1980, for a survey). He was first to obtain rigorous experimetric results on the importance of randomization, independence and blocking, and he created many powerful analysis tools that remain widely used, including Fisher's nonparametric Exact Test (Fisher, 1926; see also Fisher, 1935).

Controlled experiments allow compelling scientific inferences with respect to hypotheses of interest. Many economic experiments inform hypotheses regarding primitives assumed to be constant within an experiment (for example, preferences or decision strategies), or the effects on economic outcomes of changes in institutions (for example, comparing different auction rules or unemployment regulations; see EXPERIMENTAL ECONOMICS). One conducts controlled experiments to inform economic hypotheses because relevant naturally occurring data typically include noise of unknown form and magnitude outside the investigator's control. Econometric procedures can go some distance towards solving this problem, but even sophisticated approaches often allow only limited conclusions.

For example, suppose one wanted to investigate the (causal) effect of caffeine on heart rhythms. One approach is to obtain a random sample of 'heavy' coffee drinkers and compare them with a random sample of people who do not use caffeine. Because it is not possible with naturally occurring data to control the reason a person falls into a category, discovering that people with greater caffeine consumption have more cardiac episodes need not imply a causal caffeine effect. The reason is that a preference for coffee may stem from a biological characteristic that is itself causally tied to irregular cardiac events.

An advantage of designed investigations is that they allow cogent inference regarding causal effects through the appropriate use of randomization, independence and blocking.

1.1 Randomization

Experiments with randomized designs allow compelling causal inference. The reason is that randomly assigning participants to treatments, and randomly assigning treatments to dates and times, minimizes the possibility of systematic error. In the caffeine example, intentionally assigning heavy caffeine drinkers exclusively to a caffeine treatment generates a systematic error and invalidates causal inference. However, an experiment where subjects are randomly assigned to caffeine and no-caffeine treatments independent of their typical caffeine use allows one to draw appropriate inferences regarding causal relationships.

1.2 Independence
Randomization also helps to ensure independence both within and between treatments' observations. Loosely speaking, observations are independent if information about one observation does not provide information about another. Independence is critical for many experimetric analyses, and its failure can lead to misleading conclusions. An objective randomization procedure for treatment assignments insures against the possibility that participants in one treatment might unintentionally systematically vary from other treatments' participants.

1.3 Blocking
Causal relationships can be assessed with greater precision through 'blocking'. Blocking is a design procedure with which an experimenter can separate treatment effects from nuisance sources of data variation. In the above, heart rhythms might be affected by both caffeine and anxiety over the process of measuring heart rhythms. Especially because it is expected to differ between participants, anxiety is a source of nuisance variation that clouds inferences regarding caffeine effects. To address this one could 'block' by participant. This involves measuring each subject both with and without caffeine (in separate, randomly ordered trials). Caffeine effects are measured as the difference between trials, thus mitigating noise due to individual anxiety effects.

2. Experimetrics toolbox
Although many specialized experimetric tools have been developed, the experimetrics toolbox also includes a large number of general purpose procedures that have become standard in the experimental economics literature. A regular concern is that independence is not satisfied. The failure of independence can occur because of 'session' effects, meaning that there is less behavioural variation within than between sessions. Violations of independence can also occur if repeated measurements are taken on the same individual due to individual effects. Standard procedures can address this. Sessions can be treated as fixed effects, and random effects can be used to control for individual differences. The resulting 'mixed effect' model can be analysed using standard parametric, panel-data procedures (see, for example, Frechette, 2005).

Also in the toolbox is the McKelvey and Palfrey (1995) 'quantal response equilibrium' (QRE) framework (see QUANTAL RESPONSE EQUILIBRIA). QRE is a parametric procedure for analysing data from finite games. The key idea is to incorporate errors into players' best response functions, thus creating 'quantal response' functions. This results in an extremely flexible model that can rationalize a wide variety of behaviours. Haile, Hortacsu and Kosenok (2006) point out that this flexibility comes at a cost: in general QRE can rationalize any distribution of behaviour in any normal form game, and imposes no falsifiable restrictions without additional assumptions on the stochastic components of the model. Thus, those who wish to implement QRE analyses face the experimetric challenge of creating designs within which such assumptions are defensible.

For reasons including sample size and robustness, the experimetrics toolbox includes many nonparametric procedures (see Siegel and Castellan, 1988, for a user-friendly textbook treatment of popular nonparametric approaches). For example, Mann–Whitney tests, and their k-sample generalization due to Jonckheere (1954), are frequently used to compare medians among treatments' data. Also common is Fisher's Exact Test, which uses all the information in the data and is the most powerful nonparametric approach to inference with respect to differences among treatments. Its use is limited by the fact that it can be computationally cumbersome to implement when the numbers of treatments or observations are large.

3. External validity

An experiment's conclusions are 'externally valid' if they can be extrapolated to other environments. To rigorously address external validity requires that the source of treatment effects can be identified, which in turn implies a fundamental rule of experiment design: within any good experiment, any treatment can be matched with another that differs from it in exactly one way.

External validity is both important and subtle. For example, consider the well-known 'dictator game' where one participant is assigned the role of 'dictator', and the other 'receiver'. The dictator is given $20, and the receiver nothing. The dictator is told to split the $20 between herself and her receiver in any way she likes, after which the experiment ends. A widely replicated result is that a large fraction of dictators send half ($10) to an anonymous stranger, and one might question whether this finding is externally valid. In particular, there is no evidence that this behaviour is prevalent among winners of naturally occurring lotteries.

There are clear similarities between the situations of lottery winners and dictators. Still, the fact that actions of dictators in laboratory games do not match actions of lottery winners does not necessarily mean that dictator games lack external validity. The reason is that identical decision strategies can imply different decisions in different environments. For example, recent research provides compelling evidence that dictators' decisions are tightly connected to their beliefs regarding the decisions of others who have faced this same situation: dictators give because they believe other dictators give (Bicchieri and Xiao, 2007). This mechanism plausibly guides decisions in naturally occurring environments. In particular, lottery winners do not give because they believe other lottery winners do not give large fractions of their winnings to anonymous strangers. Thus, external validity does not require that one be able to match actions in an experiment to actions in another environment. Rather, an experiment is externally valid if one can extrapolate to novel contexts its conclusions with respect to individual or strategic decision processes.

4. Applied experimetrics research

An important application of experimetrics is to discriminate between many competing theories of learning that have emerged (see INDIVIDUAL LEARNING IN GAMES). Doing this includes significant experimetric challenges, as it requires one to account for heterogeneity in the way subjects learn. The reason is that not doing so will tend to bias fit statistics in favour of reinforcement (and hybrid) models. Wilcox (2006) shows the reason is that reinforcement models condition behaviour on informative functions of past choices, and in the presence of learning heterogeneity these choices will carry idiosyncratic parameter information not otherwise incorporated into the specification. Having said this, it is also the case that many data-sets from typical learning experiments can be roughly equally well described by many different learning models (Salmon, 2001). Consequently, the 'best' model can be highly sensitive to the particular criterion one uses for model selection, as well as the particular experiment under consideration (Feltovich, 2000). As a result, in-sample fit is often good, but this does not necessarily imply that much has been learned about the way in which people actually learn and make choices (Salmon, 2001).

Knowing how people make choices is critical to advance both economic theory and institution design. Consequently, a significant experimetric literature explores how people make decisions in complex environments, with a focus on characterizing the nature and number of different 'decision rules' at use in a population. Most approaches to accomplishing this require pre-specifying the decision rules the researcher believes people could follow, and then using choice data to assign one of those rules to each member of the population (see, for example, El-Gamal and Grether, 1995). However, in some cases one might be unwilling or unable to pre-specify the decision rules, and it turns out that doing so is not necessary. In particular, Houser, Keane and McCabe (2004) detail a Bayesian experimetric procedure that uses individual choice data to determine endogenously the nature and number of decision rules in a population. The approach requires only that one specify the information relevant to individuals' decisions.

Substantive experimetric advances have been obtained in far too many areas to detail here. Although no general survey is available, Houser, Keane and McCabe (2004), Ashley, Ball and Eckel (2005), and Loomes (2005), include excellent summaries of experimetric contributions to a variety of widely-studied games and decision problems.

5. Conclusion

Experimetrics continues to evolve as scholars adopt highly sophisticated design and analysis procedures to inform new questions. A ready example is the rapidly expanding research in neuroeconomics. The massive spatial-panel data structure that characterizes brain images poses unique inferential problems. Progress on these problems requires significant complementary innovations to both design and analysis strategies. The resulting experimetric advances are sure to have significant impact on economic theory and policy analysis.

DANIEL E. HOUSER

See also **experimental economics; experimental economics, history of; experimental methods in economics; individual learning in games; quantal response equilibria.**

Bibliography

Ashley, R., Ball, S. and Eckel, C. 2005. Motives for giving. A reanalysis of two classic public goods experiments, Manuscript, Virginia Institute of Technology.

Bicchieri, C. and Xiao, E. 2007. Do the right thing: But only if others do. Manuscript, University of Pennsylvania.

Box, J.F. 1980. R.A. Fisher and the design of experiments, 1922–1926. *American Statistician* 34, 1–7.

Feltovich, N. 2000. Reinforcement-based vs. belief-based learning models in experimental asymmetric-information games. *Econometrica* 68, 605–41.

Fisher, R.A. 1926. The arrangement of field experiments. *Journal of the Ministry of Agriculture of Great Britain* 33, 503–13.

Fisher, R.A. 1935. *Design of Experiments*. Edinburgh: Oliver and Boyd.

Frechette, G. 2005. Session effects in the laboratory. Manuscript, New York University.

El-Gamal, M.A. and Grether, D.M. 1995. Are people Bayesian? Uncovering behavioral strategies. *Journal of the American Statistical Association* 90, 1137–45.

Haile, P.A., Hortacsu, A. and Kosenok, G. 2006. On the empirical content of quantal response equilibrium. Mimeo, Yale University.

Houser, D., Keane, M. and McCabe, K. 2004. Behavior in a dynamic decision problem: an analysis of experimental evidence using a Bayesian type classification algorithm. *Econometrica* 72, 781–822.

Jonckheere, A.R. 1954. A distribution-free k-sample test against ordered alternatives. *Biometrika* 41, 133–45.

Loomes, G. 2005. Modelling the stochastic component of behavior in experiments: some issues for the interpretation of data. *Experimental Economics* 8, 301–23.

McKelvey, R.D. and Palfrey, T.R. 1995. Quantal response equilibria for normal form games. *Games and Economic Behavior* 10, 6–38.

Salmon, T.C. 2001. An evaluation of econometric models of adaptive learning. *Econometrica* 69, 1597–628.

Siegel, S. and Castellan, N., Jr. 1988. *Nonparametric Statistics for the Behavioral Sciences*, 2nd edn. Boston: McGraw Hill.

Wilcox, N. 2006. Theories of learning in games and heterogeneity bias. *Econometrica* 74, 1271–92.

field experiments

Field experiments occupy an important middle ground between laboratory experiments and naturally occurring field data. The underlying idea behind most field experiments is to make use of randomization in an environment that captures important characteristics of the real world. Distinct from traditional empirical economics, field experiments provide an advantage by permitting the researcher to create exogenous variation in the variables of interest, allowing us to establish causality rather than mere correlation. In relation to a laboratory experiment, a field experiment potentially gives up some of the control that a laboratory experimenter may have over her environment in exchange for increased realism.

The distinction between the laboratory and the field is much more important in the social sciences and the life sciences than it is in the physical sciences. In physics, for example, it appears that every hydrogen atom behaves exactly alike. Thus, when astronomers find hydrogen's signature wavelengths of light coming from the Andromeda Galaxy, they use this information to infer the quantity of hydrogen present there. By contrast, living creatures are much more complex than atoms and molecules, and they correspondingly behave much more heterogeneously. Despite the use of 'representative consumer' models, we know that not all consumers purchase the same bundle of goods when they face the same prices. With complex, heterogeneous behaviour, it is important to sample populations drawn from many different domains – both in the laboratory and in the field. This permits stronger inference, and one can also provide an important test of generalizability, testing whether laboratory results continue to hold in the chosen field environment.

We find an apt analogy in the study of pharmaceuticals, where randomized experiments scientifically evaluate new drugs to treat human diseases. Laboratory experiments evaluate whether drugs have desirable biochemical effects on tissues and proteins *in vitro*. If a drug appears promising, it is next tested *in vivo* on several species of animals, to see whether it is absorbed by the relevant tissues, whether it produces the desired effects on the body, and whether it produces undesirable side effects. If it remains with significant promise after those tests, it is then tested in human clinical trials to explore efficacy and measure any side effects.

Even after being tested thoroughly in human clinical trials and approved by regulators, a drug may sometimes reveal new information in large-scale use. For example, *effectiveness* may be different from the *efficacy* measured in clinical trials: if a drug must be taken frequently, for example, patients may not remember to take it as often as they are supposed to or as often as they did in closely supervised clinical trials. Furthermore, rare side effects may show up when the drug is finally exposed to a large population.

Much like this stylized example, in economics there are a number of reasons why insights gained in one environment might not perfectly map to another. Field experiments can lend insights into this question (see also Bohm, 1972; Harrison and List, 2004; Levitt and List, 2007; List, 2007). First, different types of subjects might behave differently; university students in the laboratory might not exhibit the same behaviour as financial traders or shopkeepers. In particular, the people who undertake a given economic activity have selected into that activity and market forces might have changed the composition of players as well; you might expect regular bidders to have more skill and interest in auctions than a randomly selected laboratory subject, for example.

A second reason why a field experiment might differ from a laboratory experiment is that the laboratory environment might not be fully representative of the field environment. For example, a typical donor asked to give money to charity might behave quite differently if asked to participate by choosing how much money to contribute to the public fund in a public-goods game (List, 2007). The charitable-giving context could provide familiar cognitive cues that make the task easier than an unfamiliar laboratory task. Even the mere fact of knowing that one's behaviour is being monitored, recorded, and subsequently scrutinized might alter choices (Orne, 1962).

Perhaps most important is the fact that any theory is an approximation of reality. In the laboratory, experimenters usually impose all the structural modelling assumptions of a theory (induced preferences, trading institutions, order of moves in a game) and examine whether subjects behave as predicted by the model. In a field experiment, one accepts the actual preferences and institutions used in the real world, jointly testing both the structural assumptions (such as the nature of values for a good) and the behavioural assumptions (such as Nash equilibrium).

For example, Vickrey (1961) assumes that in an auction there is a fixed, known number of bidders who have valuations for the good drawn independently from the same (known) probability distribution. He uses these assumptions, along with the assumption of a risk-neutral Nash equilibrium, to derive the 'revenue equivalence' result: that Dutch, English, first-price, and second-price auctions all yield the same expected revenue. However, in the real world the number of bidders might actually vary with the good or the auction rules, and the bidders might not know the probability distribution of values. These exceptions do not mean that the model should be abandoned as 'wrong'; it might well still have predictive power if it is a reasonable approximation to the truth. In a field experiment (such as Lucking-Reiley, 1999, for this example), we approach the real world; we do not take the structural assumptions of a theory for granted.

Such an example raises the natural question related to the actual difference between laboratory and field experiments. Harrison and List (2004) propose six factors that can be used to determine the field context of an experiment: the nature of the subject pool, the nature of the information that the subjects bring to the task, the nature of the commodity, the nature of the task or trading rules applied, the nature of the stakes, and the environment in which the subjects operate. Using these factors, they discuss a broad classification scheme that helps to organize one's thoughts about the factors that might be important when moving from the laboratory to the field.

A first useful departure from laboratory experiments using student subjects is simply to use 'non-standard' subjects, or experimental participants from the market of interest. Harrison and List (2004) adopt the term 'artefactual' field experiment to denote such studies. While one might argue that such studies are not 'field' in any way, for consistency of discussion we denote such experiments as artefactual field experiments for the remainder of this article, since they do depart in a potentially important manner from typical laboratory studies. This type of controlled experiment represents a useful type of exploration beyond traditional laboratory studies.

Moving closer to how naturally occurring data are generated, Harrison and List (2004) denote a 'framed field experiment' as the same as an artefactual field experiment but with field context in the commodity, task, stakes, or information set of the subjects. This type of experiment is important in the sense that a myriad of factors might influence behaviour, and by progressing slowly towards the environment of ultimate interest one can learn about whether, and to what extent, such factors influence behaviour in a case-by-case basis.

Finally, a 'natural field experiment' is the same as a framed field experiment but where the environment is one where the subjects naturally undertake these tasks and where the subjects do not know that they are participants in an experiment. Such an exercise represents an approach that combines the most attractive elements of the laboratory and naturally occurring data – randomization and realism. In this sense, comparing behaviour across natural and framed field experiments permits crisp insights into whether the experimental proclamation, in and of itself, influences behaviour.

Several examples of each of these types of field experiments are included in List (2006). Importantly for our purposes, each of these field experimental types represents a distinct manner in which to generate data. As List (2006) illustrates, these field experiment types fill an important hole between laboratory experiments and empirical exercises that make use of naturally occurring data. Yet an infrequently discussed question is: why do we bother to collect data in economics, or in any science?

First, we use data to collect enough facts to help construct a theory. Several prominent broader examples illustrate this point. After observing the anatomical and behavioural similarities of reptiles, one may theorize that reptiles are more closely related to each other than they are to mammals on the evolutionary tree. Watson and Crick used data from Rosalind Franklin's X-ray diffraction experiment to construct a theory of the chemical structure of DNA. Careful observations of the motions of the planets in the sky led Kepler to theorize that planets (including Earth) all travel in elliptical orbits around the Sun, and Newton to theorize the inverse-square law of gravitation. After observing with a powerful telescope that the fuzzy patches called 'spiral nebulae' are really made up of many stars, one may theorize that our solar system is itself part of its own galaxy, and the spiral nebulae are external to our Milky

Way galaxy. Robert Boyle experimented with different pressures using his vacuum pump in order to infer the inverse relationship between the pressure and the volume of a gas. Rutherford's experiments of shooting charged particles at a piece of gold foil led him to theorize that atoms have massive, positively charged nuclei.

Second, we use data to test theories' predictions. Galileo experimented with balls rolling down inclined planes in order to test his theory that all objects have the same rate of acceleration due to gravity. Pasteur rejected the theory of spontaneous generation with an experiment that showed that microorganisms grow in boiled nutrient broth when exposed to the air, but not when exposed to carefully filtered air. Arthur Eddington measured the bending of starlight by the sun during an eclipse in order to test Einstein's theory of general relativity.

Third, we use data to make measurements of key parameters. On the assumption that the electron is the smallest unit of electric charge, Robert Millikan experimented with tiny, falling droplets of oil to measure the charge of the electron. On the assumption that radioactive carbon-14 decays at a constant rate, archaeologists have been able to provide dates for various ancient artifacts. Similarly, scientists have assumed theory to be true and designed careful measurements of many other parameters, such as the speed of light, the gravitational constant, and various atomic masses.

Field experiments can be a useful tool for each of these purposes. For example, Anderson and Simester (2003) collect facts useful for constructing a theory about consumer reactions to nine-dollar endings on prices. They explore the effects of different price endings by conducting a natural field experiment with a retail catalogue merchant. Randomly selected customers receive one of three catalogue versions that show different prices for the same product. Systematically changing a product's price varies the presence or absence of a nine-dollar price ending. For example, a cotton dress may be offered to all consumers, but at prices of 34, 39, and 44 dollars, respectively, in each catalogue version. They find a positive effect of a nine-dollar price on quantity demanded, large enough that a price of 39 dollars actually produced higher quantities than a price of 34 dollars. Their results reject the theory that consumers turn a price of 34 dollars into 30 dollars by either truncation or rounding. This finding provides empirical evidence on an interesting topic and demonstrates the need for a better theory of how consumers process price endings.

List and Lucking-Reiley (2000) present an example of a framed field experiment designed to test a theory. The theory of multi-unit auctions predicts that a uniform-price sealed-bid auction will produce bids that are less than fully demand-revealing, because such bids might lower the price paid by the same bidder on another unit. By contrast, the generalized Vickrey auction predicts that bidders will submit bids equal to their values. In the experiment, List and Lucking-Reiley conduct two-person, two-unit auctions for collectible sportscards at a card trading show. The uniform-price auction awards both items to the winning bidder(s) at an amount equal to the third-highest bid (out of four total bids), while the Vickrey auction awards the items to the winning bidder(s) for amounts equal to the bids that they displaced from winning.

List and Lucking-Reiley find that, as predicted by the theory of demand reduction, the second-unit bids submitted by each bidder were lower in the uniform-price treatment than in the Vickrey treatment. The first-unit bids were predicted to be equal across treatments, but in the experiment they find that the first-unit bids were anomalously higher in the uniform-price treatment. Subsequent laboratory experiments (see, for example, Engelmann and Grimm, 2003; Porter and Vragov, 2003), have confirmed this finding.

Finally, Karlan and List (2007) is an example of a natural field experiment designed to measure key parameters of a theory. In their study, they explore the effects of 'price' changes on charitable giving by soliciting contributions from more than 50,000 supporters of a liberal organization. They randomize subjects into several different groups to explore whether solicitees respond to upfront monies used as matching funds. They find that simply announcing that a match is available considerably increases the revenue per solicitation – by 19 per cent. In addition, the match offer significantly increases the probability that an individual donates – by 22 per cent. Yet, while the match treatments relative to a control group increase the probability of donating, larger match ratios – 3:1 dollars (that is, 3 dollars match for every 1 dollar donated) and 2:1 dollar – relative to smaller match ratios (1:1 dollar) have no additional impact.

In closing, we believe that field experiments will continue to grow in popularity as scholars continue to take advantage of the settings where economic phenomena present themselves. This growth will lead to fruitful avenues, both theoretical and empirical, but it is clear that regardless of the increase in popularity, the various empirical approaches should be thought of as strong complements, and combining insights from each of the methodologies will permit economists to develop a deeper understanding of our science.

JOHN A. LIST AND DAVID REILEY

See also **experimental economics; experimental methods in environmental economics; experimental methods in economics; experiments and econometrics; experimental economics, history of.**

Bibliography
Anderson, E.T. and Simester, D. 2003. Effects of $9 price endings on retail sales: evidence from field experiments. *Quantitative Marketing and Economics* 1, 93–110.
Bohm, P. 1972. Estimating the demand for public goods: an experiment. *European Economic Review* 3, 111–30.
Engelmann, D. and Grimm, V. 2003. Bidding behavior in multi-unit auctions—an experimental investigation and some theoretical insights. Working paper, Centre for Economic Research and Graduate Education, Economic Institute, Prague.
Harrison, G.W. and List, J.A. 2004. Field experiments. *Journal of Economic Literature* 42, 1009–55.
Karlan, D. and List, J.A. 2007. Does price matter in charitable giving? Evidence from a large-scale natural field experiment. *American Economic Review*, forthcoming.
Levitt, S.D. and List, J.A. 2006. What do laboratory experiments measuring social preferences tell us about the real world? *Journal of Economic Perspectives* 21(2), 153–74.

List, J.A. 2006. Field experiments: a bridge between lab and naturally occurring data. *Advances in Economic Analysis & Policy* 6(2), Article 8. Abstract online. Available at: http://www.bepress.com/bejeap/advances/vol6/iss2/art8, accessed 26 May 2007.

List, J.A. and Lucking-Reiley, D. 2000. Demand reduction in a multi-unit auction: evidence from a sportscard field experiment. *American Economic Review* 90, 961–72.

Lucking-Reiley, D. 1999. Using field experiments to test equivalence between auction formats: magic on the Internet. *American Economic Review* 89, 1063–80.

Orne, M.T. 1962. On the social psychological experiment: with particular reference to demand characteristics and their implications. *American Psychologist* 17, 776–83.

Porter, D. and Vragov, R. 2003. An experimental examination of demand reduction in multi-unit versions of the uniform-price, Vickrey, and English auctions. Working paper, Interdisciplinary Center for Economic Science, George Mason University.

Vickrey, W. 1961. Counterspeculation, auctions, and competitive sealed tenders. *Journal of Finance* 16, 8–37.

individual learning in games

1. Introduction

Economic experiments on strategic games typically generate data that, in early rounds, violate standard equilibrium predictions. However, subjects normally change their behaviour over time in response to experience. The study of learning in games is about how this behavioural change works empirically. This empirical investigation also has a theoretical payoff: if subjects' behaviour converges to an equilibrium, the underlying learning model becomes a theory of equilibration. In games with multiple equilibria, this same model can also serve as a theory of equilibrium selection, a long-standing challenge for theorists.

There are two general approaches to studying learning: population models and individual models.

Population models make predictions about how the aggregate behaviour in a population will change as a result of aggregate experience. For example, in replicator dynamics, a population's propensity to play a certain strategy will depend on its 'fitness' (payoff) relative to the mixture of strategies played previously (Friedman, 1991; Weibull, 1995). Models like this submerge differences in individual learning paths.

Individual learning models allow each person to choose differently, depending on the experiences each person has. For example, in Cournot dynamics, subjects form a belief that other players will always repeat their most recent choice and best-respond accordingly. Since players are matched with different opponents, their best responses vary across the population. Aggregate behaviour in the population can be obtained by summing individual paths of learning.

This article reviews three major approaches to individual learning in games: experience-weighted attraction (EWA) learning, reinforcement learning, and belief learning (including Cournot and fictitious play). These models of learning strive to explain, for every choice in an experiment, how that choice arose from players' previous behaviour and experience. These models assume strategies have numerical evaluations, which are called 'attractions'. Learning rules are defined by how attractions are updated in response to experience. Attractions are then mapped into predicted choice probabilities for strategies using some well-known statistical rule (such as logit).

The three major approaches to learning assume players that are adaptive (that is, they respond only to their own previous experience and ignore others' payoff information) and that their behaviour is not sensitive to the way in which players are matched. Empirical evidence suggests otherwise. There are subjects who can anticipate how others learn and choose actions to influence others' path of learning in order to benefit themselves. So we describe a generalization of these adaptive learning models to allow for this kind of sophisticated behaviour. This generalized model assumes that there is a mixture of adaptive learners and sophisticated players. An adaptive learner adjusts his behaviour according to one of the above learning rules. A sophisticated player does not learn and rationally best-responds to his forecast of others' learning behaviour. This model therefore allows 'one-stop shopping' for investigating the various statistical comparisons of learning and equilibrium models.

2. EWA learning

Denote player i's jth strategy by s_i^j and the other player(s)' strategy by s_{-i}^k. The strategy actually chosen in period t is $s_i(t)$. Player i's payoff for choosing s_i^j in period t is $\pi_i(s_i^j, s_{-i}^k(t))$. Each strategy has a numerical evaluation at time t, called an attraction $A_i^j(t)$. The model also has an experience weight, $N(t)$. The variables $N(t)$ and $A_i^j(t)$ begin with prior values and are updated each period. The rule for updating attraction sets $A_i^j(t)$ to be the sum of a depreciated, experience-weighted previous attraction $A_i^j(t-1)$ plus the (weighted) payoff from period t, normalized by the updated experience weight:

$$A_i^j(t) = \frac{\phi \cdot N(t-1) \cdot A_i^j(t-1) + [\delta + (1-\delta) \cdot I(s_i^j, s_i(t))] \cdot \pi_i(s_i^j, s_{-i}(t))}{N(t)} \quad (2.1)$$

where indicator variable $I(x, y)$ is 1 if $x = y$ and 0 otherwise. The experience weight is updated by:

$$N(t) = \rho \cdot N(t-1) + 1. \quad (2.2)$$

Let $\kappa = \frac{\phi - \rho}{\phi}$. Then $\rho = \phi \cdot (1 - \kappa)$ and $N(t)$ approaches the steady-state value of $\frac{1}{1 - \phi \cdot (1-\kappa)}$. If $N(0)$ begins below this value, it steadily rises, capturing an increase in the weight placed on previous attractions and a (relative) decrease in the impact of recent observations, so that learning slows down.

Attractions are mapped into choice probabilities using a logit rule (other functional forms fit about equally well; Camerer and Ho, 1999):

$$P_i^j(t+1) = \frac{e^{\lambda \cdot A_i^j(t)}}{\sum_k e^{\lambda \cdot A_i^k(t)}}, \quad (2.3)$$

where λ is the payoff sensitivity parameter. The key parameters are δ, ϕ and κ (which are generally assumed to be in the [0,1] interval).

The most important parameter, δ, is the weight on forgone payoffs relative to realized payoffs. It can be interpreted as a kind of 'imagination' of forgone payoffs, or responsiveness to forgone payoffs (when δ is larger players move more strongly toward *ex post* best responses). We call it 'consideration' of forgone payoffs. The weight on forgone payoff δ is also an intuitive way to formalize the 'learning direction' theory of Selten and Stoecker (1986). Their theory consists of an appealing property of learning: subjects move in the direction of *ex post* best-response. Broad applicability of the theory has been hindered by defining 'direction' only in terms of numerical properties of ordered strategies (for example, choosing 'higher prices' if the *ex post* best response is a higher price than the chosen price). The parameter δ defines the 'direction' of learning set-theoretically by shifting probability towards the set of strategies with higher payoffs than the chosen ones.

The parameter ϕ is naturally interpreted as depreciation of past attractions, $A_i^j(t-1)$. In a game-theoretic context, ϕ will be affected by the degree to which players realize other players are adapting, so that old observations on what others did become less and less useful. So we can interpret ϕ as an index of (perceived) 'change' in the environment.

The parameter κ determines the growth rate of attractions, which in turn affects how sharply players converge. When $\kappa = 0$, the attractions are weighted averages of lagged attractions and payoff reinforcements (with weights $\phi \cdot N(t-1)/(\phi \cdot N(t-1)+1$ and $1/(\phi \cdot N(t-1)+1)$. When $\kappa = 1$ and $N(t) = 1$, the attractions are cumulations of previous reinforcements rather than averages (that is, $A_i^j(t) = \phi \cdot A_i^j(t-1) + [\delta + (1-\delta) \cdot I(s_i^j, s_i(t))] \cdot \pi_i(s_i^j, s_{-i}(t)))$. In the logit model, the *differences* in strategy attractions determine their choice probabilities. When κ is high the attractions can grow furthest apart over time, making choice probabilities closer to zero and one. We therefore interpret κ as an index of 'commitment'.

3. Reinforcement learning

In cumulative reinforcement learning (Harley, 1981; Roth and Erev, 1995), strategies have levels of attraction which are incremented by only received payoffs. The initial reinforcement level of strategy j of player i, s_i^j, is $R_i^j(0)$. Reinforcements are updated as follows:

$$R_i^j(t) = \begin{cases} \phi \cdot R_i^j(t-1) + \pi_i(s_i^j, s_{-i}(t)) & \text{if } s_i^j = s_i(t), \\ \phi \cdot R_i^j(t-1) & \text{if } s_i^j \neq s_i(t). \end{cases} \tag{3.1}$$

Using the indicator function, the two equations can be reduced to one:

$$R_i^j(t) = \phi \cdot R_i^j(t-1) + I(s_i^j, s_i(t)) \cdot \pi_i(s_i^j, s_{-i}(t)). \tag{3.2}$$

This updating formula is a special case of the EWA rule, when $\delta = 0$, $N(0) = 1$, and $\kappa = 1$.

In average reinforcement learning, updated attractions are *averages* of previous attractions and received payoffs (for example, Mookerjhee and Sopher, 1994; 1997; Erev and Roth, 1998). For example

$$R_i^j(t) = \phi \cdot R_i^j(t-1) + (1-\phi) \cdot I(s_i^j, s_i(t)) \cdot \pi_i(s_i^j, s_{-i}(t)). \tag{3.3}$$

A little algebra shows that this updating formula is also a special case of the EWA rule, when $\delta = 0$, $N(0) = \frac{1}{1-\phi}$, and $\kappa = 0$. Since the two reinforcement models are special cases of EWA learning, their predictive adequacy can be tested empirically by setting the appropriate EWA parameters to their restricted values and seeing how much fit is compromised (adjusting, of course, for degrees of freedom).

4. Belief learning

In belief-based models, adaptive players base their responses on beliefs formed by observing their opponents' past plays. While there are many ways of forming beliefs, we consider a fairly general 'weighted fictitious play' model, which includes fictitious play (Brown, 1951; Fudenberg and Levine, 1998) and Cournot best-response (Cournot, 1960) as special cases. It corresponds to Bayesian learning if players have a Dirichlet prior belief.

In weighted fictitious play, players begin with prior beliefs about what the other players will do, which are expressed as ratios of strategy choice counts to the total experience. Denote total experience by $N(t) = \sum_k N^k_{-i}(t)$. Express the belief that others will play strategy k as $B^k_{-i}(t) = \frac{N^k_{-i}(t)}{N(t)}$, with $N^k_{-i}(t) \geq 0$ and $N(t) > 0$.

Beliefs are updated by depreciating the previous counts by ϕ, and adding one for the strategy combination actually chosen by the other players. That is,

$$B^k_{-i}(t) = \frac{\phi \cdot N^k_{-i}(t-1) + I(s^k_{-i}, s_{-i}(t))}{\sum_h [\phi \cdot N^h_{-i}(t-1) + I(s^h_{-i}, s_{-i}(t))]}. \tag{4.1}$$

This form of belief updating weights the belief from one period ago ϕ times as much as the most recent observation, so ϕ can be interpreted as how quickly previous experience is discarded. When $\phi = 0$ players weight only the most recent observation (Cournot dynamics); when $\phi = 1$ all previous observations count equally (fictitious play).

Given these beliefs, we can compute expected payoffs in each period t,

$$E^j_i(t) = \sum_k B^k_{-i}(t)\pi(s^j_i, s^k_{-i}). \tag{4.2}$$

The crucial step is to express period t expected payoffs as a function of period $t-1$ expected payoffs. This yields:

$$E^j_i(t) = \frac{\phi \cdot N(t-1) \cdot E^j_i(t-1) + \pi(s^j_i, s_{-i}(t))}{\phi \cdot N(t-1) + 1}. \tag{4.3}$$

By expressing expected payoffs as a function of lagged expected payoffs, we make the belief terms disappear. This is because the beliefs are only used to compute expected payoffs, and when beliefs are formed according to weighted fictitious play, the expected payoffs which result can also be generated by generalized reinforcement according to previous payoffs. More precisely, if the initial attractions in the EWA model are expected payoffs given some initial beliefs (that is, $A^j_i(0) = E^j_i(0)$), $\kappa = 0$ (or $\phi = \rho$), and foregone payoffs are weighted as strongly as received payoffs ($\delta = 1$), then EWA attractions are *exactly* the same as expected payoffs. Put differently, belief learning is 'mathematically equivalent' or 'observationally equivalent' to EWA learning with $\delta = 1$, $\kappa = 0$ and $A^j_i(0) = E^j_i(0)$.

This demonstrates a close kinship between reinforcement and belief approaches. Belief learning is nothing more than generalized attraction learning in which strategies are reinforced equally strongly by actual payoffs and foregone payoffs and attractions are weighted averages of past attractions and reinforcements. Hopkins (2002) compares the convergence properties of reinforcement and fictitious play and finds that they are quite similar in nature and that they will in many cases have the same asymptotic behaviour.

5. A graphical representation

Since reinforcement and belief learning are special cases of EWA learning, it is possible to represent all three learning models in a three-dimensional EWA cube (see Figure 1). The vertex $\delta = 1$ and $\kappa = 0$ corresponds, to weighted fictitious play models. The corners $\phi = 0$ and $\phi = 1$ correspond to Cournot best-response dynamics and fictitious play, respectively. Reinforcement models in which only chosen strategies are reinforced according to their payoffs correspond to vertices in which $\phi = 0$, and $\kappa = 1$ (cumulative reinforcement) or $\kappa = 0$ (averaged reinforcement). Interior configurations of parameter values incorporate both the intuition behind reinforcement learning, that realized payoffs weigh most heavily ($\delta < 1$), and the intuition implicit in belief learning, that foregone payoffs matter too ($\delta > 0$).

The cube shows that contrary to popular belief for many decades, reinforcement and belief learning are simply two extreme configurations on opposite edges of a three-dimensional cube, rather than fundamentally unrelated models. Figure 1 also

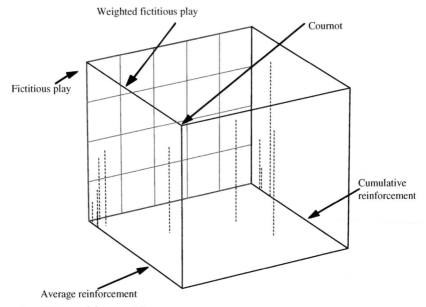

Figure 1   EWA's model parametric space

shows estimates of the three parameters in 20 different studies (Camerer, Ho and Chong, 2002). Each point is a triple of estimates. These parameter estimates were typically obtained by the maximum likelihood method. Initial attractions could be either estimated using data or set to plausible values using the cognitive hierarchy model of one-shot games; see Camerer, Ho and Chong (2004) for details. Most points are sprinkled throughout the cube, rather than at the extreme vertices mentioned in the previous paragraph, although some (generally from games with mixed-strategy equilibria) are near the averaged reinforcement corner $\delta = 0$ and $\kappa = \phi = 1$. Ho, Camerer and Chong (2007) provide an explanation for how δ and ϕ vary across games by endogenizing them as functions of game experience. Parameter estimates are generally significantly inside the interior of the cube rather than near the vertices. Thus, we may conclude that subjects' behaviour is often neither belief nor reinforcement learning.

6. Linking learning and equilibrium models

The adaptive learning models presented above do not permit players to anticipate learning by others. Omitting anticipation logically implies that players do not use information about the payoffs of other players, and that whether players are matched together repeatedly or are randomly re-matched should not matter. Both of the latter implications are unintuitive, and experiments with experienced subjects have provided evidence to show otherwise.

In Camerer, Ho and Chong (2002) and Chong, Camerer and Ho (2006), we proposed a simple way to include 'sophisticated' anticipation by some players that others are learning, using two additional parameters. We assume a fraction α of players are sophisticated. Sophisticated players think that a fraction $(1 - \alpha')$ of players are adaptive and the remaining fraction α' of players are sophisticated like themselves. They use the EWA model (which nests reinforcement and belief learning as special cases) to forecast what the adaptive players will do, and choose strategies with high expected payoffs given their forecast.

All the adaptive models discussed above (EWA, reinforcement, belief learning) are special cases of this generalized model with $\alpha = 0$. The assumption that sophisticated players think some others are sophisticated creates a small whirlpool of recursive thinking which implies that quantal response equilibrium (QRE; McKelvey and Palfrey, 1995) and Nash equilibrium are special cases of this generalized model. Our specification also shows that equilibrium concepts combine two features which are empirically and psychologically separable: 'social calibration' (accurate guesses about the fraction of players who are sophisticated, $\alpha = \alpha'$); and full sophistication ($\alpha = 1$). Psychologists have identified systematic departures from social calibration called 'false uniqueness' or overconfidence ($\alpha > \alpha'$) and 'false consensus' or curse of knowledge ($\alpha > \alpha'$).

Formally, adaptive learners follow the EWA updating equations given above (that is, (2.1) and (2.2)). Sophisticated players have attractions $B_i^j(t)$ and choice probabilities $Q_i^j(t+1)$ specified as follows:

$$B_i^j(t) = \sum_k [(1-\alpha') \cdot P_{-i}^k(t+1) + \alpha' Q_{-i}^k(t+1)] \cdot \pi_i(s_i^j, s_{-i}^k), \tag{6.1}$$

$$Q_i^j(t+1) = \frac{e^{\lambda \cdot B_i^j(t)}}{\sum_k e^{\lambda \cdot B_i^k(t)}}. \tag{6.2}$$

The generalized model has been applied to experimental data from ten-period p-beauty contest games (specific details of data collection are given in Ho, Camerer and Weigelt, 1998). In these games, seven subjects choose numbers in [0,100] simultaneously. The subject whose number is closest to p times the average (where $p = .7$ or .9) wins a fixed prize. Subjects playing for the first time are called 'inexperienced'; those playing another ten-period game (with a different p) are called 'experienced'.

The estimation results show that for inexperienced subjects, adding sophistication to adaptive EWA improves log likelihood (LL) substantially both in- and out-of-sample. The estimated fraction of sophisticated players is $\hat{\alpha} = .24$ and their estimated perception $\hat{\alpha}' = 0$. Experienced subjects show a much larger improved fit from sophistication, and a larger estimated proportion, $\hat{\alpha} = .75$. Their perceptions are again too low, $\hat{\alpha}' = .41$, showing a degree of overconfidence. The increase in sophistication due to experience reflects a kind of 'learning about learning', which is similar to rule learning (that is, subjects switch their learning rule over time (Stahl, 2000; Ho, Camerer and Chong, 2007). Overall, these results suggest that subjects are not socially calibrated, that not all subjects are sophisticated, and that the proportion of sophistication grows with experience.

7. Conclusions and future research

We describe three major approaches of adaptive learning models. We show that EWA learning is a generalization of reinforcement and belief learning and that the latter two nested models are intimately related. Specifically, they differ mainly in the way they treat forgone payoffs; reinforcement learning ignores them and belief learning treats them the same as actual payoffs. Estimation results from dozens of studies show that the emergence of behaviour is neither reinforcement nor belief learning in most games. The EWA cube provides a simple way for detecting how these simpler models fail and why.

We also describe a generalization of these adaptive models to study anticipation by some players that others are learning. This generalized model nests equilibrium and the adaptive learning models as special cases and is a powerful framework for analysing both equilibrium and learning simultaneously. We show that it can improve the predictive performance of the adaptive learning models when players are experienced and able to anticipate how others learn.

There are three promising areas of future research, all of which aim to make the above learning models more amenable to field applications.

1. *Transfer of learning across similar games.* In practice, it is unreasonable to expect people play the identical game again and again. Since people are more likely to face with similar but non-identical strategic situations, it is important to determine whether they are able to transfer learning from one situation to another. Cooper and Kagel (2004) provide evidence that subjects who have learned to play strategically in one signalling game can transfer most of this knowledge to related games. This transfer of learning occurs because the proportion of sophisticated players grows with experience (just like what we observed in *p*-beauty contest games discussed above). This positive evidence is encouraging but more work is necessary to determine whether this finding indeed generalizes to other games.

2. *Learning in extensive-form games.* Most of the learning literature focuses on strategic or normal-form games (for an exception see Anderson and Camerer, 2000). This is done in part to simplify the learning context to situations where each action unambiguously corresponds to a final outcome. In extensive-form games or many field settings, where a final outcome is typically a result of a series of actions taken sequentially over time, there is a natural question how an action step taken at a particular time contributes to the final outcome. This 'credit assignment' problem is important because different agents might be responsible for different action steps, and some steps might be more crucial than others at determining the final outcome. A good learning model should assign credit appropriately to each action step.

3. *Learning in noisy experiments.* There is a general belief that, given a sufficiently high stake and that people play repeatedly with a clear feedback, their behaviour will converge to equilibrium in the long run. However many real-world environments provide noisy feedback. So it is important to study how noise in feedback affects rates of learning and the likelihood of convergence to equilibrium.

TECK H. HO

See also **experimental economics.**

Bibliography

Anderson, C. and Camerer, C. 2000. Experience-weighted attraction learning in sender-receiver signaling games. *Economic Theory* 16, 689–718.

Brown, G. 1951. Iterative solution of games by fictitious play. In *Activity Analysis of Production and Allocation* New York: Wiley.

Camerer, C.F. and Ho, T.-H. 1999. Experience-weighted attraction learning in normal-form games. *Econometrica* 67, 827–74.

Camerer, C., Ho, T.-H. and Chong, J.-K. 2002. Sophisticated learning and strategic teaching. *Journal of Economic Theory* 104, 137–18.

Camerer, C.F., Ho, T.-H. and Chong, J.-K. 2004. A cognitive hierarchy model of one-shot games. *Quarterly Journal of Economics* 119, 861–98.

Chong, J.-K., Camerer, C. and Ho, T.-H. 2006. A learning-based model of repeated games with incomplete information. *Games and Economic Behavior* 55, 340–71.

Cooper, D. and Kagel, J. 2004. Learning and transfer in signaling games. Working paper, Ohio State University.

Cournot, A. 1960. *Recherches sur les principes mathématiques de la théorie des richesses*. Trans. N. Bacon as *Researches in the Mathematical Principles of the Theory of Wealth*. London: Haffner.

Erev, I. and Roth, A. 1998. Modelling predicting how people play games: reinforcement learning in experimental games with unique, mixed-strategy equilibria. *American Economic Review* 88, 848–81.

Friedman, D. 1991. Evolutionary games in economics. *Econometrica* 59, 637–66.

Fudenberg, D. and Levine, D. 1998. *The Theory of Learning in Games*. Cambridge, MA: MIT Press.

Harley, C. 1981. Learning the evolutionary stable strategies. *Journal of Theoretical Biology* 89, 611–33.

Ho, T.-H., Camerer, C. and Weigelt, K. 1998. Iterated dominance and iterated best-response in *p*-beauty contests. *American Economic Review* 88, 947–69.

Ho, T.-H., Camerer, C. and Chong, J.-K. 2007. Self-tuning experience-weighted attraction learning in games. *Journal of Economic Theory* 133, 177–98.

Hopkins, E. 2002. Two competing models of how people learn in games. *Econometrica* 70, 2141–66.

McKelvey, R. and Palfrey, T. 1995. Quantal response equilibria for normal form games. *Games and Economic Behavior* 10, 6–38.

Mookerjhee, D. and Sopher, B. 1994. Learning behavior in an experimental matching pennies game. *Games and Economic Behavior* 7, 62–91.

Mookerjee, D. and Sopher, B. 1997. Learning and decision costs in experimental constant-sum games. *Games and Economic Behavior* 19, 97–132.

Roth, A.E. and Erev, I. 1995. Learning in extensive-form games: experimental data and simple dynamic models in the intermediate term. *Games and Economic Behavior* 8, 164–212.

Selten, R. and Stoecker, R. 1986. End behavior in sequences of finite Prisoner's Dilemma supergames: a learning theory approach. *Journal of Economic Behavior and Organization* 7, 47–70.

Stahl, D. 2000. Rule learning in symmetric normal-form games. *Games and Economic Behavior: Theory and Evidence* 32, 105–38.

Weibull, J. 1995. *Evolutionary Game Theory*. Cambridge, MA: MIT Press.

information cascade experiments

Cascade experiments test the theory that conformity can result from individuals receiving private imperfect information and making public decisions in a sequence.

Cascade theories provide a rational explanation for imitation even when people receive different private information. If a person gathers additional information by observing others' decisions, then a sequence of decisions that matches one alternative might be strong enough to outweigh that person's contrary private information. When the initial decisions in a sequence are correct, cascades can lead to better overall decision-making than private information alone. However, information cascades are problematic when the initial decision-makers in a queue receive incorrect information and convey it to others through their public (incorrect) decisions.

Anderson and Holt (1997) designed the first laboratory cascade experiment to test the theory described in Bikhchandani, Hirshleifer and Welch (1992). Participants were shown two cups labelled A and B. Cup A contained two light marbles and one dark marble. Cup B contained two dark marbles and one light marble. A six-sided die was used to determine whether Cup A or Cup B was selected at the start of each decision-making round. The cups were equally likely to be selected by the die throw. Once a cup was selected, each person saw one private draw from the cup, with the marble being returned to the cup after each draw. Each participant made a public prediction about which cup (A or B) was being used for the draws in a randomly determined sequence that changed from round to round. Sessions included six decision-makers who were paid two dollars for a correct prediction and nothing otherwise for each of 15 rounds.

In any given round, if the first two public predictions matched (AA or BB) it was rational (based on Bayes' rule) for all subsequent decision-makers to follow, regardless of which marble they saw drawn from the cup. Starting with prior probabilities of 1/2 for each cup, if the first decision-maker predicted cup A, others could rationally infer that he saw a light marble, since there were more light marbles than dark marbles in Cup A. With this new information, the probability of Cup A should have been updated to 2/3. If the second decision-maker predicted Cup A, others could infer that he also saw a light marble, and the probability of Cup A being used for the draws should have been updated to 4/5. Even if the third person observed a dark marble, it was still more likely that Cup A was being used for the draws, and a cascade should start with the third decision-maker. Alternatively, if the first two decision-makers cancelled each other out (AB or BA) and the next two matched, then a cascade could start with the fifth person in the sequence.

Cascades were possible, based on the private draws and the decision-making sequence, in about half the Anderson and Holt (1997) experiments and actually formed in about 70 per cent of these cases. Almost all the people who did not join rational cascades were following private information that conflicted with the cascade. This type of deviation is explained by cascade models with small amounts of noisy behaviour, as described in Anderson and Holt (1997) and Goeree et al. (2007), who showed that incorrect cascades are not likely to persist in experiments with long sequences of decisions.

From a policy perspective, cascades are a concern because they hide information, since the private information of cascade followers is not revealed by their decisions. Kübluer and Weizsäcker (2004) studied whether or not people recognized the lack of information in conforming decisions by making participants pay a fee to see a private signal. In one version of their experiment, it was rational for only the first person in the sequence to purchase information, but the authors found that many people made irrational purchases. Some of this behaviour can be explained by a model with error, since it is rational to buy information if one cannot completely trust the quality of public decisions.

In addition to the studies discussed above, laboratory experiments have been used to test other variations of the seminal cascade theory including applications to voting (Hung and Plott, 2001), investment (Alsopp and Hey, 2000), markets (Drehmann, Oechssler and Roider, 2005; and Cipriani and Guarino, 2005) and advice-giving (Çelen, Kariv and Schotter, 2005).

LISA ANDERSON AND CHARLES A. HOLT

Bibliography

Alsopp, L. and Hey, J.D. 2000. Two experiments to test a model of herd behavior. *Experimental Economics* 3, 121–36.

Anderson, L.R. and Holt, C.A. 1997. Information cascades in the laboratory. *American Economic Review* 87, 847–62.

Bikhchandani, S., Hirshleifer, D. and Welch, I. 1992. A theory of fads, fashion, custom and cultural change as information cascades. *Journal of Political Economy* 100, 992–1026.

Çelen, B., Kariv, S. and Schotter, A. 2005. Words speak louder than actions and improve welfare: an experimental test of advice and social learning. Working paper, Center for Experimental Social Science, New York University.

Cipriani, M. and Guarino, A. 2005. Herd behavior in a laboratory financial market. *American Economic Review* 95, 1227–443.

Drehmann, M., Oechssler, J. and Roider, A. 2005. Herding and contrarian behavior in financial markets: an internet experiment. *American Economic Review* 95, 1203–426.

Goeree, J.K., Palfrey, T.R., Rogers, B.W and McKelvey, R.D. 2007. Self-correcting information cascades. *Review of Economic Studies* (forthcoming).

Hung, A.A. and Plott, C.R. 2001. Information cascades: replication and an extension to majority rule and conformity-rewarding institutions. *American Economic Review* 91, 1508–20.

Kübler, D. and Weizsäcker, G. 2004. Limited depth of reasoning and failure of cascade formation in the laboratory. *Review of Economic Studies* 71, 425–41.

intertemporal choice

Models of intertemporal choice

Most choices require decision-makers to trade-off costs and benefits at different points in time. Decisions with consequences in multiple time periods are referred to as intertemporal choices. Decisions about savings, work effort, education, nutrition, exercise, and health care are all intertemporal choices.

The theory of discounted utility is the most widely used framework for analysing intertemporal choices. This framework has been used to *describe* actual behaviour (positive economics) and it has been used to *prescribe* socially optimal behaviour (normative economics).

Descriptive discounting models capture the property that most economic agents prefer current rewards to delayed rewards of similar magnitude. Such time preferences have been ascribed to a combination of mortality effects, impatience effects, and salience effects. However, mortality effects alone cannot explain time preferences, since mortality rates for young and middle-aged adults are at least 100 times too small to generate observed discounting patterns.

Normative intertemporal choice models divide into two approaches. The first approach accepts discounting as a valid normative construct, using revealed preference as a guiding principle. The second approach asserts that discounting is a normative mistake (except for a minor adjustment for mortality discounting). The second approach adopts zero discounting (or near-zero discounting) as the normative benchmark.

The most widely used discounting model assumes that total utility can be decomposed into a weighted sum – or weighted integral – of utility flows in each period of time (Ramsey, 1928):

$$U_t = \sum_{\tau=0}^{T-t} D(\tau) \cdot u_{t+\tau}.$$

In this representation: U_t is total utility from the perspective of the current period, t; T is the last period of life (which could be infinity for an intergenerational model); $u_{t+\tau}$ is flow utility in period $t+\tau$ ($u_{t+\tau}$ is sometimes referred to as felicity or as instantaneous utility); and $D(\tau)$ is the discount function. If delaying a reward reduces its value, then the discount function weakly *declines* as the delay, τ, *increases*:

$$D'(\tau) \leq 0.$$

Economists normalize $D(0)$ to 1. Economists assume that increasing felicity, $u_{t+\tau}$, weakly increases total utility, U_t. Combining all of these assumptions implies,

$$1 = D(0) \geq D(\tau) \geq D(\tau') \geq 0,$$

where $0 < \tau < \tau'$.

Time preferences are often summarized by the rate at which the discount function declines, $\rho(\tau)$. For differentiable discount functions, the discount rate is defined as

$$\rho(\tau) \equiv -\frac{D'(\tau)}{D(\tau)}.$$

(See Laibson, 2003, for the formulae for non-differentiable discount functions.) The higher the discount rate the greater the preference for immediate rewards over delayed rewards.

The discount factor is the inverse of the continuously compounded discount rate $\rho(\tau)$. So the discount factor is defined as

$$f(\tau) = \lim_{\Delta \to 0} \left(\frac{1}{1 + \rho(\tau)\Delta} \right)^{1/\Delta} = e^{-\rho(\tau)}.$$

The lower the discount factor the greater the preference for immediate rewards over delayed rewards.

The most commonly used discount function is the exponential discount function:

$$D(\tau) = \delta^\tau,$$

with $0 < \delta < 1$. For the exponential discount function, the discount rate is independent of the horizon, τ. Specifically, the discount rate is $-\ln(\delta)$ and the discount factor is δ, Figure 1.

The exponential discount function also has the property of dynamic consistency: preferences held at one point in time do not change with the passage of time (unless new information arrives). For example, consider the following investment opportunity: pay a utility cost of C at date $t = 2$ to reap a utility benefit of B at date $t = 3$. Suppose that this project is viewed from date $t = 1$ and judged to be worth pursuing. Hence, $-\delta C + \delta^2 B > 0$. Imagine that a period of time passes, and the agent reconsiders the project from the perspective of date $t = 2$. Now the project is still worth pursuing, since $-C + \delta B > 0$. To prove that this is true, note that the new expression is equal to

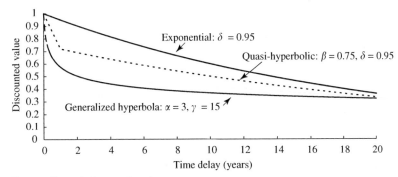

Figure 1   Three calibrated discount functions

the old expression multiplied by $1/\delta$. Hence, the $t=1$ preference to complete the project is preserved at date $t=2$. The exponential discount function is the *only* discount function that generates dynamically consistent preferences.

Despite its many appealing properties, the exponential discount function fails to match several empirical regularities. Most importantly, a large body of research has found that measured discount functions decline at a higher rate in the short run than in the long run. In other words, people appear to be more impatient when they make short-run trade-offs – today vs. tomorrow – than when they make long-run trade-offs – day 100 vs. day 101. This property has led psychologists (Herrnstein, 1961; Ainslie, 1992; Loewenstein and Prelec, 1992) to adopt discount functions in the family of generalized hyperbolas:

$$D(\tau) = (1 + \alpha\tau)^{-\gamma/\alpha}.$$

Such discount functions have the property that the discount rate is higher in the short run than in the long run. Particular attention has been paid to the case in which $\gamma=\alpha$, implying that $D(\tau) = (1 + \alpha\tau)^{-1}$.

Starting with Strotz (1956), economists have also studied alternatives to exponential discount functions. The majority of economic research has studied the quasi-hyperbolic discount function, which is usually defined in discrete time:

$$D(\tau) = \left\{ \begin{array}{ll} 1 & \text{if } \tau = 0 \\ \beta \cdot \delta^\tau & \text{if } \tau = 1, 2, 3, \ldots \end{array} \right\}.$$

This discount function was first used by Phelps and Pollak (1968) to study intergenerational discounting. Laibson (1997) subsequently applied this discount function to intra-personal decision problems. When $0 < \beta < 1$ and $0 < \delta < 1$ the quasi-hyperbolic discount function has a high short-run discount rate and a relatively low long-run discount rate. The quasi-hyperbolic discount function nests the exponential discount function as a special case ($\beta = 1$). Quasi-hyperbolic time preferences are also referred to as 'present-biased' and 'quasi-geometric'.

Like other non-exponential discount functions, the quasi-hyperbolic discount function implies that intertemporal preferences are not dynamically consistent. In other words, the passage of time may change an agent's preferences, implying that preferences are dynamically inconsistent. To illustrate this phenomenon, consider an investment project with a cost of 6 at date $t=2$ and a delayed benefit of 8 at date $t=3$. If $\beta = 1/2$ and $\delta=1$ (see Akerlof, 1991), this investment is desirable from the perspective of date $t=1$. The discounted value is positive:

$$\beta(-6 + 8) = \tfrac{1}{2}(-6 + 8) = 1.$$

However, the project is undesirable from the perspective of date 2. Judging the project from the $t=2$ perspective, the discounted value is negative:

$$-6 + \beta(8) = -6 + \tfrac{1}{2}(8) = -2.$$

This is an example of a preference reversal. At date $t=1$ the agent prefers to do the project at $t=2$. At date $t=2$ the agent prefers not to do the project. If economic agents foresee such preference reversals they are said to be sophisticated and if they do not foresee such preference reversals they are said to be naive (Strotz, 1956). O'Donoghue and Rabin (2001) propose a generalized formulation in which agents are partially naive: the agents have an imperfect ability to anticipate their preference reversals.

Many different microfoundations have been proposed to explain the preference patterns captured by the hyperbolic and quasi-hyperbolic discount functions. The most prominent examples include temptation models and dual-brain neuroeconomic models (Bernheim and Rangel, 2004; Gul and Pesendorfer, 2001; McClure et al., 2004; Thaler and Shefrin, 1981). However, both the properties and mechanisms of time preferences remain in dispute.

Individual differences in measured discount rates

Numerous methods have been used to measure discount functions. The most common technique poses a series of questions, each of which asks the subject to choose between a sooner, smaller reward and a later, larger reward. Usually the sooner, smaller reward is an *immediate* reward. The sooner and later rewards are denominated in the same goods, typically amounts of money or other items of value. For example: 'Would you rather have $69 today, or $85 in 91 days?' The subject's discount rate is inferred by fitting one or more of the discount functions described in the previous section to the subject choices. Most studies assume that the utility function is linear in consumption. Most studies also assume no intertemporal fungibility – the reward is assumed to be consumed the moment it is received. Many factors may confound the analysis in such studies, leading numerous researchers to express scepticism about the conclusions generated by laboratory studies. Table 1 provides a summary of such critiques.

Discount functions may also be inferred from field behaviour, such as consumption, savings, asset allocation, and voluntary adoption of forced-savings technologies (Angeletos et al., 2001; Shapiro, 2005; Ashraf, Karlan and Yin, 2006). However, field studies are also vulnerable to methodological critiques. There is currently no methodological gold standard for measuring discount functions.

Existing attempts to measure discount functions have reached seemingly conflicting conclusions (Frederick, Lowenstein and O'Donoghue, 2003). However, the fact that different methods and samples yield different estimates does not rule out consistent individual differences. Dozens of empirical studies have explored the relationship between individuals' estimated discount rates and a variety of behaviours and traits. A significant subset of this literature has focused on delay discounting and behaviour in clinical populations, most notably drug users, gamblers, and those with other impulsivity-linked psychiatric disorders (see Reynolds, 2006, for a review). Other work has explored the relationship between discounting and traits such as age and cognitive ability. Table 2 summarizes representative studies.

Table 1   *Potential confounds that may arise in attempts to measure discount rates in laboratory studies*

Factor	Description
Unreliability of future rewards	A subject may prefer an earlier reward because the subject thinks she is unlikely to actually receive the later reward. For example, the subject may perceive an experimenter as unreliable.
Transaction costs	A subject may prefer an immediate reward because it is paid in cash, whereas the delayed reward is paid in a form that generates additional transaction costs. For example, a delayed reward may need to be collected, or it may arrive in the form of a cheque that needs to be cashed.
Hypothetical rewards	A subject may not reveal her true preferences if she is asked hypothetical questions instead of being asked to make choices with real consequences. However, researchers who have directly compared real and hypothetical rewards have concluded that this difference does not arise in practice (Johnson and Bickel, 2002).
Investment versus consumption	Some subjects may interpret a choice in a discounting experiment as an *investment* decision and not a decision about the timing of consumption. For example, a subject might reason that a later, larger reward is superior to a sooner, smaller reward as long as the return for waiting is higher than the return available in financial markets.
Consumption versus receipt	Rewards, especially large ones, may not be consumed at the time they are received. For example, a $500 reward is likely to produce a stream of higher consumption, not a lump of consumption at the date of receipt. Such effects may explain why large-stake experiments are associated with less measured discounting than small-stake experiments
Curvature of utility function	A subject may prefer a sooner, smaller reward to a later, larger reward if the subject expects to receive other sources of income at that later date. In general, a reward may be worth less if it is received during a period of relative prosperity.
Framing effects	The menu of choices or the set of questions may influence the subject's choices. For example, if choices between $1.00 now and delayed amounts ranging between $1.01 and $1.50 were offered, subjects may switch preference from early to later rewards at an interior threshold – for example $1.30. However, if choices between $1.00 and delayed amounts ranging between $1.51 and $2.00 were offered, the switch might happen at a much higher threshold – for example $1.70 – implying a much higher discount rate.
Demand characteristics	Procedures for estimating discount rates may bias subject responses by implicitly guiding their choices. For example, the phrasing of an experimental question can imply that a particular choice is the right or desired answer (from the perspective of the experimenter).

Smoking. A number of investigations have explored the relationship between cigarette smoking and discounting, together providing strong evidence that cigarette smoking is associated with higher discount rates (Baker, Johnson and Bickel, 2003; Bickel, Odum and Madden, 1999; Kirby and Petry, 2004; Mitchell, 1999; Ohmura, Takahashi and Kitamura, 2005; Reynolds et al., 2004).

Excessive alcohol consumption. While the association with alcoholism has received relatively little attention, the available data suggest that problematic drinking is associated with higher discount rates. Heavy drinkers have higher discount rates than controls (Vuchinich and Simpson, 1998), active alcoholics discount rewards more

Table 2 *Representative empirical studies linking estimated discount rates for monetary rewards to various individual behaviours and traits*

Variable	Study	N	Discount rate findings
Nicotine	Bickel, Odum and Madden (1999)*	66	Current smokers > never-smokers and ex-smokers
Alcohol	Bjork et al. (2004)	160	Abstinent alcohol-dependent subjects > controls
Cocaine	Coffey et al. (2003)*	25	Crack-dependent subjects > matched controls[a]
Heroin	Kirby, Petry and Bickel (1999)	116	Heroin addicts > age-matched controls
Gambling	Petry (2001b)*	86	Pathological gamblers[b] > controls
Risky Behaviour	Odum et al. (2000)*	32	Heroin addicts agreeing to share needle in a hypothetical scenario > non-agreeing
Age	Green, Fry and Myerson (1994)*	36	Children > young adults > older adults
Psychiatric disorders	Crean, de Wit and Richards (2000)	24	'High risk' patients[c] > 'low risk' patients
Cognitive ability	Benjamin, Brown and Shapiro(2006)	92	Low scorers on standardized mathematics test > high scorers

Notes: N = total number of participants in study.
* These studies used hypothetical rewards; others used real rewards.
[a] Results based on those choices falling within the delay range of 1 week to 25 years. Overall analyses including shorter delays (5 minutes to 5 days) also revealed the same effect, but with smaller magnitude.
[b] Gamblers with comorbid substance abuse disorders showed a greater effect than gamblers without such disorders.
[c]'High risk' patients were those diagnosed with disorders carrying high risk for impulsive behaviour, according to *DSM-IV* criteria, such as patients with borderline personality disorder, bipolar disorder, and substance abuse disorders.

than abstinent alcoholics, who in turn discount at higher rates than controls (Petry, 2001a), and detoxified alcohol-dependents have higher discount rates than controls (Bjork et al., 2004).

Illicit drug use. Recent studies document a positive association between discount rates and drug use for a variety of illicit drugs, most notably cocaine, crack-cocaine, heroin and amphetamines (Petry, 2003; Coffey et al., 2003; Bretteville-Jensen, 1999; Kirby and Petry, 2004).

Gambling. Pathological gamblers have higher discount rates than controls, both in the laboratory (Petry, 2001b) and in a more natural setting (Dixon, Marley and Jacobs, 2003), and among a population of gambling and non-gambling substance abusers (Petry and Casarella, 1999). Moreover, Alessi and Petry (2003) report a significant, positive relationship between a gambling severity measure and the discount rate within a sample of problem gamblers. Petry (2001b) finds that gambling frequency during the previous three months correlates positively with discount rate.

Age. Patience appears to increase across the lifespan, with the young showing markedly less patience than middle-aged and older adults (Green, Fry and Myerson, 1994; Green et al. 1996; Green, Myerson and Ostazewski, 1999). Read and Read (2004) report that older adults (mean age = 75) are the most patient age group when delay horizons are only one year. However, this study also finds that older adults are the *least* patient group when delay horizons are from three to ten years. This reversal probably reflects the fact that 75-year-olds face significant mortality/disability risk at horizons of three to ten years.

Cognitive ability. Kirby, Winston and Santiesteban (2005) report that discount rates are correlated negatively with grade point average in two college samples. Benjamin, Brown and Shapiro (2006) find an inverse relationship between individual discount rates and standardized (mathematics) test scores for Chilean high school students. Silva and Gross (2004) show that students scoring in the top third of their introductory psychology course have lower discount rates than those scoring in the middle and lower thirds. Frederick (2005) shows that participants scoring high on a 'cognitive reflection' problem-solving task demonstrate more patient intertemporal choices (for a variety of rewards) than those scoring low. Finally, in a sample of smokers, Jaroni et al. (2004) report that participants who did not attend college had higher discount rates than those attending at least some college.

All of these empirical regularities are consistent with the neuroeconomic hypothesis that prefrontal cortex is essential for patient (forward-looking) decision-making (McClure et al., 2004). This area of the brain is slow to mature, is critical for general cognitive ability (Chabris, 2007), and is often found to be dysfunctional in addictive and other psychiatric disorders.

More research is required to clarify the cognitive and neurobiological bases of intertemporal preferences. Future research should evaluate the usefulness of measured discount functions in predicting real-world economic decisions (Ashraf, Karlan and Yin, 2006). Finally, ongoing research should improve the available methods for measuring intertemporal preferences.

CHRISTOPHER F. CHABRIS, DAVID I. LAIBSON AND JONATHON P. SCHULDT

Bibliography

Ainslie, G. 1992. *Picoeconomics*. New York: Cambridge University Press.

Akerlof, G.A. 1991. Procrastination and obedience. *American Economic Review* 81, 1–19.

Alessi, S.M. and Petry, N.M. 2003. Pathological gambling severity is associated with impulsivity in a delay discounting procedure. *Behavioural Processes* 64, 345–54.

Angeletos, G.-M., Laibson, D.I., Repetto, A., Tobacman, J. and Weinberg, S. 2001. The hyperbolic consumption model: calibration, simulation, and empirical evaluation. *Journal of Economic Perspectives* 15(3), 47–68.

Ashraf, N., Karlan, D.S. and Yin, W. 2006. Tying Odysseus to the mast: evidence from a commitment savings product in the Philippines. *Quarterly Journal of Economics* 121, 673–97.

Baker, F., Johnson, M.W. and Bickel, W.K. 2003. Delay discounting in current and never-before cigarette smokers: similarities and differences across commodity, sign, and magnitude. *Journal of Abnormal Psychology* 112, 382–92.

Benjamin, D.J., Brown, S.A. and Shapiro, J.M. 2006. Who is 'behavioral'? Cognitive ability and anomalous preferences. Unpublished manuscript, University of Michigan.

Bernheim, B.D. and Rangel, A. 2004. Addiction and cue-triggered decision processes. *American Economic Review* 94, 1558–90.

Bickel, W.K., Odum, A.L. and Madden, G.J. 1999. Impulsivity and cigarette smoking: delay discounting in current, never, and ex-smokers. *Psychopharmacology* 146, 447–54.

Bjork, J.M., Hommer, D.W., Grant, S.J. and Danube, C. 2004. Impulsivity in abstinent alcohol-dependent patients: relation to control subjects and type 1-/type 2-like traits. *Alcohol* 34, 133–50.

Bornovalova, M.A., Daughters, S.B., Hernandez, G.D., Richards, J.B. et al. 2005. Differences in impulsivity and risk-taking propensity between primary users of crack cocaine and primary users of heroin in a residential substance-use program. *Experimental and Clinical Psychopharmacology* 13, 311–8.

Bretteville-Jensen, A.L. 1999. Addiction and discounting. *Journal of Health Economics* 18, 393–407.

Chabris, C.F. 2007. Cognitive and neurobiological mechanisms of the law of general intelligence. In *Integrating the Mind*, ed. M.J. Roberts. Hove, UK: Psychology Press.

Coffey, S.F., Gudleski, G.D., Saladin, M.E. and Brady, K.T. 2003. Impulsivity and rapid discounting of delayed hypothetical rewards in cocaine-dependent individuals. *Experimental and Clinical Psychopharmacology* 11, 18–25.

Crean, J.P., de Wit, H. and Richards, J.B. 2000. Reward discounting as a measure of impulsive behavior in a psychiatric outpatient population. *Experimental and Clinical Psychopharmacology* 8, 155–62.

Dixon, M.R., Marley, J. and Jacobs, E.A. 2003. Delay discounting by pathological gamblers. *Journal of Applied Behavior Analysis* 36(4), 449–58.

Field, M., Santarcangelo, M., Sumnall, H., Goudie, A. et al. 2006. Delay discounting and the behavioural economics of cigarette purchases in smokers: the effects of nicotine deprivation. *Psychopharmacology* 186, 255–63.

Frederick, S. 2005. Cognitive reflection and decision making. *Journal of Economic Perspectives* 19(4), 24–42.

Frederick, S., Loewenstein, G. and O'Donoghue, T. 2003. Time discounting and time preference: a critical review. In *Time and Decision: Economic and Psychological Perspectives on Intertemporal Choice*, ed. G. Loewenstein, D. Read and R. Baumeister. New York: Sage.

Giordano, L.A., Bickel, W.K., Loewenstein, G., Jacobs, E.A. et al. 2002. Mild opioid deprivation increases the degree that opioid-dependent outpatients discount delayed heroin and money. *Psychopharmacology* 163, 174–82.

Green, L., Fry, A.F. and Myerson, J. 1994. Discounting of delayed rewards: a life-span comparison. *Psychological Science* 5, 33–7.

Green, L., Myerson, J. and Ostazewski, P. 1999. Discounting of delayed rewards across the life span: age differences in individual discounting functions. *Behavioural Processes* 46, 89–96.

Green, L., Myerson, J., Lichtman, D., Rosen, S. and Fry, A. 1996. Temporal discounting in choice between delayed rewards: the role of age and income. *Psychology and Ageing* 11, 79–84.

Gul, F. and Pesendorfer, W. 2001. Temptation and self-control. *Econometrica* 69, 1403–35.

Herrnstein, R.J. 1961. Relative and absolute strength of response as a function of frequency of reinforcement. *Journal of the Experimental Analysis of Behavior* 4, 267–72.

Hinson, J.M., Jameson, T.L. and Whitney, P. 2003. Impulsive decision making and working memory. *Journal of Experimental Psychology: Learning, Memory, and Cognition* 29, 298–306.

Holt, D.D., Green, L. and Myerson, J. 2003. Is discounting impulsive? Evidence from temporal and probability discounting in gambling and non-gambling college students. *Behavioural Processes* 64, 355–67.

Jaroni, J.L., Wright, S.M., Lerman, C. and Epstein, L.H. 2004. Relationship between education and delay discounting in smokers. *Addictive Behaviors* 29, 1171–5.

Johnson, M.W. and Bickel, W.K. 2002. Within-subject comparison of real and hypothetical money rewards in delay discounting. *Journal of the Experimental Analysis of Behavior* 77, 129–46.

Kirby, K.N. and Petry, N.M. 2004. Heroin and cocaine abusers have higher discount rates for delayed rewards than alcoholics or non-drug-using controls. *Addiction* 99, 461–71.

Kirby, K.N., Petry, N.M. and Bickel, W.K. 1999. Heroin addicts have higher discount rates for delayed rewards than non-drug-using controls. *Journal of Experimental Psychology: General* 128, 78–87.

Kirby, K.N., Winston, G.C. and Santiesteban, M. 2005. Impatience and grades: delay-discount rates correlate negatively with college GPA. *Learning and Individual Differences* 15, 213–22.

Laibson, D. 2003. Intertemporal decision making. In *Encyclopedia of Cognitive Science*. London: Nature Publishing Group.

Laibson, D. 1997. Golden eggs and hyperbolic discounting. *Quarterly Journal of Economics* 112, 443–77.

Loewenstein, G. and Prelec, D. 1992. Anomalies in intertemporal choice: evidence and an interpretation. *Quarterly Journal of Economics* 107, 573–97.

Madden, G.J., Begotka, A.M., Raiff, B.R. and Kastern, L.L. 2003. Delay discounting of real and hypothetical rewards. *Experimental and Clinical Psychopharmacology* 11, 139–45.

McClure, S.M., Laibson, D.I., Loewenstein, G. and Cohen, J.D. 2004. Separate neural systems value immediate and delayed monetary rewards. *Science* 306, 503–7.

Mitchell, S.H. 1999. Measures of impulsivity in cigarette smokers and non-smokers. *Psychopharmacology* 146, 455–64.

Mitchell, S.H. 2004. Effects of short-term nicotine deprivation on decision-making: delay, uncertainty, and effort discounting. *Nicotine and Tobacco Research* 6, 819–28.

O'Donoghue, T. and Rabin, M. 2001. Choice and procrastination. *Quarterly Journal of Economics* 116, 121–60.

Odum, A.L., Madden, G.J., Badger, G.J. and Bickel, W.K. 2000. Needle sharing in opioid-dependent outpatients: psychological processes underlying risk. *Drug and Alcohol Dependence* 60, 259–66.

Ohmura, Y., Takahashi, T. and Kitamura, N. 2005. Discounting delayed and probabilistic monetary gains and losses by smokers of cigarettes. *Psychopharmacology* 182, 508–15.

Ortner, C.N.M., MacDonald, T.K. and Olmstead, M.C. 2003. Alcohol intoxication reduces impulsivity in the delay-discounting paradigm. *Alcohol and Alcoholism* 38, 151–6.

Petry, N.M. 2001a. Delay discounting of money and alcohol in actively using alcoholics, currently abstinent alcoholics, and controls. *Psychopharmacology* 154, 243–50.

Petry, N.M. 2001b. Pathological gamblers, with and without substance use disorders, discount delayed rewards at high rates. *Journal of Abnormal Psychology* 3, 482–7.

Petry, N.M. 2003. Discounting of money, health, and freedom in substance abusers and controls. *Drug and Alcohol Dependence* 71, 133–41.

Petry, N.M. and Casarella, T. 1999. Excessive discounting of delayed rewards in substance abusers with gambling problems. *Drug and Alcohol Dependence* 56, 25–32.

Phelps, E.S. and Pollak, R.A. 1968. On second-best national saving and game-equilibrium growth. *Review of Economic Studies* 35, 185–99.

Ramsey, F. 1928. A mathematical theory of saving. *Economic Journal* 38, 543–9.

Read, D. and Read, N.L. 2004. Time discounting over the lifespan. *Organizational Behavior and Human Decision Processes* 94, 22–32.

Reynolds, B. 2006. A review of delay-discounting research with humans: relations to drug use and gambling. *Behavioural Pharmacology* 17, 651–67.

Reynolds, B., Richards, J.B., Horn, K. and Karraker, K. 2004. Delay discounting and probability discounting as related to cigarette smoking status in adults. *Behavioral Processes* 65, 35–42.

Shapiro, J.M. 2005. Is there a daily discount rate? Evidence from the food stamp nutrition cycle. *Journal of Public Economics* 89, 303–25.

Silva, F.J. and Gross, T.F. 2004. The rich get richer: students' discounting of hypothetical delayed rewards and real effortful extra credit. *Psychonomic Bulletin & Review* 11, 1124–8.

Strotz, R.H. 1956. Myopia and inconsistency in dynamic utility maximization. *Review of Economic Studies* 23, 165–80.

Thaler, R.H. and Shefrin, H.M. 1981. An economic theory of self-control. *Journal of Political Economy* 89, 392.

Vuchinich, R.E. and Simpson, C.A. 1998. Hyperbolic temporal discounting in social drinkers and problem drinkers. *Experimental and Clinical Psychopharmacology* 6, 292–305.

laboratory financial markets

Laboratory financial markets allow human subjects to trade assets under conditions controlled by the researcher. By varying the conditions – such as the trading format, or the timing and content of private information – the researcher can make direct and sharp inferences.

Such inferences are crucial to achieve insight into the ongoing debate about the importance of behavioural anomalies in financial markets (see BEHAVIOURAL FINANCE). Efficient markets and related theories provide a satisfying explanation for many of the properties of modern financial markets, but they are hard to reconcile with well documented 'market anomalies' such as home bias, the large equity premium and excessive volatility. Should financial economists force a reconciliation, or should they embrace prospect theory and other behavioural theories?

These issues are not just academic. Since the collapse of the Soviet bloc around 1990, a dominant share of the world economy has relied on financial markets to choose its economic future. If the efficient markets theory is wrong, and asset prices do not necessarily reflect all available information, then major restructuring may be in order. Perhaps the global economy would be stronger with information disclosures that cater to our behavioural idiosyncrasies, or even with non-market allocation of investment.

Laboratory asset markets inform the debate by offering evidence that complements field data. The strength of experimental methodology is that the researcher can precisely control information, public and private, and can elicit beliefs as well as track offers, transactions and allocations. Thus, in a simplified setting, researchers can systematically dissect the process of asset price formation. In conjunction with theory and field empirical work, laboratory investigations help us understand how financial markets really work.

Early laboratory markets

Experimental economics cut its teeth on laboratory commodity markets. Reacting to Edward Chamberlin's casual classroom experiments, Vernon Smith pioneered the scientific study of markets in the laboratory. He refined the idea of *induced value and cost*: the experimenter promises to pay a subject the amount v if she buys a unit, and charges another subject the amount c if he sells a unit. If they transact at price p, she earns $v-p$ and he earns $p-c$, generating surplus of $v-c$. The payments are in cash and large enough for the subjects to take seriously.

Smith introduced *stationary repetition* – several consecutive trading periods with the same endowed values and costs but no carry-over from one period to the next, so that subjects have the opportunity to adapt to the trading environment. He also brought the *continuous double auction* (CDA) market (sometimes referred to as the double oral auction) format into the laboratory: traders can make public, committed offers to buy and to sell and can accept others' offers at any time during a trading period. Variants of the CDA format predominate in modern financial markets, including the New York Stock Exchange (NYSE), NASDAQ, and the Chicago Mercantile Exchange.

Numerous laboratory studies, beginning with Smith (1962), show that CDA markets with only a few buyers and sellers (say, four of each) reliably produce highly efficient outcomes, where efficiency is defined as the fraction of potential surplus in the market that is captured by the buyers and sellers. Typically, over 95 per cent of total surplus is realized after a few periods of stationary repetition.

Such perishable commodity markets provide no interesting role for time or uncertainty, both important dimensions of financial assets. Laboratory financial markets should allow two-way traders who can both buy and sell, and who trade assets with a payout that is uncertain and/or carries over several periods. Experimenters at Caltech first introduced such markets in the early 1980s. For example, Plott and Sunder (1982) created a single period asset that was traded by six uninformed traders, who knew only that one of two states would occur with given probabilities independently each period, and six informed traders, who knew the realized state. Both informed and uninformed traders were distributed evenly across three types of state-contingent dividend schedules. Within a few periods, prices became highly efficient, and the trading patterns demonstrated that the market fully disseminated the private information. About the same time, several teams of researchers found very efficient asset prices in laboratory markets with assets paying individual- and state-contingent dividends over several trading periods. These and other early laboratory experiments demonstrated that futures and options contracts can speed convergence towards efficient asset prices. See Sunder (1995) for a thorough survey.

The main lesson from these studies is that financial markets can process information very efficiently. As Hayek (1945) conjectured, markets can fully aggregate and disseminate dispersed private information, and can do so quite rapidly. A few bids and asks in the CDA suffice to fully inform experienced traders, dealing appropriate assets, in moderately complex environments.

Dissecting financial markets

These positive early results encourage us to look more deeply at how financial markets process information. The process has several logical stages. Investors and other participants acquire relevant information from diverse sources, public and private. Individual investors incorporate the information into their beliefs about future asset prices. Acting on their beliefs, investors try to buy assets they expect to appreciate relatively rapidly and to sell assets that they expect to do less well. Their buy and sell orders in turn produce observable market outcomes such as asset price and trading volume. The market outcomes provide further public information for investors, other new information arrives from time to time, and so the process continues. We now know that the process can work quite well in favourable circumstances. But even the early laboratory studies show that it is sometimes fallible. When and where might it go wrong?

Each stage of the process can be examined in the laboratory and compared with theoretical predictions. Cognitive scientists focus on the first stage, the formation of beliefs given arriving information, and have documented many biases that might distort beliefs. Examples include overconfidence, the gambler's fallacy (believing that a coin that has come up 'heads' many times in succession is the more likely to come up 'tails') and the hot-hand fallacy (believing that basketball players who have made ten free throws in succession are especially likely to make the next). In the next stage, investors may make decision errors when they buy and sell assets, even when their beliefs are realistic. There are numerous examples, including hyperbolic (or quasi-hyperbolic) discounting, the disposition effect, and the sunk-cost fallacy.

It is often tempting to explain financial market anomalies simply by pointing to one or more of these biases and errors. But such explanations are incomplete and potentially erroneous. One problem is that there are so many documented biases and errors; indeed, a complete list seems not to exist. Given any market anomaly A, a diligent student can always find some decision error or bias B that superficially seems connected, whether or not B really causes A. Even more important, investors' biases and decision errors never translate directly into financial market imperfections. Asset prices are non-trivial functions of investors' buy and sell orders, and they provide information that affects subsequent orders and prices. These later stages of the process depend on the market format, and they can attenuate or amplify investors' biases and errors.

Attenuating biases and errors

Three different market forces can greatly attenuate the financial market impact of erratic investors. First, it is a powerful learning experience to lose money in a financial market, or even to see other investors do better when they have no informational advantage. Friedman (1998) and later studies demonstrate that people can overcome even the strongest biases and errors in a suitable learning environment. To the extent that a bias or error leads to clearly inferior performance, an investor will learn to do better over time. Subjects in most laboratory financial markets commit fewer errors and trade more efficiently in later periods than in earlier periods, and subjects with previous experience in a particular laboratory market do better yet.

Second, the market shares of investors with inferior trading strategies tend to shrink over time, reducing their influence on market performance. Blume and Easley (1992) demonstrate theoretically that wealth redistribution eventually eliminates all but the most effective investors. Laboratory studies routinely cancel out this force via stationary repetition, but it can easily be inferred by compounding relative profits across periods.

Third, persistent costly errors and biases create profit opportunities for entrepreneurs whose efforts attenuate (or even eliminate) the market impact. For example, yellow pages and speed dials help us overcome our cognitive limitations in remembering phone numbers. Similarly, mutual funds and a host of investor advisory services allow investors to sidestep their personal biases. Such entrepreneurs can create new problems but, as noted below, those problems also can be studied in the laboratory. Arbitrage is the most direct form of such entrepreneurship. If error-prone investors create an asset price discrepancy, this will attract profit-seeking arbitrageurs whose buy and sell orders tend to make it disappear. Laboratory studies, including those of Plott and Sunder (1982), confirm the power of arbitrage.

Amplifying biases and errors

There are also three strong forces that can amplify the market impact of errant investors. First, raw information is often gathered, analysed and released by individuals who have major personal stakes in the market reaction. Despite oversight by authorities such as the US Securities and Exchange Commission, these individuals may use their discretion to distort the market reaction. Bloomfield and O'Hara (1999) and subsequent laboratory studies confirm the possibility.

Second, professional fund managers typically are compensated (directly or indirectly, via competing job offers) for returns that rank highly relative to their peers. It is difficult to infer from field data whether such incentives have an impact, but inference is straightforward in the laboratory. James and Isaac (2000) find major distortions of laboratory asset prices when traders have rank-based performance incentives, and the distortions disappear in otherwise identical markets when traders are paid only their own realized returns.

Third, and most intriguingly, investors may go astray when they try to glean information from the trades of informed investors. Information mirages (for example, Camerer and Weigelt, 1991) can arise as follows. Uninformed trader A observes trader B attempting to buy (due to some slight cognitive bias, say) and mistakenly infers that B has favorable inside information. Then A tries to buy. Now trader C infers that A (or B) is an insider and tries to mimic their trades. Other traders follow, creating a price bubble.

Several research teams (including the author's) have occasionally observed such episodes in the laboratory. They cannot be produced consistently, because incurred losses teach traders to be cautious when they suspect the presence of better-informed traders. The lesson does not necessarily improve market efficiency, since excessive caution impedes information aggregation.

Price bubbles deserve longer discussion, as bubbles have produced important distortions in market prices. Asset prices seemed to disconnect from fundamental value in Japan in the late 1980s, in the dot.com bubble and crash of 1997–2002, and in a number of other episodes since the famous 17th and 18th century events now known as tulipmania and the South Sea bubble. Do such episodes indicate dysfunctional financial markets? Perhaps, but the field data also can be interpreted merely as unusual movements in fundamental value (Garber, 1989). By contrast, in the laboratory the experimenter can always observe (or more typically, control) the fundamental value, so bubbles can be detected and measured precisely.

Smith, Suchanek and Williams (1988) found large positive bubbles, and subsequent crashes, for long-lived laboratory assets and inexperienced traders. Figure 1 shows a representative example. The expected dividend is constant, so the fundamental value (the sum of expected remaining dividends) declines steadily over the 15 trading periods. Ask ('offer') and bid prices start low, but by the second period the transaction prices (indicated by lines connecting accepted bids and asks) rise above fundamental

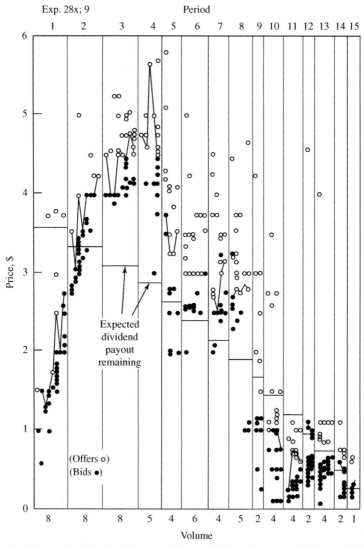

Figure 1   A bubble and crash in the laboratory. *Source*: Smith, Suchanek and Williams (1988, Figure 9).

value. The bubble inflates rapidly until late in period 4. In period 9, prices crash below fundamental value.

Keynes's 'greater fool' theory provides a possible interpretation. Traders who themselves have no cognitive bias might be willing to buy at a price above fundamental value because they expect to sell later at even higher prices to other traders dazzled by rising prices. Subsequent studies confirm that such dazzled traders do exist, and that bubbles are more prevalent when traders are less experienced (individually and as a group), have larger cash endowments, and have less conclusive information.

Current frontiers: market formats, agents, and prediction markets

Which underlying biases and errors are most important? When does attenuation predominate, and when does amplification? Accumulating laboratory evidence inspires new theoretical and empirical field work as well as follow-up laboratory studies.

It is increasingly clear that answers hinge on the market format or institution – the rules that transform bids and asks into transactions. In particular, the CDA format allows all traders to observe other traders' attempts to buy and sell in real time, and thereby encourages information dissemination. The CDA format attenuates the impact of erratic traders because the closing price is not set by the most biased trader or even by a random trader. The most optimistic traders buy (or already hold) and the most pessimistic traders sell (or never held) the asset, so the closing price reflects the moderate expectations of marginal traders.

Other traditional formats include the call market (CM), in which bids and asks (or limit orders) are gathered and executed simultaneously at a uniform price, and the posted offer (PO), in which one side (usually sellers) simultaneously announces prices and the other side (buyers) choose transaction quantities at the given prices. Many other formats and hybrids are possible in the Internet age. Which formats are most efficient? Which can attract market share from other formats? Work so far indicates that the CM format does relatively well for thinly traded assets and the PO format works best when the posting side is more concentrated; but the questions remain far from settled.

Related new work blurs the line between computer simulations and laboratory markets. Computer algorithms for artificial agents, or bots, incorporate specified cognitive limitations, and simulations examine the market level impact (for example, Arthur et al., 1997). Gode and Sunder (1993) showed that simple perishables CDA markets are quite efficient even when populated by zero intelligence (ZI) agents, bots that are constrained not to take losses but are otherwise quite random. Current work puts ZI and more intelligent bots into the same asset markets as human traders, and compares efficiency and the distribution of surplus. Such work should help inform regulators, reformers, and entrepreneurs creating new asset markets. Early published examples of policy-oriented research includes performance assessment of (*a*) trader privileges such as price posting and access to order flow information (for example, Friedman, 1993), and (*b*) transaction taxes, price change limits and trading suspensions intended (typically ineffectively) to mitigate price bubbles and panics (for example, Coursey and Dyl, 1990).

Prediction markets, which use the information-aggregation property of markets to forecast events such as election outcomes, are gaining increased attention. The Iowa Electronic Market, designed and operated by experimental economists (Berg et al., 2008), offers various assets that pay the holder ten dollars if (and only if) a specified event occurs by a specified date. Participants self-select, are not representative of the general public, and their trades exhibit partisan bias – for example, self-styled Democrats are more likely to buy assets that pay off when the Democratic Party candidates win. Nevertheless, political event asset prices have consistently out-performed opinion polls and all other available predictors. Prediction markets are a growing presence on the Internet, for example tradesports.com, and some corporations such as HP are beginning to rely on them when making business decisions. The line between laboratory and field financial markets is beginning to blur.

DANIEL FRIEDMAN

See also **behavioural finance.**

Bibliography

Arthur, W.B., Holland, J.H., LeBaron, B., Palmer, R. and Taylor, P. 1997. Asset pricing under endogenous expectations in an artificial stock market. In *The Economy as an Evolving Complex System II*, ed. W.B. Arthur, S.N. Durlauf and D.A. Lane. Reading, MA: Addison-Wesley.

Berg, J., Forsythe, R., Nelson, F. and Rietz, T. 2008. Results from a dozen years of election futures markets research. In *Handbook of Experimental Economics Results*, ed. C. Plott and V. Smith. Amsterdam: North-Holland (forthcoming).

Bloomfield, R.J. and O'Hara, M. 1999. Market transparency: who wins and who loses? *Review of Financial Studies* 12, 5–35.

Blume, L. and Easley, K. 1992. Evolution and market behavior. *Journal of Economic Theory* 58, 9–40.

Camerer, C. and Weigelt, K. 1991. Information mirages in experimental asset markets. *The Journal of Business* 64, 463–93.

Coursey, D.L. and Dyl, E.A. 1990. Price limits, trading suspension, and the adjustment of prices to new information. *Review of Futures Markets* 9, 343–60.

Friedman, D. 1993. How trading institutions affect financial market performance: some laboratory evidence. *Economic Inquiry* 31, 410–35.

Friedman, D. 1998. Monty Hall's three doors: construction and deconstruction of a choice anomaly. *American Economic Review* 88, 933–46.

Garber, P.M. 1989. Tulipmania. *Journal of Political Economy* 97, 535–60.

Gode, D.K. and Sunder, S. 1993. Allocative efficiency of markets with zero intelligence traders: market as a partial substitute for individual rationality. *Journal of Political Economy* 101, 119–37.

Hayek, F.A. 1945. The use of knowledge in society. *American Economic Review* 35, 519–30.

Holt, C.A. 1999. Y2K bibliography of experimental economics and social science asset market experiments. Online. Available at http://people.virginia.edu/~cah2k/assety2k.htm, accessed 19 February 2007.

James, D. and Isaac, R.M. 2000. Asset markets: how they are affected by tournament incentives for individuals. *American Economic Review* 90, 995–1004.

Plott, C.R. and Sunder, S. 1982. Efficiency of experimental security markets with insider information: an application of rational-expectations models. *Journal of Political Economy* 90, 663–98.

Smith, V.L. 1962. An experimental study of competitive market behavior. *Journal of Political Economy* 70, 111–37.

Smith, V.L., Suchanek, G.L. and Williams, A.W. 1988. Bubbles, crashes, and endogenous expectations in experimental spot asset markets. *Econometrica* 56, 1119–51.

Sunder, S. 1995. Experimental asset markets: a survey. In *The Handbook of Experimental Economics*, ed. J.H. Kagel and A.E. Roth. Princeton, NJ: Princeton University Press.

market power and collusion in laboratory markets

The robustness of competitive market predictions stands as one of the most impressive results in experimental economics. Laboratory markets regularly generate competitive outcomes in environments populated by just two or three sellers. However, as in natural contexts, competitive outcomes do not always emerge. This article reviews results of laboratory markets in which price increases are driven by factors such as the exercise of unilateral market power or by collusion.

Before reviewing the main concepts and contributions in this area, I offer two observations. First, laboratory methods represent an important but limited complement to existing empirical tools for investigating market performance. Given the stark simplicity and limited duration of laboratory markets, experimentalists can aspire to say little about specific naturally occurring markets. Experiments can, however, provide important insights into the behavioural relevance of theories upon which antitrust policies are based.

Second, the trading rules defining negotiations and contracting can exert first-order effects on market competitiveness. For example, markets organized under the double auction trading rules used in many financial exchanges, are much more robustly competitive than markets organized under the posted-offer trading rules used in most retail exchanges: duopoly or even monopoly sellers are less able to increase market prices in double-auction than in posted-offer markets (Davis and Holt, 1993, chs 3, 4; Holt, 1995). Indeed, one of the motivating factors in the emerging field of institutional design was an interest in developing institutional rules that promoted efficient market outcomes.

For specificity I focus here on results from posted-offer markets, primarily because posted-offer markets allow a particularly intuitive illustration of the factors affecting market competitiveness. However, a host of other trading institutions exist, ranging from single and multi-unit auctions, to multi-sided computerized 'smart' markets, and again to institutions that exist primarily as theoretical constructs, such as quantity-setting Cournot mechanisms. The competitive implications of each of these institutions must be evaluated independently.

Posted-offer markets and unilateral market power

Unilateral market power is perhaps the most frequently observed reason why prices in laboratory markets deviate from competitive predictions. This market power exists when one or more sellers, acting on their own, find it profitable to raise prices above the competitive level. The supply and demand structures shown in the two panels of Figure 1 illustrate how capacity restrictions can create market power. In each panel, the market consists of three sellers, S1, S2 and S3, each of whom offers four units for

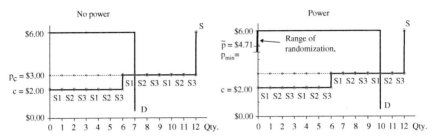

Figure 1   Supply and demand arrays for markets without and with unilateral market power

sale, under the conditions that two units cost $2.00 and two units cost $3.00. A buyer will purchase a fixed number of units (seven in the left panel or ten in the right panel) at prices less than or equal to $6.00.

Exchange in these markets proceeds in a number of trading periods. At the outset of each period, sellers simultaneously make price decisions. Production is 'to order' in the sense that sellers incur costs only for the units that actually sell. Once all sellers post prices, a simulated fully revealing buyer makes all possible purchases, starting with the least expensive units first. In the case of a tie, the buyer rotates purchases among the tied sellers.

In the market shown in the left panel of Figure 1 the buyer will purchase at most seven units. Given an aggregate supply of 12 units, sellers in this market have no market power: at any common price above $3.00, each seller can increase sales from an expected 2.33 units to four units by posting a price just slightly below the common price. For any vector of heterogeneous prices above $3.00 only the seller posting the lowest price will sell all four units. The seller posting the second highest price will sell three units, while the high-pricing seller will sell nothing. The unique Nash equilibrium for the stage game has each seller posting the competitive price of $3.00, selling 2.33 units in expectation and earning $2.00.

Expanding demand to ten units, as shown in the right panel of Figure 1, limits excess supply, and thus creates market power. Given that the highest price seller is now certain to sell at least two units, the competitive price of $3.00 is no longer a Nash equilibrium for the stage game. At a common price of $3.00 each seller sells 3.33 units (in expectation) and earns $2.00. By posting a price of $6.00, any seller can sell two units and increase earnings to $8.00. A common price of $6.00 is not an equilibrium for the stage game, since any seller would find that deviating from $6.00 increases sales to four units. Sellers have similar incentives to undercut any common price down to a minimum $p_{min} = \$4.50$, where the profits from selling four units as the lowest pricing seller equals earnings at the limit price. The equilibrium for this game involves mixing over the range from $4.50 to $6.00. As shown in the figure, the unique symmetric equilibrium is $4.71.

An extensive series of experiments show that sellers respond to unilateral market power by raising prices. Further, power drives pricing outcomes more powerfully than do changes in the number of sellers. For example, when they reallocated units among five sellers to create market power, Davis and Holt (1994) observed substantial price increases. However, reducing the number of sellers from five to three in a way that held market power conditions fixed, Davis and Holt observed only modest additional price increases. Market power of the sort illustrated in the right panel of Figure 1 has wide applications, ranging from distortions in markets for emissions trading (Godby, 2000) and for electricity transmission (Rassenti, Smith and Wilson, 2003), to price stickiness in the face of aggregate demand shocks (Wilson, 1998).

Tacit collusion

Experimentalists have also observed supra-competitive prices in repeated market games where sellers have no market power. This *tacit collusion* has been observed most frequently in duopolies (for example, Alger, 1987; Fouraker and Seigel, 1963). However, tacit collusion has also been observed in thicker markets where sellers possess no market power. For example, Cason and Williams (1990) observe persistently high prices in a four-seller design similar to that shown as the left panel of Figure 1. Experimentalists often measure tacit collusion as the difference between observed prices and prices consistent with the Nash equilibrium for the market analysed as a stage game. Importantly, other than exceeding equilibrium price predictions, tacitly collusive laboratory outcomes typically exhibit no obvious signs of coordinated activity.

Tacit collusion may coexist with market power. For example, prices in the market power sessions reported by Davis and Holt (1994) were significantly above prices consistent with the equilibrium mixing distribution. In this context, the difference between mean observed prices and the mean of the equilibrium mixing distribution may be reasonably taken as a measure of tacit collusion.

Tacit collusion is not yet well understood, and isolating the causes of tacit collusion represents an important project for future experimental work. Price signalling activity at least partially explains tacit collusion (for example, Durham et al., 2004). However, evidence suggests that more than price signals and responses may be at play. Dufwenberg and Gneezy (2000) report an experiment where duopolists deviate from the static Nash (competitive) prediction for a game, even when sellers are rematched into different markets after each decision. In such a context price signalling is not possible.

Explicit collusion

Given opportunities to explicitly discuss pricing, laboratory sellers quite persistently organize profit-increasing cartels (Isaac, Ramey and Williams, 1984). However, a capacity to monitor agreements and prevent secret discounts appears critical to the success of these arrangements (Davis and Holt, 1998). Given the illegality of explicit agreements, the more interesting questions regarding explicit collusion concern the capacity of authorities to detect such arrangements through the actions of sellers in the market (Davis and Wilson, 2002).

Other factors affecting pricing

A host of experimental studies indicate that standard 'facilitating practices' can contribute to price increases. Experimental studies where supra-competitive prices have been attributed to facilitating practices include 'most favoured nation' and 'meet-or-release' clauses (Grether and Plott, 1984), non-binding price signals (Holt and Davis, 1990) and multi-market competition (Phillips and Mason, 1991).

Buyer behaviour can also affect market outcomes. When buyer decisions are simulated, details of the purchasing rules can have a large effect on prices (Kruse, 1993). Powerful human buyers can substantially undermine both market power and tacit collusion (Ruffle, 2000). However, the use of real rather than simulated buyers appears to generate more competitive prices even when the human buyers engage in no strategic behaviour (Coursey et al., 1984).

Finally, information conditions and even sellers' expectations can significantly affect pricing outcomes. For example, Huck, Norman and Oechssler (2000) report that information regarding underlying supply and demand conditions facilitates the exercise of predicted market power (markets are drawn to static Nash predictions). However, information on rival sellers' profits made markets more competitive in a market where the high-profit seller has the highest market share, so imitation by others will tend to expand quantity and reduce price. Also, in a Cournot context, Huck et al. (2007) report that seller aspirations for increased profits helped consolidated sellers maintain prices substantially above static Nash levels.

DOUGLAS D. DAVIS

Bibliography

Alger, D. 1987. Laboratory tests of equilibrium predictions with disequilibrium price data. *Review of Economic Studies* 54, 105–45.

Cason, T.N. and Williams, A.W. 1990. Competitive equilibrium convergence in posted-offer markets with extreme earnings inequities. *Journal of Economic Behavior and Organization* 14, 331–52.

Coursey, D., Isaac, R.M., Luke, M. and Smith, V.L. 1984. Market contestability in the presence of sunk (entry) costs. *RAND Journal of Economics* 15, 69–84.

Davis, D.D. and Holt, C.A. 1993. *Experimental Economics*. Princeton: Princeton University Press.

Davis, D.D. and Holt, C.A. 1994. Market power and mergers in laboratory markets with posted prices. *RAND Journal of Economics* 25, 467–87.

Davis, D.D. and Holt, C.A. 1998. Conspiracies and secret discounts in laboratory markets. *Economic Journal* 108, 736–56.

Davis, D.D. and Wilson, B. 2002. An experimental investigation of methods for detecting collusion. *Economic Inquiry* 40, 213–30.

Dufwenberg, M. and Gneezy, U. 2000. Price competition and market concentration: an experimental study. *International Journal of Industrial Organization* 18, 7–22.

Durham, Y., McCabe, K., Olson, M.A., Rassenti, S. and Smith, V. 2004. Oligopoly competition in fixed cost environments. *International Journal of Industrial Organization* 22, 147–62.

Fouraker, L.E. and Siegel, S. 1963. *Bargaining Behavior*. New York: McGraw-Hill.

Godby, R. 2000. Market power and emission trading: theory and laboratory results. *Pacific Economic Review* 5, 349–64.

Grether, D.M. and Plott, C.R. 1984. The effects of market practices in oligopolistic markets: an experimental examination of the ethyl case. *Economic Inquiry* 24, 479–507.

Holt, C.A. 1995. Industrial organization: a survey of laboratory research. In *The Handbook of Industrial Organization*, ed. J.H. Kagel and A.E. Roth. Princeton: Princeton University Press.

Holt, C.A. and Davis, D.D. 1990. The effects of non-binding price announcements on posted-offer markets. *Economics Letters* 34, 307–10.

Huck, S., Normann, H. and Oechssler, J. 2000. Does information about competitors' actions increase or decrease competition in experimental oligopoly markets? *International Journal of Industrial Organization* 18, 39–57.

Huck, S., Konrad, K.A., Müller, W. and Normann, H.T. 2007. The merger paradox and why aspiration levels let it fail in the laboratory. *Economic Journal* 117, 1073–95.

Isaac, R.M., Ramey, V. and Williams, A. 1984. The effects of market organization on conspiracies in restraint of trade. *Journal of Economic Behavior and Organization* 5, 191–222.

Kruse, J.B. 1993. Nash equilibrium and buyer rationing rules: experimental evidence. *Economic Inquiry* 31, 631–66.

Phillips, O.R. and Mason, C.F. 1991. Mutual forbearance in experimental congolomerate markets. *RAND Journal of Economics* 23, 395–414.

Rassenti, S.J., Smith, V.L. and Wilson, B.J. 2003. Controlling market power and price spikes in electricity networks: demand-side bidding. *Proceedings of the National Academy of Sciences* 100, 2998–3003.

Ruffle, B.J. 2000. Some factors affecting demand withholding in posted-offer markets. *Economic Theory* 16, 529–44.

Wilson, B.J. 1998. What collusion? Unilateral market power as a catalyst for countercyclical markups. *Experimental Economics* 1, 133–45.

mechanism design experiments

Mechanism design is the art of designing institutions that align individual incentives with overall social goals. Mechanism design theory was initiated by Hurwicz (1972) and is surveyed in Groves and Ledyard (1987). To bridge the gap between a theoretical mechanism and an actual economic process that solves fundamental social problems, it is important to observe and evaluate the performance of the mechanism in the context of actual decision problems faced by real people with real incentives. These situations can be created and carefully controlled in a laboratory. A mechanism design experiment takes a theoretical mechanism, recreates it in a simple environment in a laboratory with human subjects as economic agents, observes the behaviour of human subjects under the mechanism, and assesses its performance in relation to what it was created to do and to the theory upon which its creation rests. The laboratory serves as a wind tunnel for new mechanisms, providing evidence which one can use to eliminate fragile ones, and to identify the characteristics of successful ones.

When a mechanism is put to test in a laboratory, behavioural assumptions made in theory are seriously challenged. Theory assumes perfectly rational agents who can compute the equilibrium strategies via introspection. When a mechanism is implemented among boundedly rational agents, however, characteristics peripheral to theoretical implementations, such as transparency, complexity and dynamic stability, become important, or even central, to the success of a mechanism in a laboratory, and we suspect, ultimately in the real world. Mechanism design experiments cover several major domains, including public goods and externalities, matching, contract theory, auctions, market design and information markets. In what follows, we will review the experimental results of some of these topics.

Public goods and externalities

With the presence of public goods and externalities, competitive equilibria are not Pareto optimal. This is often referred to as market failure, since competitive markets on their own either result in underprovision of public goods (that is, the free-rider problem) or overprovision of negative externalities, such as pollution. To solve the free-rider problem in public goods economies, incentive-compatible mechanisms use innovative tax-subsidy schemes that utilize agents' own messages to achieve the Pareto optimal levels of public goods provision. A series of experiments test these mechanisms in the laboratory (see Chen, 2008, for a comprehensive survey).

When preferences are quasi-linear, the Vickrey–Clarke–Groves (VCG) mechanism (Vickrey, 1961; Clarke, 1971; Groves, 1973) is strategy-proof, in the sense that reporting one's preferences truthfully is always a dominant strategy. It has also been shown that any strategy-proof mechanism selecting an efficient public decision at every profile must be of this type (Green and Laffont, 1977). Two forms of the VCG mechanism have been tested in the field and laboratory by various groups of researchers. The pivot mechanism refers to the VCG mechanism when the public project choice is binary, while the cVCG mechanism refers to the VCG mechanism when the level of the public good is selected from a continuum. Under the pivot mechanism, misrevelation can be prevalent. Attiyeh, Franciosi and Isaac (2000) show that about ten per cent of the bids were truthfully revealing their values. Furthermore, there was no convergence tendency towards value revelation. In a follow-up study, Kawagoe and Mori (2001) show that more information about the payoff structure helps reduce the degree of misrevelation. More recently, Cason et al. (2006) provide a novel explanation for the problem of misrevelation in strategy-proof mechanisms. As Saijo et al. (2005) point out, the standard strategy-proofness concept in implementation theory has serious drawbacks, that is, almost all strategy-proof mechanisms have a continuum of Nash equilibria. They propose a new implementation concept, secure implementation, which requires the set of dominant strategy equilibria and the set of Nash equilibria to coincide. Cason et al. (2006) compare the performance of two strategy-proof mechanisms in the laboratory: the Pivot mechanism where implementation is not secure and truthful preference revelation is a weakly dominant strategy, and the cVCG mechanism with single-peaked preferences where implementation is secure. Results indicate that subjects play dominant strategies significantly more often in the secure cVCG mechanism (81 per cent) than in the non-secure Pivot mechanism (50 per cent). The importance of secure implementation in dominant strategy implementation is replicated in Healy (2006), where he compares five public goods mechanisms, voluntary contributions, proportional taxation, Groves–Ledyard, Walker and cVCG. The cVCG is found to be the most efficient of all mechanisms.

Although the VCG mechanism admits dominant strategies, the allocation is not fully Pareto-efficient. In fact, it is impossible to design a mechanism for making collective allocation decisions, which is informationally decentralized, non-manipulable and Pareto optimal. This impossibility has been demonstrated in the work of Hurwicz (1975), Green and Laffont (1977), Roberts (1979), Walker (1980) and Mailath and Postlewaite (1990) in the context of resource allocation with public goods.

Many 'next-best' mechanisms preserve Pareto optimality at the cost of non-manipulability, some of which preserve 'some degree' of non-manipulability. Some mechanisms have been discovered which have the property that Nash equilibria are Pareto optimal. These can be found in the work of Groves and Ledyard (1977), Hurwicz (1979), Walker (1981), Tian (1989), Kim (1993), Peleg (1996), Falkinger (1996) and Chen (2002). Other implementation concepts include perfect Nash equilibrium (Bagnoli and Lipman, 1989), undominated Nash equilibrium (Jackson and Moulin, 1992), subgame perfect equilibrium (Varian, 1994), strong equilibrium (Corchon and Wilkie, 1996), and the core (Kaneko, 1977), and so forth. Apart from the above non-Bayesian mechanisms, Ledyard and Palfrey (1994) propose a class of Bayesian Nash mechanisms for public goods provision.

Experiments on Nash-efficient public goods mechanisms underscore the importance of dynamic stability, that is, whether a mechanism converges under various learning dynamics. Most of the experimental studies of Nash-efficient mechanisms focus on the Groves–Ledyard mechanism (Smith, 1979a; 1979b; Harstad and Marrese, 1981; 1982; Mori, 1989; Chen and Plott, 1996; Arifovic and Ledyard, 2006). Chen and Tang (1998) also compare the Walker mechanism with the Groves–Ledyard mechanism. Falkinger et al. (2000) study the Falkinger mechanism. Healy (2006) compares Nash-efficient mechanisms to cVCG and other benchmarks.

Among the series of experiments exploring dynamic stability, Chen and Plott (1996) first assessed the performance of the Groves–Ledyard mechanism under different punishment parameters. They found that by varying the punishment parameter the dynamics and stability changed dramatically. For a large enough parameter, the system converged very quickly to its stage game Nash equilibrium and remained stable; while under a small parameter, the system did not converge to its stage game Nash equilibrium. This finding was replicated by Chen and Tang (1998) with more independent sessions and a longer time series in an experiment designed to study the learning dynamics.

Figure 1 presents the time series data from Chen and Tang (1998) for two out of five types of players. Each graph presents the mean (the black dots) and standard deviation (the error bars) for each of the two different types averaged over seven

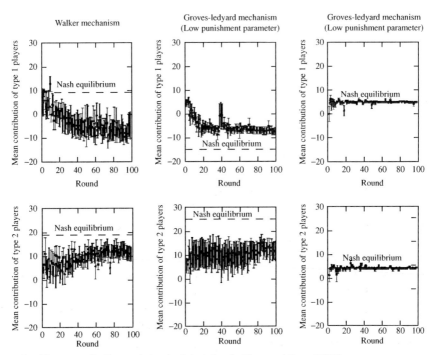

Figure 1 Mean contribution and standard deviation in Chen and Tang (1998)

independent sessions for each mechanism – the Walker mechanism, the Groves–Ledyard mechanism under a low punishment parameter (GL1), and the Groves–Ledyard mechanism under a high punishment parameter (GL100). From these graphs, it is apparent that GL100 converged very quickly to its stage game Nash equilibrium and remained stable, while the same mechanism did not converge under a low punishment parameter; the Walker mechanism did not converge to its stage game Nash equilibrium either.

Because of its good dynamic properties, GL100 had significantly better performance than GL1 and Walker, evaluated in terms of system efficiency, close to Pareto optimal level of public goods provision, fewer violations of individual rationality constraints and convergence to its stage game equilibrium.

These past experiments serendipitously studied supermodular mechanisms. Two recent studies systematically vary the parameters from below, close to, at and above the supermodularity threshold to assess the effects of supermodularity on learning dynamics.

Arifovic and Ledyard (2006) conduct computer simulations of an individual learning model in the context of a class of the Groves–Ledyard mechanisms. They vary the punishment parameter systematically, from extremely small to extremely high. They find that their model converges to Nash equilibrium for all values of the punishment parameter. However, the speed of convergence depends on the value of the parameter. As shown in Figure 2, the speed of convergence is U-shaped: very low and very high values of the punishment parameter require long periods for convergence, while a range of intermediate values requires the minimum time. In fact, the optimal punishment parameter identified in the simulation is much lower than the supermudularity threshold. Predictions of the computation model are validated by experimental data with human subjects.

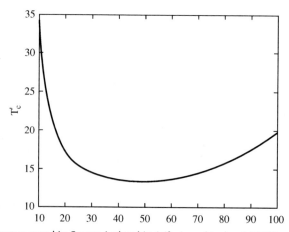

Figure 2   Convergence speed in Groves–Ledyard in Arifovic and Ledyard (2006)

In a parallel research project on the role of supermodularity on convergence, Chen and Gazzale (2004) experimentally study the generalized version of the compensation mechanism (Varian, 1994), which implements efficient allocations as subgame-perfect equilibria for economic environments involving externalities and public goods. The basic idea is that each player offers to compensate the other for the 'costs' incurred by making the efficient choice. They systematically vary the free parameter from below, close to, at and beyond the threshold of supermodularity to assess the effects of supermodularity on the performance of the mechanism. They have three main findings. First, in terms of proportion of equilibrium play and efficiency, they find that supermodular and 'near supermodular' mechanisms perform significantly better than those far below the threshold. This finding is consistent with previous experimental findings. Second, they find that from a little below the threshold to the threshold, the improvement in performance is statistically insignificant. This implies that the performance of 'near supermodular' mechanisms, such as the Falkinger mechanism, ought to be comparable to supermodular mechanisms. Therefore, the mechanism designer need not be overly concerned with setting parameters that are firmly above the supermodular threshold – close is just as good. This enlarges the set of robustly stable mechanisms. The third finding concerns the selection of mechanisms within the class of supermodular mechanisms. Again, theory is silent on this issue. Chen and Gazzale find that within the class of supermodular mechanisms, increasing the parameter far beyond the threshold does not significantly improve the performance of the mechanism. Furthermore, increasing another free parameter, which is not related to whether or not the mechanism is supermodular, does improve convergence.

In contrast to the previous stream of work which identifies supermodularity as a robust sufficient condition for convergence, Healy (2006) develops a k-period average best response learning model and calibrates this new learning model on the data-set to study the learning dynamics. He shows that subject behaviour is well approximated by a model in which agents best respond to the average strategy choices over the last five periods under all mechanisms. Healy's work bridges the behavioural hypotheses that have existed separately in dominant strategy and Nash-efficient mechanism experiments.

In summary, experiments testing public goods mechanisms show that dominant strategy mechanisms should also be secure, while Nash implementation mechanisms should satisfy dynamic stability, if any mechanism is to be considered for application in the real world in a repeated interaction setting.

While experimental research demonstrates that incentive-compatible public goods mechanisms can be effective in inducing efficient levels of public goods provision, almost all the mechanisms rely on monetary transfers, which limit the scope of implementation of these mechanisms in the real world. In many interesting real world settings, such as open source software development and online communities, sizable contributions to public goods are made without the use of monetary incentives. We next review a related social psychology literature, which studies contribution to public goods without the use of monetary incentives.

Social loafing

Analogous to free riding, social loafing refers to the phenomenon whereby individuals exert less effort on a collective task than they do on a comparable individual task. To determine conditions under which individuals do or do not engage in social loafing, social psychologists have developed and tested various theoretical accounts. Karau and Williams (1993) present a review of this literature and develop a collective effort model, which integrates elements of expectancy value, social identity and self-validation theories, to explain social loafing. A meta-analysis of 78 studies shows that social loafing is robust across studies. Consistent with the prediction of the model, several variables are found to moderate social loafing. The following factors are of particular interests to a mechanism designer.

1. *Evaluation potential*: Harkins (1987) and others show that social loafing can be reduced or sometimes eliminated when a participant's contribution is identifiable and evaluable. In a related public goods experiment, Andreoni and Petrie (2004) find a substantial increase (59 per cent) in contribution to public goods compared to the baseline of a typical VCM experiment, when both the amount of individual contribution and the (photo) identification of donors are revealed.
2. *Task valence*: the collective effort model predicts that the individual tendency to engage in social loafing decreases as task valence (or perceived meaningfulness) increases.
3. *Group valence and group-level comparison standards*: Social identity theory (Tajfel and Turner, 1986) suggests that 'individuals gain positive self-identity through the accomplishments of the groups to which they belong' (Karau and Williams, 1993, p. 686). Therefore, enhancing group cohesiveness or group identity might reduce or eliminate social loafing. In a closely related economics experiment, Eckel and Grossman (2005) use induced group identity to study the effects of varying strength of identity on cooperative behaviour in a repeated public goods game. They find that while cooperation is unaffected by simple and artificial group identity, actions designed to enhance group identity contribute to higher levels of cooperation. This stream of research suggests that high degrees of group identification may limit individual shirking and free riding in environments with a public good.
4. *Expectation of co-worker performance influences individual effort*. This set of theories might be sensitive to individual valuations for the public good as well as the public goods production functions. The meta-analysis indicates that individuals loafed when they expected their co-workers to perform well, but did not loaf otherwise.
5. *Uniqueness of individual inputs*: individuals loafed when they believed that their inputs were redundant, but did not loaf when they believe that their individual inputs to the collective product were unique. In an interesting application, Beenen et al. (2004) conducted a field experiment in an online community called MovieLens. They found that users who were reminded of the uniqueness of their contributions rated significantly more movies than the control group.

6. *Task complexity*: individuals were more likely to loaf on simple tasks, but less likely on complex tasks. This finding might be related to increased interests when solving complex tasks.

Exploring non-monetary incentives to increase contribution to public goods is an important and promising direction for future research. Mathematical models of social psychology theories are likely to shed insights on the necessary and sufficient conditions for a reduction or even elimination of social loafing.

Matching

Matching theory has been credited as 'one of the outstanding successful stories of the theory of games' (Aumann, 1992). It has been used to understand existing markets and to guide the design of new markets or allocation mechanisms in a variety of real world contexts. Matching experiments serve two purposes: to test new matching algorithms in the laboratory before implementing them in the real world, and to understanding how existing institutions evolved. We focus on one-sided matching experiments, and refer the reader to MATCHING AND MARKET DESIGN for a summary of the two-sided matching experiments.

One-sided matching is the assignment of indivisible items to agents without a medium of exchange, such as money. Examples include the assignment of college students to dormitory rooms and public housing units, the assignment of offices and tasks to individuals, the assignment of students to public schools, the allocation of course seats to students (mostly in business schools and law schools), and timeshare exchange. The key mechanisms in this class of problems are the top trading cycles (TTC) mechanism (Shapley and Scarf, 1974), the Gale–Shapley deferred acceptance mechanism (Gale and Shapley, 1962), and variants of the serial dictatorship mechanism (Abdulkadiroglu and Sonmez, 1998). Matching experiments explore several issues. For strategy-proof mechanisms, they explore the extent to which subjects recognize and use their dominant strategies without prompting. For mechanisms which are not strategy-proof, they explore the extent of preference manipulation and the resulting efficiency loss. As a result, they examine the robustness of theoretical efficiency comparisons when the mechanisms are implemented among boundedly rational subjects and across different environments.

For the class of house allocation problems, two mechanisms have been compared and tested in the laboratory. The random serial dictatorship with squatting rights (RSD) is used by many US universities for on-campus housing allocation, while the TTC mechanism is theoretically superior. Chen and Sonmez (2002) report the first experimental study of these two mechanisms. They find that TTC is significantly more efficient than RSD because it induces significantly higher participation rate of existing tenants.

Another application of one-sided matching is the time-share problem. Wang and Krishna (2006) study the top trading cycles chains and spacebank mechanism

(TTCCS), and two status quo mechanisms in the time-share industry, that is, the deposit first mechanism and the request first mechanism, neither of which is efficient. In the experiment, the observed efficiency of TTCCS is significantly higher than that of the deposit first mechanism, which in turn, is more efficient than the request first mechanism. In fact, efficiency under TTCCS converged to 100 per cent quickly, while the other two mechanisms do not show any increase in efficiency over time.

More recently, the school choice problem has received much attention. We review two experimental studies. Chen and Sonmez (2006) present an experimental study of three school choice mechanisms. The Boston mechanism is influential in practice, while the Gale–Shapley and TTC mechanisms have superior theoretical properties. Consistent with theory, this study indicates a high preference manipulation rate under Boston. As a result, efficiency under Boston is significantly lower than that of the two competing mechanisms in the designed environment. However, contrary to theory, Gale–Shapley outperforms TTC and generates the highest efficiency. The main reason is that a much higher proportion of subjects did not realize that truth-telling was a dominant strategy under TTC, and thus manipulated their preferences and ended up worse off. While Chen and Sonmez (2006) examine these mechanisms under partial information, where an agent only knows his own preference ranking, and not those of other agents, a follow-up study by Pais and Pinter (2006), investigates the same three mechanisms under different information conditions, ranging from complete ignorance about the other participants' preferences and school priorities to complete information on all elements of the game. They show that information condition has a significant effect on the rate of truthful preference revelation. In particular, having no information results in a significantly higher proportion of truth-telling than under any treatment with additional information. Interestingly, there is no significant difference in the efficiency between partial and full information treatments. Unlike Chen and Sonmez (2006), in this experiment, TTC outperforms in terms of efficiency. Furthermore, TTC is also less sensitive to the amount of information in the environment.

Owing to their important applications in the real world, one-sided matching experiments provide insights on the actual manipulability of the matching mechanisms which are valuable in their real world implementations. Some issues, such as the role of information on the performance of the mechanisms, remain open questions.

Combinatorial auctions

In many applications of mechanism design, theory is not yet up to the task of identifying the optimal design or even comparing alternative designs. One case in which this has been true is in the design of auctions to sell collections of heterogeneous items with value complementarities, which occur when the value of a combination of items can be higher than the sum of the values for separate items. Value complementarities arise naturally in many contexts, such as broadcast spectrum rights auctioned by the Federal Communications Commission, pollution emissions allowances for consecutive years bought and sold under the RECLAIM programme of the South Coast Air Quality Management District in Los Angeles, aircraft take-off and landing slots, logistics services, and advertising time slots. Because individuals may want to express bids for combinations of the items for sale, requiring up to 2^N bids per person when there are N items, these auctions have come to be known as combinatorial auctions.

As was discussed earlier under public goods mechanisms, theory has identified the VCG mechanism as the unique auction design that would implement an efficient allocation assuming bidders use dominant strategies. Theory has not yet identified the revenue-maximizing combinatorial auction, although Ledyard (2007) shows that it is not the VCG mechanism. Theory has also been of little use in comparing the expected revenue collection between different auction designs. This has opened the way for many significantly different auction designs to be proposed, and sometimes even deployed, with little evidence to back up various claims of superiority.

To give some idea of the complexity of the problem we describe just some of the various design choices one can make. Should the auctions be run as a sealed bid or should some kind of iterative procedure be used? And, if the latter, should iteration be synchronous or asynchronous? What kinds of bids should be allowed? Proposals for allowable bids include only bids for a single item, bids for any package, and some which allow only a limited list of packages to be bid on. What stopping rule should be used? Proposals have included fixed stopping times, stop after an iteration in which revenue does not increase by more than x per cent, stop if demand is less than or equal to supply, and an imaginative but complex system of eligibility and activity rules created for the Federal Communications Commission (FCC) auctions. Should winners pay what they bid or something else? Alternatives to pay what you bid include VCG prices and second-best prices based on the dual variables to the programme that picks the provisional winners. What should bidders be told during the auction? Some designs provide information on all bids and provisional winners and the full identity of the bidders involved in them. Some designs provide minimal information such as only the winning bids without even the information as to who made them. The permutations and combinations are many. Because theory has not developed enough to sort out what is best, experiments have been used to provide some evidence.

The very first experimental analysis of a combinatoric auction can be found in Rassenti, Smith and Bulfin (1982), where they compared a sealed bid auction (RSB) allowing package bids to a uniform price sealed bid auction (GIP), proposed by Grether, Isaac and Plott (1981), that did not allow package bids. Both designs included a double auction market for re-trading after the auction results were known. The RSB design yielded higher efficiencies than the GIP design. Banks, Ledyard and Porter (1989) compared a continuous, asynchronous design (AUSM), a generalization of the English auction with package bidding, to a synchronous iterative design with myopic VCG pricing and found AUSM to yield higher efficiencies and revenues on average. Ledyard, Porter and Rangel (1997) compare the continuous AUSM to a synchronous iterative design (SMR) developed by Millgrom (2000) for the FCC auctions, which only allowed simultaneous single item bids. The testing found that ASUM yielded significantly higher efficiencies and revenues. Kwasnica et al. (2005) compare an iterative design (RAD) with package bidding and price feedback to both AUSM and SMR. RAD and SMR use the same stopping rule. Efficiencies observed with RAD and AUSM are similar and higher than those for SMR, but revenue is higher in SMR since many bidders lose money due to a phenomenon known as the exposure problem, which is identified in Bykowsky, Cull and Ledyard (2000). If it is assumed that bidders default on bids on which they make losses and thus set the prices of such bids to zero, revenues are in fact higher under AUSM and RAD than under SMR. At the behest of the FCC, Banks et al. (2003) ran an experiment to compare an iterative, package bidding design (CRA) from Charles River Associates and Market Design (1998) with the FCC SMR auction format. They also found that the package bidding design provides more efficient allocations but less revenue, due to bidder losses in the SMR.

Parkes and Unger (2000) proposed an ascending price, generalized VCG auction (iBEA) that maintains nonlinear and non-anonymous prices on packages, and charges VCG prices to the winners. The design would theoretically produce efficient allocations as long as bidders bid in a straightforward manner. Straightforward bidding is myopic and non-strategic and involves bidding on packages that yield the locally highest payoff in utility. There is no evidence that actual bidders will behave this way. Chen and Takeuchi (2005) have experimentally tested iBEA against the VCG sealed bid auction and found that VCG was superior in both revenue generation and efficiency attained. Takeuchi et al. (2006) tested RAD against VCG and found that RAD generated higher efficiencies, especially in the earlier auctions. They were using experiments to test combinatoric auctions as a potential alternative to scheduling processes in situations with valuation complementarities. In many cases current procedures request orderings from users and then employ a knapsack algorithm of some kind to choose good allocations without any concern for incentive compatibility. Takeuchi et al. (2006) find that both RAD and VCG yield higher efficiencies than the knapsack approach. Ledyard, Porter and Noussair (1996) found similar results when comparing a more vanilla combinatoric auction to an administrative approach. These findings suggest there are significant improvements in organization performance being overlooked by management.

Porter et al. (2003) proposed and tested a combinatorial clock (CC) auction. After bids are submitted, a simple algorithm determines the demand for each item by each bidder and for those items that have more than one bidder demanding more units than are available the clock price is raised. They test their design against the SMR and CRA. They do not report revenue but in their tests the CC design attained an almost perfect average efficiency of 99.9 per cent. CRA attained an average of 93 per cent, while SMR attained only 88 per cent. Brunner et al. (2006) have carried out a systematic comparison of SMR and three alternatives, CC, RAD and a new FCC design called SMRPB, which takes the basic RAD design and changes two things. SMRPB allows bidders to win at most one package and the pricing feedback rule includes some inertia that RAD does not. They find that in terms of efficiency RAD is better than CC which is equivalent to SMRPB which is better than SMR. In terms of revenue, they find CC is better than RAD which is better than SMRPB which is better than SMR.

Most of these papers compare only two or three auction designs at a time and the environments used as the basis for comparison is often different in different papers. Further, environments can often be chosen that favour one auction over another. To deal with this, many research teams stress test their results by looking at boundary environments' collections of payoff parameters that give each auction under examination its best or worst chance of yielding high revenue or efficiency. But it is still unusual for a research team to report on a comparative test of several auctions in which their own design ends up being out-performed by another. Nevertheless, there are some tentative conclusions one can draw from this research.

The easiest and most obvious conclusion is that allowing package bidding improves both efficiency and revenue. In all the studies listed, anything that limits bidders' ability to express the full extent of their willingness to pay for all packages does interfere with efficiency and revenue. Less obvious but also easy to see is that simultaneity and iteration are also good design features. Bidding in situations in which value complementarities exist can be difficult since bidders need to discover where their willingness to pay is more than others but also where they fit with others interests. Getting this right improves both efficiency and revenue. Iteration and relevant price feedback both help here. Stopping rules also matter. Although this is an area that could benefit from more research, it is clear that in many cases complicated stopping rules that allow auctions to proceed for very long periods of time provide little gain in revenue or efficiency.

Summary

Mechanism design experiments identify features of mechanisms that lead to good performance when they are implemented among real people. Experiments testing public goods mechanisms show that dominant strategy mechanisms should also be secure, while Nash-efficient mechanisms should satisfy dynamic stability if it is to be considered for application in the real world in a repeated interaction setting. For matching mechanisms, transparency of the dominant strategy leads to better performance in the laboratory. Lastly, in combinatorial auctions, package bidding, simultaneity and iteration are shown to be good design features. In addition to the three domains covered in this article, there has been a growing experimental literature on market design, information markets and contract theory. We do not cover them in this article, due to lack of robust empirical regularities. However, they are excellent areas in which to make a new contribution.

YAN CHEN AND JOHN O. LEDYARD

Bibliography

Abdulkadiroglu, A. and Sönmez, T. 1998. Random serial dictatorship and the core from random endowments in house allocation problems. *Econometrica* 66, 689–701.

Andreoni, J. and Petrie, R. 2004. Public goods experiments without confidentiality: a glimpse into fund-raising. *Journal of Public Economics* 88, 1605–23.

Arifovic, J. and Ledyard, J. 2006. Computer testbeds and mechanism design: application to the class of Groves-Ledyard mechanisms for provision of public goods. Caltech working paper. Pasadena, CA.

Attiyeh, G., Franciosi, R. and Isaac, M. 2000. Experiments with the pivot process for providing public goods. *Public Choice* 102, 95–114.

Aumann, R. 1992. Foreword. In *Two-Sided Matching: A Study in Game-Theoretic Modeling and Analysis*, ed. E. Alvin, M.A. Roth, O. Sotomayor. Cambridge: Cambridge University Press.

Bagnoli, M. and Lipman, B. 1989. Provision of public goods: fully implementing the core through private contributions. *Review of Economic Studies* 56, 583–602.

Banks, J.S., Ledyard, J.O. and Porter, D.P. 1989. Allocating uncertain and unresponsive resources: an experimental approach. *Rand Journal of Economics* 20, 1–25.

Banks, J., Olson, M., Porter, D., Rassenti, S. and Smith, V. 2003. Theory, experiment and the federal communications commission spectrum auctions. *Journal of Economic Behavior and Organization* 51, 303–50.

Beenen, G., Ling, K., Wang, X., Chang, K., Frankowski, D., Resnick, P. and Kraut, R. 2004. In *Proceedings of ACM Computer Supported Cooperative Work 2004*, Conference on Computer Supported Cooperative Work. Chicago, IL: ACM.

Brunner, C., Goeree, J., Holt, C. and Ledyard, J. 2006. Combinatorial auctioneering, Caltech working paper. Pasadena, CA.

Bykowsky, M., Cull, R. and Ledyard, J. 2000. Mutually destructive bidding: the FCC auction design problem. *Journal of Regulatory Economics* 17, 205–28.

Cason, T., Saijo, T., Sjöström, T. and Yamato, T. 2006. Secure implementation experiments: do strategy-proof mechanisms really work? *Games and Economic Behavior* 57, 206–35.

Charles River Associates Inc. and Market Design Inc. 1998. Report No. 1351–00.

Chen, Y. 2002. A family of supermodular Nash mechanisms implementing Lindahl allocations. *Economic Theory* 19, 773–90.

Chen, Y. 2008. Incentive-compatible mechanisms for pure public goods: a survey of experimental literature. In *The Handbook of Experimental Economics Results*, ed. C. Plott and V. Smith. Amsterdam: Elsevier.

Chen, Y. and Gazzale, R. 2004. Supermodularity and convergence: an experimental study of the compensation mechanism. *American Economic Review* 94, 1505–35.

Chen, Y. and Plott, C.R. 1996. The Groves–Ledyard mechanism: an experimental study of institutional design. *Journal of Public Economics* 59, 335–64.

Chen, Y. and Sonmez, T. 2002. Improving efficiency of on-campus housing: an experimental study. *American Economic Review* 92, 1669–86.

Chen, Y. and Sonmez, T. 2006. School choice: an experimental study. *Journal of Economic Theory* 127, 202–31.

Chen, Y. and Tang, F.-F. 1998. Learning and incentive compatible mechanisms for public goods provision: an experimental study. *Journal of Political Economy* 106, 633–62.

Chen, Y. and Takeuchi, K. 2005. Multi-object auctions with package bidding: an experimental comparison of Vickrey and iBEA. Working paper.

Clarke, E.H. 1971. Multipart pricing of public goods. *Public Choice* 11, 17–33.

Corchon, L. and Wilkie, S. 1996. Double implementation of the ratio correspondence by a market mechanism. *Review of Economic Design* 2, 325–37.

Eckel, C. and Grossman, P. 2005. Managing diversity by creating team identity. *Journal of Economic Behavior & Organization* 58, 371–92.

Falkinger, J. 1996. Efficient private provision of public goods by rewarding deviations from average. *Journal of Public Economics* 62, 413–22.

Falkinger, J., Fehr, E., Gächter, S. and Winter-Ebmer, R. 2000. A simple mechanism for the efficient provision of public goods: experimental evidence. *American Economic Review* 90, 247–64.

Gale, D. and Shapley, L. 1962. College admissions and the stability of marriage. *American Mathematical Monthly* 69, 9–15.

Green, J. and Laffont, J.-J. 1977. Characterization of satisfactory mechanisms for the revelation of the preferences for public goods. *Econometrica* 45, 427–38.

Grether, D., Isaac, M. and Plott, C. 1981. The allocation of landing rights by unanimity among competitiors. *American Economic Review* 71, 166–71.

Groves, T. 1973. Incentives in Teams. *Econometrica* 41, 617–31.

Groves, T. and Ledyard, J. 1977. Optimal allocation of public goods: a solution to the 'free rider' problem. *Econometrica* 45, 783–809.

Groves, T. and Ledyard, J. 1987. Incentive compatibility since 1972. In *Essays in Honor of Leonid Hurwicz*, ed. T. Groves, R. Radner and S. Reiter. Minneapolis: University of Minnesota Press.

Harkins, S.G. 1987. Social loafing and social facilitation. *Journal of Experimental Social Psychology* 23, 1–18.

Harstad, R.M. and Marrese, M. 1981. Implementation of mechanism by processes: public good allocation experiments. *Journal of Economic Behavior & Organization* 2, 129–51.

Harstad, R.M. and Marrese, M. 1982. Behavioral explanations of efficient public good allocations. *Journal of Public Economics* 19, 367–83.

Healy, P.J. 2006. Learning dynamics for mechanism design: an experimental comparison of public goods mechanisms. *Journal of Economic Theory* 129, 114–49.

Hurwicz, L. 1972. On informationally decentralized systems. In *Decision and Organization*, ed. C. McGuire and R. Radner. Amsterdam: North-Holland.

Hurwicz, L. 1975. On the existence of allocation systems whose manipulative Nash equilibria are Pareto-optimal. Paper presented at Third World Congress of the Econometric Society, Toronto.

Hurwicz, L. 1979. Outcome functions yielding Walrasian and Lindahl allocations at Nash equilibrium points. *Review of Economic Studies* 46, 217–25.

Isaac, R. and James, D. 2000. Robustness of the incentive compatible combinatorial auction. *Experimental Economics* 3, 31–53.

Jackson, M. and Moulin, H. 1992. Implementing a public project and distributing its cost. *Journal of Economic Theory* 57, 125–40.

Kaneko, M. 1977. The ratio equilibria and the core of the voting game in a public goods economy. *Econometrica* 45, 1589–94.

Kauru, S.J. and Williams, K.D. 1993. Social loafing: a meta-analytic review and theoretical integration. *Journal of Personality and Social Psychology* 65, 681–706.

Kawagoe, T. and Mori, T. 2001. Can pivotal mechanism induce truth-telling? An experimental study. *Public Choice* 108, 331–54.

Kim, T. 1986. On the nonexistence of a stable Nash mechanism implementing Lindahl allocations. Mimeo. University of Minnesota.

Kim, T. 1993. A stable Nash mechanism implementing Lindahl allocations for quasi-linear environments. *Journal of Mathematical Economics* 22, 359–71.

Kwasnica, A.M., Ledyard, J.O., Porter, D. and DeMartini, C. 2005. A new and improved design for multi-object iterative auctions. *Management Science* 51, 419–34.

Ledyard, J. 2007. Optimal combinatoric auctions with single-minded bidders. *Proceedings of the 8th ACM Conference on Electronic Commerce*. San Diego, CA: ACM.

Ledyard, J., Olson, M., Porter, D., Swanson, J. and Torma, D. 2002. The first use of a combined value auction for transportation services. *Interfaces* 32, 4–12.

Ledyard, J. and Palfrey, T. 1994. Voting and lottery drafts as efficient public goods mechanisms. *Review of Economic Studies* 61, 327–55.

Ledyard, J., Porter, D. and Noussair, C. 1996. The allocation of a shared resource within an organization. *Economic Design* 2, 163–92.

Ledyard, J., Porter, D. and Rangel, A. 1997. Experiments testing multiobject allocation mechanisms. *Journal of Economics and Management Strategy* 6, 639–75.

Mailath, G. and Postlewaite, A. 1990. Asymmetric information bargaining problems with many agents. *Review of Economic Studies* 57, 351–67.

McAfee, P.R. and McMillan, J. 1996. Analyzing the airwaves auction. *Journal of Economic Perspectives* 10(1), 159–75.

McCabe, K., Rassenti, S. and Smith, V. 1989. Designing 'Smart' computer assisted markets. *European Journal of Political Economy* 5, 259–83.

Millgrom, P. 2000. Putting auction theory to work: the simultaneous ascending auction. *Journal of Political Economy* 108, 245–272a.

Milgrom, P. and Roberts, J. 1990. Rationalizability, learning and equilibrium in games with strategic complementarities. *Econometrica* 58, 1255–77.

Milgrom, P. and Shannon, C. 1994. Monotone comparative statics. *Econometrica* 62, 157–80.

Mori, T. 1989. Effectiveness of mechanisms for public goods provision: an experimental study. *Economic Studies* 40, 234–46.

Pais, J. and Pintér, A. 2006. School choice and information: an experimental study on matching mechanisms. Working Paper, Institute for Economics and Business Administration (ISEG). Lisbon: Technical University.

Parkes, D. and Unger, L. 2000. Iterative combinatorial auctions: theory and practice. In *Proceedings of the 17th National Conference on Artificial Intelligence* (AAAI-00).

Peleg, B. 1996. Double implementation of the Lindahl equilibrium by a continuous mechanism. *Economic Design* 2, 311–24.

Porter, D.P. 1999. The effect of bid withdrawal in a multi-object auction. *Review of Economic Design* 4, 73–97.

Porter, D., Rassenti, S., Roopnarine, A. and Smith, V. 2003. Combinatorial auction design. *Proceedings of the National Academy of Sciences* 100, 11153–7.

Rassenti, S., Smith, V. and Bulfin, R. 1982. A combinatorial auction mechanism for airport time slot allocation. *Bell Journal of Economics* 13, 402–17.

Roberts, J. 1979. Incentives and planning procedures for the provision of public goods. *Review of Economic Studies* 46, 283–92.

Saijo, T., Sjöström, T. and Yamato, T. 2005. Secure Implementation. Working Paper, No. 567-0047. Osaka: Institute of Social and Economic Research, Osaka University.

Shapley, L.S. and Scarf, H. 1974. On cores and indivisibilities. *Journal of Mathematical Economics* 1, 23–37.

Smith, V. 1979a. Incentive compatible experimental processes for the provision of public goods. In *Experimental Economics*, vol. 1, ed. R. Smith. Greenwich, CT: JAI Press.

Smith, V. 1979b. An experimental comparison of three public goods decision mechanisms. *Scandinavian Journal of Economics* 81, 198–251.

Tajfel, H. and Turner, J.C. 1986. The social identity theory of intergroup behaviour. In *Psychology of Intergroup Relations*, ed. S. Worchel and W. Austin. Chicago: Nelson-Hall.

Takeuchi, K., Lin, J., Chen, Y. and Finholt, T. 2006. Shake it up baby: scheduling with package auctions. Working paper. School of Information, University of Michigan.

Tian, G. 1989. Implementation of the Lindahl correspondence by a single-valued, feasible, and continuous mechanism. *Review of Economic Studies* 56, 613–21.

Varian, H. 1994. A solution to the problems of externalities when agents are well-informed. *American Economic Review* 84, 1278–93.

Vickrey, W. 1961. Counterspeculation, auctions and competitive sealed tenders. *Journal of Finance* 16, 8–37.

Walker, M. 1980. On the impossibility of a dominant strategy mechanism to optimally decide public questions. *Econometrica* 48, 1521–40.

Walker, M. 1981. A simple incentive compatible scheme for attaining Lindahl allocations. *Econometrica* 49, 65–71.

Wang, Y. and Krishna, A. 2006. Timeshare exchange mechanisms. *Management Science* 52, 1123–37.

preference reversals

Preference reversal (PR) is a widely observed behavioural tendency for the preference ordering of a pair of alternatives to depend, in a predictable way, on the process used to elicit it.

The existence of preference reversal sets an empirical challenge to fundamental assumptions of conventional economic theory: PR is an apparent failure of procedure invariance (that is, the traditional presumption that preferences should be independent of the method of eliciting them). Some see it as a challenge to the very idea that human decisions are governed by preferences.

Much of the empirical PR literature has examined decisions relating to pairs of simple gambles. One of the gambles (typically called the 'P-bet') will offer a relatively good chance of winning a modest prize, otherwise nothing (or sometimes a small loss); the other bet (the '$-bet'), offers a relatively small chance of winning a larger prize. In classic PR experiments, subjects are required to make straight choices between such pairs of bets and to provide separate (usually monetary) valuations for each bet. For any individual and gamble pair, conventional economic theory implies that the chosen gamble would also be the more highly valued of the pair. But while many individuals are so consistent, a significant proportion, typically, are not. The existence of some such inconsistency, by itself, is not especially surprising. People might, for instance, make a mistake in one or more task, leading to some level of inconsistency in comparisons of rankings. Interest in PR, however, stems largely from the fact that observed inconsistencies tend to be patterned in a highly predictable way: the typical finding is that considerable numbers of subjects choose the P-bet and value the $-bet more highly (let us call this the standard reversal), while very few commit the opposite reversal ($-bet chosen and P-bet valued more highly). It is this *asymmetric* pattern of inconsistencies between rankings based on choice and valuation that constitutes the intriguing PR phenomenon.

Evidence

PR was first predicted and then observed by psychologists (Lichtenstein and Slovic, 1971; Lindman, 1971). It was later brought to the attention of economists by Grether and Plott (1979) who described its potential significance for economics in the following passage:

> Taken at face value the data are simply inconsistent with preference theory and have broad implications for research priorities within economics. The inconsistency is deeper than mere lack of transitivity or even stochastic transitivity. It suggests that no optimisation principles of any sort lie behind even the simplest of human choices. (Grether and Plott, 1979, p. 623)

Table

	State 1	State 2	State 3
$	x	0	0
P	y	y	0
M	m	m	m

Like many economists who have followed in their footsteps, Grether and Plott did not immediately accept this face-value interpretation and, instead, looked for ways of explaining PR while retaining the assumption that individuals do have a unique preference ordering over gambles. A substantial body of research in this spirit has examined whether PR might be an experimental artefact arising from imperfectly designed experiments. Early research of this genre – including Grether and Plott (1979); Reilly (1982) and Pommerehne, Schneider and Zweifel (1982) – investigated issues such as whether PR might be a consequence of subjects failing to understand the tasks confronting them, or of having insufficient motivation to take those tasks seriously. But a large body of evidence now shows that PR is a highly replicable phenomenon, robust to many variations in experimental procedures. Seidl (2002) provides a review.

A more subtle critique of PR experiments and evidence emerged in the late 1980s with the publication of a series of theoretical papers (Holt, 1986; Karni and Safra, 1987; Segal, 1988) arguing that PR might be a spurious artefact of experimental design after all. These papers shared a common strategy, pointing to a potential weakness of two experimental procedures which had been commonly used to incentivize decision tasks in PR experiments: the Becker–DeGroot–Marschak (1964) mechanism and the random lottery incentive system. The thrust of these papers is to show that, if individuals have non-expected utility preferences (violating either the independence axiom of expected utility theory, or the reduction of compound lotteries principle, or both), these standard incentive mechanisms could be biased and might generate the spurious appearance of PR. On this interpretation, PR would not be evidence against procedure invariance: instead it would be evidence of consistent, but non-expected utility, preferences interacting with specific features of experimental design. This interpretation has, however, been largely discounted in the light of subsequent research (including Tversky, Slovic and Kahneman, 1990 and Cubitt, Munro and Starmer, 2004) which reproduces the PR phenomenon in experiments using incentive mechanisms immune to this critique of earlier studies.

Theory

There remains considerable interest in trying to find a satisfactory explanation of PR. In what follows, we discuss three types of theory that may contribute to that objective: *regret theory, reference-dependent theory,* and *constructed preference theory.*

Regret theory (Loomes and Sugden, 1982; 1983) explains PR as a form of intransitivity. In this theory preferences are defined over pairs of acts which map from states of the world to consequences (as in Savage, 1954). Suppose A_i and A_j are two potential acts that result in, respectively, outcomes x_{is} and x_{js}, in state of the world s. If A_i is chosen, the resulting utility in each state is given by a 'modified utility function' $M(x_{is}, x_{js})$. Notice that this function allows the consequences of the chosen act to depend upon those that *might have been* experienced under the forgone act A_j. In particular, the utility from having x_{is} may be suppressed by 'regret' when x_{is} is worse than x_{js}. Regret theory assumes that individuals attempt to maximize the expectation of modified utility $\Sigma_s p_s.M(x_{is}, x_{js})$ where p_s is the probability of state s. Regret theory reduces to expected utility theory in the special case where $M(x_{is}, x_{js}) = u(x_{is})$ and $u(.)$ is a von Neumann–Morgenstern utility function.

Loomes and Sugden (1982) show that, if preferences in this theory satisfy particular restrictions, then regret theory provides a possible explanation of several well-known violations of expected utility theory including some cases of the famous Allais paradox. The most important of these restrictions is a property (subsequently) called regret aversion and, in a follow-up paper, Loomes and Sugden (1983) show that regret aversion may also explain PR. The argument works roughly as follows. Consider the following three acts labelled \$, P and M with monetary consequences $x > y > m > 0$ defined over three states.

The acts labelled \$ and P have the structure of typical \$- and P-bets: they are binary gambles where \$ has the higher prize, and P the higher probability of 'winning'; the third act gives payoff m for sure. Regret theory allows choices over acts with this structure to be non-transitive and, if preferences are regret averse, if a cycle occurs it will be in a specific direction: P chosen over \$; M over P; and \$ over M. Now recall that, in a typical PR experiment, the standard reversal occurred when a subject chose P over \$ but valued \$ more highly than P. So, if we interpret choices from {\$, M} and {P, M} as analogues of valuation tasks asking 'is \$ (or P) worth more or less than M?', then the cycle predicted by regret theory can be interpreted as a form of PR.

This explanation for PR has been tested via experiments designed to look for the pure choice analogue of PR by confronting subjects with pairwise choices among triples of bets with the structure of \$, P and M above. The outcome of this strand of research has produced good and bad news for regret theory. The good news is that the non-transitive choice cycles predicted by it have been observed and replicated (Loomes, Starmer and Sugden, 1991). Since these choice cycles occur in studies that involve no valuation tasks at all, this is evidence for the intransitivity interpretation of PR. The bad news is that subsequent research (Starmer and Sugden, 1998) has cast considerable doubt on regret theory's account of these choice cycles. The current state of play appears to be that regret theory has led to the discovery of a surprising new choice phenomenon, but it turns out not to be the right explanation for it! It remains possible that these intransitive choice cycles are manifestations of regret-type influences at work but that formal models of regret must be refined to properly account for them. Another possibility is that they have nothing to do with 'regret' and that their discovery, as a consequence of testing regret theory, was just accidental.

A new account of PR has emerged in the form of reference-dependent subjective expected utility theory (Sugden, 2003). In this model, preferences are again defined over acts. The key structural departure from Savage's (1954) subjective expected utility theory is that consequences in each state are modelled as gains and losses relative to a *reference act* (the status quo). The resulting theory is a formulation of expected utility (that is, a model that is linear in probabilities) that can accommodate loss aversion (that is, losses of a given size being weighted more highly than corresponding magnitude gains). Sugden demonstrates that, when preferences are loss averse, this model predicts standard PR in experiments where values are elicited as selling prices (which they usually are). This prediction depends on the assumption that, in selling tasks, an agent's reference act is the lottery being sold: given this, seemingly reasonable, assumption, $ valuations become particularly 'inflated' by consideration of the large $ prize which becomes a (probabilistic) loss if the $-bet is given up for a certain amount of cash. Hence, on this account, PR is the consequence of loss aversion operating through selling tasks. As yet, there have been no direct tests of this explanation, though the evidence of loss aversion operating in other contexts (see Starmer, 2000, for some discussion) perhaps gives it some initial credibility.

Thus far we have discussed various preference-theoretic accounts of PR. The final type of explanation we discuss is the oldest and belongs to a class of theory that has evolved in the psychology literature. From the outset, most psychologists accepted PR as evidence against the very thing that economists have invested their efforts in defending: the presumption that behaviour can be adequately explained in terms of unique underlying preferences. Psychologists have, instead, focused on accounts of PR which attribute it to aspects of human *decision processes*. Viewed from this perspective, there is nothing fundamentally surprising about the fact that rankings delivered via choice and valuation tasks differ; those working within this paradigm will, typically, attempt to read such inconsistencies as clues to the, potentially distinct, mental heuristics invoked in those different tasks.

Numerous theories in this spirit have been proposed as putative accounts of PR, and one of the best known examples is the scale-compatibility hypothesis due to Tversky, Sattath and Slovic (1988). The general hypothesis assumes that the way in which an individual is required to respond to a task ('the response mode') can affect the weights that he or she places on particular dimensions of alternatives being evaluated. In application to PR, the hypothesis implies that, because valuation tasks require a money amount as output, individuals place particularly high (low) weight on the money (probability) dimension, leading to relatively 'inflated' values for $ bets. Some recent support for this particular hypothesis is reported in Cubitt, Munro and Starmer (2004). There is, however, a vast theoretical and empirical literature connecting PR with the constructed preference approach and, for those interested in pursuing it, an excellent source is Lichtenstein and Slovic (2006).

Developing themes

One developing theme in empirical PR research examines the persistence of PR in environments where individuals receive feedback on the consequences of their decisions. A famous experiment by Chu and Chu (1990) exposed preference reversers to 'money pumps': subjects who committed PR had their stated preferences implemented across a series of trades which ultimately resulted in monetary losses. Individuals quickly learned to avoid PR in this environment. While this is an interesting finding, since Chu and Chu use such an explicit method for disciplining inconsistent preferences, it would be a mistake to view this as persuasive evidence that PR would be eroded in any naturally occurring market. There is some limited evidence to suggest that PR may decay in some specific experimental markets (Cox and Grether, 1996) but the findings here are both tentative and mixed, and further investigation is warranted before any firm conclusions can be drawn.

Another theme of current research explores the implications of preference anomalies (including PR) for the formulation of economic policy. A discussion of this topic is contained in Braga and Starmer (2005).

CHRIS STARMER

See also **prospect theory.**

Bibliography

Becker, G.M., DeGroot, M.H. and Marschak, J. 1964. Measuring utility by a single-response sequential method. *Behavioral Science* 9, 226–32.

Braga, J. and Starmer, C. 2005. Preference anomalies, preference elicitation and the discovered preference hypothesis. *Environmental and Resource Economics* 32, 55–89.

Chu, Y.P. and Chu, R.L. 1990. The subsidence of preference reversals in simplified and marketlike experimental settings: a note. *American Economic Review* 80, 902–11.

Cox, J.C. and Grether, D.M. 1996. The preference reversal phenomenon: response mode, markets and incentives. *Economic Theory* 7, 381–405.

Cubitt, R.P., Munro, A. and Starmer, C. 2004. Testing explanations of preference reversal. *Economic Journal* 114, 709–26.

Grether, D. and Plott, C.R. 1979. Economic theory of choice and the preference reversal phenomenon. *American Economic Review* 69, 623–38.

Holt, C.A. 1986. Preference reversals and the independence axiom. *American Economic Review* 76, 508–15.

Karni, E. and Safra, Z. 1987. 'Preference reversal' and the observability of preferences by experimental methods. *Econometrica* 55, 675–85.

Lichtenstein, S. and Slovic, P. 1971. Reversals of preferences between bids and choices in gambling decisions. *Journal of Experimental Psychology* 89, 46–55.

Lichtenstein, S. and Slovic, P. 2006. *The Construction of Preference*. New York: Cambridge University Press.

Lindman, H.R. 1971. Inconsistent preferences among gambles. *Journal of Experimental Psychology* 89, 390–7.

Loomes, G., Starmer, C. and Sugden, R. 1991. Observing violations of transitivity by experimental methods. *Econometrica* 59, 425–39.

Loomes, G.C. and Sugden, R. 1982. Regret theory: an alternative theory of rational choice under uncertainty. *Economic Journal* 92, 805–24.

Loomes, G.C. and Sugden, R. 1983. A rationale for preference reversal. *American Economic Review* 73, 428–32.

Pommerehne, W.W., Schneider, F. and Zweifel, P. 1982. Economic theory of choice and the preference reversal phenomenon: a re-examination. *American Economic Review* 73, 569–74.

Reilly, R.J. 1982. Preference reversal: further evidence and some suggested modifications in experimental design. *American Economic Review* 73, 576–84.

Segal, U. 1988. Does the preference reversal phenomenon necessarily contradict the independence axiom? *American Economic Review* 78, 233–36.

Seidl, C. 2002. Preference reversal. *Journal of Economic Surveys* 6, 621–55.

Savage, L. 1954. *The Foundations of Statistics*. New York: Wiley.

Starmer, C.V. 2000. Developments in non-expected utility theory: the hunt for a descriptive theory of choice under risk. *Journal of Economic Literature* 38, 332–82.

Starmer, C. and Sugden, R. 1998. Testing alternative explanations of cyclical choices. *Economica* 65, 259–347.

Sugden, R. 2003. Reference-dependent subjective expected utility. *Journal of Economic Theory* 111, 172–91.

Tversky, A., Sattath, S. and Slovic, P. 1988. Contingent weighting in judgement and choice. *Psychological Review* 95, 371–84.

Tversky, A., Slovic, P. and Kahneman, D. 1990. The causes of preference reversal. *American Economic Review* 80, 204–17.

prospect theory

Prospect theory (PT) was developed by psychologists Daniel Kahneman and Amos Tversky to try to account for a number of patterns of response to risky choices which departed systematically from the conventional wisdom about rational decision making in the form of von Neumann and Morgenstern's (1944) expected utility (EU) hypothesis.

Kahneman and Tversky's (1979) paper 'Prospect Theory: An Analysis of Decision Under Risk' has proved to be enormously influential. According to Kim, Morse and Zingales (2006), it is the second most frequently cited paper published in economics journals since 1970, with more than 4,000 citations in the 25 years since its publication. It provided a major stimulus to the development of a number of other 'non-expected-utility' theories in the 1980s and 1990s – see Starmer (2000) for a survey and review. It has also inspired much work in behavioural economics and in economic and psychological experiments exploring individual decision making under risk and uncertainty.

The following subsections consider what PT set out to do and how it did it. There then follows a discussion of the importance of the theory as well as its possible limitations.

Background

In the 1950s and 1960s, evidence had begun to accumulate which suggested that EU failed as a general *descriptive* model of risky choice. Two of the most influential 'paradoxes' had been identified by Maurice Allais in the early 1950s (see Allais, 1953). These were renamed by Kahneman and Tversky (henceforth K&T) and are now widely known as the 'common ratio effect' and the 'common consequence effect'. Briefly, they are as follows, starting with the common ratio effect.

Consider the choice between two 'prospects' A and B where A offers a sum of money x with probability p (and 0 with probability $1-p$) while B offers a smaller sum y with a larger probability q (and 0 with probability $1-q$). An extreme form of this might involve setting $q=1$, so that B offers the certainty of y: in an example used by K&T, B offered the certainty of 3,000 Israeli pounds while A offered a 0.8 chance of 4,000 (and a 0.2 chance of 0). EU does not predict which of A and B an individual will choose – that depends on the individual's personal tastes concerning risk – but what the independence axiom of EU *does* entail is that, if p and q are scaled down by the same factor so that the ratio of 'winning' probabilities is maintained, the preference between the scaled-down prospects will be consistent with the preference between A and B.

So – to continue the example used by K&T – suppose that both p and q are scaled down to a quarter of their original values, generating prospects C and D, where C offers a 0.2 chance of 4,000 and a 0.8 chance of 0, while D offers a 0.25 chance of 3,000 and a 0.75 chance of 0. Then EU entails that anyone who prefers A over B should also prefer C over D, and vice versa. However, the common ratio effect form of the Allais paradox is manifested when a substantial proportion of those who choose the safer option B in the first case switch to the riskier prospect C in the second case, while the combination of choosing A in the first case and D in the second case is relatively rare.

In the above case, the scaling down operated on the *magnitudes* of the winning probabilities, while *maintaining the ratio* between them. Another way of manipulating the prospects could work in terms of replacing some probability of a particular sum common to both prospects by the same probability of a different sum. Consider another example used by K&T. This time, E offers 2,500 with probability 0.33, 2,400 with probability 0.66 and 0 with probability 0.01, while F offers 2,400 with certainty. Now, for both prospects, replace the 0.66 probability of 2,400 by a 0.66 probability of 0: this transforms E into a prospect G which offers a 0.33 chance of 2,500 and a 0.67 chance of 0, and transforms F into a prospect H which offers a 0.34 chance of 2,400 and a 0.66 chance of 0. Once again, EU entails that individuals should either choose E in the first case and G in the second, or else they should choose F and H. However, the common consequence effect form of Allais paradox involves many more individuals switching from safer to riskier (that is, choosing F and G) than switch from riskier to safer (that is, choose E and H).

In addition to the common ratio and common consequence effects, two other 'effects' were influential in the formulation of PT. One of these is the 'isolation effect'. Consider again the 'scaled-down' pair of prospects from the common ratio example. In the way they were presented there, C offered a 0.2 chance of 4,000 together with a 0.8 chance of 0, while D offered a 0.25 chance of 3,000 alongside a 0.75 chance of 0. In this case, the implication is that the uncertainty is resolved in a single stage: perhaps a 20-sided die is rolled, and if a number from 1 to 4 comes up C pays 4,000 (and 0 otherwise), whereas D pays 3,000 if the number is anything in the range 1 to 5.

However, there is another way of presenting this choice which EU would regard as amounting to exactly the same thing, but which PT suggests people are likely to treat differently. Suppose that the uncertainty is resolved in two stages, as follows. In the first stage, there is a 0.75 chance of being 'knocked out' and getting 0, and there is a 0.25 chance of getting through to the second stage – at which point the choice is between, on the one hand, a 0.8 chance of 4,000 and, on the other hand, the certainty of 3,000. The logic of EU entails that the two stages can be 'reduced' to a single stage by multiplying through the probabilities: a 0.25 chance of getting through and facing a 0.8 chance of 4,000 can thus be reduced to a 0.2 chance of 4,000, as offered by prospect C; and a 0.25 chance of getting through to receive the certainty of 3,000 is regarded as just the same as a direct 0.25 chance of 3,000, as offered by prospect D.

Put another way, a 0.25 chance of what was prospect A in the common ratio example is equivalent to C, and a 0.25 chance of prospect B is regarded as the same as D. Yet the evidence of what K&T called the 'isolation effect' shows that people do not process the two-stage game in the way presumed by EU. When faced with such a two-stage problem and told that they have to make a commitment ahead of the first stage, most individuals appear to disregard (or isolate) the common first stage, focus on the alternatives that are contingent on getting through to the second stage, and then make much the same choices as they do when presented with the simple one-stage choice between A and B. In other words, when asked to commit ahead of this two-stage resolution of uncertainty, there is a much stronger tendency to pick the safer option than when presented with the one-stage choice between C and D where the calculus of probability 'reduction' has already been applied.

The fourth regularity that played a significant role in the formulation of PT was the 'reflection effect'. Essentially, this refers to the observations that changing payoffs from gains to losses (relative to the status quo) tended to reverse individuals' choices. Thus if A and B above were transformed into A' and B' such that A' offered a 0.8 probability of *losing* 4,000 (and a 0.2 probability of losing nothing) while B' entailed the certainty of a 3,000 loss, the modal preference for B over A would often be 'reflected' into a modal preference for A' over B'. Thus, what appears as a predominant pattern of risk aversion in the choice between prospects such as A and B which involve gains seems to transform into a predominant pattern of risk seeking when the non-zero payoffs are losses.

Combining the reflection effect with the isolation effect can produce striking 'framing' effects. For example, consider first a scenario where an individual is given a lump sum of 1,000 and then asked to choose between a further 500 for sure or else a risky prospect offering a 50–50 chance of either 0 or an extra 1,000. If the individual isolates the initial 1,000 and displays risk aversion towards the 50–50 gamble involving gains, she will end up with a sure 1,500 rather than a portfolio consisting of a 0.5 chance of a net 1,000 and a 0.5 chance of a net 2,000. But now consider a scenario framed somewhat differently. The individual is given a lump sum of 2,000 and then asked to choose between the certainty of losing 500 or else a 50–50 chance of either losing 1,000 or losing 0. If the individual again isolates the lump-sum but now displays risk seeking towards the 50–50 gamble involving losses, she will end up with exactly the opposite portfolio preference: that is, she will choose the portfolio consisting of a 0.5 chance of a net 1,000 and a 0.5 chance of a net 2,000 rather than 1,500 for sure. K&T presented evidence which showed that this was indeed a strong tendency among those who answered their hypothetical questions framed in these various ways.

The aims and structure of prospect theory

PT can be seen as offering a descriptive (rather than a prescriptive/normative) model of a particular area of decision making. K&T were careful to specify the domain to which their model applied: it was a theory of *choice* over pairs of prospects each involving *no more than two non-zero payoffs* where the *objective probabilities were given to decision makers*. As formulated in the 1979 paper, the theory did *not* apply to valuation tasks (for example, tasks that asked people how much they would pay or accept in exchange for some risky prospect), nor to prospects involving larger numbers of possible payoffs, nor to cases where there was ambiguity about the likelihood of different events occurring (although in their concluding remarks K&T expressed some optimism that the model could be extended to accommodate the latter two features, while relevant valuations might be inferred via some iterative procedure involving a series of choices between a prospect and different sure sums). Most importantly, because it set out to provide an account of *actual* behaviour rather than a prescription for how decision makers *ought* 'rationally' to behave, PT allowed the possibility of patterns of behaviour that decision makers might wish to modify if they ever became aware of the 'inconsistencies' involved (although, in the absence of opportunities for such realization, the 'anomalies' implied by PT could be expected to occur and persist).

To *some* extent, the elimination of some potentially undesirable possible implications of PT was handled by dividing the modelling of people's decision processes into two phases: first, the editing phase, which involved simplifying prospects and screening out transparent transgressions of reasonable behaviour; and then the evaluation phase, in which the preferred alternative was identified.

The editing phase prepared the ground for the evaluation phase in various intuitively appealing ways. It involved the detection of *transparent* dominance and the discarding/rejection of dominated alternatives in such cases (while allowing the possibility that dominance might be violated if more complicated ways of presenting the prospects obscured the dominance relationship). There was also scope for some *simplification* of prospects (for example, *rounding* of payoffs and/or probabilities). In cases where there were transparently common and/or riskless components, these were liable to be *segregated* and/or *cancelled*. It was also supposed that, when a prospect offered the same payoff contingent on different events with separately expressed probabilities, those probabilities would be added together. For example, suppose a prospect offered a payoff of 100 if a card drawn at random from a standard pack of playing cards turned out to be a spade, and offered the same payoff if the card turned out to be a heart: then the probabilities of these two events – each 0.25 – would be *combined* to give an overall 0.5 chance of receiving 100. Finally, all payoffs were *coded* into gains or losses relative to some reference point – this latter normally being the status quo, although in some circumstances it might be otherwise (as discussed in the penultimate subsection of the 1979 paper).

The evaluation phase involved the interaction of two components: the *value* function, and the *decision weight* function.

A careful reading of the 1979 exposition makes it clear that the subjective value associated with a particular payoff should, strictly speaking, be expected to be a function of *two* factors: the asset position that constitutes the individual's reference point, and the positive or negative change from that point represented by the payoff in question. However, K&T argued that, over quite broad ranges of initial asset positions and for many practical purposes, it is sufficient to focus just on one argument, namely, the size of the gain or loss entailed by any particular payoff.

Drawing on existing evidence, including a substantial body of work from the realm of psychophysics, K&T argued that such a value function is characterized by two key characteristics.

First, the marginal value of both gains and losses is presumed to diminish as the magnitudes increase. Thus the difference between a gain (or loss) of 100 and a gain (or loss) of 150 registers more strongly than the difference between a gain (loss) of 1,100 and a gain (loss) of 1,150. Such diminishing sensitivity means that the gradient of the value function becomes progressively less steep as payoffs are located further from the reference point. Denoting the value of any monetary payoff x by $v(x)$, diminishing sensitivity in the domain of gains can be more formally represented as

$$v(x + a) - v(x) > v(x + a + k) - v(x + k) \text{ for all } x, \ a, \ k > 0;$$

in the domain of losses, it entails

$$v(-x) - v(-x - a) > v(-x - k) - v(-x - a - k).$$

Second, the marginal value of losses is modelled as being greater than the marginal value of gains of the same magnitude: that is, for all x, the gradient of the function is steeper at $-x$ than at x. More formally, $v'(-x) > v'(x)$ wherever the derivative of x exists. In conjunction with the first characteristic, this implies a value function as shown in Figure 1: that is, concave in the domain of gains, convex and steeper in the domain of losses, and kinked at the (0) reference point.

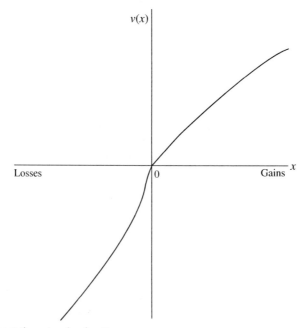

Figure 1   Prospect theory's value function

Thus one part of the evaluation of any prospect involves converting money payoffs to their values via the $v(\cdot)$ function as specified above. The other part of the evaluation requires decision weights to be attached to the various values. These decision weights are not the objective probabilities, nor even degrees of belief of the kind that are conventionally supposed to constitute subjective probabilities. In the context of the 1979 exposition, they represent a psychological transformation, or modification, of the objectively given probabilities, with the weighting function being denoted by $\pi(\cdot)$.

The key assumptions about $\pi(\cdot)$ are as follows. First, the weight attached to a zero probability event is 0, and the weight attached to a certainty is 1: that is, $\pi(0) = 0$ and $\pi(1) = 1$. Second, for low probability events, $\pi(p) > p$; but for higher probability events, $\pi(p) < p$; the 'crossover point', where $\pi(p) = p$, may vary from one individual to another, but is often depicted as being somewhere in the region of $p = 0.15$. Third, it is generally supposed that $\pi(p) + \pi(1 - p) < 1$: this property, labelled *subcertainty*, conveys the idea that complementary intermediate probabilities are jointly disadvantaged relative to certainty.

Taken together, the above assumptions are consistent with a decision weighting function of the kind depicted in Figure 2. Over most of its range, the fact that $\pi(\cdot)$ is flatter than the 45° line suggests that the evaluation of a prospect is less sensitive to changes in the probability of its non-zero payoff(s) than would be the case under EU where the utilities of payoffs are weighted in exact proportion to their respective probabilities of occurring. It also has the implication that for any given ratio of probabilities, the ratio tends to get closer to 1 as the magnitudes of the probabilities fall: more formally, $\pi(pq)/\pi(p) \leq \pi(pqr)/\pi(pr)$ for all p, q, $r < 1$.

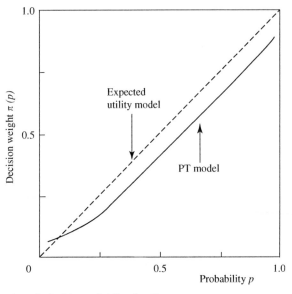

Figure 2   Prospect theory's decision weighting function

However, such a formulation also has the property that it entails abrupt changes/ jumps in the vicinities of $p = 0$ and $p = 1$. It might be said that the function is not 'well-behaved' – or indeed, not defined – in those regions, where there are 'quantal effects'. And this allows at least one pattern of behaviour that many decision theorists would find normatively undesirable/unacceptable, as follows. Consider a case where prospect C offers the certainty of some gain x, while A offers x with probability p and $x + a$ with probability $1 - p$, where a is some (small) positive amount. Evaluating each prospect separately,

$$v(C) = v(x) \text{ and } v(A) = \pi(p)v(x) + \pi(1 - p)v(x + a).$$

However, because $\pi(p) + \pi(1 - p)$ is liable to sum to less than 1, $v(A)$ may be less than $v(C)$, even though A dominates C. In a direct choice between the two, PT supposes that this dominance (if transparent) will be detected as part of the editing process, so that A will be chosen. But it should be possible to construct some other prospect B which neither dominates nor is dominated by either A or C but whose value lies between the two, so that $v(C) > v(B) > v(A)$. Hence in separate pairwise choices, C will be preferred to B and B will be preferred to A, while A will be chosen over C on the basis of transparent dominance, thereby giving a violation of transitivity.

More recent developments in theory and evidence

Because PT *does* allow such violations of principles that many decision theorists regard as normatively compelling, various modifications have been proposed to 'fix' this supposed defect: in particular, a method of deriving decision weights which ensured that they summed to 1 and disallowed any violations of stochastic dominance or transitivity was proposed by Quiggin (1982) and was subsequently incorporated into a revised and extended form of PT known as cumulative prospect theory (CPT) (see Tversky and Kahneman, 1992).

The essence of Quiggin's proposal involved ranking the possible outcomes $x_1 \ldots x_n$ offered by a prospect according to their values and then assigning weights to each of the cumulative probabilities that the prospect pays at least x_i, for all $i = 1 \ldots n$. (Hence this kind of model came to be labelled as 'rank-dependent'.) The function used to transform cumulative probabilities – call it $w(\cdot)$ to distinguish it from the $\pi(\cdot)$ discussed above – is fully defined in $[0, 1]$ space, with $w(0)=0$ and $w(1)=1$. Like $\pi(\cdot)$, it is usually supposed to have an increasing inverse-S shape (although by contrast with $\pi(\cdot)$, the 'crossover point' in CPT is more often regarded as lying in the 0.3–0.4 region – see Figure 3.

As a consequence of being steeper in the vicinities of 0 and 1, and less steep across the intermediate range, this form of $w(\cdot)$ gives greater weight to extreme than to intermediate outcomes. Although it may be psychologically implausible that most individuals transform probabilities *strictly* according to the rather cumbersome procedure specified by CPT and other rank-dependent models, the approach captures the general intuition that extreme outcomes may attract more attention and receive relatively more weight in decisions. And it appeals to those theorists who are

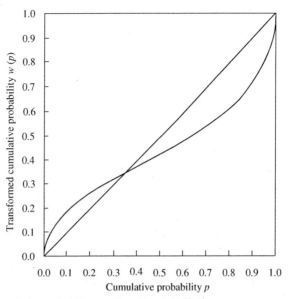

Figure 3   CPT's cumulative probability transformation function

inclined towards models that respect what are perceived to be 'fundamental' requirements of rationality such as transitivity, while also having the advantage of being applicable to prospects involving probability distributions over any number and range of outcomes.

However, the spirit of PT was to provide a *descriptive* model of risky choice, so that violations of transitivity of the kind outlined earlier were an implication of the model; and, to the extent that they occur in practice, PT can claim to be descriptively successful. And indeed there is evidence of such violations (see Starmer, 1999).

On the other hand, as K&T acknowledge, there are limitations to the scope of PT. As discussed above, the domain of the theory was very specific and excluded a number of tasks that are of economic significance (such as the formulation of certainty equivalence values). Moreover, certain assumptions made in the model are open to question. For example, the phenomenon of 'event-splitting' (see Humphrey, 1995) suggests that people may only imperfectly add the probabilities of the same payoff under different 'states of the world', contrary to the supposed process of combination in the editing phase. There may also be questions about just how transparent dominance needs to be before it is detected in the editing phase. And some researchers – see, for example, Birnbaum (2006) – have amassed evidence of patterns of choice which appear to run counter to the claims of prospect theories to provide a satisfactory description even of the behaviour which should lie within their domain.

All that having been said, there can be no doubt whatsoever of the success of PT in focusing the attention of decision theorists on patterns of behaviour that do not conform with the conventional (and still predominant) wisdom of EU, and in stimulating a very substantial body of experimental, empirical and theoretical work exploring behaviour outside of the strictures of standard economic 'rationality'.

GRAHAM LOOMES

See also **experimental economics.**

Bibliography

Allais, M. 1953. Le comportement de l'homme rationnel devant le risque: critique des postulats et axiomes de l'école américaine. *Econometrica* 21, 503–46.

Birnbaum, M. 2006. Evidence against prospect theories in gambles with positive, negative and mixed consequences. *Journal of Economic Psychology* 27, 737–61.

Humphrey, S. 1995. Risk aversion or event-splitting effects? More evidence under risk and uncertainty. *Journal of Risk and Uncertainty* 11, 263–74.

Kahneman, D. and Tversky, A. 1979. Prospect theory: an analysis of decision under risk. *Econometrica* 47, 263–91.

Kim, E., Morse, A. and Zingales, L. 2006. What has mattered to economics since 1970. *Journal of Economic Perspectives* 20(4), 189–202.

Quiggin, J. 1982. A theory of anticipated utility. *Journal of Economic Behavior and Organization* 3, 323–43.

Starmer, C. 1999. Cycling with rules of thumb: an experimental test for a new form of non-transitive behaviour. *Theory and Decision* 46, 139–57.

Starmer, C. 2000. Developments in non-expected utility theory: the hunt for a descriptive theory of choice under risk. *Journal of Economic Literature* 38, 332–82.

Tversky, A. and Kahneman, D. 1992. Advances in prospect theory: cumulative representation of uncertainty. *Journal of Risk and Uncertainty* 5, 297–323.

von Neumann, J. and Morgenstern, O. 1944. *Theory of Games and Economic Behavior.* Princeton: Princeton University Press.

public goods experiments

Since the vivid description of the Prisoner's Dilemma game and the accompanying tension between self-interest and efficiency, economists, political scientists, psychologists, sociologists and others have wondered about how individuals resolve these conflicting motivations. Many have investigated this question by experimentally examining behaviour when individual interest and group interest conflict. This research goes under different names – for example, social dilemmas in psychology, commons dilemmas in political science and public goods problems in economics.

This article does not provide a comprehensive review of this research; other excellent reviews aimed at economists (Ledyard, 1995), psychologists (Dawes, 1980) or sociologists (Kollock, 1998) exist. Instead, I highlight the different categories of public goods problems and introduce their commonalities.

The rest of this article is organized as follows. First, I offer some definitions of characteristics that public goods problems share. Next I discuss some dimensions on which they differ, and how these dimensions translate into different equilibrium and efficient outcomes. Then I describe three specific public goods problem types that have been extensively studied in the economics literature: the voluntary contribution mechanism, the provision point mechanism and the common pool resource. I conclude with a description of other games that have been studied, but where more work could be done.

Similarities

The common feature in public goods settings is the existence of externalities. In public *goods* problems, individuals can use private resources to provide goods that have positive externalities for others. Since some social benefits are not captured by the individual making the decision, this results in under-provision relative to the socially optimum level. Self-interested economic theory, then, argues that these goods will be under-provided, justifying taxation as a role for government.

Parallel to the public goods situation is the case of public *bads*. Here, individuals receive private resources by producing goods that have a negative externality for others. Since some social costs are not captured by the individual making the decision, this results in overprovision of public bads relative to the socially optimum level. Self-interested economic theory, then, argues that these goods will be over-provided, again justifying a role for government, here in regulation. (A number of models have extended the existing theory to internalize the externalities. In models of altruism – for example, Becker, 1974; Andreoni, 1989 – the utility function of one party includes the consumption of others. Thus, when an action creates positive externalities, the value from it is increased over the self-interested model. Charness and Rabin, 2002, posit that individuals care not only about their own consumption but also about social welfare directly. These other-regarding preferences can internalize some of the externalities in public goods problems, but typically the over- or under-provision problems are not eliminated.)

The defining characteristic of the public goods problems described here, however, is the existence of positive externalities. My actions affect others, and I do not take this effect (sufficiently) into account in my own maximization problem. Often these problems are symmetric; each individual faces the identical conflict, but this is not necessary for there to be a public goods problem. For a problem to exist, it must only be that the individual's welfare and the group's (social) welfare conflict.

Differences

The largest, most important and least-recognized difference in public goods situations is the production function. How does an individual's action create positive or negative externalities for others? Different production functions have different implications for equilibrium predictions as well as socially optimal outcomes.

A second important dimension on which these situations differ is the decision space. Public goods problems can involve acting to provide goods with positive externalities at a private cost, refraining from acting so as to avoid imposing negative externalities on others at a personal cost, or acting to capture what would otherwise be public benefits for private consumption. Unlike the first dimension, these differences in the decision space have only a superficial impact on the equilibria; that is, one can easily describe 'not polluting' as 'producing a public good'. However, they may affect how individuals think about (and act in) these problems.

To clarify these differences, let's examine the three classic games discussed below in terms of the production function and decision space. In the voluntary contribution mechanism (VCM), the decision space involves *giving*. Individuals are given an endowment, which they can use for their private consumption or to produce the public good. Their allocations toward the public good provide value for others in the experiment (positive externalities). The production function of the VCM game most extensively studied is *linear* (thus it is sometimes also called a linear public goods game). The more that is allocated toward the public good, the greater are the social benefits in a linear fashion. This linearity means that (with appropriate parameters as discussed below) this game has a unique Nash equilibrium in which no participant allocates any resources towards producing the public good. Deviations from the equilibrium are both welfare-enhancing and represent deviations from pure self-interest maximization. They are thus referred to as 'cooperation', and concepts like altruism, warm glow and reciprocity are offered as their explanation.

In contrast, consider the provision point mechanism (PPM). Again, this game typically has a *giving* decision space. Individuals are given an endowment which can be allocated to private consumption or towards providing the public good. But, in contrast with the VCM, in the PPM the production function involves a *threshold*. If enough resources are collected, then the public good is provided and all receive its benefits. If too few resources are collected, then the public good is not provided and no positive externalities are enjoyed. The threshold nature of this production function has critical implications for the equilibria of this game. With appropriate parameters (discussed below), the full free-riding equilibrium still exists. But there also exist a set of efficient equilibria, in which the public good is exactly provided with each individual contributing a share of its cost. In each of these equilibria, the share contributed by each individual varies. (For example, there may be one equilibrium in which I contribute 80 per cent and you contribute 20 per cent of the cost of providing the public good, and another where I contribute 20 per cent and you contribute 80 per cent.) The problem then becomes one not of cooperation but primarily one of coordination; how do we select among these efficient equilibria? Formally, this game can be thought of as a large battle-of-the-sexes game (a game of impure coordination), with multiple equilibria each of which is somebody's favourite.

Finally, consider the common pool resource (CPR) game. Here the decision space involves *taking*; for example, individuals can harvest grass from the commons for personal gain. Surprisingly, these experiments are often described as *giving* games, with negative externalities rather than positive, as in the VCM or PPM. So the decision is made on 'how many hours to spend grazing' with the resulting negative externalities as cattle eat more grass. The production function used in CPR games is typically *nonlinear*. A small amount of harvesting creates more benefit for the individual than harm to the society (and is thus socially efficient). However, as the individual harvests more, the personal benefits decrease and the social costs increase until societal costs outweigh private benefits (the socially optimal point). With appropriate parameters (described below), however, private benefit is still above private costs, leading individuals to continue harvesting past the socially efficient point. Eventually, private benefits equal private costs, leading individuals to stop harvesting. These equilibria are thus internal (individuals typically harvest more than zero but less than the full amount) but still suboptimal (total harvesting is larger than the socially optimum level).

There are many additional dimensions on which these games can vary. For example, experimenters have varied the number of players from two (the classic Prisoner's Dilemma game) to as many as 100 (Isaac, Walker and Williams, 1994). The particular parameters can vary, subject to constraints that preserve the public goods nature of the problem. The institutional rules can vary, participants can decide simultaneously or sequentially, they can discuss the game in advance or not, and so on. The games can be (finitely) repeated or one-shot. I discuss some of these variations in the sections below, but their impacts on the equilibria of the games are straightforward.

In summary, the set of public goods games is broad. When one looks at a game, however, it is critical to understand the production function that is being used to translate decisions into outcomes (positive/negative, linear/threshold/nonlinear), and the decision space that participants face (giving/taking/refraining from action). These dimensions have important impacts on the equilibrium predictions, the observed behaviour and the attributions that one can make about the causes of differences between the two.

The voluntary contribution mechanism (VCM)

The work of Marwell and Ames (1979; 1980; 1981) is often cited as the earliest VCM experiments. Unfortunately these early experiments did not involve a linear production function. Instead the return from the public account was discrete (chunky) although some of the experiments involved a linear approximation (for example, 1981, study I). Furthermore, the experiments were relatively uncontrolled; subjects had instructions mailed to them at home, were individually called and had the instructions explained to them, and then called back one week later and made their (one-shot) decision by phone.

The first paper using a linear VCM in a controlled lab setting was Isaac, Walker and Thomas (1984). This paper set a number of precedents for how such experiments are run. In this experiment, participants were brought into the lab and arranged into fixed groups of four. In each period, each group member was given tokens, which he could allocate between a private account and a group account. Tokens allocated to the private account earned 1¢ per token. Tokens allocated to the group account earned 0.3¢ per token for each member of the group, whether or not he had contributed to the group account. As the production function is linear, these parameters remain constant regardless of how much is contributed.

More generally, for there to be a public goods problem in these linear games, a few conditions must be satisfied. First, the return from the public good to the individual must be lower than the return from the private good (0.3 < 1). This ensures that individuals do not have an individual incentive to contribute, and that the dominant strategy equilibrium in the stage game is thus to contribute zero tokens. Furthermore, the social benefit from contributing toward the public good must be greater than the social cost (0.3*4 = 1.2 > 1). This ensures that contributing toward the public good is socially efficient.

The game is finitely repeated for ten periods, to allow for convergence to (and learning of) the equilibrium. In the finitely repeated game, backward induction results in the unique Nash equilibrium of zero contributions. Deviations from that equilibrium are attributed to cooperation, altruism, reciprocity or various other-regarding preferences.

A number of precedents set in this original article have been used in subsequent research. Many papers use a group size of four, although some have gone as low as two and others as high as 100. Most experiments have participants 'allocate' tokens between multiple funds rather than 'contribute' towards a public good, as this experiment did. Participants typically have multiple tokens to allocate rather than simply one. Most papers use repetition with fixed groups, and many choose ten periods.

The results from this wide variety of experiments are quite robust. First, on average, contributions to the public good begin at about half the endowment of tokens.

Second, there is considerable variation in the decisions of individuals. Third, those contributions reduce over time until the contributions in the final round are 10–20 per cent of the endowment. An example of this pattern of contributions is depicted in Figure 1. A number of interesting papers have hypothesized and tested for the source of these regularities. Some explanations include errors (Palfrey and Prisbrey, 1997), confusion (Andreoni, 1995b), strategies and learning (Andreoni and Croson, 2008), and reciprocity or conditional cooperation (Croson, 2007), among others.

Variations in the parameters have been explored as well; individual papers manipulate group size (Isaac and Walker, 1988b), the ratio of the return from the public good to the return from the private good (Isaac and Walker, 1988b), the existence of communication (Isaac and Walker, 1988a), fixed groups (Andreoni and Croson, 2008), anonymity (Laury, Walker and Williams, 1995) and framing (Andreoni, 1995a). Recent work in this area extends the paradigm to incorporate more realistic assumptions, including heterogeneity of players (Buckley and Croson, 2006), endogenous group formation (Croson, Fatas and Neugebauer, 2005), and punishment/reward (Fehr and Gächter, 2000). Data has been collected from various subject pools, including children (Krause and Harbaugh, 2000) and residents of Asian slums (Carpenter, Daniere and Takahashi, 2004). (For a fascinating look into underappreciated but related psychology literature, see research on *social loafing*, reviewed in Karau and Williams, 1993.)

In summary, the VCM captures the pure tension between individual gains and social efficiency. It is thus used in many settings and by many researchers to investigate the causes (and consequences) of this tension, as well as to describe behaviour in the world.

The provision point mechanism (PPM)

One concern with the VCM is that in equilibrium the public good is not provided at the socially efficient level. Bagnoli and Lipman (1989) discuss a logical response to this problem: add a threshold (or provision point) to the production process. The

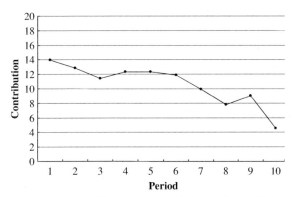

Figure 1   Average contributions to public account in VCM. *Source*: Croson (2007).

threshold needed to provide the public good is announced. If at least that much is allocated to the group account, then the public good is produced; if not, no public good is produced.

It is straightforward to see that a VCM can be 'discretized' to the PPM by adding a threshold. With the appropriate parameters (discussed below) this game now has a set of efficient Nash equilibria in which the public good is exactly provided. There are also inefficient equilibria of this game, in which the public good is not provided, but this mechanism nonetheless represents a theoretical improvement over the VCM.

There are some parameter values necessary for the existence of these efficient equilibria. In particular, imagine the threshold is T, the value from private consumption is 1 and individual endowments are E_i. Define v_i as an individual's value from the public good. For an efficient equilibrium there must exist a set of contributions $\{\sigma_i\}$ such that $\sum \sigma_i \geq T$. Furthermore, the individual rationality constraints must be satisfied $(\forall_i)\sigma_i \leq \min \{E_i, v_i\}$ and providing the public good must be efficient $T \leq \sum v_i$.

Additional assumptions are needed before this mechanism is completely described. When the threshold is not reached, the resources contributed to it can be returned or can be lost. This feature has been called the 'money back guarantee' in psychology, and in economics is the *refund* (Isaac, Schmidtz and Walker, 1989; Bagnoli and McKee, 1991). The existence of a refund does not affect the set of efficient equilibria, but does change the set of inefficient equilibria. With no refund, there is one (unique) inefficient equilibrium of zero contribution. With a refund, there are many (weak) inefficient equilibria in which some is contributed towards the public good, but not so much that any player can supplement to reach the threshold. Those contributions are then refunded, making the contributors indifferent between these strategies and contributing zero.

The second dimension is the disposition of resources above the threshold. This is referred to as the *rebate* (Marks and Croson, 1998). Experiments have been run including no rebate (excess contributions are lost), proportional rebates (excess contributions are returned proportionally based on contributions), and utilization rebates (excess contributions are used to provide the public good in a VCM fashion). None of these changes the set of equilibria.

While the PPM has the advantage of the existence of efficient equilibria, it has the disadvantage of too many equilibria. For example, in a typical parameterization used by Croson and Marks (1998), five players each had 55 tokens to allocate. Tokens allocated to the private account earned 1¢ each. If there were at least 125 tokens allocated to the public account, each participant in the group received 50¢. These parameters satisfy the conditions above; the collective benefit from the public good (5 people × 50¢ = $2.50) is greater than the social cost of provision ($1.25). There exists a set of allocations such that the public good is provided; one is the unique symmetric equilibrium in which each player allocates 25 tokens, the threshold is exactly met, and each participant receives their value of 50¢, strictly greater than their costs of 25¢.

Unfortunately, this is not the only efficient equilibrium. In particular, the set of allocations {25, 25, 25, 24, 26} is also an equilibrium, as is {25, 25, 25, 26, 24}, although player 4 prefers the former and player 5 the latter. All told, there are 4,052,751 efficient equilibria using these parameters. Thus the main problem in the PPM is not one of *cooperation*; avoiding the inefficient outcome as in the VCM. It's a problem of *coordination*, of choosing which of the many efficient equilibria the group will play.

The coordination problem is difficult enough in the stage game. However, in the lab this game is typically finitely repeated. In the repeated game, the number of potential equilibria grows exponentially, as any sequence of stage-game equilibria are themselves an equilibrium of the repeated game.

In practice, almost no instances of the inefficient equilibria are observed. Group contributions tend to cycle around the efficient equilibrium level, although they are almost equally likely to be above the threshold as below. Examples of group contributions in the PPM can be seen in Figure 2.

Further research has investigated other dimensions of the PPM. These include the effect of subject pool (Cadsby and Maynes, 1998), binary versus continuous giving (Cadsby and Maynes, 1999), heterogeneous valuations (Croson and Marks, 1999), identifiability of contributions (Croson and Marks, 1998), incomplete information (Marks and Croson, 1999), and framing (Sonnemans, Schram and Offerman, 1998).

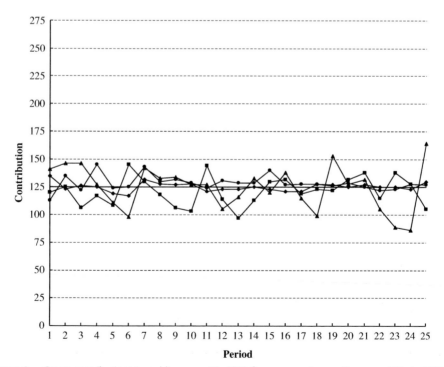

Figure 2   Group contributions to public account in PPM, four groups. *Source*: Croson and Marks (2000).

The PPM has a number of important and interesting properties. It allows for efficient equilibria, thus to some extent 'solving' the public goods problem. However, this solution brings costs: too many equilibria and the need to coordinate among them. This distinction, between the cooperation motive of the VCM and the coordination motive of the PPM is a critical and often-overlooked one.

The common pool resource game

The structure of the CPR game is based on work by Gordon (1954) and Hardin (1968) on the tragedy of the commons. In the typical tragedy, ranchers graze their herds either on their private land or on the commonly owned land in each village. Since grazing on the commons is free, individuals prefer it to using their own land, which can be used to grow cash crops. However, grazing imposes a negative externality on others; if my cows eat the grass, there is less left for your herd. The CPR game, thus, is a *continuous taking* game; each unit of grass that I take exerts a negative externality on the rest of the village.

Unlike the VCM, the externalities imposed are typically nonlinear, with public costs initially being lower than private benefit, but rising until the two cross. Thus the game has internal equilibria, in which more grazing than is optimal is predicted. (These games are similar to a class of *rent-seeking* games, which have recently been experimentally explored. Rent-seeking games are beyond the scope of this article; but see Önçüler and Croson, 2005, for some recent work.)

In the first CPR economics experiment, Walker, Gardner and Ostrom (1990) arranged subjects into groups of eight. Each participant was given a homogeneous endowment and was told he could allocate this endowment between two markets. Like the VCM, the private market paid a fixed amount, 5¢ per token. The public market (the common pool) had externalities for other group members' consumption. Unlike the VCM this externality was negative rather than positive. Also unlike the VCM, the externality was nonlinear, with increasing social cost. Conceptually, allocating resources to the public market captures the idea of grazing the herd on public land.

When x_i is the amount player i allocates to the public market, the earnings from the public market for player i are:

$$x_i / \sum x_i \left(23 \sum x_i - 0.25 \left(\sum x_i \right)^2 \right).$$

The negative squared term creates the nonlinearity. If no one is allocating resources to the public market, an individual earns more from that market than the private one (the first token allocated there earns 22.5¢ versus 5¢ in the private market). However, this return quickly diminishes, so the value from investing in the public market falls below the value from investing in the private market as the number of tokens increases. This captures the negative externalities. For each token that player i invests in the public market, the marginal value of player's j's investment in that market is lowered.

The self-interested, symmetric Nash equilibrium in this game is for each player to invest eight tokens in the public market (for a total investment of 64 tokens). (When each participant invests nine tokens in the public market, the return for that marginal token is exactly $5\,\text{¢}$. The authors assume that, when indifferent participants choose not to impose negative externalities on others, thus the equilibrium of eight tokens is used.) This equilibrium prediction is parallel to the prediction of full free-riding in the VCM. In contrast, the symmetric, socially efficient solution is for each participant to invest five tokens in the public market. This is not an equilibrium, however, since each individual privately captures more by investing further in the public market. This capturing is at the expense of the other players, who suffer the negative externality imposed. So five tokens is the socially optimal level, and is parallel to the prediction of full contributing in the VCM.

If behaviour in the CPR were parallel to that in the VCM, we should see allocations to the common market of between eight tokens (the equilibrium) and five tokens (the social optimum). As in the VCM, the stage game described above is repeated finitely many times, either 20 or 30 rounds, depending on the particular parameters. (A parallel literature in CPR games examines *dynamic* versions of the game, in which the resource replenishes itself round to round, with the replenishment rate being dependent on the harvesting rate observed. These are sometimes referred to as *renewable* CPR games. Equilibria in these dynamic games are more complicated, and Herr, Gardner and Walker, 1997, experimentally compare the different games.)

The results from the experiment can be seen in Figure 3. The solid line represents the equilibrium prediction, while the dotted line represents the social welfare maximizing outcome. Unlike the VCM, where contributions lay between these two, here contributions lie on the opposite side of the equilibrium. This indicates excessive allocation to the public market, and excessive negative externalities, over and above the equilibrium prediction.

This result of less-than-Nash levels of cooperation is replicated in other experiments, reviewed in Ostrom, Gardner and Walker (1994). Other work also

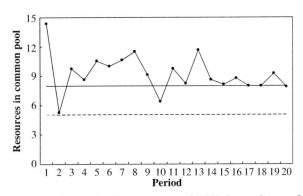

Figure 3   Average resources allocated to the common pool (CPR). *Source*: Ostrom, Gardner and Walker (1994).

reviewed there examines other questions in CPR games, including probabilistic destruction, communication, monitoring and sanctions, voting and heterogeneity.

One lingering puzzle remains: why are subjects more generous/cooperative than the equilibrium in the VCM and less generous/cooperative than the equilibrium in the CPR game? A number of studies have investigated this question by adding complexity to the VCM to make it resemble the CPR (for example, the stream of research on nonlinear VCM games below). Others investigate framing, suggesting it is the difference between providing a positive externality in the VCM and a negative externality in the CPR game. Unfortunately no study has offered either a definitive experiment or compelling data to explain why the outcomes from these games differ.

Other public goods settings

In addition to the games described above, a small literature explores different types of public goods games. A number of papers examine nonlinear VCMs, with internal equilibria (see Laury and Holt, 2008, for a review). Here the production of public good is nonlinearly related to the amount allocated to the public account. This yields an internal social optimum and Nash equilibrium level of contributions. As before, parameters are set so that the public good is under-provided in equilibrium.

Others have explored markets with externalities rather than public goods per se (for example, Plott, 1983). Still other researchers combine these games in creative ways, for example a PPM with a VCM for excess contributions (as in the utilization rebate of Marks and Croson, 1998), or a PPM with a VCM for under-contributions (as in Vesterlund, Duffy and Ochs 2005).

Finally, a number of papers have experimentally tested other proposed mechanisms for solving the public goods problem. For example, Chen and Plott (1996) provide a test of the Groves–Ledyard mechanism (a mechanism designed to elicit individuals values for public goods). Reviews of experiments using incentive-compatible mechanisms can be found in Chen (2008). These literatures are less developed than the previous three games, a disadvantage when trying to summarize a stream of research but an advantage when seeking a new contribution.

Commonalities and puzzles

The underlying similarity between all public goods experiments is the existence of externalities. These externalities can be positive or negative, and they can be linear, nonlinear or involve thresholds. The decisions participants make can be described as giving or taking. These varying situations affect the equilibrium predictions of the games.

Individuals are 'cooperative' in the VCM; they contribute more towards the public good than equilibrium behaviour would predict. There are many explanations for why this may be the case, including altruism, reciprocity (conditional altruism), warm-glow and errors, but no one causal factor has emerged as dominant.

In the PPM, the issue is not one of cooperation but coordination. On average the efficient equilibrium outcomes describe the data. However, there is also 'gaming', with groups sometimes failing to provide the public good as one individual attempts to move towards a more attractive equilibrium. Thus, while outcomes from these mechanisms are more efficient than those from the VCM, the coordination problem is severe and unsolved.

Finally, individuals harvest *more* than the Nash equilibrium predictions in CPR games. This result contrasts with the VCM; here individuals are more competitive than the equilibrium prediction. The source of these differences is still unexplored and represents an excellent direction for future research.

Summary

The tension between self-interest and social efficiency is one we experience every day. Experiments like those discussed in this article have been developed to explore how humans resolve this tension. Results from these experiments highlight the impact of different public goods structures, institutional arrangements and repeated interactions on human behaviour. Ultimately they help us to design mechanisms to better provide public goods, and allow for a deeper understanding of human motivations in the wide set of activities involving externalities for others.

RACHEL T.A. CROSON

See also **coordination problems and communication; experimental economics; reciprocity and collective action.**

Bibliography

Andreoni, J. 1989. Giving with impure altruism: applications to charity and Ricardian equivalence. *Journal of Political Economy* 97, 1447–58.

Andreoni, J. 1995a. Warm-glow versus cold-prickle: the effects of positive and negative framing on cooperation in experiments. *Quarterly Journal of Economics* 110, 1–21.

Andreoni, J. 1995b. Cooperation in public-goods experiments: kindness or confusion? *American Economic Review* 85, 891–904.

Andreoni, J. and Croson, R.T.A. 2008. Partners versus strangers: random rematching in public goods experiments. In Plott and Smith (2008).

Bagnoli, M. and Lipman, B.L. 1989. Provision of public goods: fully implementing the core through private contributions. *Review of Economic Studies* 56, 583–601.

Bagnoli, M. and McKee, M. 1991. Voluntary contribution games: efficient provision of public goods. *Economic Inquiry* 29, 351–66.

Becker, G.S. 1974. A theory of social interactions. *Journal of Political Economy* 82, 1063–93.

Buckley, E. and Croson, R.T.A. 2006. Income and wealth heterogeneity in the voluntary provision of linear public goods. *Journal of Public Economics* 90, 935–55.

Cadsby, B. and Maynes, E. 1998. Choosing between a socially efficient and free-riding equilibrium: nurses versus economics and business students. *Journal of Economic Behavior and Organization* 37, 183–92.

Cadsby, B. and Maynes, E. 1999. Voluntary contribution of threshold public goods with continuous provisions: experimental evidence. *Journal of Public Economics* 71, 53–73.

Carpenter, J.P., Daniere, A.G. and Takahashi, L.M. 2004. Cooperation, trust, and social capital in Southeast Asian urban slums. *Journal of Economic Behavior and Organization* 55, 533–51.

Charness, G. and Rabin, M. 2002. Understanding social preferences with simple tests. *Quarterly Journal of Economics* 117, 817–69.

Chen, Y. 2008. Incentive-compatible mechanisms for pure public goods: a survey of experimental literature. In Plott and Smith (2008).

Chen, Y. and Plott, C.R. 1996. The Groves–Ledyard mechanism: an experimental study of institutional design. *Journal of Public Economics* 59, 335–64.

Croson, R.T.A. 2000. Feedback in voluntary contribution mechanisms: an experiment in team production. *Research in Experimental Economics* 8, 85–97.

Croson, R.T.A. 2007. Theories of commitment, altruism and reciprocity: evidence from linear public goods games. *Economic Inquiry* (forthcoming).

Croson, R.T.A., Fatas, E. and Neugebauer, T. 2005. Excludability in three public goods games. Working paper, Wharton School, University of Pennsylvania.

Croson, R.T.A. and Marks, M. 1998. Identifiability of individual contributions in a threshold public goods experiment. *Journal of Mathematical Psychology* 42, 167–90.

Croson, R.T.A. and Marks, M. 1999. The effect of heterogeneous valuations for threshold public goods: an experimental study. *Risk, Decision and Policy* 4, 99–115.

Croson, R.T.A. and Marks, M. 2000. Step returns in threshold public goods: a meta- and experimental analysis. *Experimental Economics* 2, 239–59.

Croson, R.T.A. and Marks, M. 2001. The effect of recommended contributions in the voluntary provision of public goods. *Economic Inquiry* 39, 238–49.

Dawes, R. 1980. Social dilemmas. *Annual Review of Psychology* 31, 169–93.

Fehr, E. and Gächter, S. 2000. Cooperation and punishment in public goods experiments. *American Economic Review* 90, 980–94.

Gordon, H.A. 1954. The economic theory of a common property resource: the fishery. *Journal of Political Economy* 62, 124–42.

Hardin, G. 1968. The tragedy of the commons. *Science* 162, 1243–8.

Herr, A., Gardner, R. and Walker, J.M. 1997. An experimental study of time-independent and time-dependent externalities in the commons. *Games and Economic Behavior* 19, 77–96.

Isaac, R.M., Schmidtz, D. and Walker, J.M. 1989. The assurance problem in a laboratory market. *Public Choice* 62, 217–36.

Isaac, R.M and Walker, J.M. 1988a. Communication and free-riding behavior: the voluntary contribution mechanism. *Economic Inquiry* 26, 585–608.

Isaac, M.R. and Walker, J.M. 1988b. Group size effects in public goods provision: the voluntary contributions mechanism. *Quarterly Journal of Economics* 53, 179–200.

Isaac, R.M., Walker, J.M. and Thomas, S.H. 1984. Divergent evidence on free riding: an experimental examination of possible explanations. *Public Choice* 43, 113–49.

Isaac, R.M., Walker, J.M. and Williams, A.W. 1994. Group size and the voluntary provision of public goods: experimental evidence utilizing large groups. *Journal of Public Economics* 54, 1–36.

Karau, S.J. and Williams, K.D. 1993. Social loafing: a meta-analytic review and theoretical integration. *Journal of Personality and Social Psychology* 65, 681–706.

Kollock, P. 1998. Social dilemmas: the anatomy of cooperation. *Annual Review of Sociology* 24, 183–214.

Krause, K. and Harbaugh, W.T. 2000. Children's contributions in public good experiments: the development of altruistic and free-riding behaviors. *Economic Inquiry* 38, 95–109.

Laury, S.K. and Holt, C.A. 2008. Voluntary provision of public goods: experimental results with interior Nash equilibria. In Plott and Smith (2008).

Laury, S.K., Walker, J.M. and Williams, A.W. 1995. Anonymity and the voluntary provision of public goods. *Journal of Economic Behavior & Organization* 27, 365–80.

Ledyard, J. 1995. Public goods: a survey of experimental research. In *Handbook of Experimental Economics*, ed. J. Kagel and A. Roth. Princeton: Princeton University Press.

Marks, M. and Croson, R.T.A. 1998. The effect of alternative rebate rules in the provision point mechanism of voluntary contributions: an experimental investigation. *Journal of Public Economics* 67, 195–220.

Marks, M. and Croson, R.T.A. 1999. The effect of incomplete information and heterogeneity in the provision point mechanism of voluntary contributions: an experimental investigation. *Public Choice* 99, 103–18.

Marwell, G. and Ames, R.E. 1979. Experiments on the provision of public good I: resources, interest, group size, and the free-rider problem. *American Journal of Sociology* 84, 1336–60.

Marwell, G. and Ames, R.E. 1980. Experiments on the provision of public goods II: provision points, stakes, experience, and the free-rider problem. *American Journal of Sociology* 85, 926–37.

Marwell, G. and Ames, R.E. 1981. Economists free ride, does anyone else? Experiments on the provision of public goods, IV. *Journal of Public Economics* 15, 295–310.

Önçüler, A. and Croson, R.T.A. 2005. Rent-seeking for a risky rent: a model and experimental investigation. *Journal of Theoretical Politics* 17, 403–29.

Ostrom, E., Gardner, R. and Walker, J.M. 1994. *Rules, Games, and Common-Pool Resources*. Ann Arbor: University of Michigan Press.

Palfrey, T.R. and Prisbrey, J.E. 1997. Anomalous behavior in public goods experiments: how much and why? *American Economic Review* 87, 829–46.

Plott, C.R. 1983. Externalities and corrective policies in experimental markets. *Economic Journal* 93, 106–27.

Plott, C.R and Smith, V.L., eds. 2008. *Handbook of Experimental Economics Results*. Amsterdam: North-Holland (forthcoming).

Sonnemans, J., Schram, A. and Offerman, T. 1998. Public good provision and public bad prevention: the effect of framing. *Journal of Economic Behavior & Organization* 34, 143–61.

Vesterlund, L., Duffy, J. and Ochs, J. 2005. Giving little by little: dynamic voluntary contribution games. Working Paper, University of Pittsburgh.

Walker, J.M., Gardner, R. and Ostrom, E. 1990. Rent dissipation in a limited-access common-pool resource: experimental evidence. *Journal of Environmental Economics and Management* 19, 203–11.

quantal response equilibria

Economic theory relies extensively on the assumption of perfect rationality, which makes it possible to construct general models with strong (and sometimes surprising) predictions. The evaluation of these models using field data requires the incorporation of random errors representing unobserved and omitted elements, measurement error, and so on. Evaluation of these models using data from laboratory experiments also requires an error structure, since choice behaviour in the laboratory is also noisy, showing clear mistakes and inconsistencies over time.

Probabilistic choice models (for example, logit, probit) have long been used to incorporate stochastic elements in to the analysis of individual decisions, and the quantal response equilibrium (QRE) is the analogous way to model games with noisy players. These probabilistic choice models are based on quantal response functions, which have the intuitive feature that deviations from optimal decisions are negatively correlated with the associated costs. That is, individuals are more likely to select better choices than worse choices, but do not necessarily succeed in selecting the very best choice. Formally, a quantal response function maps the vector of expected payoffs from available choices into a vector of choice probabilities that is monotone in the expected payoffs.

In a strategic game environment, a player's expected payoffs from different strategies are determined by beliefs about other players' actions, so beliefs determine expected payoffs, which in turn, generate choice probabilities according to some quantal response function. A QRE imposes the requirement that the beliefs match the equilibrium choice probabilities. Thus, QRE requires solving for a fixed point in the choice probabilities, analogous to the Nash equilibrium.

In fact, QRE is a generalization of Nash equilibrium, which converges to the Nash equilibrium as the quantal response functions become very steep, and approximate best response functions. This approach provides a useful theoretical framework for looking at comparative statics effects of parameter changes that may not alter Nash predictions. The incorporation of random elements also provides a foundation for standard statistical analysis of field and laboratory data in game theoretic applications.

A motivating example: generalized matching pennies

Before providing general definitions, it is useful to begin with a simple two-person matching pennies game in which the Row player chooses Top (T) or Bottom (B) and the Column player chooses left (L) or right (R). Row wins a penny (and Column loses a penny) if the outcome is (Top, Right) or (Bottom, Left) and Column wins a penny otherwise. Thus Row's expected payoff for Top (U_T) is a function of Column's probability of choosing Right (p_R), which is easily calculated as $U_T(p_R) = p_R - (1 - p_R) = 2p_R - 1$, and similarly, $U_B(p_R) = 1 - 2p_R$, so the optimal decision is to choose Top if Column is more likely to choose Right, that is, if $p_R > \frac{1}{2}$. Column's expected payoffs are computed analogously, as a function of Row's probability of choosing Top (p_T).

Figure 1 illustrates the best response functions in the unit square of mixed strategies in the game, with the y-axis representing the row player's Top choice probability and the x-axis representing the column player's Right choice. The best response for Row is indicated by the dark step function that jumps from 0 to 1 at $p_R = \frac{1}{2}$. Similarly, the Column player's best response line is the step function, shown in light grey, which crosses over from left to right at a height of $\frac{1}{2}$.

Using the same figure, we can represent a quantal response function, which smooths out the discontinuous best response function, reflecting the monotone and continuous choice probability as a function of payoffs. Such a quantal response function is illustrated by Row's dark curved line that rises smoothly from the bottom-left corner to the top-right corner. The probabilistic choice equals $\frac{1}{2}$ exactly at the point where row player is indifferent between Top and Bottom. A quantal response function is also drawn for Column. The intersection of these two quantal response functions occurs in the centre of the figure, and is the quantal response equilibrium, just as the intersection of the sharp best response function at the same point is the Nash equilibrium in mixed strategies ($\frac{1}{2}$ for each decision).

Now suppose that all payoffs stay the same except for the Top-Right outcome, which gives Row a higher payoff of 9 and Column a payoff of -1 as before. The increase in Row's Top-Right payoff shifts Row's best response line leftward, as indicated by the dashed line step function in the figure, and it also shifts Row's quantal response (smooth dashed line). The new Nash equilibrium (dot at the intersection of

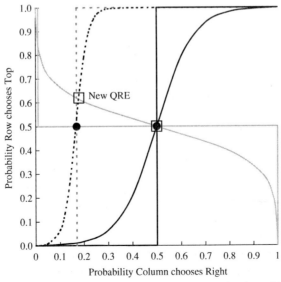

Figure 1   Players' best responses and quantal responses for a generalized matching pennies game

the step functions) is still at $p_T = 0.5$, whereas the new QRE is at a higher level $p_T = 0.62$. This intuitive 'own payoff' effect contrasts with the Nash equilibrium prediction of no change in Row's choice probabilities (since they are determined by the requirement that Column is indifferent). The own-payoff effect predicted by regular QRE accords with data from laboratory experiments that employ an asymmetric matching-pennies structure – for example, Ochs (1995), McKelvey, Palfrey and Weber (2000), Goeree and Holt (2001), and Goeree, Holt, and Palfrey (2003).

Definitions

Let $G = (N, S_1, \ldots, S_n, \pi_1, \ldots, \pi_n)$ be a normal-form game, where $N = \{1, \ldots, n\}$ is the set of players, $S_i = \{s_{i1}, \ldots, s_{iJ(i)}\}$ is player i's set of strategies and $S = S_1 \times \cdots \times S_N$ is the set of strategy profiles, and $\pi_i: S_i \to R$ is player i's payoff function. Furthermore, let $\Sigma_i = \Delta^{J(i)}$ be the set of probability distributions over S_i. An element $\sigma_i \ \varepsilon \ \Sigma_i$ is a mixed-strategy, which is a mapping from S_i to Σ_i, where $\sigma_i(s_i)$ is the probability that player i chooses pure-strategy s_i. Let $\Sigma = \Sigma_1 \times \cdots \times \Sigma_N$ be the set of mixed-strategy profiles. Given a mixed-strategy profile $\sigma \ \varepsilon \ \Sigma$, player i's expected payoff is $\pi_i(\sigma) = \Sigma_{s \ \varepsilon \ S} \ p(s) \pi_i(s)$, where $p(s) = \Pi_{i \ \varepsilon \ N} \ \sigma_i(s_i)$ is the probability distribution over pure-strategy profiles induced by σ.

Let P_{ij} denote the probability that player i selects strategy j. Recall that the main idea behind QRE is that strategies with higher expected payoffs are more likely to be chosen, although the best strategy is not necessarily chosen with probability 1. In other words, QRE replaces players' strict rational choice best-responses by smoothed best responses or *quantal responses*.

Definition 1 $P_i: R^{J(i)} \to \Delta^{J(i)}$ is a ***regular quantal-response*** *function if it satisfies the following four axioms.*

- **Interiority:** $P_{ij}(\pi_i) > 0$ for all $j = 1, \ldots, J(i)$ and for all $\pi_i \ \varepsilon \ R^{J(i)}$.
- **Continuity:** $P_{ij}(\pi_i)$ is a continuously differentiable function for all $\pi_i \ \varepsilon \ R^{J(i)}$.
- **Responsiveness:** $\partial P_{ij}(\pi_i)/\partial \pi_{ij} > 0$ for all $j = 1, \ldots, J(i)$ and for all $\pi_i \ \varepsilon \ R^{J(i)}$.
- **Monotonicity:** $\pi_{ij} > \pi_{ik}$ implies that $P_{ij}(\pi_i) > P_{ik}(\pi_i)$ for all $j, k = 1, \ldots, J(i)$.

These axioms are economically and intuitively compelling. Interiority ensures the model has full domain, that is, it is logically consistent with all possible data-sets. This is important for empirical applications of the model. Continuity is a technical restriction, which ensures that P_i is non-empty and single-valued. Furthermore, it seems a natural assumption since arbitrarily small changes in expected payoffs should not lead to jumps in choice probabilities. Responsiveness requires that if the expected payoff of an action increases, *ceteris paribus*, the choice probability must also increase. Monotonicity is a weak form of rational choice that involves binary comparisons of actions: an action with higher expected payoff is chosen more frequently than an action with a lower expected payoff.

Define $P(\pi) = (P_1(\pi_1), \ldots, P_n(\pi_n))$ to be regular if each P_i satisfies the above regularity axioms. Since $P(\pi) \ \varepsilon \ \Sigma$ and $\pi = \pi(\sigma)$ is defined for any $\sigma \ \varepsilon \ \Sigma$, $P \bigcirc \sigma$ defines a mapping from Σ into itself.

Definition 2 *Let P be regular. A **regular quantal response equilibrium** of the normal-form game G is a mixed-strategy profile σ^* such that $\sigma^* = P(\sigma^*)$.*

Since regularity of P includes continuity, $P \circ \sigma$ is a continuous mapping. Existence of a regular QRE therefore follows directly from Brouwer's fixed-point theorem.

Theorem *There exists a regular quantal response equilibrium of G for any regular P.*

Empirical implications of regular QRE

The axioms underlying regular QRE collectively have strong empirical implications, even without any parametric assumptions on P. To illustrate the nature of these restrictions, consider again the generalized matching-pennies game, where Row's payoff is X when the outcome is (top, right). If $X > 1$, it is readily verified that Row's expected payoff of choosing 'top' is higher than of choosing 'bottom' when $p_R < 2/(X+3)$ ($p_R > 2/(X+3)$). Monotonicity therefore implies that, if $(p_R{}^*, p_T{}^*)$ defines a regular QRE, it must satisfy the inequalities: $p_T^* \geq \frac{1}{2}$ if $p_R \geq 2/(X+3)$ and vice versa. Likewise, Column's expected payoff of choosing 'right' is higher (lower) than of choosing 'left' when $p_T < \frac{1}{2} (p_T > \frac{1}{2})$. Thus $(p_R{}^*, p_T{}^*)$ must satisfy $p_R^* \leq \frac{1}{2}$ if $p_T \geq \frac{1}{2}$, and vice versa. The region defined by these inequalities defines the set of possible regular QRE. For the specific case of $X = 9$, this area is shown by the dark gray shaded area in Figure 2. The three black dots show the Nash equilibria for $X = 9$ (left), $X = 1$ (centre) and $X = 0$ (right).

The case $-1 < X < 1$ can be analysed in a similar way. The set of regular QRE for $X = 0$, for instance, is given by the light shaded area in Figure 2. Note that the Row player is predicted to choose 'top' more often than 'bottom' in any regular QRE when

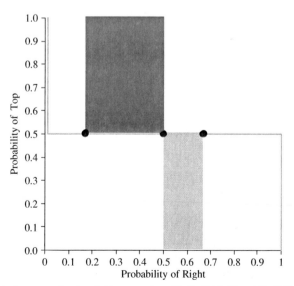

Figure 2   QRE Sets for generalized matching pennies with $X = 9$ (dark) and $X = 0$ (light)

$X > 1$, while the reverse is true for $X < 1$. In fact, the responsiveness axiom can be used to show that if Row's payoff of the (top, right) outcome rises, Row's probability of choosing 'top' increases.

Proposition (Goeree, Holt and Palfrey, 2005). *In any regular QRE of the asymmetric matching pennies game, Row's probability of choosing Top is strictly increasing in X and Column's probability of choosing Right is strictly decreasing in X.*

Quantal response equilibrium: a structural definition

The original definition of QRE (McKelvey and Palfrey, 1995) adopts an approach in the spirit of Harsanyi (1973) and McFadden (1974) whereby the choice probabilities are rationalized by privately observed, mean zero random disturbances to the expected payoffs. These disturbances are assumed to be private information to the players, thereby converting the original game into special kind of game of incomplete information. Any Bayesian equilibrium of this disturbed game is a QRE of the underlying game. The quantal response function generating the QRE is determined by the probability distribution of the random payoff disturbances.

Thus a smoothed response line can be interpreted to be the (inverse) distribution function of the differences between the disturbances, which has a value of $\frac{1}{2}$ when the expected payoffs are equal. For example, if the disturbances are i.i.d. and normally distributed, then the quantal response functions will take the shape of a 'probit' curve, while if the i.i.d. disturbances are distributed according to an extreme value distribution, the quantal response functions will have a logistic form. For example, the logit QRE for the generalized matching pennies game is a pair of probabilities that solve:

$$p_T = \frac{\exp(\lambda[(X+1)p_R - 1])}{\exp(\lambda[(X+1)p_R - 1]) + \exp(\lambda[1 - 2p_R])}, p_R = \frac{\exp(\lambda[1 - 2p_T])}{\exp(\lambda[1 - 2p_T]) + \exp(\lambda[2p_T - 1])}$$

where the numerators are exponential functions of the expected payoffs for the corresponding decision (T or R), and the denominators are normalizing factors that force probabilities to sum to 1. As the logit precision parameter λ increases, the response functions become more responsive to payoff differences, and the logit response functions converge to the sharp step functions shown in Figure 1.

The disturbances in the structural approach to QRE can be interpreted in several ways. One possibility is to interpret them literally. That is, one views the underlying game as simply a model of the average game being played, with each actual game player being a mean zero perturbation of the basic game. With this view, one can think of the payoff disturbances as reflecting the effects of unobservable components such as a player's mood or perceptual variations. A second possibility is to think of the players as statisticians, whose objective is to estimate the payoff of each strategy using some unknown set of instruments to perform the estimation. For general abstract games, a reasonable first cut is to suppose that their estimation errors are unbiased. The players then choose the strategy with the highest estimated expected payoffs, implicitly taking into account the fact that the other players are also estimating payoffs with some error, with the resulting equilibrium corresponding to QRE.

One can show that the quantal response function generated by i.i.d disturbances will always have the continuity and monotonicity properties of regular quantal response functions, and therefore will lead to regular QRE. In particular, the comparative static result of the previous section holds for the logit QRE (McKelvey and Palfrey, 1996). If disturbances are not i.i.d., however, non-monotonicities are possible. Haile, Hortacsu and Kosenok (2006) use this observation to show that, without restrictions on the disturbances, structural QRE can explain *any* data. One way to avoid this problem is to make the i.i.d. assumption or impose the weaker notion of *interchangeability* (Goeree, Holt and Palfrey, 2005). A second way to generate testable restrictions is to constrain the same structural assumptions to hold across different data-sets, thereby generating comparative static predictions.

Another solution is to simply work directly with the regularity axioms of Definition 1 – the resulting quantal response functions do impose empirical restrictions on the data and do not inherit the unintuitive features of the structural approach such as symmetry and strong substitutability. *Symmetry* requires that the effect of an increase in strategy k's payoff on the probability of choosing strategy j is the same as the effect of an increase in strategy j's payoff on the probability of choosing strategy k. *Strong substitutability* implies, among other things, that, if the payoff of strategy k rises, the probability of choosing *any* of the other strategies $j \neq k$ falls.

Applications: quantal response equilibrium in normal-form games

In an individual choice problem, the addition of 'noise' spreads out the distribution of decisions around the expected-payoff-maximizing decision. In contrast, expected payoffs in a game depend on other players' choice probabilities, and this interactive element can magnify the effects of noise via feedback effects. One notable example is a coordination game where each person's payoff is the minimum of all player's efforts, minus a cost parameter, c, times a player's own effort. If $c < 1$, any common effort level is a Nash equilibrium, since a unilateral decrease below a common effort reduces the minimum and saves the cost, for a net loss of $1 - c$ for each unit reduction in effort. Conversely, a unilateral effort increase does not alter the minimum, so the loss is $-c$. Therefore, c affects the downward slopes of the expected payoff function in each direction and, if there is any uncertainty about others' decisions, low values of c make effort increases less risky. It is not surprising that reductions in the effort cost c tend to increase average efforts, both in laboratory experiments with human subjects and in a quantal response equilibrium with noisy behaviour (Anderson, Goeree and Holt, 2001). For the two-person coordination game experiments reported in Goeree and Holt (2005a), a reduction in the effort cost parameter from 0.75 to 0.25 raised average effort levels from 126 to 159 in the final five rounds. With payoffs in pennies and a precision parameter of 0.1, the logit QRE predictions for this game are 126 and 154 for the high and low effort costs. Thus the QRE tracks the strong behavioural response to the treatment change, whereas the range of Nash equilibria – from 110 to 170 – is unaffected by this change.

The Traveller's Dilemma is another game where small amounts of noise can have large effects. As in the coordination game, the payoffs depend on the minimum of all decisions ('claims'). This is a two-person 'lost luggage' problem, where the airline representative interprets unequal damage claims as evidence that the high claimant is inflated unjustly. Each player earns the minimum of the two claims, with a penalty of R subtracted from the payoff for the high claimant and added to that of the low claimant. As with the coordination game, claims must be in a specified interval, but in the Traveller's Dilemma the unique Nash equilibrium is the lowest possible claim in this interval, irrespective of the magnitude of R, as long as the benefit R from a reduction below a common claim is greater than the smallest permitted claim reduction. In contrast, intuition suggests that claims will be high when the penalty from having the higher claim is low. In the Capra et al. (1999) experiment, reductions in the penalty parameter, R, induce dramatic increases in claims, moving the average from near Nash levels for high values of R to the opposite side of the range of feasible claims for low values of R. This strong treatment effect is tracked well by the quantal response equilibrium with the same precision parameter that tracks other coordination game data.

In addition to these applications, the QRE has been used to explain 'anomalous' behaviour in a wide variety of games, including signalling games, centipede games, two-stage bargaining, and overbidding in auctions (Goeree, Holt and Palfrey, 2002). In addition, the quantal response equilibrium has proven to be quite useful in the analysis of data from political science experiments: jury voting (Guarnaschelli, McKelvey and Palfrey, 2000), voter turnout (Levine and Palfrey, 2007), and behaviour in participation games (Goeree and Holt, 2005a; Cason and Van Lam, 2005).

Applications: quantal response equilibrium in extensive form games

The QRE approach has also been developed for extensive form games (McKelvey and Palfrey 1998), where the analysis in done using behavioural strategies. In the extensive form QRE, players follow Bayes' rule and calculate expected continuation payoffs based on the QRE strategies of the other players. Interiority implies that beliefs are uniquely defined at any information set and for any QRE strategy profile. Therefore issues related to belief-based refinements do not arise, and a quantal response version of sequential rationality follows immediately. When quantal response functions approach best response functions, then the limiting QRE of the extensive form game will select a subset of the *sequential equilibria* of the underlying game.

QRE in extensive form games will typically have different implied choice probabilities than would obtain if the same quantal response function were applied to the same game in its reduced normal form. This occurs for two reasons. First, QRE is not immune to 'reduction' of equivalent strategies, since duplicate strategies will generally change the quantal response choice probabilities, for much the same reason as the 'red bus – blue bus' example in discrete choice econometrics. Second, expected payoff differences are different when one collapses an extensive form game into its normal form: with behaviour strategies, expected payoffs are computed at the interim stage, conditioning on previous actions in the game; in contrast, normal form mixed strategies are calculated *ex ante*.

Summary

The quantal response equilibrium approach to the analysis of games has proven to be a useful generalization of the Nash equilibrium, especially when dealing with 'noisy decisions' made by boundedly rational players and by subjects in experiments. It can be extended to allow for learning and cognitive belief formation in one-shot games where learning is not possible. This approach provides a coherent framework for analysing an otherwise bewildering array of 'biases' and anomalies in economics.

JACOB K. GOEREE, CHARLES A. HOLT AND THOMAS R. PALFREY

We acknowledge financial support from the Alfred P. Sloan Foundation, the National Science Foundation (SBR 0094800 and 0551014; SES 0450712 and 0214013), and the Dutch National Science Foundation (VICI 453.03.606).

Bibliography

Anderson, S.K., Goeree, J.K. and Holt, C.A. 2001. Minimum effort coordination games: stochastic potential and the logit equilibrium. *Games and Economic Behavior* 34, 177–99.

Capra, C.M, Goeree, J.K., Gomez, R. and Holt, C.A. 1999. Anomalous behavior in a traveler's dilemma? *American Economic Review* 89, 678–90.

Cason, T.N. and Van Lam, M. 2005. Uncertainty and resistance to reform in laboratory participation games. *European Journal of Political Economy* 21, 708–37.

Goeree, J.K. and Holt, C.A. 2001. Ten little treasures of game theory and ten intuitive contradictions. *American Economic Review* 91, 1402–22.

Goeree, J.K. and Holt, C.A. 2005a. An experimental study of costly coordination. *Games and Economic Behavior* 46, 281–94.

Goeree, J.K. and Holt, C.A. 2005b. An explanation of anomalous behavior in models of political participation. *American Political Science Review* 99, 201–13.

Goeree, J.K., Holt, C.A. and Palfrey, T.R. 2002. Quantal response equilibrium and overbidding in private-value auctions. *Journal of Economic Theory* 104, 247–72.

Goeree, J.K., Holt, C.A. and Palfrey, T.R. 2003. Risk averse behavior in asymmetric matching pennies games. *Games and Economic Behavior* 45, 97–113.

Goeree, J.K., Holt, C.A. and Palfrey, T.R. 2005. Regular quantal response equilibrium. *Experimental Economics* 8, 347–67.

Guarnaschelli, S., McKelvey, R.D. and Palfrey, T.R. 2000. An experimental study of jury decision rules. *American Political Science Review* 94, 407–23.

Haile, P., Hortacsu, A. and Kosenok, G. 2006. On the empirical content of quantal response equilibrium. Working paper, Yale School of Management, Yale University.

Harsanyi, J. 1973. Games with randomly disturbed payoffs: a new rationale for mixed strategy equilibrium. *International Journal of Game Theory* 2, 1–23.

Levine, D. and Palfrey, T.R. 2007. The paradox of voter participation: an experimental study. *American Political Science Review* 101, 143–58.

McFadden, D. 1974. Conditional logit analysis of qualitative choice behavior. In *Frontiers in Econometrics*, ed. P. Zarembka. New York: Academic Press.

McKelvey, R.D. and Palfrey, T.R. 1995. Quantal response equilibrium for normal form games. *Games and Economic Behavior* 10, 6–38.

McKelvey, R.D. and Palfrey, T.R. 1996. A statistical theory of equilibrium in games. *Japanese Economic Review* 47, 186–209.

McKelvey, R.D. and Palfrey, T.R. 1998. Quantal response equilibrium for extensive form games. *Experimental Economics* 1, 9–41.

McKelvey, R.D., Palfrey, T.R. and Weber, R. 2000. The effects of payoff magnitude and heterogeneity on behavior in 2×2 games with a unique mixed-strategy equilibrium. *Journal of Economic Behavior and Organization* 42, 523–48.

Ochs, J. 1995. Games with unique, mixed strategy equilibria: an experimental study. *Games and Economic Behavior* 10, 202–17.

reciprocity and collective action

Advancing the common interest of a group sometimes requires its members to sacrifice their private interests. Such situations, in which individual incentives are not properly aligned with shared goals, are called collective action problems. They arise frequently in economic and social life, for instance in the context of political mobilization, electoral turnout, pollution abatement, common property management and the provision of public goods. They can involve relatively small groups such as families, teams, or business partnerships, or very large groups that cut across national boundaries.

In his classic work on collective action, Mancur Olson (1965) conjectured that individuals would be unable to overcome such problems unless their behaviour was constrained by rules that were externally imposed and enforced. Along similar lines, Garret Hardin (1968) argued in an influential paper that, left to their own devices, individuals would face a 'tragedy of the commons' which could be overcome only by 'mutual coercion, mutually agreed upon'. This view continues to have considerable currency in economics in the form of the *free-rider hypothesis*, which maintains that voluntary contributions that are socially beneficial but privately costly will not generally be observed (Bergstrom, Blume and Varian, 1986).

Despite the compelling logic underlying the free-rider hypothesis, there are numerous instances of groups having overcome collective action problems without external pressure, sometimes by designing and abiding by their own set of rules, and sometimes on the basis of less formal arrangements codified in social norms. The success of OPEC in constraining production to maintain price levels is based on a mutually beneficial agreement among member countries that has been sustained despite strong incentives for some producers to free-ride on the restraint practised by others. On a smaller scale, many examples of successful collective action in the management of local fisheries, forests, and other renewable resources have been documented (Bromley, 1992; Ostrom, 1990). Such resources are often held as common property, and the maintenance of sustainable stocks requires restraint in individual extraction levels. Restraint is typically enforced by formal or informal sanctions, and participation in such punishment mechanisms is itself a form of collective action. There also exist examples of collective action in the absence of any sanctioning mechanism. For instance, voter turnout is often substantial in large elections, contrary to the predictions of the free-rider hypothesis.

It has been argued that many instances of successful collective action arise in small and stable groups whose members interact with each other repeatedly. Under such circumstances, pro-social behaviour can be fully consistent with the standard economic hypotheses of rationality and self-interest. When interactions are repeated, self-interested cooperation can arise if one believes that non-cooperative actions will be punished in future periods. Moreover, such threats of punishment can be credible if abstaining from punishment is itself punished. Formally, cooperative behaviour can be sustained in subgame perfect equilibrium if interactions are infinitely (or indefinitely) repeated (Fudenberg and Maskin, 1986). Hence the tension between individual and common interest is less severe and collective action more likely to arise in small and stable groups.

While the threat of future punishment or the promise of future reward might motivate collective action in some instances, there are many situations in which individual actions are unobservable or repetition too infrequent for such considerations to be decisive. Voter turnout, for instance, or private donations to charity are not easily explained as self-interested responses to material incentives. Similarly, sacrifices involving risks to life and limb, as in the case of battlefield heroism or spontaneous collective violence, are unlikely to be driven by a calculated response to future costs and benefits. What, then, could account for such phenomena?

There is now a considerable body of experimental evidence to suggest that many individuals are willing to take actions that further the common interest provided that they are reasonably sure that other group members will also take such actions. Furthermore, they are willing to sanction the opportunistic behaviour of others even at some cost to themselves (Fehr and Gächter, 2000). The widespread prevalence of such preferences for reciprocity suggests that collective action can sometimes be viewed as a coordination problem: if the members of a group confidently expect others to further the common good, such expectations can be self-fulfilling. On the other hand, expectations of widespread free-riding can also be self-fulfilling, so building confidence in the behaviour of others is a critical ingredient of successful collective action. Communication among group members can help coordinate expectations, and it is therefore not surprising that allowing for communication among experimental subjects can result in dramatically increased levels of cooperation. This is the case even if communication takes the form of 'cheap talk', with neither threats nor promises being enforceable (Ostrom, Walker and Gardner, 1992).

If preferences for reciprocity are indeed part of the explanation for successful collective action, this raises the question of how such preferences have come to be widespread in human populations in the first place. The existence of a willingness to sacrifice one's own material interest for the common good poses an evolutionary puzzle. In order to survive and spread in human populations, the possession of such preferences must confer on an individual some advantage relative to those who are entirely self-interested. One intriguing possibility is that, despite being disadvantageous to individuals within groups, traits that are advantageous for the group itself may survive because of competition among groups:

> There can be no doubt that a tribe including many members who, from possessing in a high degree the spirit of patriotism, fidelity, obedience, courage, and sympathy, were always ready to give aid to each other and to

sacrifice themselves for the common good, would be victorious over other tribes; and this would be natural selection. (Darwin, 1871, p. 166)

In order to be effective, however, this mechanism requires variability across groups to be sustained while variability within groups is suppressed (Sober and Wilson, 1998). Whether or not the conditions for this are empirically plausible remains an open question.

There exist other channels through which a preference for reciprocity can be materially advantageous to individuals. One is assortative interaction: if individuals with preferences for reciprocity are more likely to interact with each other than with opportunists, the former can end up with higher material payoffs than the latter. Such assortation arises naturally in structured populations with local interaction. Even in unstructured populations with random matching, a propensity to reciprocate or to sanction opportunistic behaviour can confer an advantage provided that such preferences are observable to others. The visible possession of such propensities can alter the behaviour of those with whom one is interacting in such a manner as to be materially rewarding. Even opportunistic individuals might be induced to behave cooperatively in interactions with those who have a credible reputation for reciprocity. Such considerations can provide the basis for an evolutionary theory of reciprocity (Sethi and Somanathan, 2001).

Reciprocity is a key feature of successful collective action, both in repeated interactions and in more spontaneous settings. The willingness to further the common good even at considerable personal cost is widespread in human populations, but is often contingent on the willingness of others to do the same. This perspective suggests that collective action problems are not insurmountable, but that communication and coordination are critical in overcoming them.

RAJIV SETHI

See also **coordination problems and communication; social preferences.**

Bibliography

Bergstrom, T.C., Blume, L. and Varian, H. 1986. On the private provision of public goods. *Journal of Public Economics* 29, 25–49.

Bromley, D.W. 1992. *Making the Commons Work: Theory, Practice and Policy.* San Francisco: Institute for Contemporary Studies.

Darwin, C. 1871. *The Descent of Man and Selection in Relation to Sex.* London: Murray.

Fehr, E. and Gächter, S. 2000. Cooperation and punishment in public goods experiments. *American Economic Review* 90, 980–94.

Fudenberg, D. and Maskin, E. 1986. The folk theorem in repeated games with discounting or with incomplete information. *Econometrica* 54, 533–54.

Hardin, G. 1968. The tragedy of the commons. *Science* 162, 1243–8.

Olson, M. 1965. *The Logic of Collective Action: Public Goods and the Theory of Groups.* Cambridge, MA: Harvard University Press.

Ostrom, E. 1990. *Governing the Commons: The Evolution of Institutions for Collective Action.* Cambridge: Cambridge University Press.

Ostrom, E., Walker, J. and Gardner, R. 1992. Covenants with and without a sword: self-governance is possible. *American Political Science Review* 86, 404–17.

Sethi, R. and Somanathan, E. 2001. Preference evolution and reciprocity. *Journal of Economic Theory* 97, 273–97.

Sober, E. and Wilson, D.S. 1998. *Unto Others: The Evolution and Psychology of Unselfish Behavior.* Cambridge, MA: Harvard University Press.

social preferences

For the longest time economists reacted allergically to preference formulations that allowed for anything but material self-interest (cf. Binmore, Shaked and Sutton, 1985). The reaction was well founded: by adding elements to the agent's utility function, potentially one allows economic theory to explain everything and, therefore, nothing. Any behaviour can be explained by assuming it is preferred. However, this strong position has sometimes made economics seem out of touch with the world economists try to explain. Even economists care about the outcomes achieved by others, in addition to their own outcomes. Moreover, they also care about how those outcomes are achieved. Only in 1982, however, was the weakness of taking material self-interest for granted demonstrated by Werner Güth and his co-authors, who showed that economic theory failed in the simplest of decision settings (Güth, Schmittberger and Schwarze, 1982), the ultimatum game. In this game a first mover offers a share of a monetary 'pie' to a second mover who either accepts the proposal, in which case it is divided as proposed, or rejects the proposal, in which case both players earn nothing. Since then this game has become the workhorse of experimenters intent on exploring carefully the extent to which people behave in ways that are contrary to their material self-interest.

While it is interesting to document the fact that people consider the outcomes of others when they make choices in experimental games, there are at least two other particularly compelling aspects of the research that has developed since the 1980s. First, these deviations from self-interest can be replicated, and have been, both inside and outside the laboratory. Replication suggests that these behaviours are not just errors or flukes, and therefore, although self-interest is a convenient modelling assumption, it should not be used as the basis for policy formulation. Second, this research illustrates that there is a difference between theory failing because of a false assumption and its failing because of flawed logic. Research shows that people do use economic reasoning, but that they, or most of them, are not narrowly self-interested.

The original results of the ultimatum game provided the impetus for a large body of research. Initially, some researchers were convinced that the explanation was not a concern for others but simple error (for example, Binmore, Shaked and Sutton, 1985). However, this explanation was soon swept aside by volumes of evidence from a variety of games that suggested that the payoffs of other players entered into the strategic choices of experimental participants (see the reviews of Bowles, 2004; or Sobel, 2005). Despite all this research, a precise definition of social preference has not been settled upon. In most cases, 'social preference' is defined loosely as *a concern for the payoffs allocated to other relevant reference agents in addition to the concern for one's own payoff.* (A largely separate branch of research has focused on altruism and warm glow motives for giving to others, especially in the context of public goods provision. This work is discussed elsewhere in the dictionary.)

Within the standard outcome-oriented definition, research has focused on identifying the more pro-social preferences for altruism and inequality aversion while considerably less attention has been given to their opposites, spite and eminence. The evidence from the hundreds of ultimatum games conducted since 1982 suggests that, on the second-mover side of the game, few people are willing to accept the low offers associated with the subgame perfect equilibrium prediction. In fact, offers of less than 20 per cent of the pie are routinely rejected, and as offers increase they are more likely to be accepted (Camerer, 2003). Turning down positive offers is clearly against one's material self-interest, but it is consistent with aversion to unequal payoffs (inequality aversion). As the stakes increase, the probability of a rejection falls, but even when the pie is as large as three months expenditures the rejection rate is not zero (Cameron, 1999).

Interpreting the motivation of the first mover in the ultimatum game is not as straightforward, though. One hypothesis is that proposers offer half the pie because they are inequality averse. We cannot, however, distinguish this reasoning from that of completely selfish, but astute, proposers who anticipate that low offers will be rejected and offer half because they know it will be accepted. The dictator game evolved to identify the motives of first movers (Forsythe et al., 1994). The dictator game is played just like the ultimatum game except for one very important design change: second movers are passive recipients of whatever they are allocated. In other words, they cannot reject offers. If the enlightened self-interest hypothesis is correct, we would expect to see first movers allocating nothing in the dictator game. This is not the case. Although allocations in the dictator game are susceptible to changes in the presentation of the game (Hoffman et al., 1994; Eckel and Grossman, 1996), it is common for people to allocate positive amounts. In fact, it is common for the behaviour of non-student participants in the two games to be indistinguishable (Carpenter, Burks and Verhoogen, 2005) suggesting that many people prefer equal outcomes.

There is some question as to whether the simple outcome-oriented definition of social preference is sufficient. An example illustrates why. Instead of offers being generated by other participants, imagine second movers in the ultimatum game being assigned offers randomly by a computer programme. If inequality aversion is a sufficient description of the motivations of participants, this change should have no impact on behaviour. However, it does: responders are much less likely to reject computer-generated offers than offers that come from real proposers (Blount, 1995). This indicates that people are also interested in the process and intentions that generate outcomes. The definition of social preference should perhaps be expanded accordingly to *a concern for the payoffs allocated to other relevant reference agents and the intentions that led to this payoff profile in addition to the concern for one's own payoff.*

Expanding the definition of social preference to include a process component allows us to also classify reciprocity – treating only kind acts with kindness – as a social preference. Pure reciprocity, however, is more elusive than inequality aversion because one needs to show that outcomes and intentions matter. Only a few experiments have been conducted to show that intentions matter, but the results are compelling. For example, imagine two binary choice versions of the ultimatum game (Falk, Fehr and Fischbacher, 2003). In game A, the proposer can decide between claiming the lion's share of a ten-dollar pie (8, 2) and sharing the pie equally (5, 5). In game B, the first option is the same (8, 2) but the second is even worse for the second mover because the proposer demands the whole pie (10, 0). Inequality aversion predicts that the (8, 2) offer will be rejected at the same rate in the two games because the other offer is irrelevant – the decision-maker should focus only on the outcome presented. Reciprocity, on the other hand, suggests that one would be much less likely to reject (8, 2) in game B because it is the kinder of the two offers. Indeed, people are almost five times more likely to reject the (8, 2) offer in game A. An alternative approach is to compare the response of participants to different outcome allocations after another participant has made a kind or unkind act to the response when there is no initial move by another participant (Charness and Rabin, 2002). Reciprocity is identified by the subtraction of the first outcomes and intentions experiment from the second baseline inequality-aversion experiment.

In the trust (or investment) game, a first mover decides how much to send to a second mover. Any amount sent is multiplied by $k > 1$ before it reaches the second-mover. The second mover then decides how much to send back. Because of the multiplication, sending money is socially efficient yet a first mover should send money only if she trusts the second mover to send back at least enough to cover the investment. The standard interpretation is that the first mover must expect the second mover to be motivated by reciprocity before it makes sense to invest in the partnership (Berg, Dickaut and McCabe, 1995). However, one can just as easily invoke inequality aversion to explain the fact that people tend to send back more when they receive more (Cox, 2004). The same problem exists with the related experiments developed to test for the notion of gift exchange in the labour market context (for example, Fehr and Schmidt, 1999).

Other, more indirect, evidence for reciprocity and the more nuanced definition of social preference comes from the experimental literature on voluntary contributions to public goods. In these settings participants are given an endowment and asked to decide how much to contribute to a 'group project'. The incentives are of a social dilemma; contributing nothing is a dominant strategy but contributing everything is socially efficient. Playing the public goods game in strategic form asks participants to decide how much they want to contribute conditional on the contributions of others. Half the participants are conditionally cooperative in that they generate contribution schedules that are increasing in the contributions of others (Fischbacher, Gächter and Fehr, 2001). The fact that people condition their contributions according to those of others suggests that intentions and reciprocity matter.

To identify reciprocity separately from inequality aversion one may employ a design in which the two forces pull in different directions. Imagine that one can punish free riders in the public goods game: a participant can impose a penalty p at a cost c. In most cases people punish despite it being dominant to free ride on the punishment done by others (that is, punishment is just a second-order public good), and this tends to stabilize contributions (Fehr and Gächter, 2000). However, in most cases $p > c$, which means cooperators reduce the inequality between themselves and the free rider by punishing. To isolate the role of, in this case negative, reciprocity one can allow $p < c$, which actually increases the inequality. Although they do it less often, people punish when the sanction delivered is lower than the cost, and this is a nice demonstration of reciprocity (Carpenter, 2007).

Several attempts have been made to organize the evidence on social preferences into parsimonious, but flexible, utility functions. One of the most successful outcome-oriented approaches is the Fehr and Schmidt (1999) specification, perhaps because it is relatively easy to work with. Here the utility of player i increases in her own payoff, x_i, but decreases in any difference between her payoff and the payoffs of other relevant players. For two-player games this is just:

$$u_i(x_i, x_j) = \left\{ \begin{array}{ll} x_i - \alpha_i(x_j - x_i) & \text{if } x_i < x_j \\ x_i - \beta_i(x_i - x_j) & \text{if } x_i \geq x_j \end{array} \right\}$$

where α_i is player i's degree of inferiority aversion and β_i is her degree of superiority aversion. It is natural to expect $\alpha_i > \beta_i$.

While this utility function is a good first approximation because it has been shown to be consistent with much of the experimental data (if one is willing to make assumptions about the distribution of α's and β's in the population) it is limited in two ways. First, as one can see in Figure 1, the predictions can be coarse. It is not hard to graph the indifference curves associated with the Fehr–Schmidt specification, but if one superimposes a budget constraint on the indifference mapping there are just two predictions: keep it all or give away half unless the constraint has exactly the same slope as the indifference curve, in which case any amount between nothing and half is possible.

The fact that intentions play no role is a second problem faced by all the outcome-oriented approaches. A trade-off does, however, exist because incorporating intentions makes the specifications considerably harder to work with. The outcome- and process-

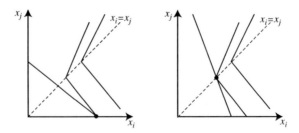

Figure 1

oriented specifications evolved from the notion of *psychological games*, which posits that utility will depend on both outcomes and beliefs (Geanakoplos, Pearce and Stacchetti, 1989). Beliefs are important because emotional responses are often triggered by expectations about how one should be treated. Perhaps the specification that is easiest to work with is the Charness–Rabin utility function, which incorporates a term θq to capture reciprocal motivations:

$$u_i(x_i, x_j) = (\rho r + \sigma s + \theta q)x_j + (1 - \rho r - \sigma s - \theta q)x_i.$$

The parameters r and s indicate which of the two players has the advantage ($r = 1$ if $x_i > x_j$, $s = 1$ if $x_j > x_i$ and $r = s = 0$ otherwise) and the parameters ρ and σ represent outcome-oriented preferences (Charness and Rabin, 2002). To recover the Fehr–Schmidt specification we simply assume $\sigma < 0 < \rho < 1$ and $\theta = 0$. Reciprocity and intentions are at work if $\theta > 0$ because we set $q = -1$ if player j has misbehaved and $q = 0$ otherwise.

Why should economists care about social preferences? By ignoring social preferences, economists have incompletely characterized many important interactions (Fehr and Fischbacher, 2002). Because many people are motivated by notions of fairness and reciprocity, social preferences can hinder the dynamics of competition that are assumed to drive equilibria, especially in the context of labour markets. For example, wages may never fall to the competitive equilibrium level because bosses understand that workers are reciprocally motivated. By lowering the wage, the boss also lowers morale and productivity (Bewley, 1999). Likewise, the economic theory of collective action is only narrowly applicable because it fails to realize that most people are predisposed to cooperate, but hate being taken advantage of (Andreoni, 1988). Designing incentives is ultimately more challenging when one accounts for the heterogeneity of social motivations identified in economic experiments.

Future research on social preferences is likely to extend in a number of interesting directions. Experimenters have begun to move from the laboratory to the field to identify the preferences of more representative samples and to investigate the external validity of these preferences (that is, what important behaviours and outcomes do social preferences correlate with?). Within the laboratory it will be interesting to better isolate the role of outcomes versus the role of intentions, to examine the co-evolution of preferences and institutions, and to examine the difference between social preferences and social norms. Is it the case, for example, that norms dictate how one should treat others regardless of whether the prescribed behaviour is consistent with one's underlying preferences?

JEFFREY CARPENTER

See also **public goods experiments; trust in experiments.**

Bibliography

Andreoni, J. 1988. Why free ride? Strategies and learning in public good experiments. *Journal of Public Economics* 37, 291–304.

Berg, J., Dickaut, J. and McCabe, K. 1995. Trust, reciprocity and social history. *Games and Economic Behavior* 10, 122–42.

Bewley, T. 1999. *Why Wages Don't Fall During a Recession*. Cambridge, MA: Harvard University Press.

Binmore, K., Shaked, A. and Sutton, J. 1985. Testing noncooperative bargaining theory: a preliminary study. *American Economic Review* 75, 1178–80.

Blount, S. 1995. When social outcomes aren't fair: the effect of causal attribution on preferences. *Organizational Behavior & Human Decision Processes* 62, 131–44.

Bowles, S. 2004. *Microeconomics: Behavior, Institutions and Evolution*. Princeton: Princeton University Press.

Camerer, C. 2003. *Behavioral Game Theory: Experiments on Strategic Interaction*. Princeton: Princeton University Press.

Cameron, L. 1999. Raising the stakes in the ultimatum game: experimental evidence from Indonesia. *Economic Inquiry* 37, 47–59.

Carpenter, J. 2007. The demand for punishment. *Journal of Economic Behavior & Organization* 62, 522–42.

Carpenter, J., Burks, S. and Verhoogen, E. 2005. Comparing students to workers: the effects of social framing on behavior in distribution games. In *Field Experiments in Economics. Research in Experimental Economics*, ed. J. Carpenter, G. Harrison and J. List. Greenwich, CT and London: JAI/Elsevier.

Charness, G. and Rabin, M. 2002. Understanding social preferences with simple tests. *Quarterly Journal of Economics* 117, 817–70.

Cox, J.C. 2004. How to identify trust and reciprocity. *Games and Economic Behavior* 46, 260–81.

Eckel, C. and Grossman, P. 1996. Altruism in anonymous dictator games. *Games and Economic Behavior* 16, 181–91.

Falk, A., Fehr, E. and Fischbacher, U. 2003. On the nature of fair behavior. *Economic Inquiry* 41, 20–6.

Fehr, E. and Fischbacher, U. 2002. Why social preferences matter – the impact of non-selfish motives on competition, cooperation and incentives. *Economic Journal* 112, 1–33.

Fehr, E. and Gächter, S. 2000. Cooperation and punishment in public goods experiments. *American Economic Review* 90, 980–94.

Fehr, E. and Schmidt, K. 1999. A theory of fairness, competition, and cooperation. *Quarterly Journal of Economics* 114, 769–816.

Fischbacher, U., Gächter, S. and Fehr, E. 2001. Are people conditionally cooperative? Evidence from a public goods experiment. *Economic Letters* 71, 397–404.

Forsythe, R., Horowitz, J., Savin, N.E. and Sefton, M. 1994. Fairness in simple bargaining experiments. *Games and Economic Behavior* 6, 347–69.

Geanakoplos, J., Pearce, D. and Stacchetti, E. 1989. Psychological games and sequential rationality. *Games and Economic Behavior* 1, 60–79.

Güth, W., Schmittberger, R. and Schwarze, B. 1982. An experimental analysis of ultimatum bargaining. *Journal of Economic Behavior and Organization* 3, 367–88.

Hoffman, E., McCabe, K., Shachat, J. and Smith, V. 1994. Preferences, property rights, and anonymity in bargaining games. *Games and Economic Behavior* 7, 346–80.

Sobel, J. 2005. Interdependent preferences and reciprocity. *Journal of Economic Literature* 43, 392–436.

trust in experiments

Trust is the willingness to make oneself vulnerable to another person's actions, based on beliefs about that person's trustworthiness.

This article focuses on interpersonal trust between two people, a trustor and a trustee. A trustee behaves trustworthily if he voluntarily refrains from taking advantage of the trustor's vulnerability. Trust applies to all transactions where the outcome is partly under the control of another person and not fully contractible, for example, between employers and employees or patients and doctors. Trust and trustworthiness are typically measured in surveys or laboratory experiments. We shortly discuss some survey evidence but focus on behavioural measures of trust.

Measurement

Trust attitudes have typically been measured by the following survey question (for example, used in the General Social Survey and the World Values Survey): 'Generally speaking, would you say that most people can be trusted, or that you can't be too careful in dealing with people?' Based on this question, trust has declined dramatically across the world since the 1960s. There are noticeable cross-country differences, with Scandinavians most and Latin Americans least likely to trust others. An empirical literature building on Knack and Keefer (1997) shows that trust attitudes are positively correlated with various measures of a country's economic performance.

Around 1990, two seminal papers started a new wave in the economic research on trust. In 1988, Camerer and Weigelt employed a binary-choice trust game, and in 1995 Berg, Dickhaut and McCabe the 'investment game' to study trust. In the binary-choice trust game, the trustor decides between a sure outcome and trust. If she chooses the sure thing, she and her trustee both receive (S, S). If she is willing to trust, both either end up with a moderate payoff exceeding S (M, M), or the trustor receives a lower payoff than if she had not trusted, and the trustee the highest possibly payoff, (L, H). Thus, for the trustor, $M > S > L$, and for the trustee, $H > M > S$. In the investment game, a trustor and a trustee are endowed with a certain amount of money, A (in some experiments, only trustors are endowed). The trustor can send any amount, $X \leq A$, to the trustee. X is multiplied by $k > 1$ by the experimenter. In most experiments, $k = 3$. Trustees receive kX and then decide how much of it, $Y \leq A + kX$, to return to their trustor. The final payoffs are $A - X + Y$ for the trustor and $A + kX - Y$ for the trustee. X is commonly referred to as trust and Y, or more precisely, Y/X, measures trustworthiness for $X > 0$. In both games, the equilibrium prediction based on selfish money-maximization and rationality is zero trustworthiness and zero trust.

The relationship between trust attitudes, as measured in surveys, and trust behaviour, as measured in experiments, is not clear. Some have found that they are related (for example, Fehr and Schmidt, 2002), others that they are not (for example,

Glaeser et al., 2000). While the investment game and the binary-choice trust game have turned out to be the most widely used games to study trust experimentally, related games include the 'gift exchange game', the 'moonlighting game,' and standard public goods games (for a review, see Camerer, 2003).

What motivates trust and trustworthiness?

Trust is based on preferences, namely, the willingness to be vulnerable to someone else, and on expectations, namely, the belief about someone else's trustworthiness. A person's willingness to be vulnerable may be related to her attitudes to risk (for example, Eckel and Wilson, 2004), her social preferences (for example, Cox, 2004), and her willingness to accept the risk of betrayal (Bohnet and Zeckhauser, 2004). Bohnet and Zeckhauser introduced an analytical framework to disentangle the various motives, and show that people dislike making themselves vulnerable to the actions of another person more than to natural circumstances. This suggests betrayal aversion: people care not only about outcomes but also about how outcomes come to be. This finding was supported by neuroscientific evidence (Kosfeld et al., 2005).

The relevance of expectations of trustworthiness for trust has typically been measured by including a question about trustors' beliefs. While this measure is not perfect, generally the relationship between expectations of trustworthiness and trust is very strong. For example, using a within-subject design with behavioural controls for risk and social preferences, Ashraf, Bohnet and Piankov (2006) found that expectations of trustworthiness explain most of the variance in trust in an investment game but that social preferences also matter.

Trustworthiness is based on trustees' social preferences, which may be related either to outcomes (for a survey, see Fehr and Schmidt, 2002) or to what the trustors' actions reveal about their intentions. In a seminal paper, Rabin (1993) introduced a theoretical model of intention-based preferences, reciprocity, into the literature. A large number of empirical studies suggests the importance of reciprocity in trust interactions (for example, Fehr, Gächter and Kirchsteiger, 1997) although outcome-based social preferences also play an important role for trustworthiness (for example, Cox, 2004; Ashraf, Bohnet and Piankov, 2006).

What influences trust and trustworthiness?

Incentives

According to most models, trustors should be more likely to trust the higher the expected returns are from trusting. Bohnet, Herrmann and Zeckhauser (2006) measured the elasticity of trust and found that trust is responsive both to changes in the likelihood and to the cost of betrayal in Western countries. However, this does not necessarily apply in other parts of the world. For example, in Persian Gulf countries people hardly responded to such changes. Instead, many basically demanded a guarantee of trustworthiness before trusting, suggesting substantial aversion to betrayal. In addition, incentives may also not work as predicted by theory if they not only affect behaviour directly but also exhibit an influence on preferences, thus either fostering or undermining people's willingness to accept vulnerability and be trustworthy voluntarily (Bohnet, Frey and Huck, 2001).

Repetition
Generally, people are more likely to trust and be trustworthy in repeated than in one-shot interactions. Theoretically, this result is expected in a traditional model when interactions are indefinitely repeated (folk theorem) but not in finitely repeated games. In support of the theory, experimental evidence suggests that trust and trustworthiness rates are generally higher in indefinitely than in finitely repeated games but they are also higher in the latter than in one-shot interactions. The equilibrium prediction of no trust and trustworthiness is generally refuted, although trust and trustworthiness rates typically drop substantially as the end of the game draws nearer (for example, Gächter and Falk, 2002).

Demographic variables
Generally, the evidence is not as conclusive as we might expect or wish. While in theory variables such as gender, race or country of origin should be easy to control for, experiments produce different results precisely because of the different sets of control variables and the different subject pools used. The most promising approaches include those identifying overarching frameworks able to account for a variety of studies. We discuss three such frameworks here: history of discrimination, societal organization and market integration.

Groups that historically have been discriminated against, such as women and minorities, are generally less likely to trust. At the same time, often these groups are more trustworthy (for example, Alesina and LaFerrara 2002; Buchan, Croson and Solnick, 2003; Eckel and Wilson, 2003).

Group-based societal organization based on long-standing relationships and repeated interactions within groups can substantially reduce the social uncertainty involved in trust. It is often referred to as 'collectivist' in contrast to the Western 'individualist' model of organization, which produces trust through more anonymous, institutional arrangements such as contracts and insurance. Trust in strangers has often been found to be higher in individualist (for example, the United States or Switzerland) than in collectivist countries (for example, Japan or the Persian Gulf countries), although the rather small number of studies and sample sizes does not allow any definite conclusions at this point (for example, Bohnet, Herrmann and Zeckhauser, 2006; but see also Croson and Buchan, 1999).

The degree of market integration is related to norms of cooperation and fairness in public goods and ultimatum games. Similarly, the norms of reciprocity typically found in trust experiments in developed countries seem to apply more strongly in societies in which goods and services are exchanged in the market rather than in informal reciprocal-exchange arrangements. Greig and Bohnet's survey of the evidence (2006) suggested that the positive relationship between trust and trustworthiness, normally taken to indicate reciprocity, is more pronounced in developed than in developing countries.

External validity

Experiments allow for maximum internal control. Concerns typically arising in field settings such as lack of randomization, selection and endogeneity can easily be addressed by experimental design. To address concerns about the subject pools experimentalists typically use, that is, North American or European students, experiments are now run with representative samples (for example, Fehr et al., 2002 in Germany) and with student and non-student subjects in other parts of the world (for example, Cardenas and Carpenter, 2005, for a survey). To directly test the external validity of trust experiments, Karlan (2005) ran investment games with members of a group lending association in Peru, and compared trustworthiness in the experiment with repayment rates. The more trustworthy subjects indeed were significantly more likely to repay their loans a year later.

IRIS BOHNET

See also **behavioural game theory; experimental economics; public goods experiments; reciprocity and collective action.**

Bibliography

Alesina, A. and LaFerrara, E. 2002. Who trusts others? *Journal of Public Economics* 85, 207–34.
Ashraf, N., Bohnet, I. and Piankov, N. 2006. Decomposing trust and trustworthiness. *Experimental Economics* 9, 193–208.
Berg, J., Dickhaut, J. and McCabe, K.A. 1995. Trust, reciprocity, and social history. *Games and Economic Behavior* 10, 290–307.
Bohnet, I., Frey, B.S. and Huck, S. 2001. More order with less law: on contract enforcement, trust and crowding. *American Political Science Review* 95, 131–44.
Bohnet, I., Herrmann, B. and Zeckhauser, R. 2006. The requirements for trust in Gulf and Western countries. *Working paper.*
Bohnet, I. and Zeckhauser, R. 2004. Trust, risk and betrayal. *Journal of Economic Behavior and Organization* 55, 467–84.
Buchan, N., Croson, R. and Solnick, S. 2003. Trust and gender: an examination of behavior, biases, and beliefs in the investment game. Working paper, Wharton School, University of Pennsylvania.
Camerer, C.F. 2003. *Behavioral Game Theory.* Princeton: Princeton University Press.
Camerer, C.F. and Weigelt, K. 1988. Experimental tests of a sequential equilibrium reputation model. *Econometrica* 56, 1–36.
Cardenas, J.C. and Carpenter, J. 2005. Experiments and economic development: lessons from field labs in the developing world. Working paper, Middlebury College.
Cox, J.C. 2004. How to identify trust and reciprocity. *Games and Economic Behavior* 46, 260–81.
Croson, R. and Buchan, N. 1999. Gender and culture: international experimental evidence from trust games. *American Economic Review* 89, 386–91.
Eckel, C.C. and Wilson, R.K. 2003. Conditional trust: sex, race and facial expressions in a trust game. Working paper, Rice University.
Eckel, C.C. and Wilson, R.K. 2004. Is trust a risky decision? *Journal of Economic Behavior and Organization* 55, 447–66.

Fehr, E. and Schmidt, K. 2002. Theories of fairness and reciprocity – evidence and economic applications. In *Advances in Economics and Econometrics*, ed. M. Dewatripont, L. Hansen and S. Turnovsky. Cambridge: Cambridge University Press.

Fehr, E., Gächter, S. and Kirchsteiger, G. 1997. Reciprocity as a contract enforcement device: experimental evidence. *Econometrica* 64, 833–60.

Fehr, E., Fischbacher, U., von Rosenbladt, B., Schupp, J. and Wagner, G. 2002. A nation-wide laboratory-examining trust and trustworthiness by integrating behavioral experiments into representative surveys. *Schmollers Jahrbuch* 122, 519–42.

Gächter, S. and Falk, A. 2002. Reputation and reciprocity: consequences for the labour relation. *Scandinavian Journal of Economics* 104, 1–26.

Glaeser, E.L., Laibson, D.I., Scheinkman, J.A. and Soutter, C.L. 2000. Measuring trust. *Quarterly Journal of Economics* 115, 811–46.

Greig, F. and Bohnet, I. 2006. Is there reciprocity in a reciprocal-exchange economy? Evidence of gendered norms from a slum in Nairobi, Kenya. Working paper, Kennedy School of Government, Harvard University.

Karlan, D. 2005. Using experimental economics to measure social capital and predict financial decisions. *American Economic Review* 95, 1688–99.

Knack, S. and Keefer, P. 1997. Does social capital have an economic payoff? A cross-country investigation. *Quarterly Journal of Economics* 112, 1251–88.

Kosfeld, M., Heinrichs, M., Zak, P.J., Fischbacher, U. and Fehr, E. 2005. Oxytocin increases trust in humans. *Nature* 435, 673–6.

Rabin, M. 1993. Incorporating fairness into game theory and economics. *American Economic Review* 83, 1281–302.

value elicitation

Why elicit values? The prices observed on a market reflect, on a good competitive day, the equilibrium of marginal valuations and costs. They do not quantitatively reflect the infra-marginal or extra-marginal values, other than in a severely censored sense. We know that infra-marginal values are weakly higher, and extra-marginal values are weakly lower, but beyond that one must rely on functional forms to extrapolate. For policy purposes this is generally insufficient to undertake cost–benefit calculations.

When producers are contemplating a new product or innovation they have to make some judgement about the value that will be placed on it. New drugs, and the R&D underlying them, provide an important example. Unless one can heroically tie the new product to existing products in terms of shared characteristics, and somehow elicit values on those characteristics, there is no way to know what price the market will bear. Value elicitation experiments can help fill that void, complementing traditional marketing techniques (see Hoffman et al., 1993).

Many goods and services effectively have no market, either because they exhibit characteristics of public goods or it is impossible to credibly deliver them on an individual basis. These non-market goods have traditionally been valued using surveys, where people are asked to state a valuation 'contingent on a market existing for the good'. The problem is that these surveys are hypothetical in terms of the deliverability of the good and the economic consequences of the response, and this understandably generates controversy about their reliability (Harrison, 2006).

Procedures

Direct methods for value elicitation include auctions, auction-like procedures and 'multiple price lists'.

Sealed-bid auctions require the individual to state a valuation for the product in a private manner, and then award the product following certain rules. For single-object auctions, the second-price (or Vickrey) auction awards the product to the highest bidder but sets the price equal to the highest rejected bid. It is easy to show, to students of economics at least, that the bidder has a dominant strategy to bid his true value: any bid higher or lower can only end up hurting the bidder in expectation. But these incentives are not obvious to inexperienced subjects. A real-time counterpart of the second-price auction is the English (or ascending bid) auction, in which an auctioneer starts the price out low and then bidders increase the price to become the winner of the product. Bidders seem to realize the dominant strategy property of the English auction more quickly than in comparable second-price sealed-bid auctions, no doubt due to the real-time feedback on the opportunity costs of deviations from that strategy (see Rutström, 1998; Harstad, 2000). Familiarity with the institution is also surely a factor in the superior performance of the English auction: first encounters with the second-price auction rules lead many non-economists to assume that there must be some 'trick'.

Related schemes collapse the logic of the second-price auction into an auction-like procedure due to Becker, DeGroot and Marschak (1964). The basic idea is to endow the subject with the product, and to ask for a 'selling price'. The subject is told that a 'buying price' will be picked at random, and that, if the buying price that is picked exceeds the stated selling price, the product will be sold at that price and the subject will receive that buying price. If the buying price equals or is lower than the selling price, the subject keeps the lottery and plays it out. Again, it is relatively transparent to *economists* that this auction procedure provides a formal incentive for the subject to truthfully reveal the certainty-equivalent of the lottery. One must ensure that the buyout range exceeds the highest price that the subject would reasonably state, but this is not normally a major problem. One must also ensure that the subject realizes that the choice of a buying price does not depend on the stated selling price; a surprising number of respondents appear not to understand this independence, even if they are told that a physical randomizing device is being used.

Multiple price lists present individuals with an ordered menu of prices at which they may choose to buy the product or not. In this manner the list resembles a menu, akin to the price comparison websites available online for many products. For any given price, the choice is a simple 'take it or leave it' posted offer, familiar from retail markets. The set of responses for the entire list is incentivized by picking one at random for implementation, so the subject can readily see that misrepresentation can only hurt for the usual revealed preference reasons. Refinements to the intervals of prices can be implemented, to improve the accuracy of the values elicited (see Andersen et al., 2006). These methods have been widely used to elicit risk preferences and discount rates, as well as values for products (see Holt and Laury, 2002; Harrison, Lau and Williams, 2002; Andersen et al., 2007).

Indirect methods work by presenting individuals with simple choices and using a latent structural model to infer valuations. The canonical example comes from the theory of revealed preference, and confronts the decision-maker with a series of purchase opportunities from a budget line and asks him to pick one. By varying the budget lines one can 'trap' latent indifference curves and place nonparametric or parametric bounds on valuations. The same methods extend naturally to variations in the non-price characteristics of products, and merge with the marketing literature on 'conjoint choice' (for example, Louviere, Hensher and Swait, 2000; Lusk and Schroeder, 2004). Access to scanner data from the massive volume of retail transactions made every day promises rich characterizations of underlying utility functions, particularly when merged with experimental methods that introduce exogenous variation in characteristics in order to statistically condition and 'enrich' the data (Hensher, Louviere and Swait, 1999). One of the attractions of indirect methods is that one can employ choice tasks which are familiar to the subject, such as binary 'take it or leave it' choices or rank orderings. The lack of precision in that type of qualitative data requires some latent structure before one can infer values, but behavioural responses are much easier to explain and motivate for respondents.

One major advantage of undertaking structural estimation of a latent choice model is that valuations can be elicited in a more fundamental manner, explicitly recognizing the decision process underlying a stated valuation. A structural model can control for risk attitudes when choices are being made in a stochastic setting, which is almost always the case in practical settings. Thus one can hope to tease apart the underlying deterministic valuation from the assessment of risk. Likewise, non-standard models of choice posit a myriad of alternative factors that might confound inference about valuation: respondents might distort preferences from their true values, they might exhibit loss aversion in certain frames, and they might bring their own home-grown reference points or aspiration levels to the valuation task. Only with a structural model can one hope to identify these potential confounds to the valuation process. Quite apart from wanting to identify the primitives of the underlying valuation free of confounds, normative applications will often require that some of these distortions be corrected for. That is only possible if one has a complete structural model of the valuation process.

A structural model also provides an antidote to those that claim that valuations are so contextual as to be an unreliable will-o'-the-wisp. If someone is concerned about framing, endowment effects, loss aversion, preference distortions, social preferences, and any number of related behavioural notions, it is impossible to generate a scientific dialogue without being able to write out a structural model and jointly estimate it.

Lessons and concerns

The most important lesson that has been learned from decades of experimental research into the behavioural properties of these procedures to elicit values is: keep it simple. This refers primarily to the nature of the task given to respondents. It can be dangerous to rely on fancy rules that ensure incentives to truthfully reveal valuations only if everyone sees a complete chain of logic, even if that logic is apparent to trained economists. Of course, one can use 'cheap talk' and just tell people to reveal the truth since it is in their best interests, but one cannot be sure that such admonitions work reliably. Cultural familiarity with institutions counts for a lot when subjects are otherwise placed in an artefactual valuation task.

The desire to keep it simple has a corollary: the use of more rigorous statistical techniques to infer valuations. This implication follows from the need to make inferences about valuations on a cardinal scale when responses are often between subject and qualitative. Progress has been made in the use of numerical simulation methods for the maximum likelihood estimation of random utility models that allow extraordinary flexibility (for example, Train, 2003).

We also have a better understanding now of the manner in which valuations may be biased by being hypothetical, due to procedural devices in the institution being employed, and because of field context (for example, Harrison, Harstad and Rutström,

2004). More constructively, methods have been developed to undertake *ex ante* 'instrument calibration' to remove biases using controlled experiments, and to implement *ex post* 'statistical calibration' to filter out any remaining systematic biases (see Harrison, 2006).

Finally, the manner in which valuations change with states of nature is starting to be understood. Insights here again come from thinking about valuation as a latent, structural decision process. If we observe the same person state a different value for the same product at two different times, is it because he has a shift in his utility function, a change in some argument of his utility function, a change in his perceived opportunity set, or something else? If valuation is viewed as a process we can begin to design procedures that can help us identify answers to these questions, and better understand the valuations that are observed.

GLENN W. HARRISON

See also **auctions (experiments); experimental economics; experimental methods in economics.**

Bibliography

Andersen, S., Harrison, G.W., Lau, M.I. and Rutström, E.E. 2006. Elicitation using multiple price lists. *Experimental Economics* 4, 383–405.

Andersen, S., Harrison, G.W., Lau, M.I. and Rutström, E.E. 2007. Valuation using multiple price list formats. *Applied Economics* 39, 675–82.

Becker, G.M., DeGroot, M.H. and Marschak, J. 1964. Measuring utility by a single-response sequential method. *Behavioral Science* 9, 226–32.

Harrison, G.W. 2006. Experimental evidence on alternative environmental valuation methods. *Environmental and Resource Economics* 34, 125–62.

Harrison, G.W., Harstad, R.M. and Rutström, E.E. 2004. Experimental methods and elicitation of values. *Experimental Economics* 2, 123–40.

Harrison, G.W., Lau, M.I. and Williams, M.B. 2002. Estimating individual discount rates for Denmark: a field experiment. *American Economic Review* 5, 1606–17.

Harstad, R.M. 2000. Dominant strategy adoption and Bidders' experience with pricing rules. *Experimental Economics* 3, 261–80.

Hensher, D., Louviere, J. and Swait, J.D. 1999. Combining sources of preference data. *Journal of Econometrics* 89, 197–221.

Hoffman, E., Menkhaus, D.J., Chakravarti, D., Field, R.A. and Whipple, G.D. 1993. Using laboratory experimental auctions in marketing research: a case study of new packaging for fresh beef. *Marketing Science* 3, 318–38.

Holt, C.A. and Laury, S.K. 2002. Risk aversion and incentive effects. *American Economic Review* 5, 1644–55.

Louviere, J.J., Hensher, D.A. and Swait, J.D. 2000. *Stated Choice Methods: Analysis and Application.* New York: Cambridge University Press.

Lusk, J.L. and Schroeder, T.C. 2004. Are choice experiments incentive compatible? A test with quality differentiated beef steaks. *American Journal of Agricultural Economics* 2, 467–82.

Rutström, E.E. 1998. Home-grown values and the design of incentive compatible auctions. *International Journal of Game Theory* 3, 427–41.

Train, K.E. 2003. *Discrete Choice Methods with Simulation.* New York: Cambridge University Press.

Index